Publications of The Pennsylvania German Society

Volume XVIII

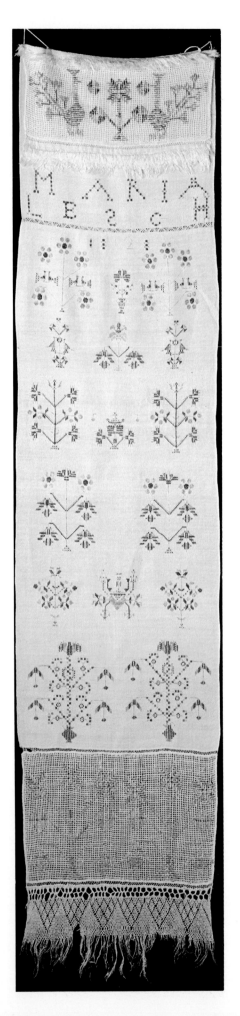

THIS IS THE WAY
I PASS MY TIME

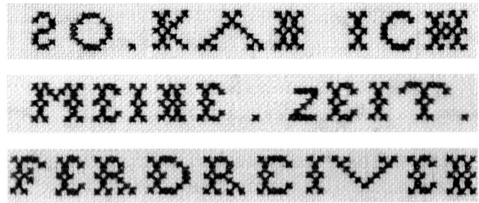

Birdsboro, Pennsylvania
The Pennsylvania German Society

A Book About Pennsylvania German
Decorated Hand Towels

by

ELLEN J. GEHRET

in cooperation with
Tandy Hersh, Alan G. Keyser and Frederick S. Weiser

The color plates in this volume were published in part
with the support of a grant
from the Arcadia Foundation, Norristown, Pennsylvania

Library of Congress Catalog Card Number: 84-62851
ISBN: 0-911122-48-6

Printed and bound in the United States of America
by Kutztown Publishing Company,
Kutztown, Pennsylvania

Needlework on the title page was made by Heidi Mayer.

JACKET DETAIL *Elizabeth Booser is my name, 1843. So Kan Ich Meine Zeit Ferdreiven* (This is the way I pass my time). Balanced plain weave linen fabric; cross stich; cotton darning stitch on drawn thread panels, w. 19''.[62]

On the title page:

PLATE 1 *Maria Lesch, 1828.* Balanced plain weave linen fabric; cotton cross stitch; cotton darning stitch on drawn thread panels. Note drawn thread panel as the flap. Self and applied plain and knotted fringes. 60'' x 15½''.[473]

PLATE 2 *CH, 1818.* Lancaster county. See Plate 39. Red wool fabric appliqued bird's breast; white silk fabric appliqued bird's wing. L. 2''; W. 2-3/8''.[285]

To The Memory Of

HATTIE KLAPP BRUNNER

(1889-1982)

PLATE 3 *Esther Niszly, Mey 2, 1821* (May 2, 1821).
Balanced plain weave linen fabric; red cotton, brown silk cross stitch; cotton darning stitch on drawn thread panels; self and applied plain fringes. The red door with yellow striping and blue door frame were last painted in 1814. 59'' x 16-7/8''.[609]

PLATE 4 *Barbara Kuns, 1824.* Balanced plain weave linen fabric; red cotton, black light blue, gold, and white silk cross stitch; red and white cotton darning stitch on drawn thread panels; needlelace; self and applied plain fringes. 61'' x 18¼''.[64]

PREFACE

This is a book about *some* Pennsylvania German decorated hand towels. As you will learn from the text, these towels call themselves *Handtuch* or its English equivalent *hand towel*. Twentieth century dealers and collectors have given them the names *Door Panel* or *Show Towel*. Modern German scholarship calls them *Zierhandtuch, Paradehandtuch, Prunkhandtuch,* or *Überhandtuch.* These names and their merits are discussed below, too. They are mentioned here only so that the reader recognizes by some name what this book concerns.

We shall never know how many towels were made, nor probably how many of those made have survived. We believe, because of their nature, their rate of survival has been relatively high. We do know, however, that in order to prepare this book, over twelve hundred towels were examined. This, therefore, is a book based on over twelve hundred of the grand total of towels that were made.

Each of these towels was assigned a number with which to identify it and its owner. It is this registration number that accompanies names in the text, notes, captions, and appendix.

Standardized data sheets were filled with detailed information about each towel's construction, embroidery, designs, and finishes. Many towels or designs were also photographed. The examination and ultimate definition of someone else's handwork, particularly if it is a personalized innovation, is at best difficult. We attempted to be as accurate as possible.

A series of features, from dated towels only, was charted in five year increments. Trends in embroidery coloration, changes in towel size, the comings and goings of embroidery stitch types, drawn thread techniques and needlelace construction, and many other such patterns in decorated towel development became apparent. These findings are reported in this study and the charts themselves, somewhat simplified, are reproduced here.

Many thousands of embroidery designs were copied onto graph paper or pin pricked in actual size. They were sorted into categories that emerged from them. Only a fraction of these designs could be reproduced here. We should have liked to reproduce more. The wide variety extant, the few exact duplicates preclude this.

There is enough material gathered for many more pages than those given here. The selection made is, however, only partly arbitrary and subjective. While we did select what we liked, we sought especially what was rare and what was typical, what represented great achievement and what illustrates points in the text. The selection of towels for photography, both in color and black and white, has been guided by a desire to show representative examples, including the variety of color combinations. They have not been selected by the canons of the antiques market. We have generally selected those towels which have not been published elsewhere.

Generally we have not given step-by-step directions for duplicating the needlework on the towels. There are references to standard needlework guides in which these instructions may be found. There is only one drawing of a needlework procedure in this book, for a simple needlelace, since this material is not available elsewhere.

All of the original data sheets, charts, and drafted designs are available for further study. We invite dialogue with other needlework historians and interested persons. Qualified persons wishing to study this material should apply in writing to the author in care of the Pennsylvania German Society.

Readers should understand that not every towel illustrating a point in the text is cited there, but that significant examples are. Footnote numbers are to the towels themselves; those with texts and those in public collections are listed with accession numbers in the appendix. A number which appears in the text, but not in the appendix, represents, therefore, a towel without any text found in a private collection. Approximately 80 percent of the towels we found have *some* text, from initials to poems, sayings, and scripture.

We believe that, although chance has directed us to the more than twelve hundred towels we saw, these towels do represent a typical cross-section of all of them and that the conclusions we have reached, therefore, are reasonably valid about all decorated towels that were made. We are intensely interested in examining towels we have not seen. They will expand our appreciation of the incredible richness this needlework tradition of Pennsylvania German women represents.

EJG
T H
AGK
FSW

Fall 1984

vii

Color	Symbol		Symbol	Color
BLUE	•		∧	PURPLE
BROWN	+		✕	RED
CREAM	–		▽	ROSE RED
DARK GREEN	◉		■	SALMON
GOLD	◸		⊞	TAN
GRAY	●		⊟	TAUPE
GRAY-GREEN	◪		ı	WHITE
LIGHT BLUE	⁄.		▲	WINE RED
MULBERRY	∨		◣	YELLOW
OLIVE	○		⬟	DRAWN WORK HORIZONTAL STITCH
ORANGE	✖			
ORANGE RED	△		◆	DRAWN WORK VERTICAL STITCH
PINK	▼			

Most drawings in this book are for cross stitch motifs. The only exceptions are those copied from drawn thread embroidery. They are denoted by a circle with either a vertical or horizontal line to indicate the direction of the darning stitch. The other symbols represent the colors used on the original towel although no distinction is made between cotton, linen, silk and wool embroidery threads. All cross stitch and drawn thread motifs have been copied from the towel whose number appears with the design. Each square in the grid represents one cross stitch. In several instances the original placement of an individual cross stitch was moved one thread on the towel fabric in which case the symbols were drawn on a line instead of in a space.

Contents

ACKNOWLEDGMENTS

A project of this magnitude necessarily involves numerous persons. We are always astounded at the eagerness with which people show and share family heirlooms and priceless collections. It has been a privilege to gain the friendship of the following generous folks who so willingly granted us permission to scrutinize their decorated towels and share information about them. Mr. and Mrs. Raymond Althouse, Mr. and Mrs. Edward Babcock, Mr. and Mrs. James Barnett, Judith B. Baxter, Patricia S. Bednar, Jane Best, Vinson Bitner, Mr. and Mrs. Edmund Bohne, Anna Catharine Bolton, Kathleen Bower, Raymond J. Brunner, Robert C. Bucher, Elizabeth Buckwalter, Kirke Bryan, Bessie and Mary Cassel, Eugene and Vera Charles, Mr. and Mrs. H. Raymond Charles, Mary Jane Clemens, Patricia J. Keller-Conner, Mrs. Robert V. Cresswell, Janet Gray Crosson, Mr. and Mrs. David Cunningham, Frederick Darnell, Pearl Detweiler, Henry P. Deyerle, Mrs. Howard J. Dietrich, Edwin C. and Margaret R. Diller, Robert Egan, Mr. and Mrs. John F. Elliott, Patricia Fedor, Arthur Feeman, Paul and Rita Flack, Mary Freeman, Albert T. and Elizabeth Gamon, Roberta Garlock, Beatrice B. Garvan, Mr. and Mrs. Philip F. Gehret, Mrs. Noah Getz, Elizabeth Gibson, Anna Gouchnauer, Mary Goetz, Mrs. Earl B. Good, Jean Good, Donald Goodyear, Mrs. Grace Graber, Charles Grove, Mr. and Mrs. Richard Hate, Anna Heebner, Iva Heilman, Robert A. Heilman, Mr. and Mrs. Gary E. Heimbach, Mrs. Donald Helfferich, Mr. and Mrs. Stephen Hench, Hope S. Henry, Dr. and Mrs. Donald M. Herr, Mr. and Mrs. Harold Herr, Lois Wismer Hernandez, Dr. and Mrs. Charles Hersh, Mr. and Mrs. Hiram Hershey, Clarke E. Hess, Arlene Hess, Helen Highouse, Sandra Highouse, Mr. and Mrs. William Hoag, Mr. and Mrs. Carroll Hopf, Mr. and Mrs. Robert G. Hostetter, Mr. and Mrs. Paul Hunsberger, Mrs. J.W.R. Hunter, Esther Keller, Mr. and Mrs. Harold Kerper, Alan G. Keyser, Joe K. Kindig, III, Mr. and Mrs. John L. Kraft, Vernon and Elizabeth Kratz, Mr. and Mrs. Gerald Kriebel, Mrs. Harold Kriebel, Mrs. Homer S. Kriebel, Clarence Kulp, Jr., the late Sidney Kutz, Miriam Lease, Mrs. Lloyd LeFever, Patricia Long, Ursula Martino, J. Lamar Mast, Beverly A. McCausland, Mary Ann McIlnay, Mrs. Isaac N. Miller, Mrs. John Miller, Marion Mizenko, Mrs. Daniel Moseman, Mrs. and Mrs. C. Edward Mosheim, Mr. and Mrs. Dennis K. Moyer, Jay Moyer, Mildred Ott, Agnes Park, Wendell and Ann Pass, the late Mrs. Claude Reinford, Mr. and Mrs. Daniel Reinford, Mr. and Mrs. H.F. Riffle, Mr. and Mrs. Donald F. Roan, Dr. and Mrs. Earl Robacker, Mr. and Mrs. Edward Rosenberry, Jackie Rothfus, Harold Royer, Elizabeth L. Sallada, Mr. and Mrs. Wilbur Seipt, Barbara Shellenberger, Donald A. Shelley, Helen Shiffer, Wendel Shiffer, Margaret and Lawrence Skromme, Hannah Jones Smith, Mr. and Mrs. Richard F. Smith, Grace Stirba, Barbara Strawser, Mary E. Suter, Mrs. Harvey Taylor, II, Rosemary Tillich, Mary Treichler, Ronald Treichler, Mr. and Mrs. A. Leroy Tyson, Carolyn Weaver, Leslie Webb, Frederick S. Weiser, Carolyn Wenger, Polly Williams, Gloria Stahl Woodland, Ruth Landes Yeakel, Mr. and Mrs. Harry Zane, Clara Zawadski.

Staff personnel and volunteers at these local, county, state and federal museums have been most generous and cooperative with their collections of decorated hand towels: The Abby Aldrich Rockefeller Folk Art Center, Williamsburg, Virginia; Adams County Historical Society Gettysburg; American Museum in Britain, Bath, England; Barnes Foundation, Merion Station; Bucks County Historical Society, Doylestown; Dauphin County Historical Society, Harrisburg; Doon Pioneer Village, Kitchener, Ontario; Goschenhoppen Folklife Museum and Library, Green Lane; Henry Francis DuPont Winterthur Museum, Winterthur, Delaware; Heritage Center of Lancaster County, Inc., Lancaster; Hershey Museum of American Life, Hershey; Historical Society of Montgomery County, Norristown; Historical Society of York County, York; Lancaster County Historical Society, Lancaster; Lebanon County Historical Society, Lebanon; Lititz Historical Foundation, Lititz; Mennonite Historians of Eastern Pennsylvania, Souderton; Metropolitan Museum of Art, New York; Moravian Museum, Bethlehem; New York Historical Society, New York; North Museum of Franklin and Marshall College, Lancaster; National Society of Daughters of the American Revolution, Washington; Pennsylvania Farm Museum of Landis Valley, Lancaster; Pennsylvania Historical and Museum Commission, Harrisburg; Philadelphia Museum of Art, Philadelphia; Renfrew Museum, Waynesboro; Schwenkfelder Museum and Library, Pennsburg; Smithsonian Institution, Washington D.C.; Westmoreland-Fayette Historical Society Museum, West Overton-Scottdale.

There were many others who gave help and advice as the project progressed. John Aungst, Louisa A. Babcock, Mr. and Mrs. Ralph Bieler, Michael S. Bird, Marion Borneman, Elaine Clark, Clair Conway, Carol Faill, Rebecca Gehret, Mr. and Mrs. Fred D. Geiselman, Clarke E. Hess, Ellen Jensen, Grace John, Wolfgang Kleinschmidt, Terry Kobyashi, Clarence Kulp, Jr., Jane LeVan, David Luthy, Salinda Matt, Heidi Mayer, John and Joyce Munro, Larry Neff, Donald and Nancy Roan, Joan Romig, Bertie Ryder, Shirley Sacks, the late Irma A. Schultz, Debbie Smith, Karen R. Strawbridge, Mary Hammond Sullivan, Susan B. Swan, Ruth Kuder Yost, and Samuel Waddington.

We appreciate the photography of Dan Arthur, Michael Bird, Chartrand Photo Service, Emmaus, J. Arthur Davis and Associates, Hummelstown, Dennis Dunda Photowork, New York, Tandy Hersh, Alan G. Keyser, John Munro, Guy F. Reinert, W. J. Taylor, Ronald Treichler, Poist's Studio, Hanover, and the Hayman Studio, York. Rebecca S. Gehret did the art work. Vevonna Kennedy prepared the drawing of the needlelace stitch.

ABBREVIATIONS

AARFAC	Abby Aldrich Rockefeller Folk Art Center, Williamsburg, Virginia
ACHS	Adams County Historical Society, Gettysburg
AMB	American Museum in Britain, Bath, England
BF	Barnes Foundation, Merion Station
BCHS	Bucks County Historical Society, Doylestown
DCHS	Dauphin County Historical Society, Harrisburg
D	Doon Pioneer Village, Kitchener, Ontario
GH	Goschenhoppen Folklife Museum and Library, Green Lane
Winterthur	Henry Francis DuPont Winterthur Museum, Winterthur, Delaware
HCLC	Heritage Center of Lancaster County, Inc., Lancaster
HMAL	Hershey Museum of American Life, Hershey
HSYC	Historical Society of York County, York
LCHS	Lancaster County Historical Society, Lancaster
LBCHS	Lebanon County Historical Society, Lebanon
LHF	Lititz Historical Foundation, Lititz
MHEP	Mennonite Historians of Eastern Pennsylvania, Souderton
MMA	Metropolitan Museum of Art, New York
MM	Moravian Museum, Bethlehem
NYHS	New York Historical Society, New York City
NMFM	North Museum of Franklin and Marshall College, Lancaster
NSDAR	National Society of Daughters of the American Revolution, Washington D.C.
PFMLV	Pennsylvania Farm Museum of Landis Valley, Lancaster
PHMC	Pennsylvania Historical and Museum Commission, Harrisburg
PMA	Philadelphia Museum of Art, Philadelphia
RM	Renfrew Museum, Waynesboro
SL	Schwenkfelder Museum and Library, Pennsburg
SI	Smithsonian Institution, Washington, D.C.
WM-FHSM	Westmoreland-Fayette Historical Society Museum, West Overton-Scottsdale

Photography Credits:

Dan Arthur: 415

Michael Bird: 3, 112, 136, 140, 154, 288, 363, 433, 436, 439, 441, 442, 444, 471, 500, 511, 515, 516, 547

Chartrand Photo Service, Emmaus: 113, 114

J. Arthur Davis, Hummelstown: 5, 6, 210, 326
Dennis Dunda Photowork, New York: 101

Tandy Hersh: 505

Alan G. Keyser: 8, 9, 11, 85, 87, 89, 93, 118, 139, 198, 212, 246, 252, 263, 299, 300, 316a, 318, 328, 330, 339, 349, 351, 352, 358, 360, 362, 367, 368, 397, 405, 419, 420, 422, 424, 425, 454, 484, 489, 491, 496, 507, 510, 512, 519, 520, 523, 524, 525, 526, 527, 531, 532, 533, 534, 535, 536, 537, 538, 539, 540, 542, 543

John Munro: 7, 84, 128, 141, 222, 229, 243, 244, 253, 269, 285, 294, 329, 369, 423, 461, 463, 486, 487, 488, 490, 498, 501, 502, 509, 513, 514, 521, 552, 560; Plates 2, 25, 26, 39

Guy F. Reinert: 110, 111, 120, 122, 123, 559

W. J. Taylor: 503, 518, 558

Ronald Treichler: 371, 389, 410, 517, 530, 541

Winterthur Photo Services: 92, 186

Poist's Studio, Hanover: 105, 152

Hayman Studio, York: 1, 2, 10, 86, 88, 91, 94, 97, 98, 99, 102, 103, 104, 106, 107, 108, 109, 115, 116, 117, 121, 124, 125, 126, 127, 130, 131, 132, 133, 134, 135, 137, 138, 143, 144, 145, 146, 147, 148, 149, 150, 151, 151a, 153, 155, 156, 157, 158, 159, 160, 161, 162, 163, 164, 165, 166, 167, 168, 169, 170, 171, 172, 173, 174, 175, 176, 179, 180, 180a, 181, 182, 183, 184, 185, 187, 188, 189, 190, 191, 192, 193, 194, 195, 200, 201, 202, 203, 204, 205, 206, 209, 211, 215, 216, 218, 220, 221, 224, 225, 226, 227, 228, 230, 231, 233, 234, 235, 236, 237, 238, 239, 240, 241, 242, 245, 247, 248, 249, 250, 251, 254, 255, 257, 266, 267, 268, 270, 271, 279, 283, 284, 289, 290, 291, 293, 295, 296, 297, 302, 309, 313, 317, 319, 320, 321, 322, 323, 324, 325, 327, 331, 333a, 336, 337, 340, 347, 348, 353, 354, 355, 356, 357, 361, 364, 366, 372, 374, 377, 378, 379, 380, 381, 382, 383, 384, 385, 386, 387, 394, 399, 400, 401, 403, 404, 406, 407, 409, 411, 412, 413, 416, 417, 418, 426, 427, 428, 429, 430, 431, 432, 434, 438, 443, 445, 446, 447, 448, 449, 452, 453, 455, 458, 462, 464, 465, 466, 467, 468, 469, 470, 472, 473, 474, 475, 476, 477, 478, 479, 481, 483, 485, 492, 493, 494, 495, 499, 504, 506, 508, 522, 528, 529, 544, 545, 546, 548, 549, 550, 551, 553, 554, 555, 556, 557, 561; Plates 1, 3-24, 27-30, 32-38, 40-45, 47-49

End Paper Towel Numbers

Front top, left to right: 611, 68, 264, 115, 365, 312, 47
Front bottom, left to right: 15, 266, 624, 761, 323, 604, 269, 344
Back top, left to right: 379, 18, 301, 273, 382, 15, 106, 271, 706
Back bottom, left to right: 233, 197, 319, 546, 15, 744, 756, 340

Towel Numbers For Chapter Heading Designs:

chapter 1: 624	chapter 4: 364
chapter 2: 212	chapter 5: 319
chapter 3: 149	chapter 6: 545

EXECUTOR'S UNRESTRICTED PUBLIC SALE
OF THE ENTIRE PRIVATE COLLECTION OF
ANTIQUES
OF THE LATE HATTIE S. BRUNNER of REINHOLD'S, PA.

Monday, Tuesday, Wednesday and Thursday — May 18 - 19 - 20 - 21
Commencing at 10 A.M. Each Day — Eastern Daylight Saving Time — Morning and Afternoon Sessions. 1936

FIGURE 1a   Hattie S. Brunner's sale May 18-21, 1936, at the Reinholds fire hall with her door panels on the line.

THIS IS THE WAY I PASS MY TIME

FIGURE 1 *MV, 1687, IF DR*. Canton Valais, Switzerland. Balanced plain weave linen fabric; red cotton and brown silk cross stitch; netted lace. This type of very long towel was used in houses of nobility and was hung over a rod so that one end hung directly above the other. Both ends of the towel are shown here side by side. Courtesy, Swiss National Museum, Zurich.

Introduction

The phenomenon of a decorated towel not intended for use is an old one in Western culture.* Like much of what is fundamental to Western life, these towels rest on Italian origins. They became popular in Germanic Europe during the Renaissance. At first the nobility and bourgeois classes displayed them, something like a tapestry. Towels from this period were woven (one from Augsburg dated circa 1460 has survived).

By the seventeenth and eighteenth centuries such towels were also to be found in the homes of the better-off peasants. Now not only woven towels, but also embroidered ones, in various stitches, and towels with other needlework techniques became evident. It is probably true that the embroidered towels were homemade examples of the expensive woven towels which could be bought, such as the "Brixener-Tücher" which were woven in South Tirol and peddled far and wide in Europe.

---

*There is no single Germanic study of the decorated hand towel. German textile scholarship and much of German folk art scholarship began with examination of the *Tracht,* the regional costumes once found in many areas of German-speaking Europe and still surviving in a few, especially worn on festive occasions. The *Tracht* has many components, whether men's or women's, some of which were decorated with techniques also found on towels. Between 1923 and 1929 a series of thirteen volumes entitled *Deutsche Volkskunst* treating various areas of German culture was published. Volume 5 by Karl Gröber concerned Swabia, 12 by Theodor Zink the Palatinate, 13 by Hermann Busse, Baden and an additional book by Ernst Polaczek, Alsace, to mention those most pertinent to Pennsylvania research. Some of these volumes have recently been reprinted. A new series was begun in 1940, including areas not covered earlier, as well as a new study of Hesse by Karl Rumpf (1951). In 1956 Erich Meyer-Heisig published the only general study of Germanic folk textiles *Weberei Nadelwerk Zengdruck.* Since 1956 there has been interest in samplers *(Stickmustertücher)* and two important catalogues have appeared: Gerhard Kaufmann, *Stickmustertücher aus dem Besitz des Altonaer Museums* (Hamburg, 1975) and Nina Gockerell, *Stickmustertücher; Kataloge des Bayrischen National-almuseums,* vol. 16 (München, 1980). Examples of Germanic towels may be found illustrated in these and similar books and articles cited in the extensive bibliography in *Meyer-Heisig.* Copies of most of those articles were kindly made available to us by Professor Wolfgang Kleinschmid, Ph.D., of the University of Bonn. The standard museums of Germanic culture folk art, including those in Nuremberg, Munich, Vienna, Innsbruck, Basel, Zurich and Strasbourg, have collections of towels and related textiles both on display and in storage. A general examination of these towels in European life will also reveal Scandinavian, Basque, and other examples.—See "Prunkhandtuch," in Oswald A. Erich, Richard Beitl and Klaus Beitl, *Wörterbuch der deutschen Volkskunde,* third ed., (Stuttgart, 1974), 652-3, and "Handtuch," in E. Hoffmann-Krayer and Hanns Bächtold-Stäubli, *Handwörterbuch des deutschen Aberglaubens* (Berlin and Leipzig, 1930/1931), III, 1412-1413.

Already in 1523 the first printed book of embroidery designs was published with the designs reproduced in woodcuts. In 1597 Johann Sibmacher's *Schön neues Modelbuch,* printed from copper engravings he made, appeared. It was often reprinted. But one may not underestimate the role of nuns and cloister schools in creating and disseminating the cross stitch designs, for instance, so popular in these textile artifacts. Such schools existed also among Protestants, in many instances until the nineteenth century taught by women of the nobililty, some of whom lived in what had been convents and conducted schools for girls there. Among peasant classes, as is true of much Germanic material culture, an aping of the moneyed classes, in means and by methods which required some skill but not *the* accomplishment of professional artisans, played a role in spreading this tradition to the humbler, poorer classes of society.

These decorated towels found a variety of uses in different parts of the Germanic world. In White Russia they were engagement gifts from the bride-to-be to her groom. At marriages the door posts of the bridal chamber were decorated with them in some areas. They also hung on the house of women in childbirth to show that the visit of neighboring women was not yet desired. In Hesse they were displayed on Easter and Pentecost and for weddings. In Westphalia they were hung on the wall for family occasions such as funerals. A common nineteenth century use for these towels was to hang them over the towel the family used to hide it. This use gave rise to the name *Überhandtuch,* covering towel, in European sources. A more inclusive name is expressed in the titles, *Zierhandtuch, Paradehandtuch,* or *Prunkhandtuch,* each of which means a decorated hand towel. [Figure 1]

In Alsace and Baden, in the Palatinate and Hesse, in areas along the Rhine which contributed extensively to the German migration to Pennsylvania, the terms *Türlappen* (door cloth) and *Türzwele* occur. (*Zwele* comes from old high German *dwahila,* middle high German *dwähele,* and is related linguistically to the English word *towel.* The term *Zwele* occurs infrequently in eighteenth century Pennsylvania German inventories). The word *Türzwele* singles out one more regional use for these towels. In this area they hung on *doors,* to decorate the room in which they were a part. It was this use which prevailed in Pennsylvania.

Although the earliest surviving towels in Pennsylvania postdate the American Revolution, there are doors with pegs in the appropriate places, or the holes where pegs once were found, in houses that predate it. We have every reason to believe that the tradition of hanging a decorated towel on the stove-room door, the *Schtubb*, came with the earliest Pennsylvania Germans from their homeland.

If they brought the towel to Pennsylvania from Europe, they also took it with them to other areas of the new world in which they settled. The evidence before us, however, demands that we qualify which element among the Pennsylvania Dutch kept the towel tradition alive by transplanting it to other places. There are towels worked by Lutheran and Reformed girls, members of the larger element of the Pennsylvania German population. But though 90 percent of the Pennsylvania Germans belonged to these churches or their daughters, the United Brethren, the Evangelical Church, or the Church of God, the *minority* of towels come from them. Schwenkfelders, a tiny religious community in central and northern Montgomery county and adjoining parts of Berks and Lehigh counties, widely practiced the making of these towels. But it was the Mennonites in both the Franconia and the Lancaster Conference, who especially made these towels—and took the practice with them to western Pennsylvania, [Figure 177] to Virginia, [Figure 2] and to Canada [Figure 3]. In spite of the high percentage of towels with texts of one sort or another, it is extremely hard to place a towel geographically without its particular precise history. It appears that the extensive migration of Mennonites from Lancaster county especially to Ontario propagated the towel there, prolonged its life and even produced a higher percentage of richly decorated towels than seems to have been made in Pennsylvania. The Pennsylvania German decorated hand towels from Ontario are worthy of a comprehensive study in their own right.

The precise history of the decorated hand towel in Pennsylvania and how and why the Mennonites came to esteem them so highly escapes us now and may always be obscure. It is easier to explain the Schwenkfelders' use of them: they lived in an area of concentrated Mennonite population and probably acquired their interest in them from their neighbors. The Mennonites and their religious kinfolk, the Amish, who have decorated towels into the twentieth century, are cultural conservators and generally cultural borrowers. Moreover, they live in intense community relationships with visits between geographical areas of settlement—including visits between Ontario and Pennsylvania—an important part of religious practice. To be specific: Sundays are days for worship and visiting—often for visits in other congregations, since until recently few met for worship weekly. And a typical women's Sunday activity to this day is examining the hostess's needlework. These circumstances may help to account for the wider prevalence of the towel in Mennonite material culture. What *may* have happened is that a folk cultural practice some Pennsylvania Germans enjoyed in the eighteenth century was increasingly discarded by all but the Mennonites and persons closely settled near them as the nineteenth century progressed.

FIGURE 2 *Anna Hiethwole, 1826.* Rockingham county, Virginia. Balanced plain weave linen fabric; red cotton and gold silk cross stitch motifs that are not sewn in mirror image; white cotton hand-knotted fringe. This is the only towel documented to the Pennsylvania Germans in the Valley of Virginia. 51" x 19".[799]

4

FIGURE 3 *Barbara Martin, 1876.* Waterloo County, Ontario, Canada. Balanced plain weave linen fabric; red and blue cotton cross stitch; self and applied plain and knotted fringes. This evergreen tree and lady in a bower motif are frequently seen on Canadian towels but not on Pennsylvania ones. 60" x 20".

At any rate, about half of the towels come from Mennonite homes in Montgomery, Bucks and eastern Berks counties on the one hand and from Lancaster county on the other. They are practically unknown in Northampton, Lehigh, York, Schuylkill and Upper Dauphin, Snyder, Union or Centre counties, for instance. Either they entered the folk culture after these more remote areas were settled—which the evidence contradicts—or they were lost already before most people went into those districts—which the evidence might be read to argue—or they simply never were known in all segments of the large German population in Pennsylvania—which may very well be the case. After all, fashion and its stepchild fad play a role at all times and in all places.

All of which simply places before us the ancient and varied pedigree the decorated hand towels discussed in this book possess.

There remains to point out that this folk artifact was almost exclusively the work of adolescent women—those few towels with men's names no doubt the gift of brides and sisters—and that while there were a few professional seamstresses who made towels to order, most were done by amateurs, in the best sense of that word. As a folk art form, the decorated towel is one of the few not done by "professional" craftsmen. Schoolmasters made *Fraktur,* joiners—apparently—painted furniture, gunsmiths (and joiners and teachers) carved tombstones, tinsmiths made cookie cutters, blacksmiths made objects of iron. All of them did what they did over and over, improving and then tiring of their skill. But few women made more than a couple decorated towels. Their achievement, both of craftsmanship and aesthetic, is the greater because of this perspective.

Well over one thousand examples of handdrawn *Fraktur* have survived to the present. All but a group of bird and flower drawings bear texts which help the student understand *Fraktur.* Well over one thousand examples of handcarved decorated gravemarkers exist in Pennsylvania German graveyards with German inscriptions and decorations not unlike those on *Fraktur.* Over a thousand decorated hand towels have survived. Over 80 percent of these have texts of one sort or another. They are more verbal than any other form of Pennsylvania German needlework with the exception of samplers. Together these three forms of folk art represent the most common decorated objects of the Pennsylvania Dutch. The iconography of *Fraktur* has been discussed and illustrated. Correlations are evident between some texts and symbols. That is equally true of the decorated hand towel. Those texts tell us why the towel was made and the place it had in the culture of these people, but they also offer clues to the meaning of some of the designs. This study is a step to understanding the mentality of the Pennsylvania Dutch as expressed in their workmanship and in their imagery. These artifacts, not quite mute, tell us more about their makers than meets the eye confronted with the relatively few spectacular colorful towels that exist.

5

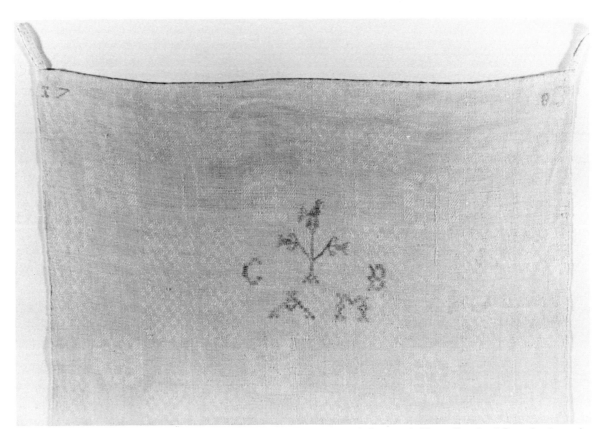

FIGURE 4 *CB AM, 1783*. Double face twill and linen fabric; red cotton cross and chain stitch. The earliest dated Pennsylvania towel recorded in this study. 57¼" x 15¼".[415] Courtesy, The State Museum, Pennsyulvania Historical and Museum Commission 69.99.1.

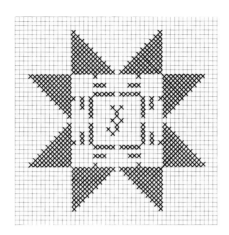

Creators and Culture

A. TOWELS AND DECORATED TOWELS

There were two kinds of hand towels in Pennsylvania German culture. The less common of these was the decorated towel which is the subject of this book. The other was the towel intended for day-to-day use. These towels were similar in size, ground fabric and color, but the decorated towel had a variety of fancy forms of needlework as embellishment. The hand towel is one of a variety of textiles found listed over and over on Pennsylvania German household inventories. These include the clothing persons owned, (Gehret) modest in quantity compared to today, the bed linens (bags for chaff and feathers, sheets, bed, bolster, and pillow cases, and bed curtains), blankets, coverlets and quilts, tablecloths, hand towels, bags, and other textile objects ranging from wagon covers to fish nets to cloths used to wrap the butter taken to market. (Gehret and Keyser) Not to be found in most Pennsylvania German homes, at least initially, were carpets, window curtains or napkins. The quantity of bed linens, hand towels and tablecloths was generally large, compared to the amount of clothing. These quantities probably reflected the *Aussteier* or wedding gift parents provided each child, if they could, as well as the bride's accumulation of her own production. Even after a lifetime of marriage, Pennsylvania German women felt secure if their clothes presses and chests had a good supply of linens stored in them. Each piece frequently had its owner's initials embroidered on it and was sometimes numbered for identification. Thus a young woman began housekeeping with series of sheets, pillowcases, tablecloths, and hand towels.

The German language estate inventories introduce us to the dialect term for towels. It is usually *Handtuch* or, reflecting its pronunciation, *Handduch*. Occasionally the word *Zwele* is found. English equivalents are towel and

hand towel. The prefix *hand* is not in contrast to other kinds of towels, such as bath towels or tea towels. Rather it distinguishes one *Tuch* from another, since this word means *cloth*. A *Handtuch* is not a *Halstuch* (a neck kerchief) or a *Schnupptuch* (a handkerchief). A 1751 Lancaster county inventory reflects this reality. It refers to a bedcloth, a table cloth, and hand clothes, by which towels are meant. (Margret Hover, inventory, Earl township, Lancaster county, 1751)

Use of the term *Handduch* to represent the decorated towel was found in the accounts Anna Weber, a professional seamstress from near Akron, Lancaster county, kept. She wrote, *"Ein handug ausgenet"* (embroidered a hand towel) in her account book when recording her work on one. (Weber, II 1838-1843, 4)

If there was a specific dialect term to distinguish the decorated towel from others, it has escaped us. Conversations with older Pennsylvania German women have not produced a specific term for decorated towels. Hattie Brunner, for instance, who probably did as much for anyone to acquaint the antiques market with this artifact, consistently called them a *Handduch* in the dialect and a *door panel* in English. Old Order Mennonite women in Canada use the term *ausgeneht Handduch* somewhat as Anna Weber does above.

The term for the decorated towel does not appear in any of the estate inventories examined. Conceivably if a decorated hand towel was appraised and listed in estate inventories, it was hidden behind the term *hand towel* or its equivalents. Rarely does one hand towel appear listed alone; they were grouped in quantities. (While inventories list towels in considerable quantities and on nearly every inventory, nothing was found that would point to a separately evaluated towel which might have been a decorated one and no designation for such a towel was found. It should be noted that inventories were made by men, that they reflected the economic value at that time of the objects listed, and that since towels were made by and for the owner, a common notion of their monetary value would not have existed. The inventories cited in this study are part of a collection of about one thousand inventories and sale bills gathered by the author during the past fifteen years in the study of the material culture of the Pennsylvania Germans. They date from 1735 to 1845 and are from Philadelphia, Montgomery, Berks, Bucks, Lancaster, Lehigh, Northampton, York, and Adams counties).

Misconceptions concerning the towel's name and original use probably began about the turn of the twentieth century when people, authors in particular, associated and confused this early decorated towel with wash stands, roller towels, and other stitchery covered towels. The persons who had made these towels were not consulted, but they were still living then and could have properly explained the old custom and practice of embroidering the linen hand towel. Instead, the current terms and usage of the day were applied to the earlier tradition of the decorated hand towel. Facts became confused.

Frances Little wrote in 1931, "Among embroideries that were employed for ornamental household purposes were the gayly colored towels of the Pennsylvania Germans, who not only wove their linens and printed them but worked them in many colors as well. These pieces were used as covers for the more utilitarian articles, and their patterns show the familiar hearts, flowers and birds, worked in cross stitch in bright hues." (Little, 183)

Richmond Huntley wrote an article in 1934 in *American Collector* attempting to see the long, narrow towel as akin to early, long and narrow samplers. Although his thesis was wrong, in that he did not know of the traditional decorated German towel, he did present material on the use of the towel which he apparently obtained verbally from Hattie Brunner. "... throughout most of the 18th and early 19th Centuries, finely worked linen panels intended to be hung on the back of the door of the best bed room were made in large quantities.... Known as door panels, they were theoretically the display towel for the guest room." It is significant that the term *show towel* is not used here, but the author seems to coin the phrase *display towel*. (Huntley, 3)

Catalogues of auctioneers Gilbert, Kleinfelter and Pennypacker of Lebanon and Reading, examined for the period 1936 to 1961, reveal no single use of the term *show towel* and consistent preference for *door panel, linen door panel* or *homespun linen door panel*. As recently as 1959 the first reference in a sale catalogue

calling the object a homespun linen towel appears, but that is the only such in the period to 1961.

Frances Lichten followed in 1946 with *Folk Art Of Rural Pennsylvania* in which she stated, "On 'show' towels, (*Parade Hand-Tuch*) the finest stitchery was lavished, for these long, embroidered panels were used only for display. Here as in Europe, they were hung as decorations on the doors, where they served not only as indisputable evidence of the house-wife's deftness with the flax wheel and the needle, but also had a practical use. In the days when water had to be drawn from a well, laundering was a tedious process; so cautious housewives, when guests came, did not set aside a slightly used towel. Instead, they covered it with a 'show' towel, always made with two tape loops for ease in hanging." (Lichten, 56) It is entirely possible that the term *show towel* was the creation of Frances Lichten. We find no earlier reference to it than hers.

By 1951 Fredric Klees used the term *show towel* in *The Pennsylvania Dutch* without the quotation marks that Frances Lichten used. "Finest of all the fancy work, and a treasured part of the *Haus-steier*, were the show towels that were hung over the everyday towel when company was expected. These were long homespun panels embroidered in cross stitch with tulips, hearts, stars, peacocks, roosters, distilfinks, and always with the maker's initials and usually the initials of her true love as well." (Klees, 379)

Most twentieth century authors have continued to follow suit by quoting from these well-meaning historians. One of them has even stated, "These towels were made by and for young women to show the proficiency of their needlework skills to suitors and as marriage dowry or special gifts." (Garvan, 261)

There is no evidence that the Pennsylvania Germans ever used these towels to cover soiled household towels, or made them to attract suitors. Nor is there any evidence from the eighteenth or nineteenth centuries when these towels were made for German terms like *Überhandtuch* or *Paradehandtuch* or English terms like *show towel*.

The decorated towel was unique in American culture to the Pennsylvania Dutch and is relatively unknown outside the folk cultural area. A related textile the sampler (or more often more precisely called a needlework picture) is found among both the Germans of Pennsylvania and other European settlers of North America.

Decorated towels reached the peak of their popularity between 1820 and 1850. The earliest towel discovered is dated 1783.[415] [Figure 4] There are others from the 1890s.[214,664] [Figure 183] And some Amish women have worked them as recently as 1948.[969] [Figure 167]

B. A WOMAN'S TASK

The preparation of household textiles was primarily women's work in the Pennsylvania German culture, a culture which had strong sex-role differentiations. Men grew the flax and broke it, but women helped harvest and process it. They spun it. Men tended the sheep and sheared their wool. Women spun it into yarn. Professional weavers, fullers and dyers, most of them men, made it into cloth. But women made the cloth into objects, including those listed here. Although preparing clothing was a lifetime activity, making bed and table linens and towels was an intense activity of adolescence, in anticipation of marriage.

It is at this point in life that the decorated towels were made. It was young, unmarried women who spent the hundreds of hours necessary to apply fancy stitchery to a linen towel. Some makers embroidered the year they completed making the towel on it as well as their date of birth. Susanna Groff[771] was eleven years old; Fronica Krebielin[408] and Anna Kreider[827] were sixteen; Susan Killefer[611] was eighteen. "Maria Young worked in the 19 teen year of her March."[798] Salome Kriebel[453] was twenty

[Figure 111] and Rebecca Gerhard[279] was twenty four. These ages agree exactly with similar information yielded from genealogical researches into the birthdates of others who put only the date of workmanship on the towel. (See Appendix II) Creating a fancy towel was, like preparing other household linens, a primary activity of adolescence.

A few towels were made by women such as Elizabeth Traub after marriage and embroidered with the husband's family name.[757] Sallie L. Alderfer made two towels in 1896 the year she married; one with her maiden name and one with her new name Sallie L. Halteman.[1011,1012]

Apparently most girls were content to make one towel—or were busy elsewhere, fatigued or bored after they had made one. Sarah Sugrist,[410,411] Deborah Heebner,[346,347] Elisabeth Erb,[426,427] [Figures 5, 6] Elisabeth Rinker,[314,319] Leah Lapp,[327,328] and Catherine Weaver[774,775]—among others—made at least two towels. Anna Kurtz made at least three towels.[627,629,630] Improved craftsmanship may usually be detected on the second towel.

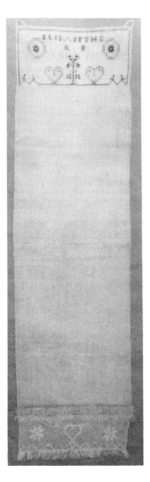

FIGURE 5 *Elisabeth Erb, 1811.* Balanced plain weave linen fabric; red cotton and brown silk cross stitch; white cotton darning stitch on drawn thread grid; self plain fringe with red cotton yarns inserted into it. This is one of two towels made by Elisabeth Erb. See Figure 6. 54½" x 15¼".[426] Courtesy, Hershey Museum of American Life.

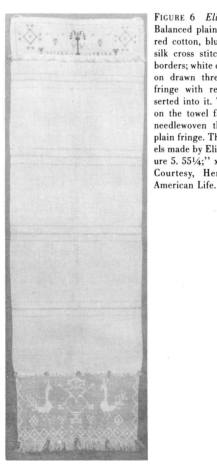

FIGURE 6 *Elisabeth Erb, 1812.* Balanced plain weave linen fabric; red cotton, blue linen, and brown silk cross stitch and needlewoven borders; white cotton darning stitch on drawn thread grid; self plain fringe with red cotton yarns inserted into it. The flap is outlined on the towel fabric by red cotton needlewoven threads and applied plain fringe. This is one of two towels made by Elisabeth Erb. See Figure 5. 55¼;" x 18¼".[427] Courtesy, Hershey Museum of American Life.

FIGURE 7 Lydia Clayton embroidered this flap on her towel for Catharine Dentzler in 1856. Balanced plain weave linen fabric; red and blue cotton cross stitch. See Figures 171, 251 for another of her towels. Flap: 4" x 18".[258]

From the generally mediocre quality of workmanship on the towels it is evident that most of those who made them were trained at home by mothers or grandmothers. In only a few instances does the stitchery indicate that the towel was made by either a professional seamstress or someone who had disciplined training by a professional. The embroidered towel is a folk phenomenon, not the result of schooling.

Some women embroidered towels for others. Ruth Hoppel made a miniature towel in 1825 for Mary Stauffer, aged twelve, and sewed RH on it.[573] [Figure 547] Other towels described themselves: "L. Clayton's Needlework for Catharine Dentzler 1856."[258] [Figure 7] Or, "This towel was mad[e] by Your Au[n]t Susana brubacheren manor township lancaster County State of Pennsylvania in march the 2 a.d. 1839 for Anna Brubacher."[1059]

Christina Hess apparently made a number of towels, not all for herself.[285,392,468] [Figure 324, Plates 39, 46] She was born in Conestoga township, Lancaster county, in 1790, a daughter of John and Elizabeth (Musser) Hess. She never married. Her father died in the second decade of the nineteenth century and she and her sister Elizabeth (1785-1851) acquired a tract of 17 acres on which they lived together until their deaths. The tax lists of Conestoga township call her Christina or Stena and refer to the two women as spinsters on the "freeholders" (unmarried persons) schedule. The census of 1850 is more specific: it names Christina Hess, age 60, seamstress, with Elizabeth Hess, age 65, seamstress, and Sarah Kreitler, age 15, in the household. Christina or Christiana (the anglicized form of the name) died January 26, 1854. Elizabeth, who died first, left a will, leaving what she had to her sister Christiana, upon whose death it was to be bequeathed to Sarah Kreitler.

Christiana's heirs were 1) her brother Christian (1777-1853), whose wife Christiana (1777-1853) has previously been mistaken as the maker of these towels; 2) her sister Fanny (1788-   ), married to Jacob Menart, Sr. (1791-1878); 3) her sister Esther, married to John Shenck; 4) her brother Samuel (1784-1866) married to Anna Menart. Christina Hess was buried on Melchior Hackman's private cemetery. An inventory of the possessions of Christiana Hess was made February 2, 1854, by Melchior Hackman and George D. Warfel. There are five lots of material items including beds and bedding and bedsteads and tablecloths and "Sundries." Nothing specifically related to the work of a seamstress is mentioned. Christina's towels are discussed below, page 58.
(For the information on Christina Hess we are indebted to Clarke E. Hess who drew from these sources: 1850 census, Conestoga township, Lancaster county; Christina's sister Elizabeth Hess will, Lancaster county, Will U I - 1043, 1851; estate records of Christina Hess, Lancaster county Orphans Court Records, Vol. 1852-1855, 386, 387; Register of Death, Lancaster county, 1852-1855, 135; tax lists, Conestoga township, Lancaster county, 1820-1854).

Rebecca J. Minnich made two towels for her siblings which have survived[18,575] as well as a sampler. Rebecca was born September 4, 1824 and died August 8, 1885, and never married. The sampler is marked "Rebeca Minnich 1843 daughter of John and Barbara Minnich." [Figure 105]. One towel was made for her brother Emanuel J. Minnich (born in 1827) and is dated 1849 and January 24, 1850.[18] [Plate 11] It is a full-sized towel and contains considerable text as well as an unusual calendar circle [Figure 201] and an "eeagle." [Plate 27] The second towel was made for Catharine Halanah Minnich and is dated March 14, 1850.[575] It is a smaller-sized towel. Catharine was born March 24, 1845; the towel was ready for her fifth birthday. It too has extensive text [Plate 48]. A third towel[1054] bears the name of a sister Maria (born February 26, 1822) who apparently made it and dated it August 25, 1842. She died February 4, 1844, and may well have been sickly which would account for the unusual August date when few people had time for needle-work. This unusual document bears several hymn verses and other sayings as well as a carefully stitched copy of "st sophia at Constantinople"—there in all its glory [Figure 477] "for my parents and my friends to look upon when I am dead and gone." [Figure 476]

Like Christina Hess, Anna Weber was a single Mennonite woman who made her living by sewing. Born in January, 1796 at Weaverland in Earl (now East Earl) township, Lancaster county, she was the eighth child of Samuel and Anna (Heatwole) Weber. Anna's mother died in 1808 and her father, a linen weaver, in 1825. Anna lived with her father until his death; in 1829 she moved to her sister Magdalena Shirk who had been widowed in 1826. The two sisters lived together on the Gravel Hill just south of present day Akron, Pennsylvania. Anna kept detailed records of her day to day finances and some of her other activities. In one entry she recorded, "*Ein*

handug ausgenet fir Mäde Scherck Julius 1838 . . . 26¢." [A handtowel embroidered for Made [Magdalena] Scherck, July 1832, 26¢.] (Weber, II 1838-1843 4) In August Anna spent three days quilting for a total of 37½ cents—12½ cents a day. Assuming that the same pay scale was obtained when she embroidered, we may say that it took her a little more than two good ten hour days to complete the towel. Unfortunately the towel she made is not one of those found in this study.

Anna Weber died September 1, 1876, and was buried on Metzler's Mennonite Cemetery next to the meeting-house where she had likely attended meeting for more than forty-five years. (Information on Anna Weber was gotten from these sources: 1850 census, West Earl township, Lancaster county; Anna Weber will, Lancaster county, Will Book C, Vol. 2, 133; Tombstone at Metzlers Mennonite Cemetery; Weber-Weaver History, 9,15).

C. DOOR PANELS

The finished towel was made to beautify a home. Sometimes one was a gift or a commemorative piece, but they were not made as substitutes for samplers. Samplers had a place in their own right in Pennsylvania German culture, as chapter four will explain. Towels are akin to the needlework pictures (that are sometimes misnamed samplers). They were intended for display, whereas the sampler was not. But in Pennsylvania German homes the towel did not hang on the wall. It hung on a door instead. [Plates 3,4]

Initially the decorated hand towel was displayed on the living room side of the door between the kitchen and the living room or stove room. Because of cold and drafts in the early Pennsylvania houses the doors were kept closed. Thus what would appear to be the back was actually the front of a door which could be seen in the main room of the house where many of the day to day activities occurred. Here the family prayed and ate. Here the women spun, sewed, and reared children. Here, in some houses, the parents and infants slept. Here guests were entertained around the warm jamb stove.

Because most doors were painted, usually red or blue, the embroidered white towels with drawn work panels would have stood in pleasing contrast to the closed doors. No wonder that antiques dealers early in the twentieth century called them door panels.

The earliest documentation of the towel hanging on a door in Pensylvania is a door, with its pegs to hang the towel, in a half-timbered one and a half story Germanic house on North Market Street in Schaefferstown, Lebanon county. The date 1757 is carved on a cornerpost. The door has been removed from its original location in the house, but the architectural evidence is clear. Glued into the walnut door on the *Schtubb* [stove room] side, 13-7/8 inches apart, are two walnut button-like pegs. Each peg is fifteen-sixteenths of an inch in diameter and seven-

eighths of an inch long. This required the use of large sized loops for hanging sewn onto the top of the towel. The pegs are placed 2-5/8 inches from the top of the door and 9¼ inches from the left side and 7¾ inches from the right side. The door itself measures 32¾ inches wide by 68½ inches high providing ample space on which to hang the embellished towel. The door and the knobs have the identical layers of paint; they are original to the door and not added at a later date. [Figures 8,9]

In another Lebanon county house, dismantled in the spring of 1984, evidence was found for hanging a towel. On the living room side of the door between the kitchen and the *Schtubb* was one brass knob in the top rail of the door, and a mark where the other knob had once been. The knob and the mark were about eighteen inches apart. The door dates to the third quarter of the eighteenth century.

It appears, however, that at some point in the nineteenth century, the towel began to be hung on the upstairs bedroom doors, for in some houses evidence of knobs is still apparent on the top rail of these doors. A strong element in support of this tradition is the prevalance of embroidered designs copied directly from Jacquard woven coverlets. Apparently some towels matched the coverlet on the bed in the room. [Figures 84,85,419-422,424,425] Lydia Martin of Blue Ball related in 1976 that a towel her mother's sister made as a gift for her mother in 1890 always hung inside on the guest room door in their home.

Phebe Earl Gibbons' book, *Pennsylvania Dutch and Other Essays*, 1882, was one of the first published sources to draw attention to this fancy towel. Miss Gibbons was specific about where the towel was hung when she described the room in which an Amish meeting was held. ". . . the floors were bare, but on one of the open doors hung a long white towel, worked at one end with colored

FIGURE 8 Painted walnut door with original wooden pegs on which to hang the towel. Schaefferstown, Lebanon County, 1757. 68½" x 32¼".

FIGURE 9 Detail of door showing turned walnut pegs to hang the towel. Schaefferstown, Lebanon County, 1757.

FIGURE 10 Towels were folded in this manner for storage in chests or bureaus during the nineteenth century. They were first folded in half lengthwise, then in half lengthwise again. Then the top was folded to the bottom and creased at the middle. This was again folded in half, middle to bottom. See Figure 126.[97]

figures, such as our mothers or grandmothers put upon samplers. These perhaps were meant for flowers." (59-61) She continues, "In Amish houses the love of ornament appears in brightly scoured utensils, - how the brass ladles are made to shine! - and in embroidered towels, one end of the towel showing a quantity of work in colored cottons." (17)

In some European cultures decorated towels were displayed only for Sundays or festival occasions. Whether that was true in Pennsylvania cannot be said. The condition of many surviving towels is sufficiently good that it is unlikely that towels were displayed endlessly. We suspect that many were never hung, but resided in chests or bureaus (the piece of furniture the Dutch called a *Draar*), folded—so permanent do some of the creases in them seem to be. [Figures 10,126] Some have never been washed. Some are so faded, however, that one wonders if they were actually used to dry hands at some point in their history, as Henry Francis DuPont in this century in fact did use them as guest towels in a powder room.

In some homes towels were treasured heirlooms passed from mother to daughter for many generations.[11,609] But most towels have been sold at household vendue and found their way into public and private collections.

D. WORK EQUIPMENT

Making a decorated hand towel required more time, patience, and imagination than expensive sewing supplies. Basic needlework tools were an integral part in the home life of Pennsylvania Dutch housewives and their daughters for great quantities of hand sewing they did. [Figure 11]

A most important self-made tool needed when preparing to embellish a towel was the needleworked sampler on which were recorded letters, numerals, and as many as one hundred separate cross stitch motifs. While the sampler was consulted when marking other household linens perhaps its most important function was to aid in designing decorative needlework, especially the towel. As listed in Pennsylvania German estate inventories and sale bills, the monetary value of a sampler was minimal. Two samplers were sold in 1837 at the vendue of Abraham Custer in Skippack, Montgomery county. One sold for eleven cents, the other sold for six cents. (Abraham Custer sale bill, Skippack township, Montgomery county, 1837) The 1835 household inventory of Susanna Gorgas, Lancaster county, listed, "2 pocket books, Several Samplers, needles, etc. $.75" (Susanna Gorgas inventory, village of Ephrata, Cocalico township, Lancaster county, 1835) Its significance to women and young girls as a marking reference was far greater than the value given to it and other tools kept in the sewing basket. See also chapter four.

It is unfortunate for needlework historians that more samplers and decorated hand towels have not stayed together until present times. Most likely when an estate was divided the sampler was given to one child and the towel was inherited by another, or they were sold at vendue. Such a legacy makes it extremely difficult today to find both the sampler and hand towel made by the same person. A few examples of towels and samplers by the same girl do exist such as those of Anna Carle,[756] Catarina Franck,[807] [Figures 98,99] Fanny Nissley,[574] [Figures 102,103] Mary Nissley,[856] Salome Kriebel,[454] [Figure 110; Plate 6] and Rebecca J. Minnich.[575] [Figure 104; Plates 11,48]

The sewing basket, *Neh Karb* (Susanna Bleyler sale bill, Milford township, Lehigh county, 1821) or *Neths Körbgen*, (Gatarina Reiben sale bill, Upper Hanover township, Montgomery county, 1802) kept in the kitchen dresser when not in use, was filled with necessary scissors, thimble, pin cushion, needlecase or box with needles and pins, threadcase, balls of handspun sewing thread and skeins of colored yarns. Appraisers seldom inventoried sewing tools or supplies, but when they did, the sewing basket ranged in value from six pence (Gatarina Reiben sale bill, Upper Hanover township, Montgomery county, 1802) to two shillings seven pence. (Henry Schleiffer inventory, Upper Hanover township, Montgomery county, 1797)

The "neatel basket" (Anna Mary Miller inventory, New Hanover township, Montgomery county, 1826) or "basket with sewing equipment" (Abraham Rex inventory, Heidelberg township, Lehigh county, 1825) was often a low coiled rye straw or willow basket—sometimes with an open or "cut" work band—lined with silk, chintz or handwoven fabric to prevent the loss of pins and needles. The coil of rye straw was small and delicate and the basket often had a footed base. Some had separate lids.

Octagonal pasteboard boxes covered with brightly printed paper also served as receptacles for sewing supplies as did little paper containers with lids sometimes called a band box. Regina Heebner (1777-1862) of Hereford township, Berks county used such a box which still exists. It is five inches across, 3½ inches deep and covered with pink paper marked in yellow and black designs. Her daughter Christina Schultz (1815-1910) from Kraussdale inherited the box and kept her sewing equipment in it including a small printed cotton threadcase, 2¼ inches wide and 6¼ inches long. Her cross stitched initials CS are sewn in blue cotton at the top.

Handmade threadcases designed with small pockets to hold skeins of embroidery thread were often made of scraps of printed cottons or hand embroidered linen. They varied in size and were not generally listed in inventories, but were nonetheless convenient and useful when sewing on the linen towel.

Needleboxes and horn or bone needlecases with screw lids stored the costly needles, *Nodle*. The estate of Ehlon Miller, 1785, Ephrata, Lancaster county, included a needlebox valued at one shilling nine pence. There are so few references to them that needlecases were probably not widely used in the Dutch country. Or were they more important to the embroiderer than the appraiser? Tape, needles, and pins were sometimes valued together, but if specified a "little needle" was worth four shillings (John Fuller inventory, Hanovertown, York county, 1786) whereas ten "darning needles" were worth one shilling. (Martin Keeler sale bill, Limerick township, Montgomery county, 1792)

Purchased household straight pins, *Spellen*, sometimes called "pens" (Willmina Licey sale bill, Hilltown township, Bucks county, 1815) were sold from one household as a "paper of pins" for one shilling one pence. (Martin Keeler sale bill, Limerick township, Montgomery county, 1792) Eighteenth and nineteenth century pins were a thin piece of brass wire with a sharp tapered point at one end and a small circular knob at the other. They were needed to secure two towel units an equal distance apart while being joined by faggotting, needlelace or other insertions. A *bax mit spellen* or box with pins was mentioned in one inventory. (Susanna Bleyler sale bill, Milford township, Lehigh county, 1821) Boxes and needlecases prevented the loss of needles and pins better

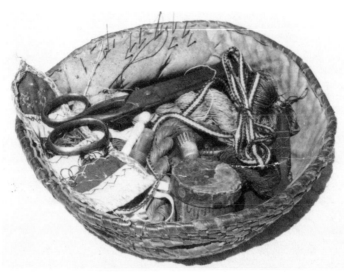

FIGURE 11 A rye straw sewing basket with needlework tools needed to decorate a hand towel.

than did pin cushions. Homemade pin cushions, *Schpella Kisse*, took on assorted shapes and sizes from the square and rectangular ones attached to the inside lining of the sewing basket to bird, spherical, and other shaped ones. Made of linen, chintz, printed cotton, silk, wool, or combinations thereof, they had more visual appeal than monetary value. A plain pin cushion belonging to Magdalena Kolb in 1823 was sold at her estate sale for 6 cents, (Magdalena Kolb sale bill, 1823, New Hanover township, Montgomery county) but another pin cushion with hook and chain was worth ten shillings. (Rebecca Brodhead inventory, Berks county, 1788) Some even had owner's initials cross stitched on them.

A combination pin cushion and sewing box was sometimes made of cardboard in the same manner as a band box. One example which has survived is from a Schwenkfelder family in Worcester township, Montgomery county. It is 3½ inches long, 2½ inches wide, and has a silk-covered pin cushion fastened on top of the lid. A long narrow mirror kept in place by the printed paper covering the box is on the front of the box. Mirrors were useful to reflect and reverse a cross stitch image or border.

Thread, *Neths* (Mary Beitler sale bill, Richland, Bucks county, 1826) or *Netz* (Anna Schultzin sale bill, Upper Hanover township, Montgomery county, 1796) was considerably more valuable than other sewing implements and it was carefully appraised. However, unless it is specified as sewing or embroidery thread the term, as it appears in inventories, is often rather general. "A bundle of white thread." (Philip Morningstar inventory, Manheim township, York county, 1789) "A box and thread." (Abraham Ziegler sale bill, Skippack township, Montgomery county, 1841) "Sowing thread." (John Christman inventory, Limerick township, Montgomery county, 1842; Willmina Licey sale bill, Hilltown township, Bucks county, 1815; Andrew Ziegler inventory, Lower Salford township, Montgomery county, 1797) "A skane of thread." (Hester Ziegler inventory, Skippack township, Montgomery county, 1798) "Three pounds of thread."

(Abraham Stout inventory, Rockhill township, Bucks county, 1812) "A lott yarn and thread." (Henry Muck inventory, Heidelberg township, Dauphin county, 1811) All these phrases described thread as found in the house. Some indicated a box as the thread container. "A box of thread." (Joseph Alderfer inventory, Lower Salford township, Montgomery county, 1831; Eve Custer inventory, Skippack township, Montgomery county, 1816) "Four small paper boxes and thread." (Joseph Alderfer inventory, Lower Salford township, Montgomery county, 1831)

Delicate hand-forged iron scissors, *eine Scheere*, were appraised more often than other sewing tools. They range in value from six pence (Chatrine Swartz sale bill, New Britain township, Bucks county, 1811) to two shillings three pence (Abraham Sell sale bill, Upper Hanover township, Montgomery county, 1799) with only one pair of scissors usually listed per household.

Brass, steel, or silver thimbles, *Fingerhiet*, were seldom included in household inventories.

During the years when towels were being embroidered, local country stores were well equipped to provide most sewing supplies. Basic needles, pins, scissors, thimbles and fancy machine-made fringes were not in short supply. Day books from the Samuel Rex store, Schaefferstown, Lebanon county, record in 1798 selling "scanes of silk thread, thimbles, lace, needles, pins, and scissors." Joseph Bombarger purchased 2¼ ounces of "Turkey yearn" on September 11, 1802 for two shillings ten pence. (Samuel Rex store accounts from 1798, Nos 1, 6, 18, 20.)

During 1839 and 1840 when decorated towels were at their peak the Stetler store in Frederick township, Montomery county had available, "skains of silk, English scissors, sewing coten, plaited thimbles, needles and insertion." (Stetler store account book.)

Young Pennsylvania German women of yesteryear have given us a rich and abundant needle art form. It deserves our attention.

14

E. AN EXERCISE FOR ADOLESCENTS

The making of towels—an activity of adolescence—was, as we have seen, a step in anticipation of married adulthood. It was more; and the more involves the Pennsylvania German understanding of adolescence. There are several twists in the fiber of the story.

Formal classroom education for many Pennsylvania Germans terminated at age thirteen or fourteen, at the end of eighth grade even after the common school act was adopted in 1834. The Amish still succeed in concluding schooling for their children at that age. But it was never part of the Pennsylvania German concept that education should terminate at that age—only that institutional education (except for certain professions) should have given the child by that point the fundamental book skills of reading, writing, and arithmetic. At that point in life it was time to learn more practical skills related to the economic reality of self-support. One way this next step was achieved, into the nineteenth century, was by apprenticeship. The master provided room, board, discipline, training, time for catechetical instruction, and a suit of clothes at the end of the training period. Apprentices were expected both to work and to acquire skills. The important feature to remember of this system was its expectation that adolescents would acquire a skill with earning power. The skill was taught almost on a one-to-one basis by a person who had mastered it. Most of these were skills of doing things with one's hands. Even in less formal learning situations than apprenticeship, such as in the home, the one-to-one teaching of a skill was common.

Even more basic was the realization that adolescence was a time for self-mastery, self-control. Pennsylvania Germans believed that that was acquired by doing things, by making things. Even if the apprentice did not have to submit a master piece for advancement, he still strove to master the skill he was about, to be able to do it as well as his master. Mastering a skill and developing self-control were closely related in Pennsylvania Dutch mentality.

Making a decorated towel was part of this development of skill/self-control. Girls made samplers, then made towels. Or they made several towels, improving as they went. One Pennsylvania German woman wrote an autobiography describing her grandmother's exercising the role of master late in the nineteenth century which catches some of the spirit of the whole transaction.

I was born February 2, 1881 (Ground Hog Day) which, as my mother told me, was a very blustery cold snowy day....
I was either six or seven when my father died.... In the few years that my father lived, the most vivid in my mind are the yearly trips he took us to Boiling Springs ... the reason for those trips, was to visit by mother's mother or my grandmother. As I got older my sister Katharyn and I would visit grandma.... Grandma died in 1895 and was all but ninety five years old.... She to[o] came to our house. She loved to make quilt patches and quilt so of course she felt my sister and I should learn the art. Of course we would rather have done anything but sit and sew, nevertheless while she was with us, we spent an hour of each day sewing with her and many a crack over the fingers did I get for making too big a stitch and have to rip it out and try again. [Written by Viola Tanger Sheely, Hanover, Pa., July 4, 1951]

Granted that quilts and not towels were the medium—the fashion had changed—the circumstances are the same. More than one girl had the same experience.

Filling time, particularly the in-between time in the life of an adolescent, also is a part of the story. The best way to understand time, in the Pennsylvania German mentality, is to keep busy, to do something. What twentieth century folk call "crafts" were popular among Pennsylvania Germans long ago. Anna Weber, the seamstress, went from towels to threadcases to wallpaper-covered cardboard boxes in addition to the many clothes she made and mended. If there appears to be a compulsion to work, it is because idleness invites temptation. The English word *pastime* invokes pleasure; the Pennsylvania German phrase *Zeitverdreib*, is harsher—literally, driving time on! Sally Landis (1867-1962) commented, *"Mei Maemm hat ihre Hend nie net uff der Schoos gelegt."* (My mother never put her hands in her lap).

If pushing time along is done gainfully, so much the better. The decorated towel was not a utilitarian piece. For a culture that demanded use for everything to allow a fancy extra like an embroidered towel was quite an exception. A purpose was served, however, the purpose of self-mastery, learning a skill, *Zeitvertreib*. Thus it was best if, when you were done, you could announce, achievement in hand, "This is the way I pass my time."—*So kann ich meine Zeit ferdreiven!*

Construction

About the only two things that all decorated hand towels have in common are that they are made with white material and that they are long and narrow. Otherwise, the various kinds of fabrics and sewing threads, the overall sizes and predominant colors, designs and design placements, and embroidery stitch combinations represent collectively and individually personalized statements from young Pennsylvania German women.

We want here to examine the common features, variations, and exceptions found on decorative hand towels in their stitchery and in the basic construction of the towels themselves. Many are similar, but no two are alike.

A. FABRIC

Linen

The beauty of the towel fabric is often overpowered by the embroidery that embellishes it. Most decorated towels were made of Z twist single handspun, handloomed, bleached linen fabric. Only a few were made of linen and cotton woven together and only a small percentage of towels were made from a handwoven all-cotton material.

A balanced plain weave linen material was readily available at minimum cost since it originated in the family's flax patch. It was the common everyday material and making a towel offered opportunity to use small pieces not suitable for family clothing or household bedding.

Domestic and professional handspinners were adept at producing finely spun single linen yarns which in turn were used to weave what was called "fine" linen fabric. Spun flaxen yarns were firm, smooth, shiny, and easy to count even in linen fabric that may not be well woven. The slight irregularities that occurred from hand spinning were not enough to prevent young embroiderers from working.

For the most part, the warp or vertical thread count on the linen towels ranged from twenty-eight to sixty-two warp threads per inch. The weft, fill, or horizontal thread count was from twenty-four to fifty-eight threads per inch. The average towel was made of "fine" linen which meant it had more than forty warp ends per inch. Linen material with less than forty warp ends per inch was called tow and fewer than 10 percent of the towels in this study were made with tow fabric.

Some of the finest linen woven by Pennsylvania German weavers had a warp end count of over fifty yarns per inch, but this was accomplished by using only the finest handspun linen yarns. Only 11 percent of the towels surveyed were made with this extra fine weave fabric.

Linen and tow fabric each produced a towel with noticeable differences in embroidery stitch and design size. Some cross stitch designs made on a "fine" linen resembled woven tapestry or petitpoint more than handsewn cross stich.[115,116,222] [Plate 12] The large stitched designs sewn by BP in 1818 on tow material with a count of twenty-eight warp ends per inch[289] and similar stitchery by Magdalena Meier, 1822[85] stand in sharp contrast. [Plate 25] Gone was the neat, tidy, controlled, and tight appearance usually associated with decorated towels.

If drawn thread work was to be "cut out" of the basic towel fabric rather than to be applied, the linen thread count per inch was doubly important. It was the thread count that regulated the size of the drawn thread grid and what designs could be logically embroidered on it.

A variation in weave structure can be seen on a towel from Montgomery county which has an entire panel woven with two weft threads per shed.[4] Apparently the panel was used intentionally for its cross stitched designs have a definite elongated appearance. [Figure 12]

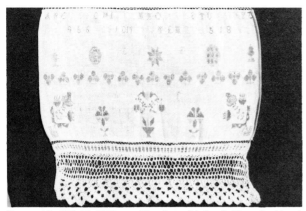

FIGURE 12 *EF AF, 1842* .... The linen fabric of this embroidered panel was woven with two yarns in each weft shot; red and blue cotton cross stitch; mill-woven lace one-half inch high; hand knit white cotton lace 4½ inches high. 9" x 14-3/8".[4] Courtesy, Goschenhoppen Folklife Museum and Library, Green Lane.

Cotton

Anything made of cotton required a cash outlay, for cotton was not a native product of the Pennsylvania farmstead. In addition, not every Pennsylvania Dutch household had what the inventories call a "cotton wheel" with which to spin it. This wheel was apparently different from the "spinning wheel" or "little wheel" used to spin flax fibers and from the "wool," "walking," or "large wheel." All three types were present in some homes. Therefore, locally spun, handwoven cotton material was indeed a luxury and its limited use for towels provided accent and prestige.

It was used as early as 1794 for a decorated towel,[35] but cotton fabric was not always practical for hand embroidery especially when counting threads. Because of its naturally short fibers, handspun cotton yarns tended to be nubby and irregular in size and weight. They were also soft, dull, and fuzzy making them difficult to count and separate when doing count thread work.

One towel has a handloomed cotton fabric panel attached to the bottom of the linen towel.[513] In this piece of cotton the single yarns were spun thick and thin and were then woven with two weft threads per shed in only certain areas of the uneven weave. The count was approximately forty-one warp ends by thirty-one weft yarns per inch. Colorful cotton and silk free-form tulips and small flowers were successfully sewn in outline, straight, and satin stitches on its surface despite all its irregularities.

Other fragments of cotton towel material are on a towel made by Elizabeth Alderfer in 1853 which utilized two separate pieces of cotton, one woven more coarsely than the other.[171] A piece of pattern woven mill-made cotton toweling was used by Anna Byler in 1861 on which she embroidered wool flowers, stars, and birds.[75] Another pattern weave cotton panel was distinguished on an 1810 towel by placing it at the bottom of the balanced plain weave linen towel and attaching fancy knotted fringes to it.[271] In Montgomery county, Sarah Kriebel chose a white

cotton batiste-type material on which she sewed all white chain stitch-type needlework.[402] [Figure 560] This towel, unusual in several aspects, is discussed in chapter six.

All in all very few towels were made of handloomed cotton material. It was more customary to use a purchased, mill-made cotton fabric when and if cotton was used at all.[43,84,92,328] Only 10 percent of the towels in this study were made of cotton.

Linen-Cotton

When linen and cotton yarns were combined in the loom the finished balanced plain weave yardage possessed a dull-shiny appearance. The brightness from the linen and the softness from the cotton added a subtle dimension to the material. This fiber blend was often used for pattern weave tablecloths, but seldom for decorated towels although examples of it date 1825,[833] 1838,[293] 1841,[445] 1851,[452] as well as a few un-dated ones.

Pattern weave

Although the weavers produced fabrics with intricate patterns for utilitarian towels, tablecloths, and coverlets, these patterns were only seldom used on embroidered towels. The most frequently used were the four harness pattern such as "M and O," the heavy twill stripe, and spot bronson. Their use for decorated towels was limited because it was difficult to count and embroider on threads that were pattern woven. When attempts were made only small cross stitch designs and initials were used which often assumed an irregular shape due to the uneven substrate. Free-form embroidery was more successful.[598] This is why only 10 percent of the towels in this study contain pattern weave fabric. [Figures 13, 14]

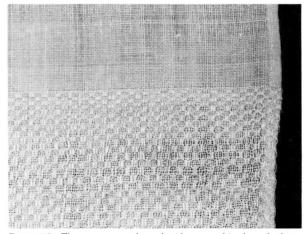

FIGURE 13 The weaver, not the embroiderer, combined on the loom a balanced plain weave linen on which to embroider motifs with huckaback weave. There were three six inch high panels of woven huckaback on the towel.[1031] Courtesy, Clarke E. Hess.

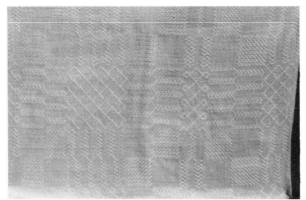

FIGURE 14 Sixteen harness broken point twill linen towel.[1293]

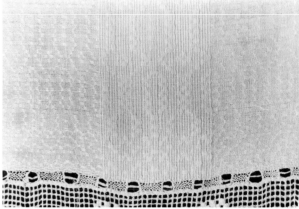

FIGURE 15 This spot weave linen fabric created its own beauty. The nature of the pattern was changed by throwing a shuttle with multiple yarns in the pattern shot (middle). The linen needlelace is three-eighth inches high and is made with the buttonhole stitch.[298]

A practical approach for those who appreciated the beauty of pattern weave linens was either to attach a balanced plain weave panel to the top or bottom of a pattern woven towel or to alternate panels of plain and pattern woven fabric throughout the length of the towel. It was usual to place the pattern weave panel at the top with the plain weave section and its fancy stitchery attached along the bottom edge. [Figure 174] MB, 1823, reversed this order and placed a narrow plain weave panel at the top of the towel on which she embroidered in red cotton and yellow silk her initials, the year, and several designs.[32] The second panel was the longest, measuring 40½ inches, and was pattern woven.

Anna Weber records the same type towel in her diary, *"Ein stick dug aus genet fir oben an ein gebilt handug fir Harriet Heiser Jenner 1839 20¾ [¢]."* [Embroidered a piece for the top of a damask twill towel for Harriet Heiser January 1839 20¾¢.] (Weber, II, 1838-1840, 8) Since Anna earned about 12½ cents daily for sewing it would appear that she spent just under two days making this panel. Again this towel has not come to the surface in this study.

Pattern woven linens used for decorated hand towels took on several other variations. One all-linen towel woven in the typical "M and O" pattern had a second pattern woven into it in a 3½ inch wide vertical stripe from the top to the bottom in the center of the towel.[298] This second pattern incorporated white cotton in the weft direction only. The contrast between the two weaves was unusual. [Figure 15]

Another variant was to team pattern weave linens, with or without woven side borders,[1183] with drawn thread work in the form of an insertion. The 1797 MA HO towel has a 3¼ inch wide vertical drawn thread insertion that extends from the top to the bottom down the center of the pattern woven towel.[581] It is full of darned hearts, diamonds, and other geometric designs. [Figure 150]

A fabric which alternated balanced plain weave material and patterned bands is a four harness pattern weave that is often mistaken for a plain weave. The pattern stripes were created by weaving heavy or multiple yarns in each shot of the shuttle in the weft direction.

Units of these stripes were woven together to make a 1¼ inch[141] to 4¾ inch high band.[697] The bands themselves were spaced every four [382] to 13½ inches.[333] Patterned bands were used as horizontal borders on decorated towels to separate areas of embroidery.[1156] [Figures 16, 381]

It should be noted that only three or four of these patterned bands appeared on any one towel. Three white linen stripes, 1¼ inches high, are on one towel;[333] others[294,833,1159] were woven with red cotton bands and still others[42,382,463] with alternate brown and white linen stripes. [Figure 17] The use of brown linen or red cotton yarns in this type of patterned fabric indicates a custom weaving job. White linen bands were the most typical.

This particular weave with its built-in woven borders should have been a natural choice for would be towel makers, but this was not the case. It was used primarily for tablecloths. Only a small percentage of towels in this study were made of this striped material.

FIGURE 16 A three harness pattern woven band in white linen three inches high. There were three of these stripes on the towel spaced 10½ and 11½ inches apart.[268]

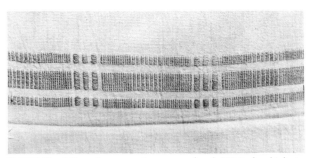

FIGURE 17 A three harness pattern woven band, 2½ inches high, in brown linen. There were three of these stripes on the towel spaced 10½ inches apart.[42]

B. THREADS

Most embroidery threads on towels were commercially produced and purchased at country stores by the towel maker. A small percentage of embroidery threads were homemade. Several things can be learned by examining the reverse side of the towel. The weight of these threads varied from light to heavy. The back of the towel, which was exposed to less daylight, often reveals embroidery thread colors closer to the original shade although frequent laundering has faded them. For those well acquainted with sewing techniques stitch construction can be scrutinized and thread connections between designs studied. Of great importance is the fact that tiny knots were always placed at each end of all embroidery strands. In general sewing, embroidery, drawn thread work, and other forms of stitchery, threads were always anchored with a knot to prevent fraying and thread loss during laundering.

Linen sewing thread

Linen sewing thread was handspun with a Z twist and plied with an S twist on the spinning wheel by distaff members of the family or by locally hired spinners and later it was bleached in the bucking tub and sunlight. It was seldom store bought.

When the basic towel and any elongating additions were cut to size all raw edges were usually hemmed with this white linen two-ply thread to prevent fraying while working on it.

This same handspun two-ply white linen thread was also used to make buttonholed loops for hanging the towel, and for certain kinds of faggotting, needleweaving, knotted fringes, needlelaces, backstitching, and general sewing work. In addition this thread was suitable for attaching tassels or ready-made fringes, butting hemmed edges, sewing flat felled or open work seams, and binding the drawn thread grid. A lighter or finer single or double ply linen thread was often sought for making fine insertions. The thread used for all these techniques was almost always white.

Linen sewing thread was also dyed blue, brown, or left in its natural color, but was used primarily for constructing clothing and other household linens. This dark or light blue and brown linen thread is easily distinguished from cotton embroidery thread by its smooth shiny appearance. It was used occasionally in count thread sewing or as accents in drawn thread work. It should also be noted that white linen yarns were sometimes used to sew free-form and counted thread designs, but more often to darn motifs on the drawn thread grid. Linen yarns for embroidery were observed on decorated towels from 1805 through 1851, but they were probably also used on eighteenth century towels which have not survived.

Weft yarns such as those removed or "drawn out" in preparation for drawn thread embroidery were sometimes used to make a tied-on fringe along the bottom edge of the towel. The crimp in these yarns caused by being woven over and under the warp yarns straightened somewhat after laundering. The re-use of these threads is a good example of the resourcefulness for which the Pennsylvania Germans are famous.

Cotton embroidery thread

Cotton embroidery threads dyed turkey red and dark or light indigo blue were the most popular choice to embellish hand towels despite the fact that they had to be purchased. Yellow, white, tan, and gray colored embroidery cottons[59,237] as well as blue and white cotton plied together[1124] were also used, but are unusual.

Prior to 1820 red cotton was used by itself [Plates 8, 40] or combined with dark brown silk [Plate 20] or blue cotton; [Plates 1, 36] after 1825 this combination of red and brown was seldom employed although there are a few examples from 1831[1137] and 1850.[1211] Between 1820 and 1850 the most popular color choices for decorating a towel were either red and blue or all-red cotton.

The red and blue single Z twist or two-ply S twist cotton embroidery thread was spun either by hand or commercially. Threads made by both types of spinning can be seen used together on the same towel although handspun single yarns were more common in the earlier period. Some single strand cotton embroidery yarns were loosely spun and thus had little abrasion resistance and low tensile strength. The back of one towel has many knots close together. One set of knots is only three-eighths of an inch apart. It appears that the thread broke frequently.[43]

Embroidery done with a two-ply cotton thread or a thickly spun single strand gave a heavier, bolder appearance than a light weight single yarn embroidered on fabrics with the same thread count. This bold, primitive effect was exemplified on a fine weave linen towel with a count of fifty-one warp and forty-six weft threads per inch that was embroidered with a heavy red and blue cotton thread.[233] In fact Lidia Bauman used such a large embroidery thread in 1834 that her cross stitches resembled an embroidered square and not the delineated cross.[65] [Figure 23]

Others preferred the extra-fine single or two-ply cotton yarns some of which have a tight twist. Such fineness was required when embroidering on linen fabric with a warp count of more than forty-five threads per inch. Susana Steinweg used both a fine two-ply and a single

19

cotton yarn for her embroidery, as well as black and gold silk.[102] [Figure 26; Plate 41]

On the towels examined, a fine two-ply cotton embroidery thread was used most often. Definite correlation was needed between the size and ply of the cotton, wool, or silk embroidery thread and the thread count of the linen fabric. Coarse threads could not be used successfully on fine fabric and fine embroidery threads would tend to be lost on coarser fabric.

Wool embroidery thread

What appear to be handspun wool yarns were sometimes used for towel embroidery, but for the most part the machine or commercially spun, mill-dyed, two-ply wool yarn was preferred. Advanced spinning technology and the development of aniline dyes in 1856 made available fine, strong, evenly spun wool threads in bright colors which presented new possibilities to creative embroiderers. Not much towel embroidery appears to be of these synthetic dyed yarns. The colors on towels embroidered with polychromed wools included bright blue, pea green, rose red, wine red, bright red, light and dark orange, gray-green, black, pink, lavender, and dark and light yellow. [Plate 12] A popular combination was yellow or gold wool and red cotton.

As early as 1813 single handspun red and yellow wool yarns were used to sew a wide floral border.[103] Blue linen, red cotton, and black silk color the remaining cross stitch designs. This is one of the few examples on which cotton, linen, wool, and silk embroidery threads were all used together on one towel. From that date on the use of wool embroidery gradually increased to a peak sometime after 1850. Women continued sewing wool onto towels, especially the color red, into the 1890s.

Problems occurred, however. The newly developed aniline dyes and some of the locally produced natural colors sometimes bled during laundering causing major discoloration on the linen towel material. If towels were washed in too hot water the wool embroidery yarns shrank and felted. Even though the motifs can still be distinguished, the needlework stitches became matted together. If the towels were not properly cleaned and stored, moths attacked the woolen threads leaving gaping holes.

Because wool accepted dyes more readily than either cotton or linen, it was a good medium for applying brilliant colors to a towel. And since the fibers were heavier and less expensive than silk it provided more color per pence.

Worsted wools were used only sparingly on towels in the period to 1830. Then it was usually in a red and yellow combination or as a red, yellow, brown or olive accent. Only occasionally was an all wool embroidery towel made with four or five colors.

Once the merino sheep with its finer fiber wool was more widely bred and dyed yarn from its wool more readily available, the towels took on brighter colors. The earliest of these begin appearing in 1830. By the early 1840s about 15 percent had, as it was called, zephyr yarns; by the late forties about a quarter of the towels were worked in it. In the 1850s more than half were done in these brightly colored wools.

Zephyr merino yarns were imported from Germany to New York and from there they were brought to Pennsylvania. The records of the Moravian community in Bethlehem, Pennsylvania show this. "Mr. [John] G. Kummer [of Bethlehem] boght of A. Schrader N.Y. 6 - July 1839 4 lb [?] Zephr $4.5 $18.00 6 oz. German worsted 2.50 .93" "May 7, 1840 160 skeins zephyr worsted $4.00 Fr. Edw. P. Wolle" (We are indebted to Susan B. Swan who gleaned these quotes from the needlework records in the Moravian Archives, Bethlehem, Pa., on March 12, 1976.) It is ironic that the same improved ease of travel which allowed the incorporation of zephyr merino yarns on the towel also hastened the disintegration of the folk culture responsible for making the towels.

Silk embroidery thread

Although embroidery silks offered a wide spectrum of colors and shades, they were seldom used by Pennsylvania German needleworkers on their decorated towels, clothing, bedding, or household linens. Their use was usually limited to samplers and needlework pictures.

Perhaps silk was not used frequently because towels were laundered more often than other pieces of decorative stitchery. Silk embroidery was not as durable as that worked in linen and cotton and was more susceptible to dirt, moths, and fading in strong sunlight. Raising silkworms and processing the filaments into useable threads was not part of the traditional Pennsylvania Dutch folk culture. The women purchased few skeins of silk and used it sparingly.

Small amounts of silk embroidery appeared on some towels before 1800; brown, white, green, and gold colored silk was mixed with red cotton to shade small flowers, initials, and borders.[377,581] Using silk to decorate hand towels continued into the early decades of the nineteenth century, but not much past 1835. Elisabeth Gotschal of Montgomery county filled her towel with silk embroidered designs in 1825, but she was an exception.[111] [Plates 15-19] Generally speaking, all-silk embroidered towels were of the finest quality with superb workmanship.[1225]

If multicolored embroidery silks were used they were pink-brown, gray, gold, pink, maroon, light blue, tan, aqua, yellow, light yellow, and green.[1211,1247,1268] [Plate 24] There were two girls, however, who used only two colors—a light tan or gold silk together with a darker brown silk—to embroider their entire towel.[334,1283] [Figure 18, Plate 38] Silk colors on towels were most often either black or dark brown combined with red cotton.[1119,1145,1152] [Plate 20] Unfortunately the dye used to make silk black-brown has caused the silk fibers to disintegrate and stain the linen fabric brown. Designs have been lost and towels disfigured by this negative chemical reaction, a reaction that has not occurred with other colored embroidery silk, however.

More silk floss than silk twist was used. Floss was softer and laid flat on the linen fabric. We have seen only a few towels on which a silk, buttonhole-twist type

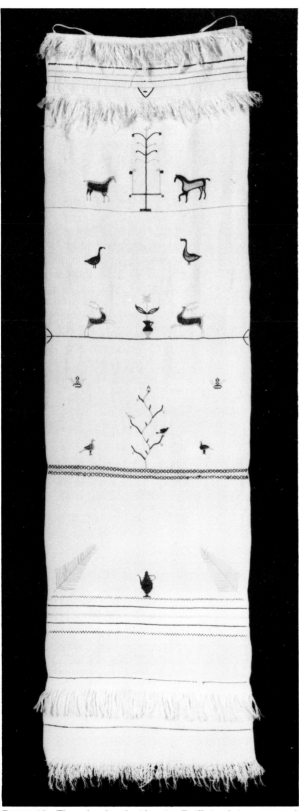

thread was used to embroider all the free-form designs.[513] Silk twist was normally used for clothing construction.

Threads for drawn thread embroidery

Two kinds of threads were required for most drawn thread embroidery. A white linen two-ply sewing thread was used most often for binding together the remaining threads in the grid after groups of warp and weft threads were removed. It also served to hem all four edges of the drawn panel. The binding was done either before or after the designs were embroidered on the grid, but hemming was done immediately after thread removal to help maintain shape and rigidity.

The second essential thread was a softly twisted white cotton yarn to make the flowers, stars, and bird motifs seen on drawn thread pieces. The loose twist of the cotton was important because its fluffy texture is what effectively filled the grid hole making designs.

At other times colored wool yarns,[384,420] red and blue cotton,[14,315,815] [Plate 1] or white [195,260] and brown[37] linen threads accented the all-white cotton drawn thread panel. Entire motifs sewn in colored linen and wool occur less often. It should be noted, however, that when a hard twisted thread such as linen was used more stitches and thread were required to fill the same space on the open grid. A few drawn thread panels were made with all linen threads between 1790 and 1850, but the majority of towels seen used white cotton for darning the designs.

FIGURE 18 The colored embroidery is all silk in chain, cross, and threaded straight stitch; balanced plain weave linen fabric; plain self fringe. See Figures 406, 481. 58" x 16¼".[1283]

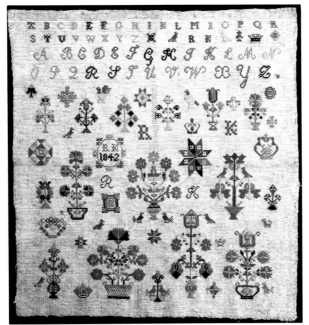

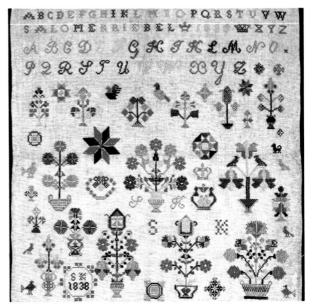

PLATE 5 Sampler. *R[osina] K[riebel], 1842* .... Montgomery county. Balanced plain weave linen fabric; silk cross stitch. Three edges are overcast with white silk. This sampler has forty-two different designs many of which are similar to those on her sister Salome Kriebel's sampler and towel. See Figures 110, 112, Plate 6. L. 15¼", W. 14¼".[457]

PLATE 6 Sampler. *S[alome] K[riebel], 1838* .... Montgomery county. Balanced plain weave linen fabric, silk cross stitch. The edges are hemmed. This sampler has forty designs. See Figures 110, 112, Plate 5. L. 14-7/8"; W. 14". [455]

PLATE 7 Balanced plain weave linen fabric; wool cross stitch; self and applied plain fringes. Bottom of the towel only. W. 16½".[63] Courtesy, Clarke E. Hess.

22

C. DETAILS

The actual construction and embellishment of the basic towel was influenced by the maker's overall concept of design, motif selection, inscriptions, and the desired general appearance. Whether plain or elaborate, the end result demonstrated not only the maker's sewing expertise, but reflected interests in flowers or animals, religious symbolism or sentimentality, genealogy, and sometimes even her sense of humor.

Seams

The towel itself could be made of one piece of cloth or of as many as five[692] or six[583] separate horizontal panels joined by fancy stitchery called openwork seams, butt or antique,[55,62,88,93,269] flat felled,[47] overlapped,[54,250,454] or overcasted seams.[447] Special attention was given to seam construction for it offered opportunity for weakness as well as beauty.

The strong, durable flat felled seam was used most often when flap material was added to the towel,[136,177] [Figure 19] the overall width or length expanded,[87,139] if small pieces of fabric were horizontally or vertically joined to the towel,[401,493] [Figure 29] or if small four inch wide pattern weave cotton strips were added as special accents.[271]

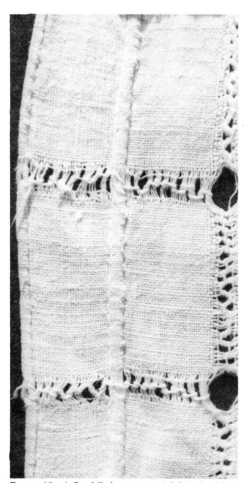

FIGURE 19 A flat felled seam one-eighth inch wide.[47]

The original flat felled seam measured from one-eighth to one-quarter inch wide and was formed by twice sewing together the cut edges of the two pieces being joined. It offered great resistance to wear and fraying. While the seam laid flat it could be bulky at times if the towel was made of coarse weave linen. Most times it was hidden from view by overlapping fringes. Other times its use was decorative.

Salome Kriebel, 1839,[454] Fanny Witmer, 1847,[250] and other towel makers[54] simply overlapped two hems or a hem and selvage edge when attaching towel units together. [Figure 20]

FIGURE 20 On few occasions an overlapped seam was used when joining two hemmed edges.[54]

The butt or antique seam was the most popular choice when joining two hemmed edges. Its use occurred most often when adding horizontal panels to extend the length of the towel.[55,88] [Figures 21, 200] Maria Kral found the butt seam a convenient way to join a fold to a hemmed edge.[368]

FIGURE 21 Two hemmed edges joined with a butt seam attaching an unbound fringe to the bottom of a towel.[55]

A different type of joining occurred when the fabric addition to the towel had a cut or raw edge instead of a hem. It was folded or turned in toward the front or right side of the towel and sewed to the towel itself along its folded edge on the back or reverse side of the towel by using a whip or backstitch.[401] This raw, overcasted edge was positioned under a fringe and not seen.[311]

Each time one panel was attached to another there was opportunity for needlework other than plain sewn seams. The joining of two pieces of fabric by means of these decorative stitches made what is called an openwork seam. Each piece must have its raw edges finished before being joined by any of the insertion stitches. The subject is more fully covered in chapter five. Expertise in many areas of sewing was needed before deciding on seam and overall towel construction.

Hems

A white, two-ply linen sewing thread was originally used to sew one-eighth to one-quarter inch wide plain hems. [Figure 22] Larger hems almost always indicate a later towel. Selvage edges were almost never hemmed.

FIGURE 22 Plain hems on linen towels were made as small as the fabric allowed and were all hand sewn. -1/8''.[697] Courtesy, Sally and Pete Riffle.

The selvage was visible on many towels in either a horizontal or vertical position. Often the length of the towel was one loom width which measured from thirty-nine to forty-two inches. The selvage, therefore, extended across the top and bottom of the towel and the cut side edges were hemmed.[61] In other instances the selvage was placed on one side of the towel with the top, bottom and opposite side hemmed. SF chose to turn and stitch a selvage edge into a rolled one-sixteenth inch wide hem.[510]

There seemed to be no rule determining how to run the warp threads or where to place the selvage edge, but fabric was never used on the bias. Women seemed to use to best advantage what linen fabric they had with little regard for the straight of grain. Practical experience, however, pointed to placing the warp vertically. It was easier to count the threads and the completed towel hung straighter.

It was good practice to hem towel fabric as soon as possible after cutting to prevent stretching and fraying. This was not done on several towels, such as Maria Leaman's, on which narrow fringes were first sewn to the surface of the towel and later the cut edges of the fringe were rolled and hemmed together with the sides of the towel.[636] She made the left hem after her embroidery was completed because every embroidered border and half of a cross stitch design were caught and turned under in the hem.

Flap

The upper area of the towel was usually accented in some way. This emphasis was accomplished by one or several techniques: needlemade four-sided borders;[42,65,191] [Figure 23] a combination of embroidered borders and designs; [Figure 26] hand-folded fabric or tape points;[205,325] [Figure 133] knitted lace;[334] knotted fringes;[45] fringe that extended beyond the top and sides;[466] [Figure 24] or the top edge of the towel was scalloped cut and a white linen blanket stitch bound all the cut edges, a

FIGURE 23 *Lidia Bauman, 1834.* Red cotton chain stitch borders created a flap effect. The other designs, name, and date are sewn in red, blue, and yellow cotton chain and cross stitch.[65]

FIGURE 24 Commercially produced fringe decorated the top edge of this towel instead of a flap. The 1½ inch long fringe was sewn on top of the towel's one-eighth inch hem with the fringe going up and not hanging down. The white linen tape used as a hanging tab is three-eighth inches wide and 1-3/8 inches long.[466]
Courtesy, Dr. and Mrs. Donald M. Herr.

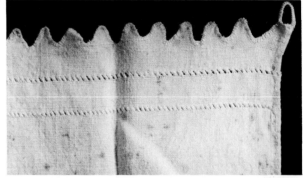

FIGURE 25 To decorate the top edge the fabric of this towel was cut into three-eighth inch deep points and the cut edges were bound with a blanket stitch in white linen thread. There are two points per inch and one inch between the top of the point and the first row of open lacing stitch border below. The buttonholed thread hanging loop is three-eighth inches long.[178]

24

FIGURE 26 A three inch high flap containing twenty-one red and blue cross stitch motifs. A row of red cotton chain stitch was embroidered one-eighth inch from the flap fold. The hanging tabs are white cotton twill tape 1½ inches long.[102]

FIGURE 27 *Lydia Bachman, 1831.* Plain fringe was the main attraction on these two flaps. Each row of fringe, from 1¼ inches to 1¾ inches long, was diagonally bound with red cotton. Balanced plain weave linen fabric; four shades of red cotton cross stitch. Width 17-1/8 inches.[719] Courtesy, Sally and Pete Riffle.

technique found in one instance.[178] [Figure 25, 126] There was also FH who in 1808 attached a one inch wide linen stroke gathered ruffle to the top edge of her towel.[1196] [Figure 174]

About half of the towels in the study have a top flap which conspicuously called out for attention. It was from one-quarter to 12½ inches high[1184] and was formed by folding the upper edge of the towel to the front on itself, or by fastening a separate piece of fabric to the towel with a butt[234] or flat felled seam. The thread count on an added flap piece often differed from that on the body of the towel which in turn created larger or smaller cross stitch designs.[234]

Susana Steinweg, in 1848, made a three inch high flap and by using small two by two thread cross stitches she managed to squeeze twenty-one designs plus two borders onto the flap's surface.[102] She sewed the rest of the towel with larger three by three thread cross stitches. [Figure 26; Plate 41] Elisabeth Dillier stitched twenty-five motifs on a four inch high flap; they did not leave room for much else.[231]

Lydia Bachman affixed on her towel not one, but two flaps in 1831, each of which had three rows of plain fringe on it.[719] [Figure 27] Instead of using added fabric, Elisabeth Erbin, 1812, innovated with needle and thread and formed a flap effect by embroidering top and side borders and then attaching a plain fringe at the bottom edge.[427] [Figure 6]

Fringes were an important element in flap construction. The flap almost always had a one to three inch long self-fringe that was overcast two to three threads deep to prevent fraying. Single or double rows of colorful red, white, yellow, or blue cotton, brown silk, white linen, or dyed wool threads were employed for this job. [Figure 27]

Fringes occasionally extended over the top and side edges of the towel particularly if the flap was made of added fabric.[466] Double rows of fringe were also effective accents and were made by placing one row of fringe above another or one on top of the first. Elaborate machine-made fringes with tassels were sometimes sewn to the bottom of the flap,[1198] [Figure 28] but they were more often attached to the lower edge of the towel.

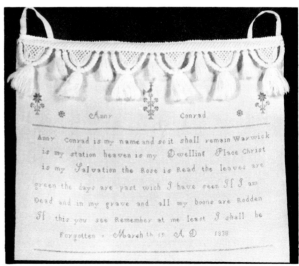

FIGURE 28 *Anny Conrad, 1838 ....* This mill-made fringe, 3½ inches long, provided an accent at the top of the towel instead of a flap. The red cotton cross stitched inscription was embroidered on "fine" balanced plain weave linen and shows examples of upper and lower case block letters, script upper case letters, and typical spelling. Each line of text had a weft thread pulled to create a line on which to place the lettering.[283]

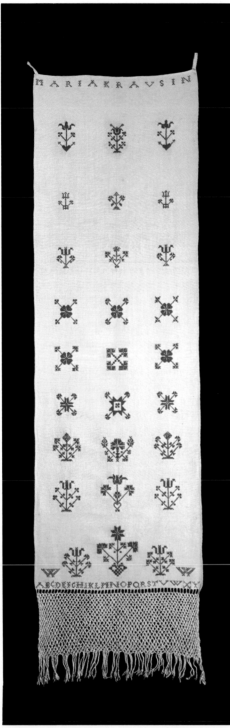

PLATE 8 *Maria Krausin* .... Lehigh County. Balanced
plain weave linen fabric; cotton cross stitch; linen knotted and braided fringe. See Figures 160, 552. 47'' x 13-
1/8''.[339]

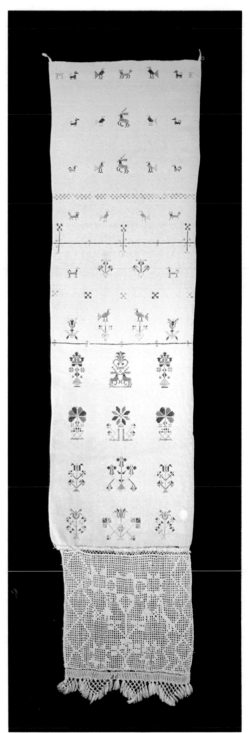

PLATE 9 *M*[aria] *K*[rauss]. Lehigh county. Balanced
plain weave linen fabric; cotton cross stitch; cotton darning stitch in drawn thread grid; applied cotton mill-
made fringe. See Figure 161, Plate 10. 54½'' x 12-
7/8''.[340]

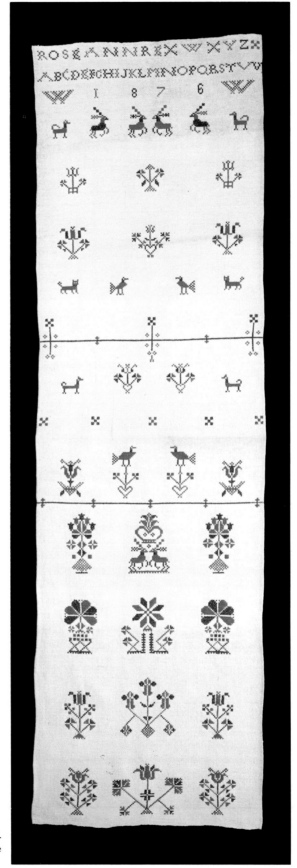

PLATE 10 *Roseann Rex, 1876* .... Lehigh county. Balanced plain weave linen fabric; cotton cross stitch. See Figure 161, Plate 9. 40½'' x 11-7/8''.[341]

Some flaps with long fringe were so large that embroidery underneath it could not be seen. Christina Lenz put the date 1817 under the top flap[109] and Elizabeth Hershey sewed her initials EH under the flap where they were not easily seen.[1278] Sara Lauch deviated a little by embroidering "1824" in plain sight, but then hid the year "1804" under the flap.[311] Was this her year of birth perhaps? [Figure 29]

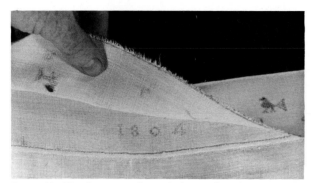

FIGURE 29   The date was underneath the top flap where it was not easily seen. A flat felled seam was used to join the flap to the towel.[311]

Regardless of the size or formation of the flap, the towel's appearance improved if the flap was anchored to the body of the towel in some way. This procedure seemed to impart a degree of support and strength when the completed towel hung on the door. This fastening was accomplished in a myriad of ways: by stitching, by using herringbone, cross, and straight stitches, by embroidering designs through the double thickness of the flap and towel fabric, by attaching buttons, or by sewing the ends of the flap to the towel's edge.

The most common method seen in this study was hand sewn "stitching." It was a form of backstitch that can be classified along with hemming as plain sewing rather than fancy work. But often because of its tiny size, placement, and the color threads used when "stitching" its decorative qualities seem to oppose this classification. Backstitching in dark brown or yellow silk, and red cotton occurs on several towels;[257,302,333,377] however, it was most often worked in white linen thread. Each backstitch was two threads in length and a single row of this finely done needlework was generally sewn within one-quarter of an inch from the top fold of the towel flap. [Figure 52] The purpose of the stitch always seemed to be to fasten two pieces of fabric, therefore "stitching" was also used to attach additional panels[360] or to bind together a double row of fringe.[257]

The herringbone stitch, a favorite of many, was another imaginative way to hold the flap in place. A row of solid or spaced-out oblique cross stitches and vertically made square cross stitches[609] that stretched across the entire width were a few of the embroidery stitches sewn through both the flap and towel fabric. Magdalena Diener fastened two small straight stitches in the exact center of the flap,[286] another needleworker made small

cross stitch squares across the flap,[232] and others embroidered all the designs through the double thickness of flap and towel fabric, plus overcasting the ends together.[301,510,707] A most creative approach was to fasten the flap with small thread buttons of the type usually seen on men's homespun linen shirts from the eighteenth and early nineteenth century.[103,756]

One of the main uses of the flap was to provide a noticeable area on which to emphasize and embellish personal information about the young towel maker. Frequently, her name, a date, and sometimes an inscription were sewn here. The flap was distinguished from the rest of the embroidery.

Applied work

The addition of fabric to the surface of a ground material to make a design has a long history. As an embroidery form applied work (also called appliqué) can be effective whether the design is simple or complicated. Even so its use on towels was minimal.

A small one-half inch square of linen fabric was sewn to the reverse side of the intersection of a one-half inch wide row of horizontal and vertical ladder hemstitching. It not only stabilized and filled in the large opened area, but embroidered in the center of the applied linen square was a tiny cross motif.[1090]

GR, 1810, applied a small rectangular piece of balanced plain weave linen to the center top of her pattern woven towel. On it she embroidered her initials and date.[1277]

A more complicated piece of applied work was accomplished by CH in 1818. She sewed to her towel a tiny piece of red wool fabric as the bird's breast over which she sewed white silk fabric denoting the wing. The tail, legs, neck, head, and beak were embroidered in chain stitch. There were two of these birds on top of a heart motif and each bird measured two inches high and 2-7/8 inches long. [Plate 2] This same needleworker applied a circle of yellow silk fabric to the center of a two inch diameter embroidered flower and held it in place with tan silk embroidered French knots. In each case the surrounding embroidery stitches covered the raw edges of the applied fabric making it unnecessary to turn them under.[285]

The practice of applying printed cotton fabric seems to have been transferred from quilts to hand towels by very few girls. Two large stylized floral motifs, made of plain and printed calico, covered the entire length of a towel. The towel contains insertions and fringe along the bottom edge, but otherwise appears atypical.[1289]

Ruffles

Ruffles were an option considered by only a small percentage of towel makers. Instead of a flap, FH, 1808, sewed a single row of linen ruffles across the top edge of her towel.[1196] [Figure 30] Elisabet Staufer, on the other hand, attached a similar common ruffle to the right and left sides of the drawn thread panel.[1285] [Figure 31] The ruffles were one inch wide, had a one-eighth inch hem

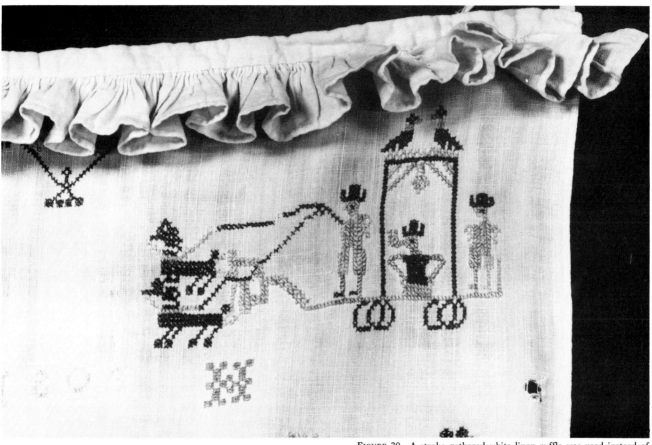

FIGURE 30 A stroke gathered white linen ruffle was used instead of a flap. This 1808 towel includes the interesting horse and carriage motif. Red cotton and brown silk cross stitch.[1198]

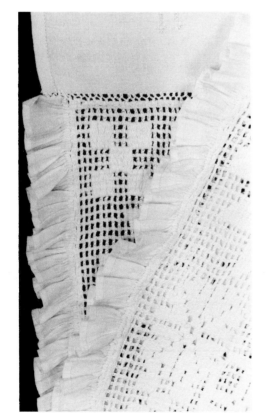

and were stroke gathered onto the linen towel fabric. The raw edges of the ruffle fabric were encased together with the edges of the towel with a separate piece of linen fabric. (For further information about stroke gathering techniques see deDillmont, 10).

Netting

"The term netting usually connotes an open textured single-element fabric with meshes of fixed dimensions secured by knots...." (Emery, 46) This describes the netted panel, much like fish netting, that is attached to the bottom of a small percentage of towels. Most are made of white cotton,[1096,1196] but one netted panel has two horizontal red cotton stripes netted into it as it was made.[1117] Tassels usually hang from the lower edge and

FIGURE 31 Elisabet Stauffer stroke gathered a white cotton ruffle to both side edges of the drawn thread panel. The reverse side is shown on the right.[1285]

29

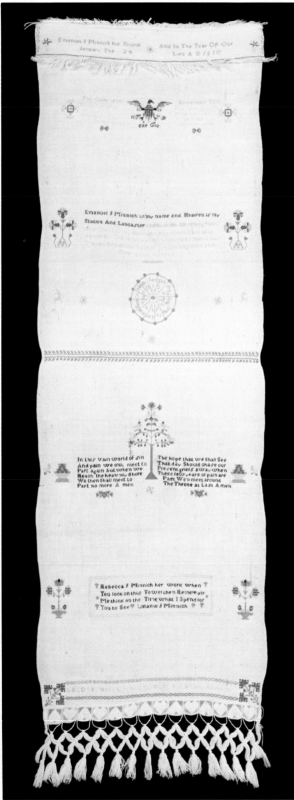

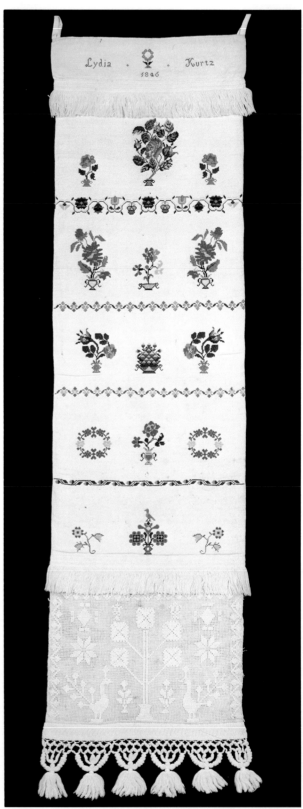

PLATE 11 *Emanuel J. Minnich, 1849, 1850 . . . .* Lancaster county. Balanced plain weave linen fabric; wool cross and chain stitch; applied cotton mill-made knotted fringes; 47-5/8'' x 16''.[18] Courtesy, Dr. and Mrs. Donald M. Herr.

PLATE 12 *Lydia Kurtz, 1846.* Balanced plain weave linen fabric; wool cross stitch; cotton darning stitch on drawn thread panel; applied mill-made plain and knotted fringes. The drawn panel has new fabric backing sewn to it. See Figure 136. 61-1/8'' x 16½''.[469] Courtesy, Dr. and Mrs. Donald M. Herr.

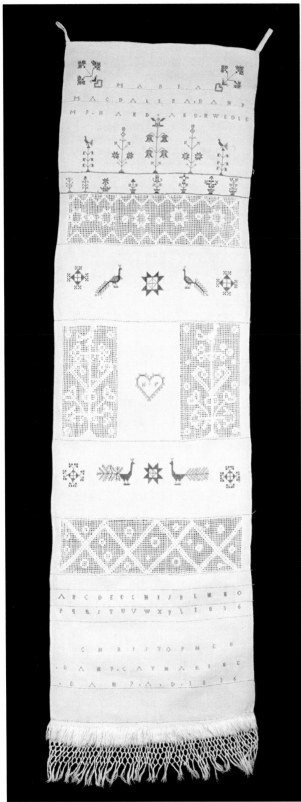

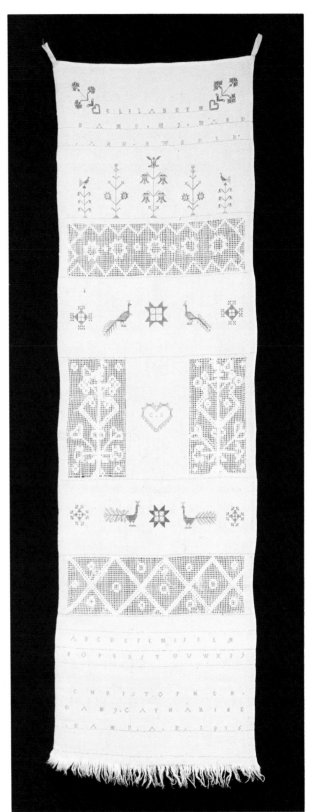

PLATE 13 *Maria Magdalina Damy, 1836* .... Maria Magdalina married Henry Fenstermacher in 1837, one year after the towel was made. She stitched his initials in the center of her towel. Balanced plain weave linen fabric; cotton cross and running stitches; cotton darning stitch on drawn thread panels; self and applied plain and knotted fringes. See Figures 236, 237, 239, 240, Plate 14.
53'' x 16½''.[1335]

PLATE 14 *Elizabeth Damy, 1836* .... Elizabeth married Christian Simon in 1837, one year after the towel was made. She stitched his initials in the center of her towel. Balanced plain weave linen fabric; cotton cross and running stitches; cotton darning stitch on drawn thread panels; self plain fringe. See Plate 13.
57¼'' x 16-3/8''.[560]
Courtesy, Mr. and Mrs. Richard F. Smith.

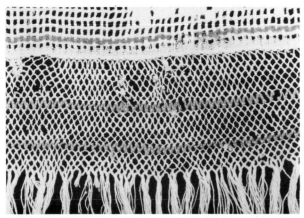

FIGURE 32 White cotton handmade netting with two red cotton horizontal stripes netted into it.[1117]

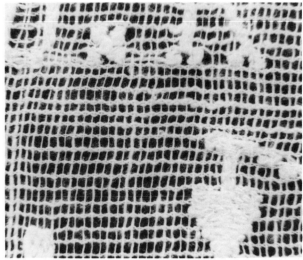

FIGURE 33 Leno weave construction.[50]

the upper edge is handsewn to the towel. The netting is not embroidered in any way, but left to hang and display its own beauty. [Figure 32] These net additions seem to have been of domestic manufacture made with a gauge rod and netting shuttle and not store bought.

Leno

A purchased, not homemade, leno weave panel was used in place of a drawn thread grid or drawn fabric embroidery by only a few girls. The leno weaving process is characterized by, "warp yarns that are arranged in pairs. Two harnesses are required and two sets of warp, the ground threads and the doup threads. The filling is shot straight across the fabric as in a plain weave, but the warp threads are alternately twisted in a right and left hand direction, crossing before each pick is inserted. The crossing threads are called doup threads, and are attached to a special harness called a doup harness which is manipulated to twist the warp threads alternately in one direction and then the other, by passing them through a heddle on each side of the ground thread. This weave gives firmness and strength to an open weave cloth, preventing slipping and displacements of warp and filling yarns." (Wingate) [Figure 33]

RS, 1835, used a white cotton chain stitch to embroider on her leno panel which in turn gave the designs an almost raised appearance.[50] [Figure 34] Another RS sewed a satin-type stitch in multicolor wool to create a large flower motif. This leno panel also had a white cotton fabric backing sewn to it to provide sturdiness.[927] [Figure 133] Still another towel maker used the more traditional darning stitch, the same as used in drawn thread work, to sew the white cotton motifs on the leno woven panel.[1204] Embroidered leno panels impart a certain delicateness not often found on drawn thread grids.

Drawn thread embroidery

Drawn thread embroidery was a technique understood and practiced by Pennsylvania Dutch women on special bedsheets and tablecloths, but most often on a fancy towel. This type of embroidery was nearly as common on the decorated towel as cross stitch. Even the lavish use of drawn thread work on towels did not overpower but complemented the other embroidery. It always seemed to be an extension of the embroidered designs and general "feel" of the towel.

Large drawn thread panels were often made separately and then attached to the bottom of the towel. Squares, rectangles, and borders could also be cut and threads drawn out or removed from the towel fabric.

The subject of drawn thread work is large, and it is so common on decorated towels that an entire section of this book is devoted to presenting our findings. See chapter three.

32

FIGURE 34 *RS, 1835,* Montgomery county, embroidered designs on a leno woven panel and attached it to the towel with a butt seam. The mill-made white cotton fringe with tassels is 4½ inches long. Panel 5'' x 14¾''.[50]

PLATE 15 *Elisabeth Gotschal, 1825* .... Montgomery county. Balanced plain weave cotton fabric; red cotton, brown, gold, blue, light brown, and green silk cross stitch; applied white cotton mill-made fringe. See Plates 16-19.
38½" x 12¾".[111]

34

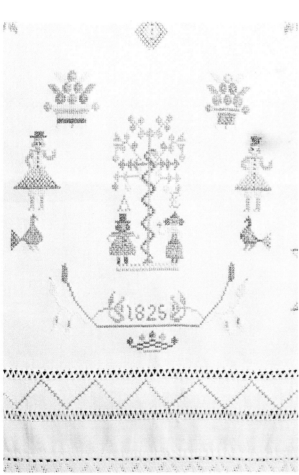

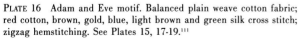

PLATE 16 Adam and Eve motif. Balanced plain weave cotton fabric; red cotton, brown, gold, blue, light brown and green silk cross stitch; zigzag hemstitching. See Plates 15, 17-19.[111]

PLATE 17 Balanced plain weave cotton fabric; red cotton, brown, gold, blue, light brown, and green silk cross stitch; zigzag hemstitching. See Plates 15, 16, 18, 19.[111]

PLATE 18 Eagle motif. Balanced plain weave cotton fabric; red cotton, brown, gold, blue, light brown, and green silk cross stitch. See Plates 15-17, 19.[111]

PLATE 19 Heart with flowers and initials *RH*. Balanced plain weave cotton fabric; red cotton, brown, gold, blue, light brown, and green silk cross stitch; zigzag hemstitching. See Plates 15-18.[111]

FIGURE 36 The red and blue cotton cross stitches inside the top tulip and on several short stems just above the heart are half-stepped or are only one thread instead of two apart. This created the illusion of a curved line. Flower buds were denoted with the double cross or star stitch.[150]

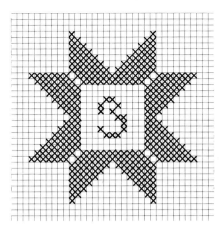

Embroidery

The general subject of embroidery is often divided into "modes" or "styles" and embroidery stitches are often grouped according to the "styles" with which they are associated. However, "the same stitch may be called by different names when used differently and different stitches by the same name when used for the same purpose. Stitchery has acquired a confusing multiplicity of terms." (Emery, 234) Who would argue with the validity of that statement?

Explanations of stitch designations used throughout the text, rather than strict definitions of needlework terms, are given here as they relate to the folk culture and needlework of the Pennsylvania German women. Illustrations and directions for some of the more obscure needle techniques and certain particular aspects of towel construction are explained. The reader is encouraged, however, to consult present-day needlework encyclopedias for basic embroidery and needle technology. Unfortunately dialect names for these stitches, if they were ever common, have not been preserved.

A. COUNT THREAD

Pennsylvania German women decorated their towels by using two general types of embroidery, count thread and free style. Count thread work, specifically cross stitch, was predominant on all their needlework. Small crosses marked everything from bags, tablecloths, bed linens, and wearing apparel to samplers, pictures, and decorated towels.

Count thread embroidery required no drawing, tracing, or transferring of design patterns, but was worked by counting the threads of the fabric and embroidering each stitch over an exact number of threads.

Although there are several count thread embroidery stitch groups, the only ones which occur on Pennsylvania German decorated towels are the cross stitch, herringbone stitch, drawn thread, and drawn fabric stitch groups.

Cross stitch

The cross stitch as seen and defined in this study was a plain cross stitch formed of two oblique stitches, placed one across the other, crossing each other in the middle. They could be made by first counting diagonally over two warp threads and then diagonally over two weft threads, a two by two cross stitch. They could be made larger, of course, by counting and sewing over three or four threads. Changing stitch size altered the height and width of a design which at times worked to the embroiderer's advantage. See chapter four.

Generally, cross stitches were sewn in rows rather than individually as the reverse side reveals. This technique had to be altered at times to accommodate two or more color threads within a design unit. Alternate rows of two colors required constantly re-threading the needle with the appropriate color or using two or more needles, one for each color. The first oblique stitch in each row of cross stitches went in the same direction, left to right or right to left, regardless of the different colors used or the vertical or horizontal direction of the row of stitching. Uniform, even, neat, and flat cross stitches resulted with the majority of the embroidery thread on the front surface. The reverse was also tidy and had no long loops or dangling ends to tangle during laundering.

There are always exceptions. Barbara Meyer painstakingly made each individual cross stitch on her 1835 towel so she used more embroidery thread than would have been necessary.[302] Even worse, Nansey Happel, 1832, left long threads stretching from point to point on the reverse side of a blue and red star.[721] Her dilemma probably stemmed from sewing with two colors and the uncertainty of how to work through the design using the shortest route. Fortunately she corrected her problem on the second star. [Figure 35]

Several variations have been found. In the center of a tulip design the cross stitches were "half-stepped" on

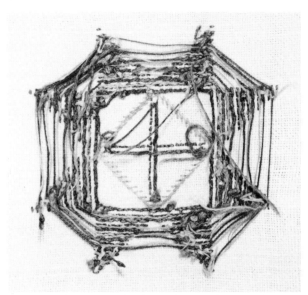

FIGURE 35 The reverse side of an eight pointed star motif showing an exceptionally excessive use of thread in embroidering from point to point. Red and blue cotton thread.[721] Courtesy, Sally and Pete Riffle.

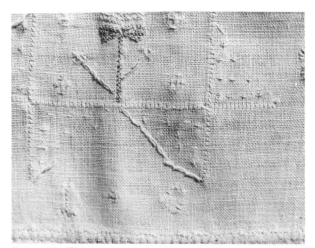

FIGURE 37 White cotton chain stitch and red cotton square and oblique cross stitches. The workmanship was that of a beginning embroiderer.[133]

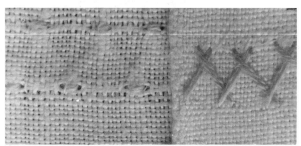

FIGURE 38 The front and reverse side of the herringbone stitch sewn in red cotton and used as a border across the upper area on the towel.[699] Courtesy, Sally and Pete Riffle.

the diagonal which enabled the seamstress to create the illusion of a curved line in less space.[150] [Figure 36] Eliza Brackbill, 1847, sewed ad lib cross stitches in the formation of a turkey, spotted cow, flowers, and birds on a tulip design.[769] Rows of small square, not oblique, crosses were used to fill the open area inside a star on another towel; elsewhere groups of five of this same style square cross were combined to make a larger design.[133] [Figure 37]

Herringbone stitch

Following cross stitch, the herringbone was the most widely used counted thread stitch on decorated towels, and its use spans the entire decorated towel era. It is a loosely worked lattice type stitch that can be worked in a single, double, or triple rows over any number of counted fabric threads. [Figure 38] Large and small, wide and narrow, shallow, steep or close examples can be found. In fact, on one towel a closed herringbone stitch was worked so tightly that the finished product closely parallels zipper teeth.[732] [Figure 39]

The herringbone stitch was used alone most often as a decorative horizontal border.[57,59,85,91] It was also intermixed with the running stitch[29] [Figure 51] and needleweaving[637] to create a wider border element. Mary Kreider used the herringbone stitch with narrow drawn thread borders to divide the bared warp threads into groups.[550]

It was a good stitch to use as a binding on rows of self-fringe to prevent fraying. [Figure 72] Anna G. Herr gained dual duty from one row of herringbone. She sewed it through the double thickness of flap and towel fabric which not only kept the flap in place, but bound the fringe as well. Hers was a large version of the stitch which extended three-eighths of an inch in height having three points per inch.[637] [Plate 47]

The stitch's decorative powers were not limited to borders. Herringbone was also positioned on a seam,[1] hem,[401] or denoted the roof covering on an embroidered house.[125] [Figure 132]

Color enhanced the stitch's decorative nature especially if two colors were used by sewing the first color left to right and the second color stitched right to left.[356] Catharine Dienner embroidered a row of herringbone in red wool and then superimposed a second row in green wool.[212] Some ladies used a double thread in the needle, instead of a single thread, to emphasize its design.

The threaded or laced herringbone is a two-step stitch which was used as an insertion stitch on only a few towels.[445] [Figure 40] This was done by making a row of herringbone across the full width of the towel and then lacing, threading, or whipping it with a second thread.

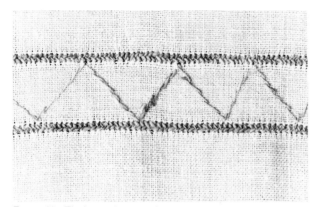

FIGURE 39 The herringbone stitch sewn on every two threads resulted in a zipper teeth effect. The chevrons were embroidered in the stem stitch. The border is one inch high; red cotton.[732] Courtesy, Sally and Pete Riffle.

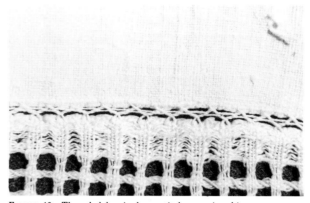

FIGURE 40 Threaded herringbone stitch sewn in white cotton, one-eighth inch high, and used as an insertion.[445] Courtesy, Goschenhoppen Folklife Museum and Library, Green Lane.

B. DRAWN THREAD WORK

Like cross stitch drawn thread work required no drawing, tracing, or transferring of design patterns.

We define drawn thread work as found on Pennsylvania German hand towels as a method of stitchery worked on a balanced plain weave linen material from which counted numbers of threads were removed. There were two ways this was done. First, groups of only the weft threads were withdrawn from the fabric; this is sometimes referred to as single openwork on linen. Wrapping, knotting, or interlacing the bared warp yarns became necessary and stitches were used to prevent fraying of cut edges. Hemstitching and some of its variations, open lacing, needleweaving, needlewoven bars, and the count thread herringbone stitch already mentioned were used in this form of openwork.

In a second type groups of both the warp and weft threads were withdrawn to make a lattice or open grid on which to work geometric patterns. This is sometimes called cut openwork referring to the groups of threads that were cut and removed. The cut edges and supporting threads in the grid were then oversewn and further stitchery added. The darning, diagonal, goose-eye, and ground stitches were used to make designs by re-filling the cut-out spaces or grid holes.

These two techniques are not to be confused with another meaning of the term "cut openwork" which denotes entire areas of fabric which have cut-out shapes removed and later are filled with fancy stitchery. This is not part of decorated towel tradition.

Both forms of drawn thread work were commonly practiced on decorated towels. Examples of one or both types can be seen on almost every towel.

Weft threads withdrawn

Constructing horizontal borders was the primary reason for removing weft threads. The prerequisite was to count and remove specified numbers of weft threads from one side of the towel to the other. This resulted in an opened area crossed only by the remaining warp yarns.

To retain the desired openness of the warp yarns after the weft was removed the woven cut edges of the towel as well as the warp yarns needed to be bound in some way. The most fundamental procedure in this type of drawn thread embroidery was a single row of plain hemstitching which was usually worked in white linen.[25] On most towels hemstitching appeared by itself or in combination with other embroidery in decorative borders throughout the towel.[383,407,419] It was seldom used to decorate a hem.[1093] Instead of a full-sized drawn thread panel, Susanna Heebner put twelve horizontal rows of hemstitching along the bottom edge,[482] and Elizabeth Cassel sewed a four inch high panel full of one inch squares formed by vertical and horizontal rows of hemstitching.[458] [Figure 41]

To make this plain hemstitching, weft threads from the towel fabric for the desired height were withdrawn. The working thread was brought out near the space of drawn threads at the right. The needle was passed behind three loose threads—the number of threads taken together here could be varied to suit the design or fabric—and passed behind the same three threads, this time bringing the needle through the fabric in readiness for the next stitch.

There were variations on the theme of hemstitching, of course. Ladder hemstitching was made exactly as plain hemstitching except the hemstitch was worked along both sides of the drawn threads instead of on one edge only. It effectively bound the warp yarns into groups of three, four,[90] or as many as nine yarns.[99] [Figure 42]

In interlaced hemstitching the top and bottom edges of the drawn thread area were bound or hemstitched, but a working thread, often red or blue, was passed through the remaining warp yarns twisting two threads together as it went. This often formed horizontal borders on towels.[59,60,234,246] [Figure 43] Other times two equal numbered groups of warp yarns were twisted together instead of the individual yarns. BR in 1848 made a one inch high border with as many as seventeen warp yarns interlaced into one group.[309] Interlaced hemstitching was usually worked horizontally, but Cadarina divided the top flap into squares by rows of vertical and horizontal interlaced hemstitching. She then cross stitched her name inside the resultant plain woven squares.[491]

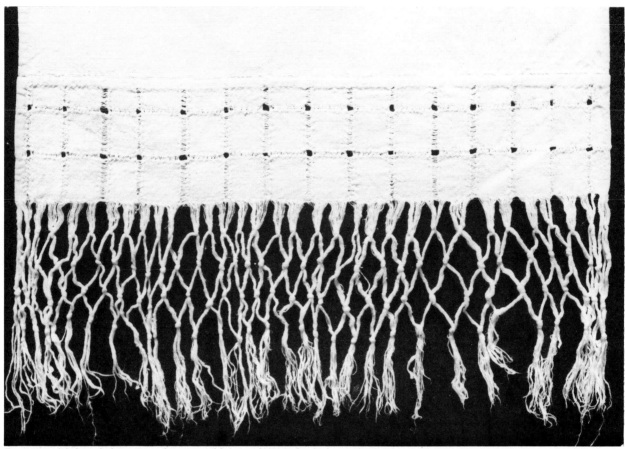

FIGURE 41 A balanced plain weave white cotton fabric panel, 2½ inches high, was divided into three-quarter inch squares by withdrawing vertical rows of threads -1/8 inch wide and horizontal rows of thread -1/8 inch wide creating an open hole at the intersection of the rows. The edges of the fabric squares were hemstitched to prevent fraying. Groups of fourteen cotton self fringed yarns were knotted together for 2½ inches.[998]

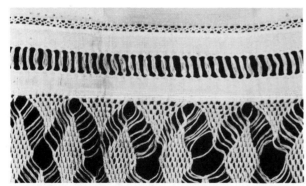

FIGURE 42 Ladder hemstitching, one-half inch high, in which groups of nine linen warp yarns were bound together at the top and bottom with two ply white linen thread. At the top the needle lace insertion was sewn along the selvage edge of the towel, and at the bottom the linen fringe was knotted into a diamond pattern seven inches long.[99]

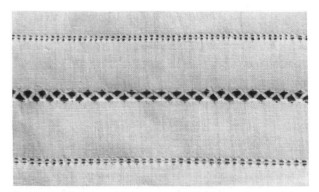

FIGURE 43 The top and bottom rows of stitching are interlaced hem stitching; the middle row is zigzag hemstitching.[989]

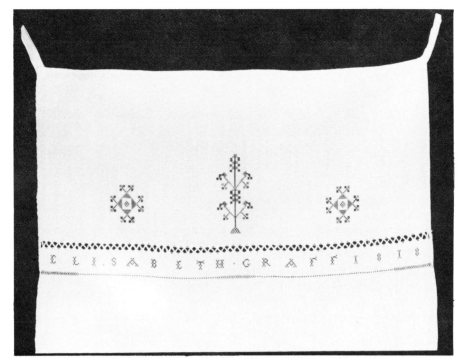

To make interlaced hemstitching one first worked the ladder hemstitch. A new long thread was fastened at the right and interlaced along the center through two groups of threads at a time. The needle passed over two groups and then from left to right under the second group. The second group was twisted over the first group by inserting the needle under the first group from right to left. The thread was pulled taut, but not too tightly or the interlaced groups would not lie in position.

Zigzag hemstitching was constructed in the same way as plain hemstitching, but there were even numbers of threads that were caught in the first row. In the second row these groups were divided in half so that each new group was made up of half the number of threads from the first group and half from an adjacent group. [Figure 44; Plate 16] This was often worked with a contrasting color such as red wool.[140] By combining three bands of alternate rows of zigzag and ladder hemstitching Lidia Sensenig created small, open, and delicate borders on her towel in 1833.[1172] Elisabeth Clemmer, 1859, made a similar panel with three rows of squares on which she embroidered the letters of the alphabet.[1273]

Additional tedious procedures tested the technical skills of a young towel maker as she fashioned borders from warp yarns.

Open lacing stitch, although seldom used, was produced by using a long working thread to go under four (or the required number) loose warp yarns and take a backward stitch over and around the same four yarns and bring the needle out eight yarns to the left in readiness for the next stitch. This was continued to the end of the row.[47] This thread was placed in the center of the warp yarns and not next to the woven edges as done in hemstitching. The working thread was white linen, red cotton, or colored wool. [Figures 45, 25]

FIGURE 44 Zigzag hemstitching, one-quarter inch high, was a major decorative feature.[306] Detail below.

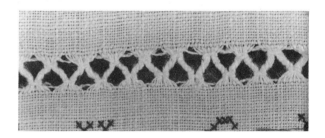

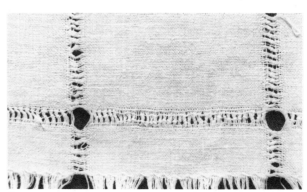

FIGURE 45 The open lacing stitch as a decorative feature on the bottom panel of a towel.[47]

41

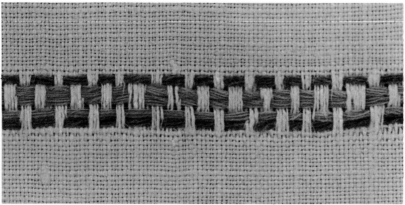

FIGURE 46 A form of needleweaving in which the removed weft threads were replaced with groups of alternate red and blue threads needlewoven over and under prescribed numbers of warp yarns. A series of three of these borders, in opposite colors of red and blue, were spaced 10-7/8 inches apart on the towel.[302]

Needleweaving consisted of using a needle and thread to weave in and out on a warp of threads in which the weft had been withdrawn. It is one of the drawn thread borders seen most often and was probably one of the easiest to make. To start, all the weft threads were removed from within a pre-determined area. A needle with a single or double thread of the first color was then woven over and under or in and out of counted groups of warp yarns such as three, six, or eight yarns. A sufficient number of passes were made with the needle and thread to make the blocks of color a nearly square shape. With that completed the thread was knotted and the needle re-threaded with the second color. This time the needle and thread were woven over and under the alternate or opposite groups of warp yarns to make a square

or block of color underneath the first, producing a checkerboard effect. It was customary to make two or three of these rows in two colors, but larger variations were produced. Combining colors and making up units of design from this simply executed technique were popular.[1,2,7,16,59] [Figures 46, 317]

Needlewoven bars were created by a procedure used to weave together diagonal blocks of warp yarns. Using needle and thread counted groups of warp yarns were woven together by an over and under figure-eight darning-type stitch. This was the same darning stitch used to make designs on the larger drawn thread panels. Borders of these bars vary from three-eighths to three-quarters of an inch high and were easily assembled in white linen or red cotton.[97,349,407,456] [Figures 47, 48]

FIGURE 47 Needlewoven bars (center), three-quarter inches high, in which alternate groups of ten warp yarns were needlewoven together. The needle lace (top) is one-eighth inch high, and the self-knotted fringe (bottom) has a heart motif worked into it.[97]

FIGURE 48 Warp yarns needlewoven together in a chevron pattern (top); cross stitched border also in a chevron design; the cretan insertion stitch followed by a spider web and diamond knotted fringe at the bottom.[1181]

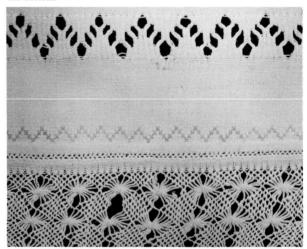

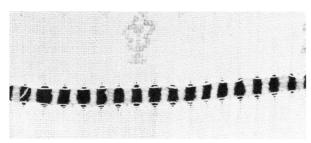

FIGURE 49 Overcast bars formed by overcasting white linen warp yarns with red cotton threads.[1135]

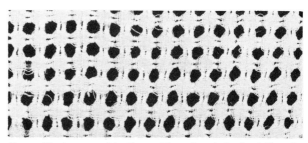

FIGURE 50 A coarse white linen grid panel made by Sarah Fretz by first removing counted warp and weft yarns, and then binding the remaining bared yarns by overcasting with white linen.[1206]

Overcast bars, borrowed from the Hardanger embroidery tradition, were made similarly to woven bars. The required number of weft threads were withdrawn from the towel fabric. One then separated the remaining warp yarns into bars by overcasting firmly over and around these threads as many times as necessary to cover completely the groups of threads. No weaving or back and forth motion was necessary.[6,386,537] In 1820 one woman used red cotton, not the usual white linen or cotton, to overcast the warp yarns which added another element of color to the towel's surface.[1135] [Figures 49,50]

Needlewoven and overcast bars were generally placed near the bottom of the towel as a narrow drawn thread border. On one towel, however, in place of knotting, the overcasting technique was applied to warp yarns before they fell into the bottom fringe.[386]

EH used the concept of weft thread removal as the primary basis for her towel decoration. Thirteen alternate rows of needlewoven bars and reversed wave stitch were spaced in three basic groups throughout the length of the towel. Her all-white stitchery was accented only by a few small red cross and satin stitch flower, diamond, and cross designs and her initials.[835]

To make the reversed wave stitch she withdrew the required number of threads from the towel fabric, missed the required number of threads, and withdrew another band of the same number of threads. She then inserted and passed the threaded needle over two loose threads to the left in the upper band of drawn threads and brought the needle out in the lower band of drawn threads, two threads to the right. The needle was inserted four threads to the left in the lower band and brought out in the upper band two threads to the right and repeated. This procedure bound together two groups of bared warp yarns with one pass of the needle. It is a drawn thread stitch not often encountered on towels. (Further directions for all the above mentioned drawn thread stitch techniques may be found in the book, Coats Sewing Group, *50 Counted Thread Embroidery Stitches*, New York, 1977). [Figure 51]

"Mice teeth," a folk name for another form of drawn thread work, consisted of tiny knots that customarily appear on men's old homespun shirt cuffs. They could be put only on a fold; the folded top edge of the flap was a natural place to make them. When sewn in red cotton their presence was accented, but more important, the "teeth" kept the top flap in place.[541] [Figure 52] (Gehret, 253)

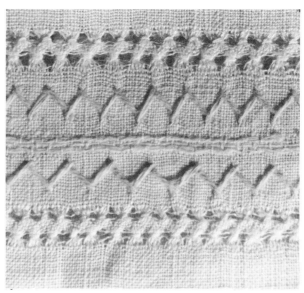

FIGURE 51 A border, 1-7/8 inches high, composed of the reversed wave stitch, herringbone, and a running stitch that went under only one of every five or six threads (center). Three of these borders were spaced 10½ inches apart on the towel.[29]

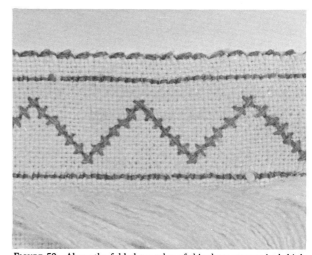

FIGURE 52 Along the folded top edge of this three-quarter inch high flap are "mice teeth" sewn in red cotton. Below are two rows of "stitching" in which each stitch was sewn over one or two threads of the linen fabric. The chevron border was sewn with two by two cross stitches in red cotton.[541] Courtesy, Pennsylvania Farm Museum of Landis Valley, Lancaster.

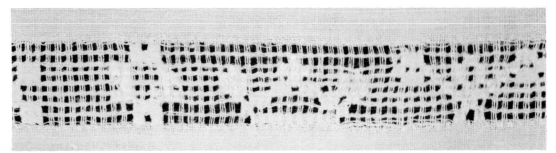

FIGURE 53   A self-drawn thread border, one inch high, cut and started inside the left side edge of the towel. The small motifs were embroidered in white linen with the darning stitch on a thread grid bound horizontally only. The designs were sewn in mirror image.[374] Courtesy, The Henry Francis duPont Winterthur Museum.

Warp and weft threads withdrawn

The second type of drawn thread work is one in which groups of both the warp and weft threads were removed. It was made in two ways. The threads were either cut and drawn out of the towel material making the grid an integral piece of the towel which we call self-drawn thread work, or a drawn thread panel was made separately and attached to the towel after its completion. We call this applied drawn thread work. Both procedures were widely used with both often represented on the same towel.[335] A third and unusual way was to make the entire towel of drawn threads excluding all balanced plain weave material. This departure from tradition is more fully described in chapter six.

Self-drawn thread work

Counting, cutting, and removing certain warp and weft threads from the towel material was exacting work especially if a fine weave linen fabric was used. One thread cut wrong spelled disaster as some towels demonstrate.[140]

Three general effects could result by withdrawing counted groups of threads from the towel fabric: 1) horizontal borders that extended the full width of the towel; 2) symmetrical square and rectangular shapes dispersed throughout the towel's surface; 3) a tall panel or series of panels.

Dividing the towel with self-drawn thread horizontal borders was preferred for their durability and stability, but these borders lacked needed versatility for insertions. They measured from three-eighths[76] to 1½ inches high[104] and were sometimes made in pairs.[521] These narrow borders could accommodate only a single row of small diamonds, crosses, hearts, or a chevron pattern rather than large designs. Very often the weft threads were not withdrawn from the outer edge of the towel, but were counted and cut one-quarter inch to the inside. This helped retain edge strength.[1260] [Figure 53]

Any number of squared or rectangular shapes were created by counting, cutting, and removing warp and weft threads from within the towel's periphery. The weave of the towel fabric governed the size of the thread grid and what could be embroidered on it, but the geometric placement of the squares throughout the towel provided major visual interest.[1200] [Figures 154-157]

Small drawn squares, without designs, were usually well-ordered and well-placed. Elisabet Eben arranged three diagonally contiguous squares at the side edges of her towel.[119] This design pattern soon developed problems, however. Too many threads were removed from the corners where the squares meet to assure stability during use and laundering. This same inherent weakness was encountered by Elisabet and other towel makers when placing four small one inch squares that met each of the outside corners of a large central square.[140,200,682,1205,1210] [Figure 54] Symmetrically positioned drawn thread squares and rectangles that alternate with equal sized areas of balanced plain weave material were a bit more successful. [Figures 154-157]

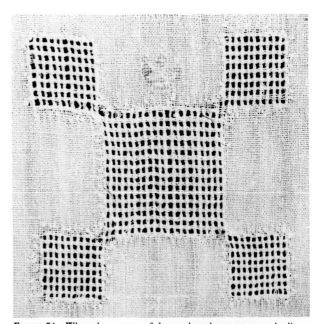

FIGURE 54   When the corners of drawn thread squares met, the linen towel fabric became weak and often pulled apart.[119]

44

When drawn thread areas were larger than a one inch square it was possible to darn small designs on their grid. This, coupled with well-balanced placements on the towel, doubled the intensity of their attractiveness. Anna Histand placed two small drawn thread squares with flower designs in each upper corner of her towel,[89] and ES devoted the bottom panel to alternating drawn thread and fabric one inch squares with designs.[198] Other women were more elaborate with this type of stitchery by re-arranging unlimited drawn thread and fabric squares and rectangles throughout the entire length and width of the towel.[62,64,320,355,358,601,704]

The third alternative was to cut and remove from the towel fabric sufficient groupings of threads to form a full-fledged vertical or horizontal panel. Feronica Witmer made four of these horizontal panels, each cut and started one-half inch from the hemmed and selvage edges of the towel. Groupings of smaller drawn thread squares are spaced between them.[200] [Figure 154]

Sara Anna Hollobush, 1840, combined the principles of alternate drawn thread and fabric squares with vertical bordering by creating a perpendicular stripe from top to bottom in the center length of her towel. It is just two squares wide and on each fabric square she cross stitched a letter in her name. The towel is long enough to accommodate all the letters needed.[576] [Figure 151a]

Another towel maker combined the intricate techniques of patterned warp and weft removal with needle weaving or a darning-type work. She developed four separate two to three inch wide decorative panels on her fine-weave linen towel by counting, cutting, and withdrawing groups of warp and/or weft threads. Square blocks, triangles, diamonds, and other geometric shapes were pre-determined by this cutting and drawing-out of threads. The blocks then had designs needlewoven inside them using one or two single red cotton yarns. These red yarns filled in the open grid area by being pattern woven over and under one, two, or every three warp threads.[516] [Figures 55, 56, 147]

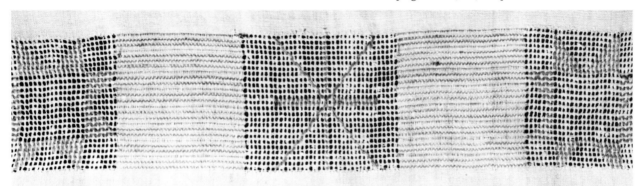

FIGURE 55 Patterned warp and weft removal together with needleweaving were used to make this 3-1/8 inch high border. First the weft yarns were removed in an alternating pattern of threes. Three were removed and three remained the full width of the towel. The star, to the right, was sewn in a red cotton darning stitch on a thread grid from which groups of warp and weft yarns were removed. The square cross was sewn with a red cotton darning stitch, but the oblique cross with diagonally placed stitches. The squares were formed by removing no warp yarns. A needle, threaded with red cotton, was inserted where the weft was removed and was woven over and under every two warp yarns in two journeys. In every third row, however, the threaded needle was woven over and under every other warp yarn which created a subtle pattern. There are four borders constructed in this manner on the same towel. See Figure 147.[516] Courtesy, Albert and Elizabeth Gamon.

FIGURE 56 The drawn stripes were formed as above [Figure 55] by weft removal. The center square on this 2-3/8 inch high border was formed on a thread grid on which groups of warp and weft yarns were removed. The spaces in the square were filled with the red cotton darning stitch sewn in a horizontal and vertical direction. The next square area had the same weft yarns removed, but no warp. A needle threaded with red cotton was alternately woven over and under every two warp yarns in two journeys to fill in the empty spaces. The triangle was formed by patterned warp and weft removal, but its shape was accented by the needlewoven area adjacent to it. The four borders made in this fashion probably represented some of the most tedious work found on any of the towels. See Figure 147.[516] Courtesy, Albert and Elizabeth Gamon.

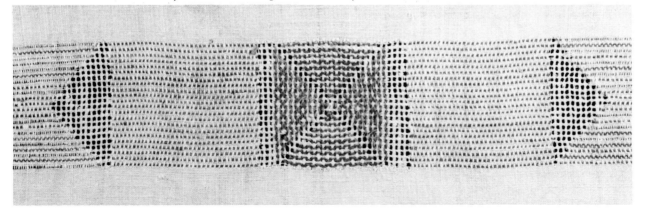

Drawn thread embroidery that is made separately and attached to the towel after its completion is what we call applied drawn thread work. It offered several options not available with self-drawn thread work in terms of fabric used, placement on the towel, and overall size.

The original fabric from which the threads were removed to form the thread grid could be finer or coarser than the towel. This, in turn, produced a tighter or looser thread grid on which to work.

Drawn thread panels were a customary decorative element sewn to the bottom edge of a hand towel. This placement on the towel reached its zenith between 1830 and 1850 after which its use abruptly stops. The handmade drawn thread panel was replaced by commercially produced white cotton fringe. It is interesting to note that the majority of undated towels in this survey have drawn thread panels along the bottom edge. They probably pre-date 1850. [Figures 124-132, 134-142]

The attached or inserted drawn thread panels extended in height from 1½[104] to 20½ inches.[35] They almost always reached the full width of the towel, or they were widened by sewing pieces of woven fabric to each side.[48,358,1223] [Figure 57] Anna Maria, 1816, expanded her panel by attaching another drawn thread panel to each end instead of using fabric.

FIGURE 57　Pieces of balanced plain weave cotton fabric, 1¾ inches wide and 7½ inches high were added to the side edges of this drawn thread panel with a butt seam making this bottom panel as wide as the linen towel. The three inch long plain fringe was also joined to the bottom edge with a butt seam. White cotton darning stitch on the drawn thread grid. 7½" x 14¾.[48]

The attached drawn thread panel that extended vertically down the center of the towel is uncommon.[926] It occurs as early as 1797 as a panel 3¼ inches wide and full of hearts, diamonds, and crosses.[581] [Figure 150] In 1838 Katarina NS filled a similar vertical panel with eight pointed stars.[586] Yet other variations alternated three or four full-width drawn thread panels with a nearly equal number of balanced plain weave or pattern woven panels.[93,94] And SH, 1827, fastened a narrow drawn thread border on top of the linen flap of her towel.[1186]

Several basic steps were necessary when making self or applied drawn thread work. The initial selection of fabric was determined by the desired number of grid holes (our term) per inch. Coarsely woven fabric produced fewer grid holes per inch than a fine weave material. Warp and weft threads were then counted and divided into groups which were alternately cut and removed. The remaining groups of warp and weft threads were bound together and designs were embroidered on them.

A balanced plain weave bleached linen material was sought for drawing threads for an attached panel, but this was obviously not necessary for self-drawn thread work. The rare exception was Nancy Weaver, who in 1836 used a half-linen half-cotton balanced plain weave fabric.[580]

Usually the number of grid holes per inch was not the same in both directions just as the warp and weft thread counts were not the same on the linen when counting cross stitch. There were from three[1172] to thirteen[348] horizontal holes per inch and from four[282] to twenty[348] vertical holes per inch.

To remove threads from the woven material the linen fabric was held over the index finger. This made it easier to count and draw up the individual threads with a blunt needle prior to cutting and removing them. One drew up three weft threads, cut them and pulled each one out, then skipped three threads, drew up the next three weft threads, cut and removed them. This manner continued until all the desired weft had been withdrawn. The linen fabric had a horizontal striped appearance at this point. The bared warp yarns had to be hemstitched or interlaced in some way if self-drawn thread borders were being made. This binding procedure prevented further thread movement or possible thread loss.

In applied drawn thread work alternate groups of three warp yarns were now drawn up, cut, and removed in the same manner as with the weft threads, adjusting the number of yarns removed, if necessary, to make as square an opening as possible. After all the groups of yarns in the warp and weft were withdrawn the material resembled a lattice or checkerboard.

It was helpful if a narrow margin of fabric remained on the four edges of the panel for easier hemming. This could be accomplished by allowing a one-half inch margin on each side before starting to remove threads. This one-half inch strip had only the horizontal or vertical threads removed, not both, which was easier to handle than an edge of all threads. Selvages were not always cut away.

These outer edges were hemmed not only to prevent fraying, but to help stabilize the weakened fabric that tended to sag and hang unevenly. A concern for permanence as well as for appearance probably prompted LK to secure the entire drawn thread panel with a cloth binding.[291] Nency Greybill sewed both folded twill tape and folded linen fabric to reinforce the panel's weakened edges.[702] [Figure 58] Elisabeth Himmelbergin bound only

FIGURE 58 White cotton twill tape was first folded over the top edge of the drawn panel. Then the edges of the tape were sewn together, binding the top edge of the drawn thread panel. The folded edge of the tape was then sewn to the back of the pattern woven linen towel just above the self fringe. The left and right side edges of the thread grid were bound with folded linen fabric. Brown silk herringbone stitches and fragments of red cotton and brown silk cross stitch remain on the top and side edges of these bindings. The bottom edge of the drawn panel was hemmed and butted to a mill-made plain white cotton fringe. 9" x 17¾".[702] Courtesy, Sally and Pete Riffle.

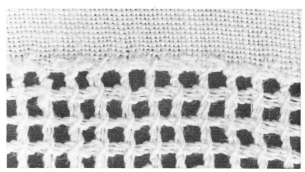

FIGURE 59 The cut edges of the drawn thread panel were firmly bound to prevent thread loss. The threads in the grid also needed to be bound together to retain a square shape.[699] Courtesy, Sally and Pete Riffle.

the sides of the panel and hemmed the top and bottom edges where it was sewn to other towel material.[301] Nancy/Anna Lang[269] and Nancy Weaver[580] combined the techniques for self and applied drawn thread by cutting and withdrawing the warp and weft threads one-quarter inch from the outside edge. This woven fabric provided a strong neat hem on the applied panel. A one-quarter inch hem was the norm on thread panels and it was made directly after all the threads were removed.

The main purpose of binding together the groups of warp and weft threads was to define and secure the square grid holes better and make them easier to count when embroidering. Binding, or the lack of binding, however, noticeably affected the appearance of the finished panel. [Figure 61]

Generally speaking, the entire grid was bound horizontally and vertically prior to darning designs on it. A finely spun two-ply white linen thread was best. The working thread was discreetly anchored on the wrong side of the hem. The needle and thread was placed between the intersections of the warp and weft threads on the right side. The groups of threads were bound by a single wrapping motion: the needle was brought up, passed over the next intersection of threads and worked down and up to wrap together the next group of threads. This is what we call the ground stitch. Working in straight rows, the seamstress wrapped together the groups of threads as she went. The thread was anchored on the far side into the hem and returned by binding the threads in the next row. On most towels all the horizontal threads were bound together row after row because all these ground or binding stitches went in one direction. With that completed the woman then bound the vertical threads row by row. She continued until all groups of warp and weft threads were bound in this manner. This produced a neat, crisp, and well defined grid on which to embroider. [Figure 59]

The degree of fineness in the thread grid was crucial to the quantity and size of individual motifs that could be put on it. Designs were created by counting numbers of available grid holes just as threads were counted for cross stitch. The grid had to be made large enough to accommodate the biggest design scheduled to be embroidered on its surface.

The number of alternate threads removed was determined by the size of the yarns, the tightness of the weave, and how much removal was necessary to make the desired square-shaped grid hole. On most towels groups of three warp yarns and groups of three weft yarns, the same number in each direction, form the latticed grid. We refer to that as a three by three grid.

CW used a three by three grid, but because she chose such finely woven material her drawn thread work is smaller and finer than usual.[137] Some women preferred a bolder, heavier grid of four threads. MK made a five by five thread grid which has the appearance of coarse lace and has no embroidered designs.[184] The beauty of this drawn thread work lay in the circular effects made by binding together the groups of five threads.

Most often white linen thread, but sometimes brown thread, was used for this binding work.[1] On one towel both the threads in the grid and the ground stitch binding were an unbleached or natural linen color with contasting white cotton designs embroidered on it.[126] [Figure 60]

FIGURE 60 A drawn thread grid made from linen fabric, bound with unbleached linen threads; the motifs embroidered with white cotton—a dark and light effect. 7½" x 15½".[126]

FIGURE 61 The upper area of the drawn thread grid was bound vertically only which gave it a more striped appearance than when bound in both directions. The woman motif was sewn by weaving the white linen thread over and under each grid thread and space instead of using the darning stitch. This technique was not often seen.[29]

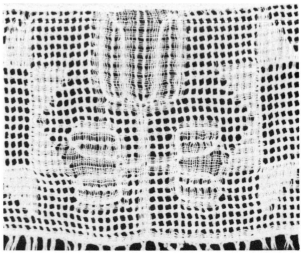

FIGURE 62 Appearance of this panel differed because: 1) motifs were embroidered on an unbound thread grid; 2) white linen threads that outlined flower petals were threaded over and under the grid holes to form round curved edges; 3) after the motifs were completed the grid threads were selectively bound together horizontally and vertically which created a gauze-like appearance within the motif.[61] Courtesy, Sally and Pete Riffle.

Binding a panel of loosely woven threads required an experienced "feel" on the part of the needleworker. A too tightly or unevenly pulled ground stitch could easily twist the empty grid into undesirable angles. This is a difficulty which may have been encountered by those women who waited to bind the grid until after the designs were in place.[45,61] But, the grid was ill-defined, limp, and confusing to count if it was not bound.

Some ladies bound the grid in one direction only to create an almost striped effect in back of the embroidered designs.[94,198,323,347] [Figures 61, 53] More decorative effects were developed by specialized binding such as those of Elisabeth Leatherman[445] who began the binding three-eighths of an inch from the hemmed edge which left the narrow area drawn, but not bound. Another skilled lady bound the entire grid in a horizontal direction only; in the open areas within a motif, the grid is bound in both directions.[235] Some grids are not bound at all, but are full of designs sewn on a gauze-like mesh.[374] Other towels have unfilled drawn thread panels attached to them.[29,125,1139] [Figures 132, 148]

Elizabeth Fry, 1818, was one of those towel makers whose drawn thread panel developed an unusual appearance. It is unconventional for several reasons. An unbound thread grid was used to create the designs and a bound grid forms the background. The open grid holes within the star design were re-filled with white linen threads by weaving over and under groups of warp yarns the length of each point of the star instead of filling each grid hole separately. After several washings all the threads within the star motif separated from their unbound groups and dissolved into a gauze-like look.[61] [Figure 62]

Embroidering designs onto a thread grid was accomplished by using what we call a darning stitch. (This is the same stitch used in making needlewoven bars. It is not to be confused, however, with the darning stitch which resembles an evenly spaced small running stitch used in so-called darned embroidery). This darning stitch literally closed or filled in the grid work one square at a time. A needle with double thread was inserted from the wrong side and worked over and under two groups of threads in a figure eight fashion filling and closing the grid hole between them. Two passes with needle and thread were usually sufficient. To close an adjoining grid hole it was necessary to tie into the first darning which in turn created an interlocked appearance of stitches within a motif. A knot secured the thread at the beginning, but the finished thread end was often inserted back into the wrong side of the design without a knot. [Figure 63]

FIGURE 63 An unfinished drawn thread panel on which the marker began to lay out the right hand half of the design which she would then copy in mirror image on the left side. 14" x 15-3/8".[1417]

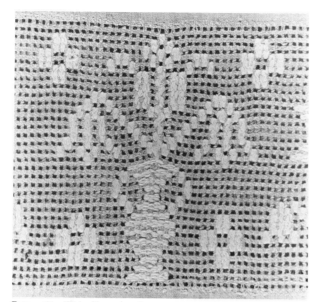

FIGURE 64 White linen two ply sewing thread was sometimes used in embroidering drawn thread panels.[418] Courtesy, The State Museum, Pennsylvania Historical and Museum Commission 73.98.37

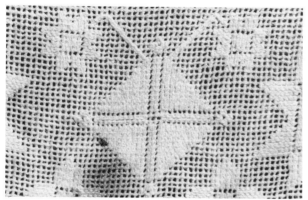

FIGURE 65 The running stitch, not the darning stitch, was used to embroider this diamond and flower motif. The stems were sewn with diagonal stitches. White cotton motifs on a white linen grid.[53]

Care was needed when darning designs not to pull or distort the squareness of the thread grid, but to keep the work flat and even. This became more difficult if the young girl did not understand the technique or attempted an original venture. Inventiveness was injected into this form of embroidery by diversifying stitch direction and stitch formation, variegating colors, and modulating embroidery thread size.

The traditional darning stitch was sewn in horizontal and vertical rows just as cross stitch was made. But, in addition, each grid hole was filled with a pattern in mind. Vertically filled stems contrasted to horizontally filled flowers; an eight pointed star, divided into quarters, had alternating quarters sewn in opposite directions; a woman's apron was distinguished from the petticoat just by changing the direction of the stitch. This conventional technique developed texture and contrasts in what could easily become monotonous stitchery. The differences were more noticeable when shiny linen embroidery threads were used. [Figure 64]

Supplementary embroidery stitches were used on the drawn thread grid. Several crosses were made on one towel with all the embroidery threads emerging from a central hole much like an eyelet.[277] Fronica Gehman in 1850 used an eyelet stitch for the eye of a bird.[318] Towel makers sewed a border on the grid with what appears to be a series of large chain stitches.[120,277] In 1795, K decorated an urn by looping a single thread around itself in the grid to form a cross rather than filling the grid hole.[195] The darning on another panel is a combination of the darning stitch and satin stitch which covered two grid holes at once.[524] One woman made flower petals by weaving over and under, and round and round following the outline of the flower itself instead of counting and developing the shape by rows.[194] There were others who used this method to achieve a more realistic curved leaf and flower, but these women badly distorted the thread grid making it impossible to bind the grid until after the embroidery was completed, if at all.

Numbers of embroiderers chose a running stitch to go over and under long lengths of grid threads diagonally[29,53] or in a straight line.[235] [Figure 65] This stitch diversion filled an entire row with two passes of the needle instead of filling each grid hole separately. This very same method allowed another young woman to run a single thread of blue the entire length of a stem. The remaining space in the grid to each side of the blue thread was later filled with white threads to devise a striped stem.[122] [Figure 66] This procedure would have been more difficult, if not impossible, to accomplish if she employed the typical darning stitch. Designs made in this way appeared somewhat detached on the surface, but were neater and flatter on the wrong side.

FIGURE 66 A drawn thread panel on which a running stitch of blue cotton was sewn for the length of the stem after which the spaces were filled with white cotton to create a striped stem. The motifs were embroidered with red, white, and blue single ply cotton; hand-knit linen lace insertion is 1½ inches high; mill-made cotton plain fringe is 2¾ inches long. 16¾" x 15½".[122]

The goose-eye stitch is a drawn thread stitch that was worked over two groups of threads alternately horizontally and vertically, diagonally left to right, and from the lower threads upward. Each group of threads was bound twice to make the round pattern of the goose-eye clearly defined. Elisabeth Sensenig, 1824, made a full-sized panel with this specialized work, but this type of embroidery on drawn threads is seldom encountered.[372]

Color selection for drawn thread embroidery was predominantly white. If other colors were chosen they were generally sewn in combination with white, although a panel of all-red cotton[375] and another of gold wool[384] have been seen.

Designs sewn in red and white were most numerous[24,104,105,195,257,282,308,317,331,367,368,373,1234] [Plate 22] followed by red, white, dark and light blue.[122,284,315,473,1188,1223] [Figure 66; Plate 32] Red and white cotton combined with brown linen were seen less often.[37]

One towel had small red and blue irregular stitches sewn on top of the embroidered white human figure to denote female face and body features.[194] [Figure 417] On another towel red colored crosses and stripes effectively filled the woman's embroidered petticoat.[195] [Figure 67]

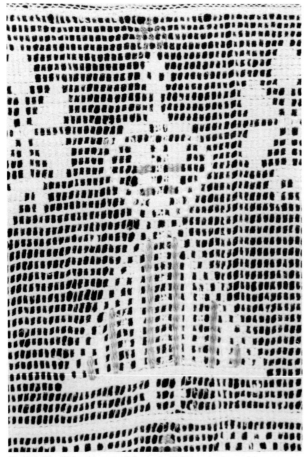

FIGURE 67 This was one of the most elaborately dressed women embroidered on a drawn thread grid. The bodice and petticoat were sewn not only in rows of red cotton and white linen darning stitch, but in vertical stripes of Greek cross filling stitches. Above her head is a red cotton diamond-shape design also embroidered with the Greek cross filling stitch. See Figure 515.[195]

Diversion from both the traditional darning stitch and white color was also practiced by Anna Gehman, 1846, who edged each side of her large drawn thread panel with two borders of gold and red wool running stitch.[420] Sara Yorty in 1831 liked the idea of framing her drawn thread work, so she ran a dark blue cotton thread over two grid holes and under one group of threads, over two grid holes and under one group of threads in running stitch fashion.[264] [Plate 36]

A loosely spun white cotton thread was most practical to fill in the open spaces on the thread grid. In some instances the two-ply cotton thread was threaded double through the needle,[35] and other times a single handspun cotton yarn was used doubled in the needle.[29,140] Generally two and not more than three passes of the needle were used to fill one grid space. There are towels which use two types of threads in their drawn thread panel: those with a tight twist and others more loosely spun.[130] As with cross stitch embroidery there needed to be a definite correlation between the thread size and the drawn grid size.

Motifs were embroidered with all-white linen thread,[175] but we have found this on only several towels dating from 1790 through 1845. One towel boasts designs embroidered with both white linen and white cotton.[129] The linen embroidery threads presented a smooth shiny finish and because it was more tightly spun more thread and more stitches were required to make designs. It was an option open to young embroiderers, but white cotton was preferred.

Most drawn thread designs were made as previously discussed by counting and filling in rows of grid spaces. The viewer, therefore, sees the zigzag border, for instance, as solid stitchery or as a positive image sewn on an open grid or mesh background.[129,387] [Figure 68]

The opposite is also true. Drawn thread borders in particular show best how the narrow grid was completely filled except for the open patterned zigzag formation in what could be termed a negative image.[24,35,392,468,1117,1214] [Figure 69] This effect is occasionally seen in individual motifs, but is more noticeable in borders.

The negative image created within a solid, stitchery-filled grid imparts a baroque-like quality to the drawn thread embroidery. Little is known about this particular form of drawn thread needlework except that is does exist in Europe. It deserves attention from future needlework historians.

Several towels contain drawn thread borders made with Greek cross filling stitch or Loop stitch.[989,1126,1180] Warp and weft threads are removed in the manner previously described, but all the grid holes are filled with this overall lacey stitch produced by sewing four diagonal loops. Individual motifs were not made. [Figures 70-72, 146] This filling stitch also served as the binding stitch.

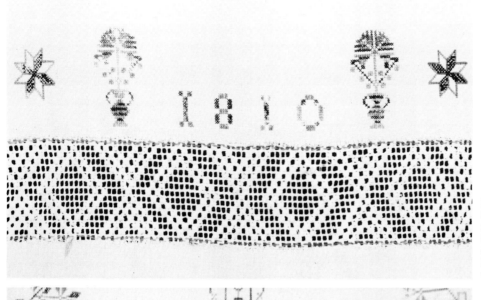

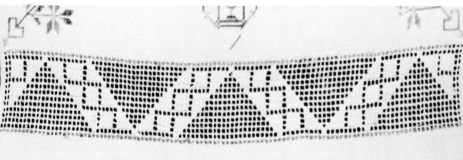

FIGURE 68 A drawn thread border, 3-3/8 inches high, with alternate cross and diamond motifs. The thread grid was bound and the designs were embroidered with white linen, but the top and bottom edges were needlewoven with red cotton.[24]

FIGURE 69 A self drawn thread border, three inches high, that started inside the side edges of the 1810 towel and is embroidered in what we call a negative image.[24]

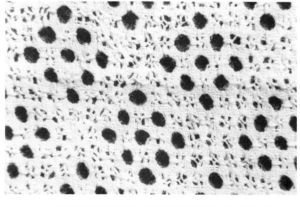

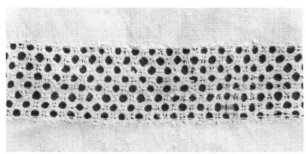

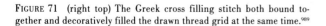

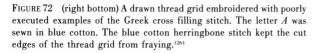

FIGURE 70 (above) A drawn thread border embroidered with the Greek cross filling stitch. This is one of three borders sewn in this manner on the towel. 1-5/8" x 19¼".[989]

FIGURE 71 (right top) The Greek cross filling stitch both bound together and decoratively filled the drawn thread grid at the same time.[989]

FIGURE 72 (right bottom) A drawn thread grid embroidered with poorly executed examples of the Greek cross filling stitch. The letter A was sewn in blue cotton. The blue cotton herringbone stitch kept the cut edges of the thread grid from fraying.[1261]

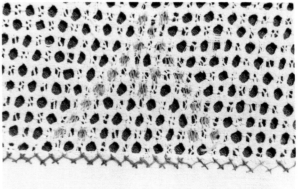

C. FREE-FORM

The second largest general type of embroidery used to decorate Pennsylvania hand towels was sewn in what we call a free-form or free-style. Free embroideries were worked over a traced, stamped, drawn or transferred design having been marked on the linen hand towel with ink, pencil or chalk. All towels are so laundered that evidence of this original transfer has been washed away. We have no positive identification of what the young Pennsylvania Dutch girls might have used. We do know that counting threads was not necessary. (Our use of the term free-embroidery is not to be confused with free-hand, free-motion, flat or free-embroidery as related to work done on a domestic or trade sewing machine invented in 1828).

Hand sewn free-style embroidery was used with some reserve during the late eighteenth and early nineteenth centuries, but its appeal became increasingly widespread. In the earlier period artistic borders and small designs that undoubtedly originated with the towel's maker accented the world of cross stitch, but their presence often goes almost unnoticed.[665]

Three stitch groups were used to make the free embroidery seen on towels: the flat, the looped, and the knotted stitches. One example of a couching and filling stitch was also seen. The flat stitches seen are the stem (sometimes called outline) stitch, the running, satin, straight, and back stitches. Looped stitches include the buttonhole sometimes called a blanket stitch, the chain and lazy daisy stitch often known as a detached chain stitch, and the feather stitch. We found only two knotted stitches called the French knot and the bullion knot/stitch, and two couching and two seeding stitch examples. Certain of these stitches such as the running, back, straight, satin, and herringbone, were used both as counted thread and free embroidery stitches.

Flat stitches

"Flat stitches are the most elementary structures added to fabric with needle and thread. They are formed by working the needle alternating in and out of the material. There is no interworking of the threads on the surface or reverse side although one stitch may overlap or cross another. All flat stitches are in a sense "straight" stitches, that is, the sewing thread is carried straight from the point where it emerges from the fabric to its next point of entry, and it is solely by variation of the location of entry and exit points that the arrangement of stitches and the appearance of the stitchery is varied." (Emery, 234, 241)

Stem stitch

The stem stitch produced a line of regularly slanted stitches which was often used to outline curved areas. Therefore, it was used to sew the rounded numerals in the year.[66,217] Maria Good used it to embroider her name.[219] [Figure 330] Maria Schultz chose the stem stitch to denote hills, a tulip, heart, star, deer, and a bird in a tree,[253] [Figure 96] but on the HA CA towel the stem stitch outlined items with straight lines such as a house,

fence with gates, six, eight, and sixteen pointed stars, and two apple trees.[125] [Figure 132] Fanny Steman, 1838, also sewed three straight border lines of stem stitch in red wool and red cotton at the top of her towel.[196] We find its use on towels as early as 1815.

Running stitch

The running stitch may be the simplest stitch there is in that the needle was passed in and out of the material at regular intervals. In certain embroideries it was desirable to have the stitches of equal length and the under stitches also of equal length, but only half the size of the upper stitches. On the towels in this study, however, the linen fabric threads were generally counted when embroidering the running stitch which governed their size. It has been used on towels since at least 1810.

It was used primarily as a border stitch, but unlike needleweaving, no weft threads were removed. Christina Lenz stitched three identical rows of running stitch, one-quarter inch apart, that ran over and under each three warp threads. The groups of three warp threads did not alternate. This border design appeared four times on the towel and two times on the flap.[109] [Figure 73]

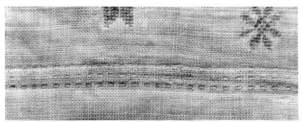

FIGURE 73   Three rows of red cotton running stitch about one-quarter inch apart. Each stitch went over and under four warp yarns and each is worked to form both horizontal and vertical rows of stitches. This border appeared four times on the towel and twice on the flap.[109]

CH, on the other hand, embroidered two different running stitch borders. The first consisted of four red cotton threads stitched over ten warp yarns and under three. The second border was made of five separate rows, each with a different number of running threads per row.[91]

The running stitch was combined with cross stitch[5] or with herringbone.[29] [Figure 51] Lidia Bauman embroidered both horizontal and vertical rows of running stitch to create 2¾ inch squares on a panel sewn to the bottom of her towel.[65] Sophia Elizabeth G. Witmer used the running stitch to sew her name,[593] and Molly Ryder sewed the running stitch to hold the top flap in place. Her stitches were placed every quarter inch with long floats on the reverse side.[335]

Susan Hochstitter ambitiously sewed the double running stitch to make groups of small, two-thread long square blocks which when combined formed her initials.[624] Anna Carle, 1825, used the same technique to embroider a large heart motif.[756] [Figure 74] Margetha Minsen sewed the stitch as early as 1797 to denote flowers,[810] and Sarah Hager, 1843, created a diamond motif by joining small squares sewed by the double running stitch.[800]

FIGURE 74   A red cotton and brown silk heart embroidered with the double running or holbein stitch.[756]

The double running or holbein stitch was made by working a row of running stitches right to left, passing the needle over and under two threads of fabric (or the desired number) following the shape of the design and on the return journey filling in the spaces left in the first row. It was worked over counted threads for best results.

Satin stitch

Satin stitching consisted of short straight flat stitches that were worked with one stitch between each two adjacent threads of fabric. They could be worked across pre-determined areas to shape and fill them, or the satin stitch could be sewn over counted groups of threads. In either case there was just as much thread on the surface as on the wrong side.

As early as 1796 a small count thread satin stitch hour glass figure was embroidered,[275] but in 1797 Elizabeth Maier used the free-form satin stitch to form the four legs on a cross stitch dog.[377] It was also used to fill in tree leaves,[125,253] apples,[125] [Figure 132] and the wing of a small bird.[253]

A slanted satin stitch, with centered "V" shape, covered solid the petals of a tulip design.[513]

Counted blocks of satin stitch formed zigzag and diamond shaped borders[76,104,194,404,429] [Figure 75] or special

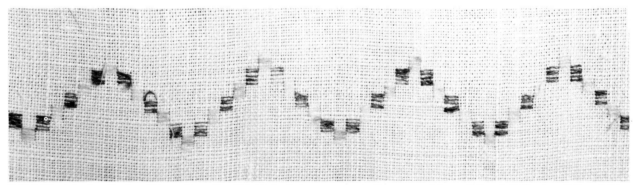

FIGURE 75   A border of red and blue cotton satin stitch blocks that were sewn over five warp and five weft threads.[104] Courtesy, Sally and Pete Riffle.

53

designs such as the crosses sewn by Abeth Ditze[451] and Maria Bollingern.[488] But, satin stitch blocks were not necessarily square. Elisabeth Diehl purposely counted and embroidered blocks that were four by six and three by four threads or similar shapes to make an entire counted satin stitch towel.[25] [Plate 49]

Straight stitch

The straight stitch, also known as a single satin stitch, could be worked in a regular or irregular manner with the stitches the same or varying lengths. The straight stitch was found on decorated towels more often than all other stitches in the flat stitch category. Its use on towels began after 1815 and disappeared by 1855.

Short and long straight stitches sewn in concentric circles formed a small flower or rosette;[5] the straight stitch represented leaves on a stem[212] or made the handle of a sgraffito incised urn;[261] [Figure 342] it formed claws on bird's feet,[268] and accented the end of a flower petal or leaf.[261,356] It created a variety of effects.

On occasion the straight stitch was used by itself to form large geometric designs. The diamond design is encountered most often.[268,553,408] Sara Schitz filled a diamond motif with rows of closely staggered straight stitch, each four threads in length, which produced an appearance that resembled the tent stitch.[261] [Figure 461] Occasionally the straight stitch was combined with other free embroidery stitches such as the chain stitch to create stylized flowers and birds.[489]

Straight stitch lent itself to sewing simple borders,[86] but was not without its diversions. Counted straight stitches two threads high were sewn diagonally on the warp yarns of one towel to form a vertical zigzag border.[39] This was a more complicated border to execute than counting and embroidering a border with an angled straight stitch ten weft threads high slanted at a ten warp thread angle.[134] Other types of borders include one made of vertical rows of short, horizontally placed straight stitches sewn on the front side edges of a top flap. They were decorative only and did not keep the flap in place.[231] Grouped straight stitches in the form of a star with many rays were sewn along the edges of a border on the 1832 Daniel Harr towel. In this instance the needle was always inserted in the center of the star as it was being made sometimes creating a small hole. Hence its name star eyelet.[83] [Figure 329]

MR, 1817, used threads in the towel fabric as a guide for sewing short zigzag straight stitches in one journey and threading them in the second journey. We call this a threaded straight stitch. Counted rows of this work filled in the geometric shape of a star motif, but ad lib placed rows filled in bird forms. She also used a single row of this zigzag threaded straight stitch to denote a tulip motif.[709] [Figure 76] A second girl created a diamond shaped border by placing horizontal rows of this stitch, one above the other, in alternate positions.[1283] [Figure 18]

To make this stitch a threaded needle was brought up at point A and inserted four threads to the right and four threads above point A at point B. The needle was brought out at point C two threads to the right and inserted four threads to the right, but four threads below point C at point D. The needle was brought out two threads to the right at point E and continued across the row. The stitch size can vary according to fabric and need. When starting the second row of zigzag straight stitches the placement was alternated so the finished design resembled a diamond shape. Where the points

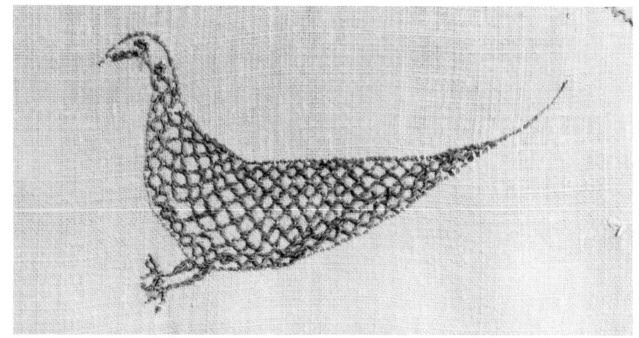

FIGURE 76 The outline of the red cotton bird was embroidered with a running stitch, but filled with rows of the threaded straight stitch. The bird is three inches high and is 5-3/8 inches from the beak to the tip of the tail. See Figure 266.[709] Courtesy, Sally and Pete Riffle.

meet the needle was inserted in the same hole which created on the wrong side two rows of short stitches each two threads long. To thread this zigzag straight stitch the needle was re-threaded and the thread laced around each point alternating top to bottom in each row being careful not to pierce the fabric. This made the sharp points appear more rounded.

Back stitch

As its name implies this stitch is made by taking a small backward stitch before advancing the needle. It follows a tight curve if the stitches are kept tiny such as when it was used to outline a bird.[312] In most instances, however, towel makers limited its use to making solid straight lines with counted threads as the stitch-size regulator. Meri Weinholt denoted a woman's fingers and claws on a bird's foot,[467] [Figure 77] and Elizabeth Kauffman sewed a row of tiny back stitches above a row of fringe to prevent fraying.[442] Its use was sporadic between 1830 and 1845.

If embroidered in a straight formation it served as a fringe binding,[1,396] a self-drawn thread grid binding,[485] and as decoration along a hemmed edge[181] and top flap.[416] When stitched in a circular direction a simple flower design could be formed with the addition of French knots for the center and lazy daisy stitches for the petals.[344] On other towels buttonholed eyelets were incorporated into a chain stitch border.[717] [Figure 78] Rayel Ziegler also expanded its use by embroidering two different flowers each with scalloped edges as well as the eyelet-type flower, but without the central hole.[718] [Figure 127]

The buttonhole was the primary stitch used to fasten and bind together the small coil of thread inside a thread button. Such buttons were generally found on homespun linen clothing, but they also appeared on towels. They either held the flap in place, as previously mentioned, or they were sewn onto the towels as border decoration. [Figures 74, 79; Plate 45] Maria Brubaker fashioned buttons from red cotton and brown silk and attached them

FIGURE 77 Two women appear to watch a turkey (or is it a pea hen?) on top of a tulip. Each woman had earrings and fingers embroidered in back stitch. The bird's curved beak, neck, and claws were also sewn in back stitch. All other embroidery is red and blue cotton cross stitch. See Figure 165.[467] Courtesy, Dr. and Mrs. Donald M. Herr.

Looped stitches

"A looped stitch is formed if the thread is made to deviate from the direct line and is held out of line by the next stitch. They have been defined as flat stitches pulled out of straight and forced into a loop, or 'pulled to one side by looping the thread under the needle.'" (Emery, 241) Those seen most often on towels are the buttonhole, chain, detached chain sometimes called the lazy daisy stitch, and feather stitch.

Buttonhole stitch

The buttonhole, and its first cousin the blanket stitch, is perhaps the basic form of the looped stitch. It could be sewn in a straight line, as a curved edging for outlining, or in a circular direction for filling. It is a simple looping stitch.

in four rows across the width of the towel as a separation for drawn thread panels. These buttons, as well as others, were not completely covered with buttonholed threads, but had only a minimum number of buttonholed threads, used as a couching-type thread, to hold the coiled button together.[794] (For directions to make these buttons see Gehret, 184).

The biggest uses for the buttonhole stitch, however, were as reinforcement at the ends of fancy insertion work [Figure 80] and as buttonholed loops for hanging the towel. [Figures 532, 533] It was also the primary stitch in needle lace which is discussed later. In these instances the buttonhole stitch was sewn in white linen thread and not in decorative colors. Its use on dated towels begins in 1820 and ends in 1845.

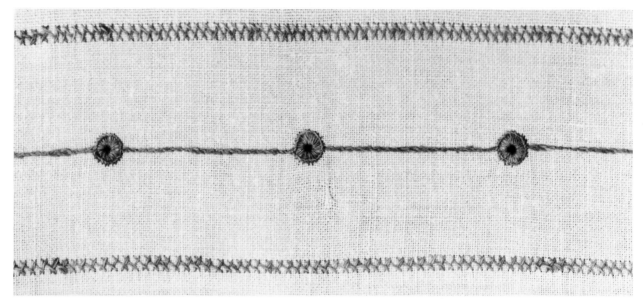

FIGURE 78 A border composed of count thread and free-form embroidery. The red cotton chain stitch connects a three-eighth inch diameter buttonholed eyelet every 2¼ inches. The red cotton counted herringbone stitch is about three by three threads.[717] Courtesy, Sally and Pete Riffle.

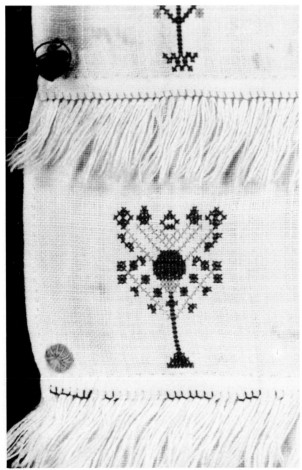

FIGURE 79 The red cotton thread button is one-quarter inch in diameter and is one of many sewn onto this towel as decoration. The tree-like motif is cross stitched in red cotton and brown silk. The plain fringe above and below was bound into groups with a blanket-type stitch.[756]

FIGURE 80 White linen buttonholed bars were often placed at each end of an insertion to stabilize and strengthen a weakened area on the towel.[1000]

Chain stitch

"If the loop of a buttonhole stitch is completed the stitch is then known as chain stitch." (Emery, 243) The chain stitch is one of the oldest and most universal of all embroidery stitches. It was the most widely used of the looped stitches seen on towels. We noted its use from before 1790 until after 1870.

There are many variations in the shape and direction of this stitch, but its use enabled embroiderers to outline bent and curved shapes as well as to fill them with interlocking flat chains of color.[289] The majority of color remains on the surface and very little can be seen on the reverse side of the design. It was an obvious stitch-choice for names [84,407] and dates, [104,320] but it found more use in borders and designs. [Figure 81a, 81b]

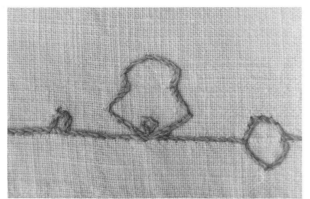

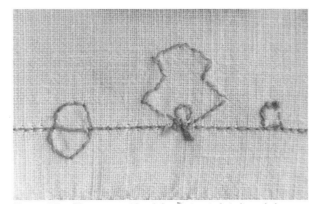

Diamond, looped, and zigzag shaped chain stitch borders were sewn alone[33,270,271,415,419,467,522,692,814] or in combination with other stitches such as the running stitch.[85,417] Because chain stitch is made in a series of links it produces a heavier, stronger appearance than does a single straight or running stitch. Perhaps this accounts for the towel makers who sewed it to hold the flap in place,[44] or those who outlined a false flap and divided it into thirds in the absence of a true flap,[65] [Figure 23] and why another young woman chained a wavy line on all four sides to frame her towel.[467] [Figure 165]

Many hearts, flowers, and birds were embroidered in chain stitch.[5,16,84,214,268,289,334,249,352,384,428,447,489,509,510,538,718] Some of these had leaves and petals made with the lazy daisy or detached chain stitch. If the design was filled with color rows of chain stitch were sewn round and round following the outline of the design until it was filled. [Figures 223,361]

Feather stitch

The feather stitch was a looped stitch not frequently encountered. It was sewn across a towel by Elisabeth

Roth in 1818 to create a vine-like border with a periodic placement of three straight stitches simulating flowers.[1049]

Knotted stitches

The knot stitches on Pennsylvania German hand towels are what Emery describes as, "a non-functional stitch used to produce a visual effect." (Emery, 244) The only knotted stitches found were the bullion stitch/knot and the French knot. Both are made by wrapping a thread around the needle before its insertion into the material.

French knots are tightly wrapped knots that resemble a small bead, and when used on towels they filled or outlined the center of a flower or flower petals.[344] [Figure 82] The bullion stitch, on the other hand, is a longer wrapped stitch that can be raised from the surface of the towel. An all-white towel had at the bottom these wrapped and coiled loops resembling flowers, and a row of similar loops decorating the top edge instead of a flap or fancy fringe.[929] [Figure 561]

FIGURE 82 French knots fill the center of this white cotton satin stitch free-form flower; 2½ inches in diameter.[518] Courtesy, Albert and Elizabeth Gamon.

FIGURE 83 A leaping spotted deer was sewn in the outline stitch in two ply red cotton. The eye, tail, and long loop in the antlers were blue cotton, but the individual points were sewn in red cotton. The spots, sewn in seed stitch, alternated between red and blue cotton. See Figure 96. 2-1/8" x 2¾".[253]

Couching and filling stitches

Couching refers to a two-part method of embroidery. The first part consists of 'laying' a thread on the surface of a fabric, and the second to tie down or couch it in place with a series of short stitches. (Emery, 247) The decorative procedure of couching was used on towels in conjunction with overcasting a fringe. Mary[440] and Fanny Witmer[250] laid two strands of red cotton embroidery thread side by side along a fringed edge. The threads were kept in place by sewing a small slanted stitch at even intervals which also served as the overcasting to prevent fraying. [Figure 511]

Seed stitches are a simple filling stitch composed of small straight stitches of equal length placed at random within the area to be filled. They were used to fill such areas as a leaping deer[253] [Figure 83] and the tail of a bird.[268]

Cross stitch, herringbone, and chain were the principal embroidery stitches on both dated and undated decorated towels and were encountered in that order of frequency. The satin stitch follows closely. All of the other embroidery stitches had sporadic use between 1815 and 1850. The diversity of embroidery stitches died before the tradition of the decorated hand towel.

In conclusion we want to focus on three towels that exemplify expertise in both counted thread and free embroidery. Each towel contains many of the same designs, stitches, and basic technical concepts, but in a different way. The towels bear the texts Christina Hessin, 1815, a miniature,[392] Anna Herr, 1816,[468] and CH, 1818,[285] not only within three years of each other, but in the early decades of the Pennsylvania decorated towel's heyday. Their work showed an obvious relationship through their use of embroidered German lettering, choice of designs, and overall workmanship. We suspect the seamstress had professional training in utilizing free embroidery stitch techniques which she then applied. These towels contained sophisticated needlework that comes only with knowledgeable schooling above the folk level. See page 10. [Figure 324; Plates 39,46]

Three of the towels' most noticeable characteristics were similarities in embroidered designs, coloration, and baroque-type drawn thread borders. On the upper panel of each towel a large heart was featured with the maker's initials and year placed inside. An elaborate vine with flowers encompassed two of the hearts, and on the CH towel confronting birds were perched in a branch on each lobe of the heart. These particular birds were unique because each had a finely applied red wool fabric breast and a white silk fabric wing. Two fanciful flowers on the same towel had yellow silk fabric applied centers held in place by tiny embroidered knots.

The blossoming carnation embroidered on each of the towels differed in size by one-quarter inch which may or may not preclude the original use of a paper or stamped pattern. The construction and design of this particular flower has not been seen on other Pennsylvania towels, although Fronica Brandt[356] and several other girls sewed a carnation nearly like it. It was a flower motif more often seen on pieces of English needlework made in Philadelphia or New England rather than in the stitchery found in the German speaking sections of southeastern Pennsylvania. We believe this to be an instance in which Pennsylvania Dutch girls borrowed motifs from outside their native folk culture and executed them with precision. (See Swan, 1976, 70, 76).

The combination of red cotton and aqua silk embroidery threads is striking and unusual. It is a color blending shared by all three towels, but it has not been seen on other towel stitchery.

Horizontal drawn thread borders appeared on each towel that contained a chevroned design. The CH, 1818, towel, which was the most elaborate of the three, has additional floral borders of all-white embroidery the patterns of which seem to be from a non-German source. This type of embellishment was seen on later-dated monochromatic towel variants.[279] Collectively these decorative towels represent an acculturation in stitchery and needlework not usually seen, especially at such an early date.

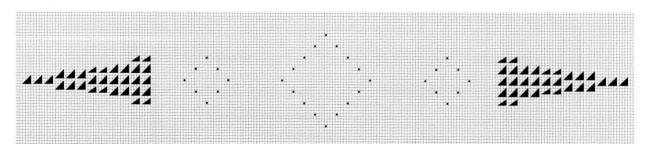

FIGURE 482 The tapered yellow ends of this tail piece are drawn here thread for thread, not stitch for stitch. Each horizontal and vertical line in the graph represents one thread of fabric. The cross stitches are not always square. The three blue diamonds in the center are also drawn thread for thread.[1116]

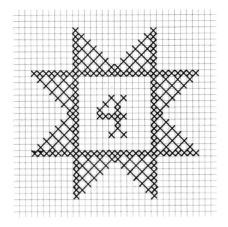

Designs

A. SOURCES

In a general sense embroidery designs, including those in the Pennsylvania Dutch folk culture, appear to have originated from two main sources: adaptations from European designs and original motifs created by needlewomen.

It is not surprising then that cross stitch designs seen on Pennsylvania decorated hand towels can be readily linked to European Germanic needlework traditions. Certain motifs on Pennsylvania towels are close approximations of designs found on textiles from the late seventeenth and early eighteenth centuries from the Netherlands, Switzerland, and portions of Germany, for it is from these areas that families migrated to Pennsylvania bringing with them traditional needle designs and stitch techniques.

Some European cross stitch design traditions never used on Pennsylvania towels were ships, mermaids, the spinning monkey, or windmills. (See Meulenbelt-Nieuwburg). Occasionally on Pennsylvania towels we find Biblical or religious scenes, church buildings, ecclesiastical objects, or the horse and carriages seen in European needlework. The Pennsylvania Dutch rendition of a European design is generally not as ornate, elaborate, or intricate as its predecessor, but relationships are obvious.

The source of a small catagory of needlemade cross stitch motifs can be traced to original inspirations from immediate surroundings rather than imported traditions. Locally woven Jacquard, twill, and double cloth coverlet patterns such as the rose, cross, star, trees, eagles, peacocks, and flowers were copied in cross stitch. [Figures 84,85]

The patriotic eagle from early United States currency was used on the front cover of Reading almanacs printed by Johann Ritter, was recreated in woven coverlets, and

was painted on dateboards on Pennsylvania German houses. The observant embroiderer was also inspired to transpose the design into cross stitch. [Figures 86,87]

Printed sources did not escape scrutiny by young eager eyes looking for ideas. A house on an advertising broadside, [Figures 88, 89] the rooster in an ABC book, [Figures 90, 91] but especially engraved lettering seemed to fascinate numbers of young girls. Most households had a family Bible, almanac, and other printed materials from which the ambitious needleworker could copy typefaces. The curved lines and flourishes in the printed *Fraktur* typeface [392,468,745,] [Figure 323] as well as in decorative tailpieces[1116,1265,1291] presented a challenge to only the most enterprising and knowledgeable embroiderers. [Figures 167, 325, 482]

Design sources for drawn thread motifs appear to parallel those of cross stitch. Embroidered drawn thread designs frequently are similar to the cross stitch motifs sewn on the same towel. Allowances are made for sewing on a thread grid instead of on fabric, but their likeness is obvious. Size more than complexity limited the choice of cross stitch designs that could be utilized in drawn thread embroidery. This meant that it was not necessary to develop a special drawn thread sampler or to draw a particular graph to record drawn thread designs. [Figures 92,93] A needlemade sampling of cross stitch motifs was sufficient for both needs.

Some free style embroidery is uniform, balanced, and has a similarity in its designs that comes from being copied in some way. Identical or very similar designs have been seen more than once. Perhaps the most frequent is a vase of flowers whose stems rise and crisscross until a tulip forms. A bird perches on that flower.[316,510,699] [Figure 94; Plates 23, 31] Other examples include a leaping deer, and a bird sitting on a spray of flowers copied from the house blessings or *Taufscheine* printed by the Baumans at Ephrata.[253,758] [Figures 95-97]

Text continues on pg. 67.

PLATE 20 *Eli Zug Ihmiahr 1842* (In the year 1842). Balanced plain weave cotton fabric; red cotton and brown silk cross stitch. W. 17-3/8".;[1014] Courtesy, Clarke E. Hess.

PLATE 22 *S[usana] R[ock].* Cotton darning stitch on drawn thread panel; applied red, white and blue cotton plain fringe. 18½" x 15-7/8.[561] Courtesy, Mr. and Mrs. Richard F. Smith.

60

PLATE 21 *Lea Stolsfusz*. Balanced plain weave linen fabric; red and blue cotton, gold silk chain, satin, straight, and cross stitch. W. 18¼".[722] Courtesy, Sally and Pete Riffle.

FIGURE 84 (above) In 1840 Susanna Miller of Annville township, Lebanon county rendered these Jacquard coverlet motifs in red cotton cross stitch on her hand towel.[254]

FIGURE 85 (left) This Jacquard border motif was used by a number of Pennsylvania coverlet weavers in the second quarter of the nineteenth century, and was the inspiration for several towel designs. This from a blue and white cotton and red and blue wool coverlet by David Steiner, Brecknock township, Lancaster county.

FIGURE 86 This cross stitch eagle by Franey Kulp in 1861 appears to be a copy of the one used on the *Readinger Calender* for many years. Red and blue cotton cross stitch.[1265] See Figure 186 for similar design.

FIGURE 87 The almanac cover was also a source of cross stitch designs. *Der Neue Readinger Calender 1827*, Reading; Johann Ritter.

FIGURE 89 (above) The house on this public sale broadside of 1853 was from a wood engraving commonly used by rural Pennsylvania printers in the middle decades of the nineteenth century. 16½" x 13½".

FIGURE 88 (left) Cross stitch house in blue and red cotton copied from a wood engraving by Barbara Bamberger, 1833.[465] See Plate 37. Courtesy, Dr. and Mrs. Donald M. Herr.

FIGURE 90 (above) Catharina Weidman, 1838 reproduced the rooster on her ABC book in red cotton cross stitch.[1047]

FIGURE 91 (right) The rooster appeared on the back cover of many Pennsylvania German ABC books. This one, from an undated edition, Schäfer and Koradi, Philadelphia, was reprinted many times. 6¾" x 4-3/8".

FIGURES 92, 93   The designs marked on this paper sampler in black ink are similar to those embroidered in white cotton by Lea Iungst on a drawn thread panel.[66] Paper sampler size: 2-3/8'' x 4''. Drawn thread panel size: 15'' x 17''.

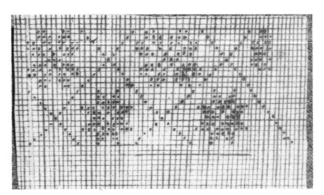

FIGURE 94 Free-form designs on a balanced plain weave cotton towel; white and blue cotton, yellow silk, and yellow wool chain stitch. The large floral design with bird is fourteen inches high.[510] See Plates 23, 31. Courtesy, Albert and Elizabeth Gamon.

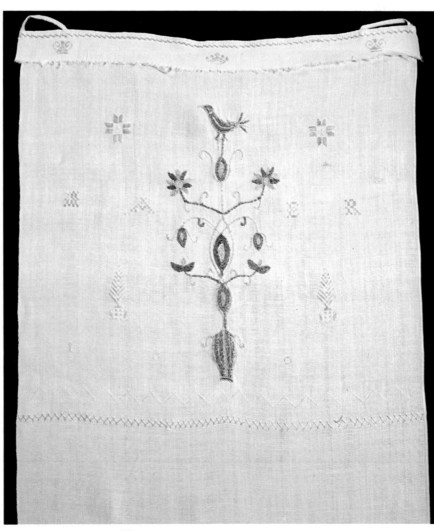

PLATE 23 *MA ER, 1808.* Balanced plain weave linen fabric, cotton chain, cross and herringbone stitches. Design: L. 11½"; W. 4¾"; towel W. 16-5/8".[699] Courtesy, Sally and Pete Riffle.

FIGURE 95 House Blessing. The motifs on the Bauman broadsides were the source for several embroiderers who attempted the birds, flowers, and deer with needle and thread. Printed by Samuel Bauman, Ephrata, 1813.

FIGURE 96 M[aria] S[chultz], Montgomery county. Balanced plain weave cotton panel; red and blue cotton outline, satin, and seeding stitches. Each initial is 1-5/8 inches high. The motifs are similar to those printed by Samuel Bauman at Ephrata, but are more poorly executed than those embroidered by Clary Hallman. See Figure 97. 9" x 15¼".[253]

The origins of some other free-form designs are not as easily traced. It is clear that many young ladies drew freely onto their towel familiar objects, flowers, and birds. They were primitive in interpretation having been executed without benefit of pattern, stamp, or stencil. The mystery deepens with the handful of towels that were decorated with sophisticted, elaborate, free-style design units that called for fine well executed stitchery.[279,285,548] [Figure 557; Plate 39] The source of these designs is also probably beyond recall.

It must be remembered that making a decorated towel was a folk tradition and not a formal exercise practiced under the watchful eye of a paid instructor. Therefore, the outside influence of schools, independent teachers, and imported ideas were at a minimum although we cannot deny these did exist in some areas.

FIGURE 97 *Clary Hallman, 1841,* Montgomery county. Balanced plain weave cotton panel; red and blue cotton outline, satin, seeding, and star stitches. The deer is two inches high and 2-3/8 inches wide. The motifs appear to have been inspired by designs on Bauman printed broadsides. 8'' x 17½''.[758] Courtesy, Sally and Pete Riffle.

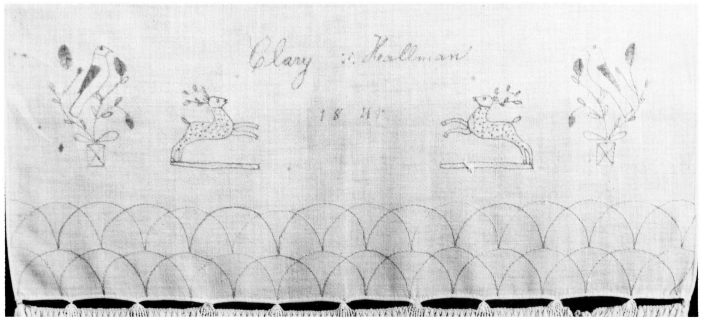

PLATE 24   *Catharina Kratz, 1838.* Balanced plain weave linen fabric; red cotton, yellow, green, tan silk cross stitch. W. 13½''.[12] Courtesy, Mary Ann McIlnay.

B. SAMPLER AND PAPER RECORDS

A practical way of recording and preserving favorite motifs was to embroider the favored cross stitch designs on fabric, having shared or traded them with family and friends. The basic purpose of the early Pennsylvania German sampler was, therefore, as a reference source and not as an object to exhibit. [Figures 98, 99]

The exchange of design patterns between women within a family is evident from similarities in motifs on several pieces of needlework from one family. It is obvious that mothers, daughters, sisters, cousins, and in-laws often influenced each other's sewing, but each woman stitched her own rendition of a design type.

The Schaeffer, [Figures 464-467] Nissley, [Figures 100-103] Minnich, [Figure 104; Plates 11, 48] Witmer, [Figures 105-109] and Leaman women are examples of this as are three sisters Salome, Susanna, and Rosina Kriebel and their sister-in-law Anna Kriebel. Salome (January 16, 1823—November 17, 1891) married Abraham Anders October 21, 1847, made a sampler[455] in 1838, [Plate 6] a towel in 1839,[454] [Figure 110] and another towel in 1843.[453] [Figure 111] Her sisters Susanna made a towel in 1843[456] [Figure 112] and Rosina a sampler in 1842.[457] [Plate 5] Anna Kriebel, their sister-in-law, also made a towel in 1842.[476] Each of the two large samplers made by Rosina and Salome contain over forty different cross stitch designs plus two alphabets. Many of the motifs on the two

FIGURE 98 Sampler. *Catharina Franck, 1820* .... Balanced plain weave linen fabric; black and tan silk cross and straight stitches; white two ply linen needlelace sewn in fourteen different designs. Self plain fringe, one-quarter inch long on sides and bottom and three-eighth inches long on top edge. L. 17¼"; W. 18¾".[808]

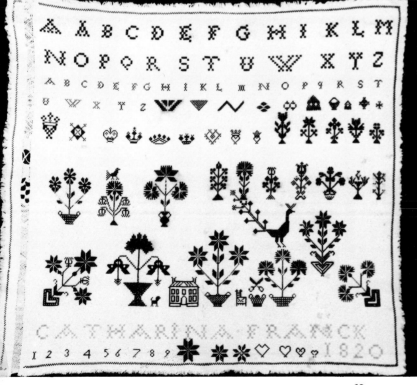

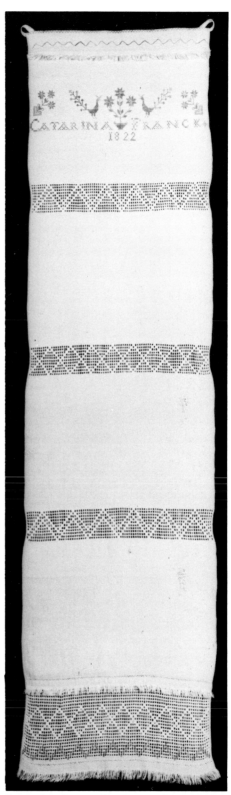

FIGURE 99 *Catarina Franck, 1822*. Balanced plain weave linen fabric; red cotton cross, herringbone, and chain stitches; hemstitching; white linen and red cotton darning stitch in drawn thread panels. Self and applied plain fringe. The embroidered motifs also appear on her 1820 sampler. See Figure 98. 62½" x 16½".[807]

FIGURE 100 Needlework picture. *Anny Nisly, 1837. Rapho township, Lancaster county* .... Anny Nisly was one of five sisters, three of whom embroidered pictures, samplers, and towels and traded motifs. Sampler seen by photograph only.

FIGURE 102 Sampler. *Fanny Nisley, 1836. Rapho township, Lancaster county* .... Balanced plain weave linen fabric; red and blue cotton cross stitch; bordered with green silk ribbon. L. 24-5/8''; W. 22'' with frame. Courtesy of Mr. and Mrs. Richard F. Smith.

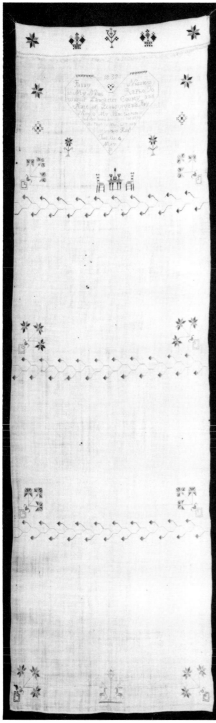

FIGURE 103 *Fanny Nissley, 1839. Rapho township, Lancaster county.* Balanced plain weave linen fabric; red and blue cotton cross stitch. These embroidered designs are similar to those sewn by all the Nissley sisters. 56" x 16½".[574]

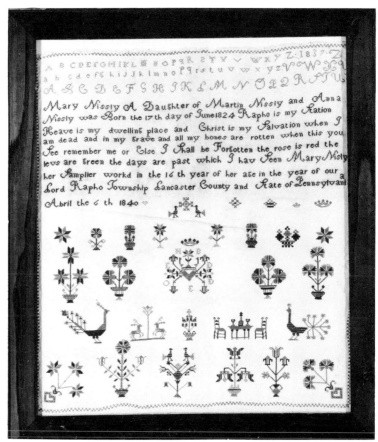

FIGURE 101 Sampler. *Mary Nissly, 1840. Rapho township Lancaster county* . . . . Balanced plain weave linen fabric; red and dark blue cotton cross stitch. Mary was one of five daughters of Martin and Anna Nissly. L. 16½"; W. 15¼".[632] Courtesy, North Museum of Franklin and Marshall College, Lancaster.

FIGURE 104 Sampler. *Rebeca Minnich, 1843. Lancaster county.* Balanced plain weave linen fabric; multicolor wool cross stitch. Bound with cream color silk ribbon. L. 16¼"; W. 16¼".[575a] Courtesy, Dr. and Mrs. Donald M. Herr.

71

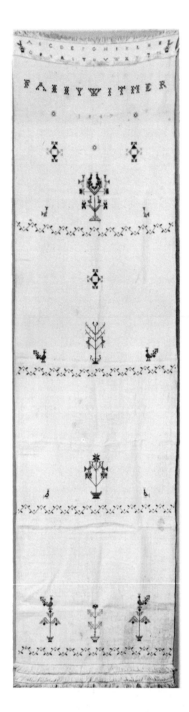

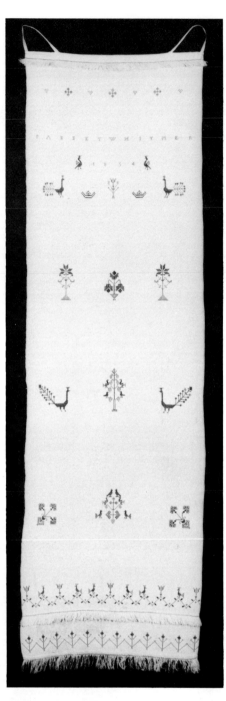

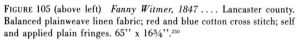

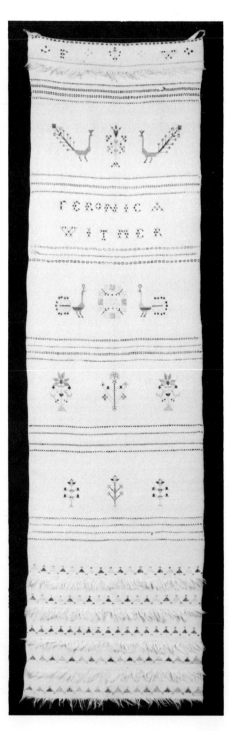

FIGURE 105 (above left) *Fanny Witmer, 1847 . . . .* Lancaster county. Balanced plainweave linen fabric; red and blue cotton cross stitch; self and applied plain fringes. 65'' x 16¾''.[250]

FIGURE 106 (above right) *Fanney Whitmer, 1854.* Lancaster county. Balanced plain weave linen fabric; red and blue cotton cross stitch; self and applied plain fringes. 55'' x 16½''.[67] Courtesy, Clarke E. Hess.

FIGURE 107 (right) *Feronica Witmer, 1826.* Lancaster county. Balanced plain weave linen fabric; red and blue cotton cross stitch; self and applied plain fringes. 63'' x 16¾''.[612] Courtesy, Collection of Paul and Rita Flack.

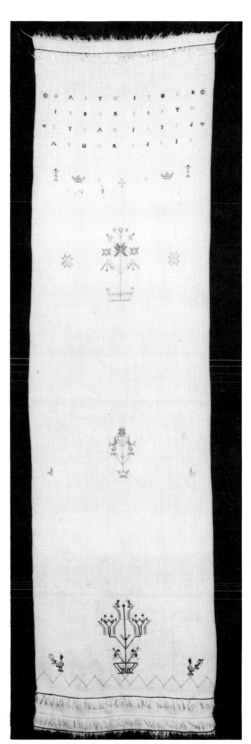

FIGURE 108 *Mary Witmer, 1847*. Rapho township, Lancaster county. Balanced plain weave linen fabric; green, gold, and red wool cross stitch; self and applied plain fringes. See Plate 7. 61'' x 16½''.[63] Courtesy, Clarke E. Hess.

FIGURE 109 *Mary Witmer*, Lancaster County. Balanced plain weave linen fabric; red, dark blue, and light blue cotton cross stitch; self and applied plain fringes. 64½'' x 17½''.[440] Courtesy, Clarke E. Hess.

FIGURE 110 *Salome Kriebel, 1839, SK*, a member of the Schwenkfelder community, Worcester township, Montgomery county. Pattern woven cotton towel and balanced plain weave linen panel; red cotton cross stitch designs not in mirror image. The mill-made white cotton applied fringe is 3½ inches long. See Plate 6 for her sampler. 5¼" x 19".[454]

FIGURE 111 *Salome Kriebel, 1843 ....*, a member of the Schwenkfelder community, Worcester township, Montgomery county. Pattern woven cotton towel and a balanced plain weave cotton panel; red cotton cross stitch; interlaced hemstitching; self plain fringe is two inches long. 5" x 19¼".[453]

FIGURE 112 *Susanna Kriebel, 1843*, a member of the Schwenkfelder community, Worcester township, Montgomery county. Pattern woven linen towel and a balanced plain weave cotton panel; red cotton cross stitch. The mill-made white cotton applied fringe and tassels is 3½ inches long. 5½" x 17½".[456]

samplers are identical in design, but differ in color combinations or have had design elements exchanged. For instance, the bouquets of flowers are alike, but they are in varied containers. [Plates 5,6] This type of individual exchange and personal interpretation continued in the thirteen designs that occur on each of Salome and Susanna's towels and the six motifs on Anna's towel. Their

sources can all be traced to each other as well as the figures sewn on the samplers. The similarity of designs and their arrangements so closely resemble each other that relative influence cannot be doubted.

Probably seeing one another's towels did as much as anything, however, to spread designs. Sundays were visiting days and women spent visiting time sharing their needlework with one another. No doubt this visual examination and the impressions left on brains not sated with images contributed to the repetition of designs and their slight modification.

Two other examples of towels with demonstrably close relationships may be cited. Hanna Brenneisen[711] and Catarina Kemper[76] prepared towels that are quite similar in design. [Figure 184] The two girls lived near one another in East Earl township, Lancaster county. Hanna was a Lutheran, Catarina probably a member of the Church of the Brethren. In 1837 Mary Carpenter embroidered a towel with initials of family members.[56] Lydia Nolt, a member of the later generation in the same family, continued the tradition.[106] [Figure 175] Examples could be multiplied to prove this point. Whether by family tie, geographic proximity, or an example seen at someone's house, the towel was frequently a copy of a related example.

There was another way to save designs for future use. Just as weavers hand-drew pattern books to record weaving drafts, and musicians lined their own staff paper, so some young girls drew an inked graph on which to record their embroidery designs. [Figure 113]

In 1828, Susanha Heebnerin, a Schwenkfelder girl from Montgomery county, made her own needlework chart on which she drew over twenty separate cross stitch motifs including hearts, tulips, a double-headed eagle, facing stags, and other geometric designs as well as five borders, her name, and the year. It was drafted on paper with the graph grid drawn in brown ink. The designs are watercolored in blue, black, pink, green, and red in color combinations often seen in stitchery. [Figure 114] Some of the designs she recorded that have been seen on towels are a small dog, simple borders, and her lettering style. [Figure 115] However, most of her floral designs have a European flavor and may have been copied from an earlier printed source.

Another diagramed registry of cross stitch designs is from the Weaverland area in Lancaster county. The graphed grid is also drawn in brown ink. The designs on the graph are filled solid with red ink and include a complete alphabet, the symbol "&", the year 1820, four large floral motifs and three smaller flowers. The name and date Abraham Weber, 1820 are written in German script at the bottom of the page. [Figure 116]

The knowledge and practice of embroidering a hand towel as a folk tradition was passed from mother to daughter without benefit of printed materials. One of the earliest Pennsylvania German printed embroidery design sources is the alphabet, seven inches high, in the Metamorphosis printed by Starck and Lange in Hanover, Pa., in 1814. [Figure 117]

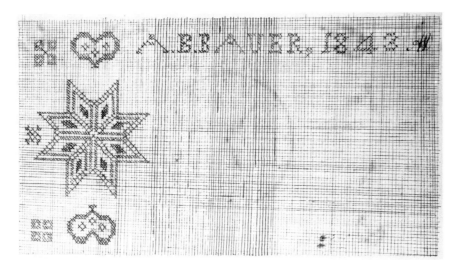

FIGURE 113 Paper sampler. A[ndreas] B. Bauer, 1843. Douglas twp. Montgomery co. Black and blue ink on wove paper. This is part of a four page booklet made by him. 20.1 cm. x 33.2 cm. Courtesy, Schwenkfelder Museum and Library, Pennsburg.

FIGURE 114 Hand drawn paper sampler of cross stitch motifs made by Susanha Heebnerin, 1828, Montgomery county. Watercolored. 20.3 x 30.4 cm. Courtesy, Schwenkfelder Museum and Library, Pennsburg.

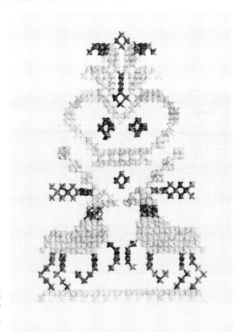

FIGURE 115 Deer and crown motif almost identical to one drawn on the paper sampler of Susanha Heebnerin, 1828. See Figure 114. Red and blue cotton cross stitch.[340]

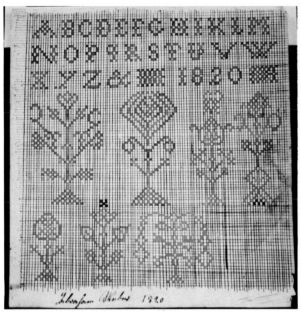

FIGURE 116 Hand drawn paper sampler with the name and date Abraham Weber, 1820 written in German script along the bottom edge. Lancaster county. 8" x 7½". Courtesy, Dr. and Mrs. Donald M. Herr.

Printer Carl F. Egelmann of Reading sensed the favorable moment in the decorated towel craze and in 1831 incorporated a page in his copybook entitled, "For Marking on Linen." It is a one page copper engraving of small cross stitches on a grid that comprises an upper and lower case alphabet with several optional letters, a full set of numerals one through zero, four borders, and five designs. [Figure 118] The impact of this one page was phenomenal. Young ladies throughout the Dutch country eagerly began copying with much frequency his designs and borders onto their towels. [Figure 119] A Folmer family towel[4] [Figure 12] and the 1854 Elisebeth Horte towel [706] have most of Egelmann's designs sewn on them. [Figure 180a] And Elizabeth Longenecker in 1838 embroidered two of his four borders on her towel.[15] A most difficult feat was accomplished by LK in 1847 who worked one of his circular designs into her drawn thread panel.[291] The younger generation welcomed Egelmann's ideas into their tradition.

In Egelmann's almanac for 1844, there is a graphic page with an upper and lower case alphabet, a complete set of numerals one through zero, two small diamond designs, and a border identical to one he printed in 1831. [Figure 198]

We are not aware of hand-drawn notebooks or printed patterns of free-form designs that might have circulated through the Dutch countryside, nor are we aware of similar drafts shared by members of a family unit. To the best of our knowledge printed free-style patterns that would have been helpful to young embroiderers were never produced by the Pennsylvania German presses. The most reliable way to record and preserve designs was to do it yourself—with needle and thread or pen and ink.

FIGURE 117 The alphabet and numerals printed in the 1814 Metamorphosis by Starck and Lange of Hanover, Pennsylvania.

76

FIGURE 118   The page "For Marking On Linen" from the 1831 Carl F. Egelmann copybook printed in Reading.

FIGURE 119   Anna Hosteter, 1842, copied designs and border units exactly as they were printed in the Egelmann copybook. Balanced plain weave linen fabric; red cotton cross stitch. W. 19¾".[1343]

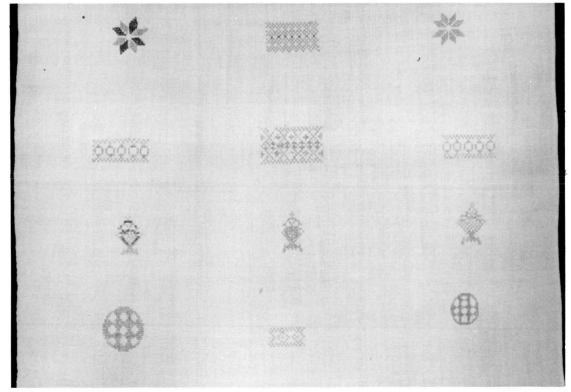

C. PLACEMENT

Regardless of the size or type design and no matter what stitches or colors were used, the placement of each design was an important consideration and helped make each towel unique. Towels were divided into horizontal panel sections throughout their length. These panels were, at times, delineated by embroidered borders, applied fringes, drawn thread borders, or by a single row of cross stitch designs. Some towels show just a top and bottom embroidered section while others utilize more surface space. Each panel can be considered a unit of designs with one central motif. To the right and left of center usually there are mirror-like designs. Their individual placement is precise and they balance each other. The impact of this symmetry is equally strong even with towels having poor workmanship. It is this traditional balanced panel design layout against which we will compare individualized placements of cross stitch, drawn thread, and free-form motifs.

There are some towels which have each panel or unit filled with motifs all of a different design, but of a nearly equal size. The overall appearance of the towel is generally balanced, but exact symmetry is missing.[909] [Figure 128]

Towel makers selected between one[148,275,415] and twenty-eight[264] different cross stitch designs and carefully arranged them throughout the towel in up to seventy-three separate places all the while maintaining balance and symmetry.[231] Christina Lenz, 1817, probably set a record when she cross stitched twenty-seven individual motifs 120 times which filled nearly every inch of available space on her towel.[109] [Plate 40]

By the maker's choice, the height of each horizontal panel varied according to the size and type of motifs. MK stretched tradition when she placed five very wide and tall cross stitch designs down the middle of the towel which left room for only one small motif to either side of each large motif with the exception of the third design from the top. This was so tall that not one, but three small vertically placed designs were required on either side for balance.[366] [Figure 129] Balli Weiser stretched tradition even further by sewing just three very large designs down the center of her 1795 towel. Each unusual motif consists of a group of long crossed lines with a round flower-like design at the end of each stem.[886] [Figure 120]

Elisabeth[466] and Anna[755] Frey, Sara Anna Hollobush[576] and Catarina Kemper[76] were among the few who ignored traditional regularity and uniformity and devoted one entire panel on their towel to illustrating a scene, dramatic event, or casually placed favored designs. The thrill of the hunt and the familiar tranquil yardscape, instead of individual symbolic motifs, were recorded with needle and thread. The cross stitch designs in these panels were harmonious, but not necessarily symmetrical. [Figures 151a, 187; Plate 29]

Drawn thread embroidery does not have its own design or design placement tradition. The drawn thread designs were not only copied from those of cross stitch,

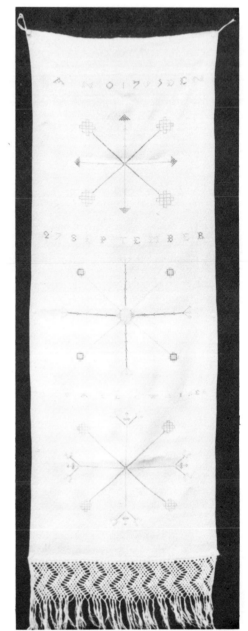

FIGURE 120 *Balli Weiser, 1795* . . . . Balanced plain weave linen fabric, red and blue cotton cross stitch; applied knotted fringe; 43" x 14".[886] Courtesy, Mary Ann McIlnay.

but they used the same symmetrical placement that featured a central motif with mirror-image designs to either side. Other panels had overall designs worked on them that included large diamonds with smaller designs sewn between or inside them.[66,124,137,299]

The quantity of drawn thread motifs sewn on any one towel was limited by the size of the drawn thread grid as well as by the number of grid panels included in the towel. The record to date of the number of designs on one towel is ninety-one drawn motifs embroidered on three separate panels.[370]

Between 1815 and 1850 free-design forms also dominated the surface of towels, but cross stitch was still included in some way even if it was just to spell the name and year.[74,356] Small free-style designs whose patterns appear to have originated with the towel maker herself were often spaced among count thread cross stitch embroidery. Most of these designs were sewn with the chain or outline stitch, but several towel makers used an uncounted cross stitch, sewed at random, to develop various free-form motifs.[769,1116] They were incorporated into each paneled unit of designs, but did not interfere with its symmetry.

Large stylized free-form motifs were often arranged in mirror-image panels much as cross stitch designs were symmetrically placed.[75,84,85,253,285] [Figures 191-194] But, variations abound. One seamstress in 1860 embroidered an outdoor scene of two birds watching a spotted rabbit run through a thicket of trees and hanging branches.[322] [Figure 558] MR, 1817, went further by arranging fifteen free-style birds, flowers, and a star design all over the towel, none of them repeated motifs.[709] [Figure 266] This freedom in design arrangement occurs more frequently with free-form than with counted thread embroidery.

Using large free-style motifs by themselves expanded the traditional paneled effect sometimes to the point of losing it.[661] In exceptional cases the sectioned units were completely disregarded. Three towels made by Schwenkfelders have just one very large free-form design that extends from the top to the bottom.[71,402,932] They are unusual and are discussed in detail in chapter six. [Figures 559,560]

The addition of these imaginative motif arrangements to the customary design placement of cross stitch, drawn thread, and free-form motifs on a single towel serves to reinforce our view that decorating hand towels was creativity expressed within a tradition-bound discipline.

A group of towels with documented Schwenkfelder origin, dating from 1819 to 1844, have certain similarities in design placement. The top three-quarters of the towel was either pattern woven or a balanced plain weave, linen or cotton fabric, but it seldom had the typical top flap. The embroidery was almost always limited to an attached bottom panel. They contained either cross stitch, drawn thread, or free-style designs, but stitchery types were seldom mixed on one panel. The width of these towels was within traditional limits, but their length was shorter than normal, seldom exceeding fifty inches. There is an absence of knotted fringes and a minimum of insertions. White cotton commercially-produced fringe was almost always sewn along the lower edge of the towel.

Several of these towels, dated from 1830[261] through 1843,[456] were cross stitched with several elements in common. There was almost always an embroidered border on one or all four sides of the decorative panel. [Figures 110, 112] The name and year was prominent although they were blended-in with symmetrically placed designs. The cross stitching was almost always sewn in all-red cotton. A variation in coloration was to combine red cotton with brown silk.[230] [Figures 121-123]

FIGURE 121 *Hanna Huebner, 1839*, a member of the Schwenkfelder community, Worcester township, Montgomery county. Balanced plain weave cotton fabric; red cotton cross stitch. The mill-made white cotton fringe is four inches long. 5¾" x 15-5/8".[229]

FIGURE 122 *Regina Schultz, 1837*, a member of the Schwenkfelder community. Towel seen by photograph only. Colors, stitches, dimensions, and family history are unknown.[889]

The three drawn thread panels also had similar characteristics. The decorative panels were attached to the bottom of the towel and embroidered borders appear on one or four sides of the thread grid panel. The name and year are embroidered on the thread grid in arrangements similar to those seen on the cross stitch versions. These towels were made by Regina K. Schultz, 1824,[262] Deborah Heebner, 1825,[347] and Susanna Kriebel, 1825,[348] all within a year of each other. It is interesting to note that a Mennonite girl, Sarah Landes, made a similar drawn thread panel employing like designs and design placement. She too attached it to the bottom of her towel.[177]

On two towels each with a panel of free form embroidery sewn to the bottom edge the girl signed her initials, not her full name: RG, [Rebecca Gerhard] 1844,[279] [Figure 558] and MH [Maria Heebner].[461] Rebecca and Maria each embroidered their free-style tulip and floral designs with all-white embroidery thread.

There are other towels with embroidered cotton panels in this group. On hers, Maria Schultz used blue and red to develop hills, tulips, birds, leaping harts, and stars.[253]

FIGURE 123 *R*[egina] *S*[chultz], *1841*, member of the Schwenkfelder community in Upper Hanover township, Montgomery county. Towels seen by photograph only. Colors, stitches, and dimensions are unknown.[891]

It is remarkable that identical designs in similar colorations were found on a second towel made by Clary Hallman in 1841.[758] Clary Hallman is not a Schwenkfelder name, but families with the name of Hallman lived as neighbors in the upper end of the Schwenkfelder settlement area near the Berks and Montgomery county line. We suspect they were friends and shared towel designs. [Figures 95, 96]

Five additional Schwenkfelder towels fit into a miscellaneous category in terms of their design placement, to prove the point that there are always exceptions. Fronica Krebielin used the more typical approach by embroidering symmetrical designs in the upper areas of the towel which were followed by a brief inscription.[408] Maria Kriebel, in 1842, made two towels each of which had the embroidered panel placed in the middle of the towel, not along the bottom edge.[645,646] Deborah Heebner, 1827, embroidered two decorative panels, one at the top and the second near the bottom edge.[346] Susanna Heebner put an embroidered panel at the bottom, but it is an example of twelve rows of horizontal hemstitching and not count thread or free-form embroidery.[482]

The choice and placement of all design elements were certainly an individual's for practically no two towels are alike. While religious convictions at one time might have influenced the selection of designs, they did not seem to affect the type of stitchery and the layout or placement of the designs onto the towel's surface. Regional contrasts, denominational variances, family distinctions, or stylistic differences are almost impossible to define by observing the organization of designs.

Some broad observations could be made, however. Lancaster county probably produced most of the finest towels in terms of quality of workmanship, quantity of motifs per towel, and color impact. But Montgomery county, with its Schwenkfelder residents, produced towels with a variety of needlework and layout.

In the placement of designs, the distribution of cross stitch, free-form, and drawn thread work embroidery, the needleworker demonstrated her sense of aesthetic value. She was untutored, copying, but varying what her friends and relatives were doing. Her selection of designs, choice of color, and the arrangement of them contributed to the first impact a towel made hanging on a door. A close examination might reveal the variety of her choices of needlework or the skill with which she executed what she did, but most people saw the towel for its visual impact. One must respect the unwritten canons by which these choices were made. In all but a few instances, the needlework hand towels from Pennsylvania German households were pleasing to the eye, an honest reflection of the neat and orderly life these people espoused.

AN ALBUM OF DECORATED HAND TOWELS
MADE BY PENNSYLVANIA GERMAN WOMEN

FIGURE 124 *Jacob Schitz, 1840, ES, 1839.* Balanced plain weave linen fabric; red cotton cross stitch; white cotton darning stitch in drawn thread panel; self plain fringe. 58" x 19-1/8".[135]

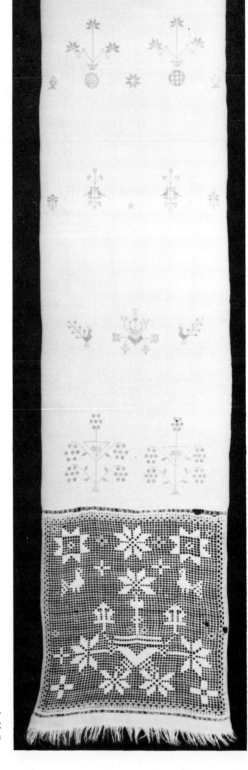

FIGURE 125 *CB, 1831.* Balanced plain weave linen fabric; red cotton cross stitch; white and red cotton darning stitch in drawn thread panel; applied plain fringe; linen needlelace. 71" x 15¾".[58]

82

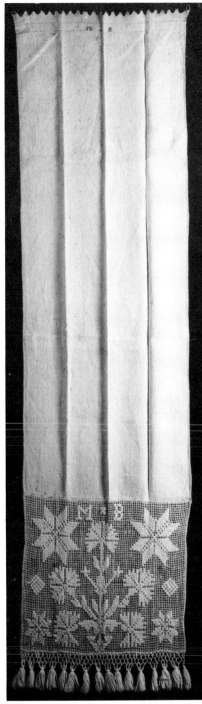

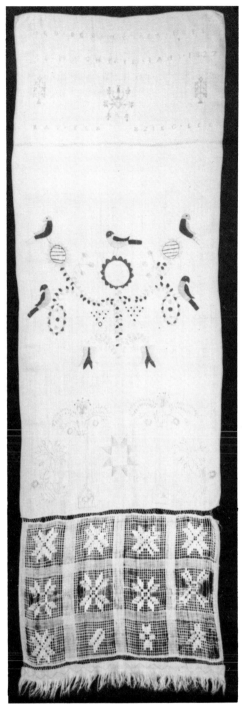

FIGURE 126 *M*[ary] *B*[auer], Skippack, Montgomery county. Balanced plain weave linen fabric; red cotton cross stitch initials; white linen darning stitch in drawn thread panel; applied knotted fringe. Creased from being folded for storage in a chest. See Figure 10. 49'' x 14''.[178]

FIGURE 127 *Hedded Meier, Rayel Ziegler, 1827* . . . . Balanced plain weave linen fabric; red and blue cotton cross, chain, satin, back, eyelet, buttonhole, and outline stitches; white linen and red cotton darning stitch in drawn thread panel; applied plain fringe. 56¼'' x 18''.[718] Courtesy, Sally and Pete Riffle.

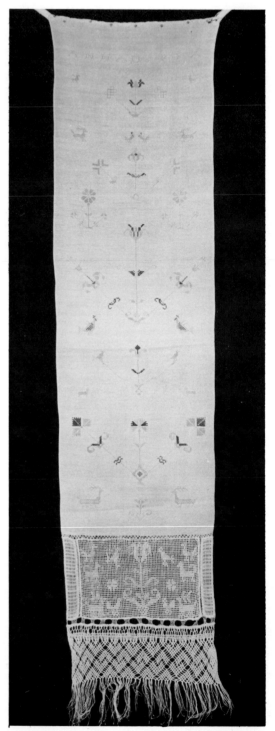

FIGURE 129 *Anna Maria, 1816.* (above) Balanced plain weave linen fabric; red and blue cotton cross stitch; red cotton darning stitch in drawn thread panel; linen needlelace; hand-knotted fringe. 51'' x 13''.[375] Courtesy, The Henry Francis duPont Winterthur Museum.

FIGURE 128 (left) *Elisabeth Dornbach, 1821.* Balanced plain weave linen fabric; red cotton, yellow wool, dark brown and yellow silk cross stitch; white and red cotton darning stitch in drawn thread panel; pattern woven bands in white linen; ladder hemstitching; hand-knotted fringe is four inches long. The designs are not sewn in mirror image. 60'' x 13''.[282]

84

FIGURE 130 (above) *Susanna Walbin, 1800.* Quakertown area, Bucks county. Balanced plain weave linen fabric; red and blue cotton cross stitch; white linen darning stitch in drawn thread panel; applied braided fringe. See Figures 33a, 374. 54½'' x 12-5/8''.[273]

FIGURE 131(right) *Anna Staman, 1839. Warwick township, Lancaster county.* Balanced plain weave linen fabric; red and blue cotton cross stitch; white cotton darning stitch in drawn thread panel; white cotton mill-made plain fringe. 65'' x 17''.[191]

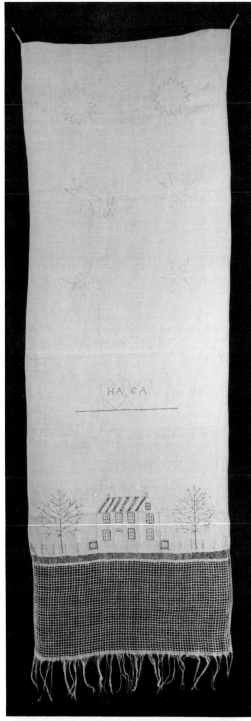

FIGURE 132   *HA CA.* Balanced plain weave linen fabric, red and blue cotton outline, satin, and herringbone stitches; white linen needlelace; self plain fringe. 50½'' x 16-1/8''.[125]

FIGURE 133   *RS.* Balanced plain weave cotton fabric; red cotton chain, satin, back and cross stitch and French knot; light green, pink, yellow, red, dark green, maroon, red-orange, and brown wool satin-type stitch on leno woven panel; white and red and white striped cotton fabric folded points; white cotton mill-made fringe. 47½'' x 14¾''.[927]

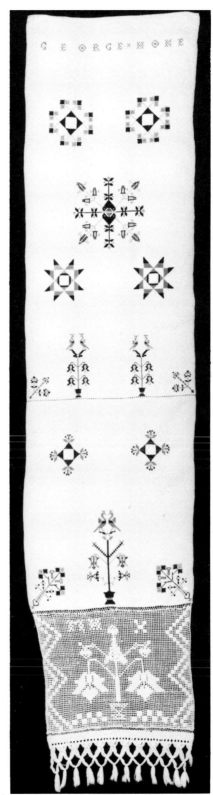

FIGURE 134 *BH, 1824*. Balanced plain weave linen fabric; red, dark blue, light blue cotton and gold and brown silk cross stitch; white cotton darning stitch on drawn thread panel; self plain fringe. 57¼" x 16¾".[1070]

FIGURE 135 *George Hoke*. Balanced plain weave linen fabric; red and blue cotton cross stitch; white cotton darning stitch on drawn thread panel; applied white cotton mill-made fringe. See Figure 148 for towel with similar motifs. 69½" x 15-7/8".[559] Courtesy, Mr. and Mrs. Richard F. Smith.

FIGURE 136 (above)   White cotton darning stitch on drawn thread panel; applied white cotton plain fringe, three inches long, covers the butt seam where the towel and thread panel are joined. The applied mill-made white cotton fringe with tassels is 5½ inches long. Multicolor wool cross stitch. See Plate 12. 10-5/8'' x 16½''.[469] Courtesy, Dr. and Mrs. Donald M. Herr.

FIGURE 137 (above)   White cotton darning stitch in drawn thread panel on which the weaver's rose motif was included five times. Balanced plain weave linen fabric; red cotton cross stitch. See Figure 143 for a similar design sewn on the drawn thread grid. Interlaced hemstitching one-half inch high; applied plain fringe. 18½'' x 17''.[608]

FIGURE 139 (below)   1833. White linen darning stitch on drawn thread panel. This is one of two towels with the same motifs, the other dated 1824.[148] The 2½ inch long applied fringe was of linen yarns inserted into each grid space and knotted in place. 10-5/8'' x 15¾''.[449] Courtesy, Goschenhoppen Folklife Museum and Library, Green Lane.

FIGURE 140 (below)   White linen running stitch in drawn thread panel. The top third of the grid was bound vertically; the lower two-thirds was bound both vertically and horizontally. The designs are not in mirror-image and their placement is asymmetric. 13¼'' x 16''.[29]

FIGURE 138 *Elisabeth Histand, EH.* Balanced plain weave linen fabric; red cotton cross stitch; white cotton darning stitch on drawn thread panel; white linen needlelace, hand knotted fringe. Note that the drawn thread panel is started five-eighth inches from the side edges. See Figure 155. 8-7/8'' x 11¼''.[625] Courtesy, North Museum of Franklin and Marshall College, Lancaster.

FIGURE 142 An eagle and shield sewn in white cotton darning stitch on drawn thread panel. 13½'' x 12½''.[412] Courtesy, The State Museum, Pennsylvania Historical and Museum Commission 65.106.143.

FIGURE 141 *CA.* White linen darning stitch in drawn thread panel; applied knotted fringe 4½ inches long. 12¾'' x 18¼''.[300]

FIGURE 143 *Dina Hautz.* Balanced plain weave linen fabric; red and blue cotton cross stitch; white cotton darning stitch in drawn thread panel; linen needlelace; applied white cotton mill-made fringe. See Figures 137, 411. 67½" x 17-1/8".[1314]

FIGURE 144 *Susanna Herr, David Herr, 1813.* Lancaster county. Balanced plain weave linen fabric; red cotton, blue linen, brown silk, red and yellow wool cross stitch and needleweaving; white cotton darning stitch in drawn thread panels; red and blue cotton thread buttons; self plain fringe and applied white cotton mill-made fringe. 65½" x 16¾".[103] Courtesy, Clarke E. Hess.

FIGURE 145 *EH, 1804.* Balanced plain weave linen fabric; black, tan, and light tan silk cross stitch; white cotton darning stitch in drawn thread panels; self and applied plain fringes. 62½" x 18¾".[1069]

90

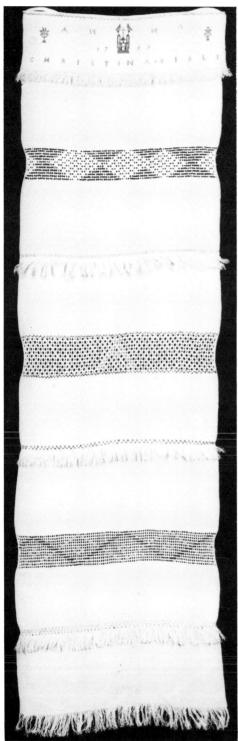

FIGURE 146 *Christina Ribli, Anno 1799*. Balanced plain weave linen fabric; red cotton and brown silk cross and herringbone stitches; red, white and blue cotton darning and Greek cross filling stitches in drawn thread panels; self and applied plain fringes. See Figures 72, 432. 57¼" x 16½".[1261] Courtesy, Mary Ann McIlnay.

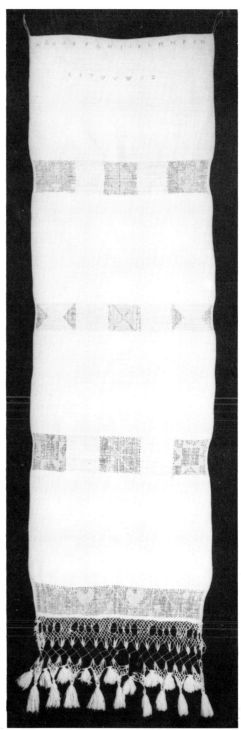

FIGURE 147 *A to Z*. Possibly from Lehigh county. Balanced plain weave linen fabric; brown silk cross stitch; red cotton needleweaving, running, and darning stitches in drawn thread panels; applied white cotton knotted fringe. See Figures 55, 56. 60" x 17".[516] Courtesy, Albert and Elizabeth Gamon.

FIGURE 148 *Sarah Shimp.* Balanced plain weave linen fabric; red and blue cotton cross stitch; applied knotted fringe. See Figure 135 for towel with similar motifs. 53¼" x 16".[562] Courtesy, Mr. and Mrs. Richard F. Smith.

FIGURE 149 *AH, Anna Herr, 1816.* Conestoga township, Lancaster county. Balanced plain weave linen fabric with pattern woven stripes; red cotton, aqua silk cross, outline, straight, seeding and satin stitches; white cotton darning stitch in drawn thread panels; self plain and knotted fringes. 57½" x 16-1/8".[468] Courtesy, Dr. and Mrs. Donald M. Herr.

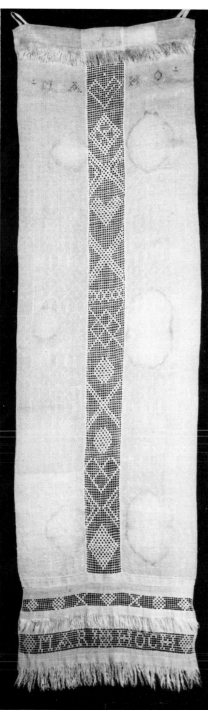

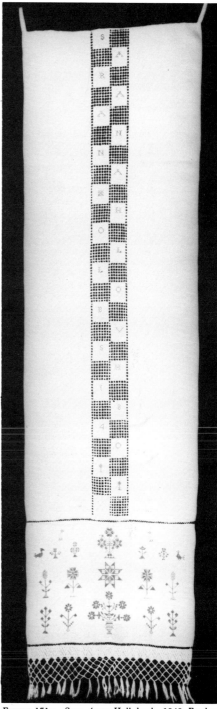

FIGURE 150   *MA HO, MARI HOCH*[stetter], 1797. Lancaster county. Spot weave linen fabric; white and brown silk cross, herringbone, and running stitches; red cotton and white linen darning stitch in drawn thread grids; self and applied plain fringes. 61'' x 17¾''.[581]

FIGURE 151   *AMC.* Balanced plain weave linen towel; red and blue cotton cross stitch symmetrical motifs are smaller at the top of the towel; white cotton darning stitch on drawn thread grids; applied plain fringe. 55½'' x 16-7/8''.[926]

FIGURE 151a   *Sara Anna Hollobush, 1840.* Frederick (now Upper Frederick) township, Montgomery county. Balanced plain weave linen fabric; red and white cotton cross stitch; white cotton mill-made knotted fringe. Some designs on bottom panel are not sewn in mirror-image. 54'' x 15-1/8''.[576]

FIGURE 152 *Elisabeth L. Frank, ABCDE.*
Balanced plain weave linen fabric; red cotton
cross stitch; white cotton darning stitch on
drawn thread panels; self and applied plain
fringes. See Figure 153 for towel with similar
motifs. 51-3/8'' x 16-3/8''.[566]

FIGURE 153 *Susannah ti Barnhardk, Catahrinek*
. . . . Balanced plain weave linen fabric; red cotton
cross stitch; white cotton darning stitch in drawn
thread panels; self plain fringe. See Figure 152 for
towel with similar motifs. 57'' x 16½''.[1266] Courtesy,
Mary Ann McIlnay.

FIGURE 154 *Feronica Witmer.* Balanced plain weave linen fabric; red cotton cross stitch; white cotton darning stitch in drawn thread panels; self and applied plain fringes. All drawn thread grids are cut and drawn from one piece of fabric. 58" x 16".[200]

FIGURE 154a (right) *1829, 1835.* Balanced plain weave linen fabric; red and blue cotton cross stitch; white cotton darning stitch on drawn thread panels; hand-knotted applied fringe. 62" x 15".[781] Courtesy, The New-York Historical Society, New York City.

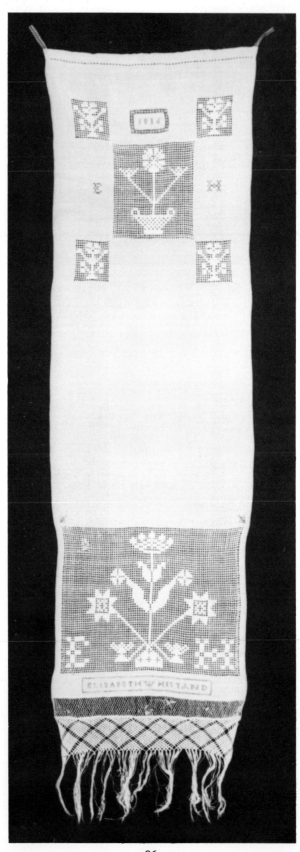

FIGURE 155 *Elisabeth Histand, 1816.* Balanced plain weave linen fabric; red cotton cross stitch; white cotton darning stitch on drawn thread panels; applied hand-knotted fringe. See Figure 138. 40½'' x 12½''.[625] Courtesy, North Museum of Franklin and Marshall College, Lancaster.

96

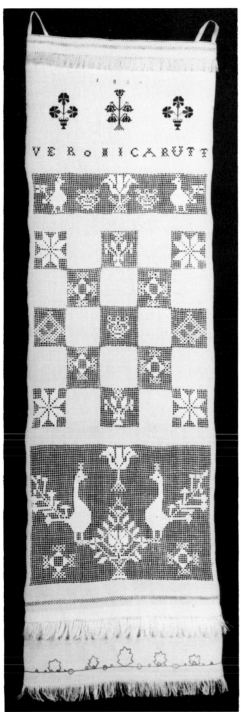

FIGURE 156 *Veronica Rutt, 1820.* Elizabethtown, Lancaster county. Balanced plain weave linen fabric; red and dark blue cotton cross, running and outline stitches; white cotton darning stitch on drawn thread panels; self and applied plain fringes. See Figure 157 for a similar towel. 53½'' x 16''.[751]

FIGURE 157 *Maria Rutt, Hornung 1828* [February 1828]. Balanced plain weave linen fabric; red cotton cross stitch; white cotton darning stitch in drawn thread panels; self and applied plain fringes. See Figure 156 for a similar towel. 58'' x 18¼''.[1133] Courtesy, Mary Ann McIlnay.

FIGURE 158 *Magdalena Gantzi, 1821.* Balanced plain weave linen fabric; red and blue cotton cross stitch; self and applied plain fringe. See Figure 443. 57" x 18¾".[1259] Courtesy, Mary Ann McIlnay.

FIGURE 159 *Magdalena Gantzie, 1819.* Balanced plain weave linen fabric; red and blue cotton cross stitch; self plain fringes. 54" x 19".[1132] Courtesy, Mary Ann McIlnay.

FIGURE 160 *MK, 1836.* Heidelberg township, Lehigh county. Balanced plain weave linen fabric; red and blue cotton cross stitch; self plain fringe. See Figure 161, Plates 8, 9, 10. 52½" x 12¾".[935]

FIGURE 161 *Sarah Ann Rex.* Heidelberg township, Lehigh county. Balanced plain weave linen fabric; red and blue cotton cross stitch. See Figure 160, Plates 8,9,10. 38" x 12¾".[934]

FIGURE 162 *Henry Kiefer, 1858.* Balanced plain weave cotton fabric; red, orange, olive green, and dark green wool cross and running stitches; self plain fringes. See Figure 163. 42" x 16-3/8".[693] Courtesy, Sally and Pete Riffle.

FIGURE 163 *Catarina Kiefer, 1854.* Balanced plain weave cotton fabric; red, orange, olive green wool, black silk, and white cotton cross and running stitches; self plain fringes. See Figure 162. 43½" x 17¼".[694] Courtesy, Sally and Pete Riffle.

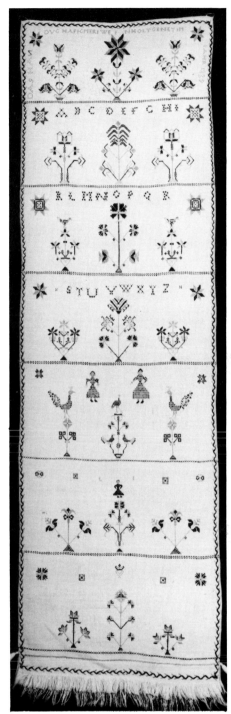

FIGURE 164 *Rebe Wein*[hold]. Lancaster county. Balanced plain weave linen fabric; red and blue cotton cross stitch and needleweaving; fringe missing. See Figure 165. 61'' x 17½''.[1416]

FIGURE 165 *Meri Weinholt, 1839 . . . .* Lancaster county. Balanced plain weave linen fabric; red and blue cotton cross and back stitches; self and applied plain fringes. See Figures 77, 164. 62¼'' x 18-7/8''. [467] Courtesy, Dr. and Mrs. Donald M. Herr.

FIGURE 166 *Freni Kinig, 1839* .... Lancaster county. Balanced plain weave linen fabric; multicolor cotton cross, outline, satin, and chain stitches; self plain fringe. 52½" x 18½".[973] Courtesy, Clarke E. Hess.

FIGURE 167 *Anna Stolzfusz, Mary Lapp, 1896* .... Lancaster county. Balanced plain weave linen fabric; multicolor cotton cross stitch; self plain and knotted fringe. 56" x 19".[969] Courtesy, Clarke E. Hess.

FIGURE 168 *Elizbeth B. Keener, 1855.* Balanced plain weave linen fabric; red and blue cotton cross stitch. Top of towel only. See Figure 284 for bottom border. 5¾" x 16½".[1279] Courtesy, Mary Ann McIlnay.

FIGURE 169 *Fianna Grube, 1850.* Balanced plain weave linen fabric; red cotton and brown silk cross stitch. Top half of towel only. 59" x 17¼".[1211] Courtesy, Mary Ann McIlnay.

FIGURE 170   Balanced plain weave linen fabric; red cotton cross and chain stitches. The top plain fringe is one inch long and is bound into groups with red cotton; the second is white cotton mill-made fringe 1½ inches long; the third is a self plain fringe, 1¼ inches long, bound into groups with red cotton; the bottom white cotton mill-made fringe is sewn to the towel underneath this self plain fringe. It is 4½ inches long including the tassels. W. 17-5/8''.[692] Courtesy, Sally and Pete Riffle.

FIGURE 171   *Mrs. Lydia Claytons' Needle work. Lydia Clayton March 4th 1859.* Balanced plain weave cotton towel fabric with a woven red stripe. The flap and bottom panel are balanced plain weave linen fabric; red and blue cotton cross stitch; plain fringes. See Figures 7, 251. 60'' x 15-1/8''.[1151] Courtesy, Mary Ann McIlnay.

FIGURE 172   Balanced plain weave linen fabric; red and blue cotton cross stitch; self plain fringe. Note the three red cotton tassels inserted into the middle and at each end of this fringe. Bottom of towel shown only. See Figure 173 for top of the towel. W. 17''.[1280] Courtesy, Mary Ann McIlnay.

FIGURE 173   *Catharina Balmer May 6, 1833.* Balanced plain weave linen fabric; red and blue cotton cross stitch; applied mill-made white cotton plain fringe. Top of towel shown only. See Figure 172 for bottom of towel. 68'' x 17''.[1280] Courtesy, Mary Ann McIlnay.

105

FIGURE 175 *Maria Nolt, 1890* .... Lancaster county. Balanced plain weave linen fabric; red and gray cotton cross stitch; self plain fringe. A family register towel with deceased people's names sewn in gray, the living in red. 50½" x 19".[106] Courtesy, Clarke E. Hess.

FIGURE 174 *FH, 1808*. Pattern woven cotton towel fabric; balanced plain weave linen fabric top panel; red cotton and brown silk cross stitch; white linen fabric stroke gathered ruffle; white cotton knotted fringe. 58" x 15½".[1196] Courtesy, Mary Ann McIlnay.

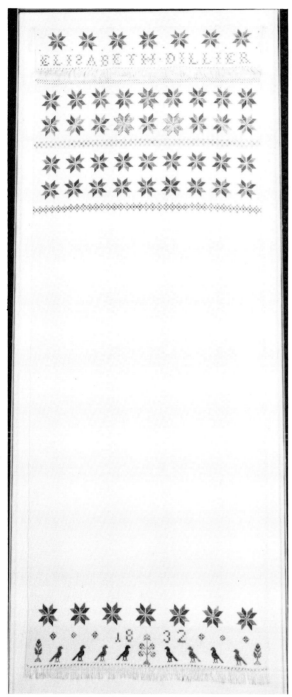

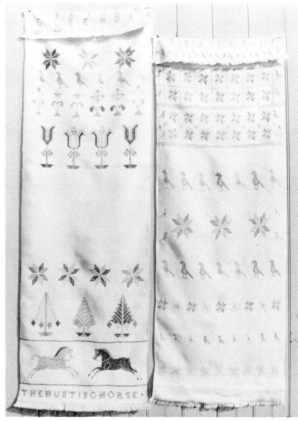

FIGURE 176a An old photograph, circa 1930, on which two towels, made by members of the Dillier family, are hung on the side of an outside shed. Note the two horses on the left towel and the identifying words, 'The Hunting Horse.'[1410, 1411]

FIGURE 176 *Elisabeth Dillier, 1832.* Probably Lancaster county. Balanced plain weave linen fabric; red and blue cotton cross stitch; self plain fringe. 51'' x 18-3/8''.[232]

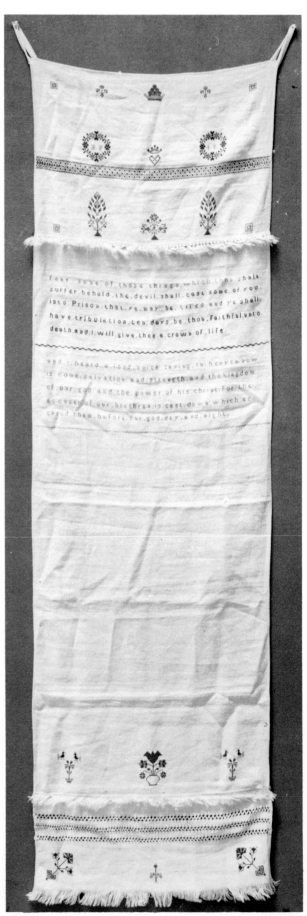

FIGURE 177 *Elisabeth Stauffer, 1821.* North Huntington township, Westmoreland county. Balanced plain weave linen fabric; light blue, yellow and tan silk cross stitch; self plain fringe. The mirror-image designs are arranged in staggered rows. 42½" x 17½".⁹⁶² Courtesy, Westmoreland-Fayette Historical Society Museum, West Overton-Scottdale.

FIGURE 178 (right) *MF IF ....* Balanced plain weave linen fabric; red and blue cross stitch; self and applied plain fringes. 58½" x 17".⁷¹⁵ Courtesy, 13.108.6 Towel. The Metropolitan Museum of Art, Rogers Fund, 1913. (13.108.6).

FIGURE 179 *Barbara Mark.* Balanced plain weave linen fabric; red and blue cotton cross stitch; fringe missing. See Plate 13. 56½'' x 16½''.[1313]

FIGURE 180 *Catarina Guth, 1852.* Balanced plain weave linen fabric; red, dark blue cotton and brown, yellow and aqua silk cross stitch; self and applied plain fringes. See Figure 379. 56'' x 17''.[1275] Courtesy, Mary Ann McIlnay.

FIGURE 180a *Elesebeth Horte, den 15 Merz 1854*
....[March 15, 1854]. Balanced plain weave linen fabric;
red cotton and red wool cross stitch; self and applied plain
fringes. 54" x 19½".[706] Courtesy, Sally and Pete Riffle.

FIGURE 181 *Fanny Meyer, 1838.* Balanced plain weave linen
fabric; red cotton and gold silk cross stitch; self and applied
plain fringes. 60¼" x 19½".[830] Courtesy, Heritage Center
of Lancaster County, Inc., Lancaster.

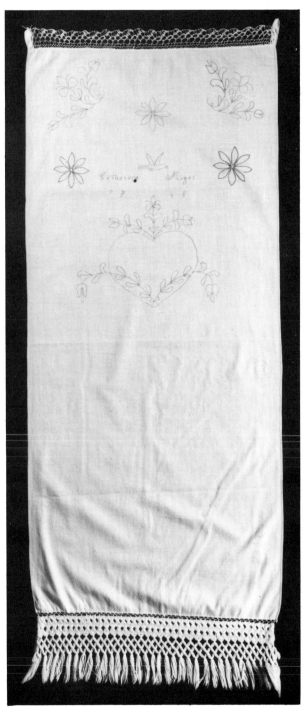

FIGURE 182 *Anna E. Habecker, 1839 . . . .* Probably from Lancaster county. Balanced plain weave linen fabric; red and blue cotton, tan and gold silk cross, running and outline stitches; self and applied plain fringes. See Figures 347, 348, 403. 58'' x 16¾''.[750]

FIGURE 183 *Catharine Moyer, 1898.* Bucks county. Balanced plain weave cotton fabric; red cotton chain and outline stitches; white cotton lace one inch high along top edge; white cotton mill-made fringe 3¾ inches long across bottom of towel. 38½'' x 16-1/8''.[214] Courtesy, Mennonite Heritage Center, Souderton.

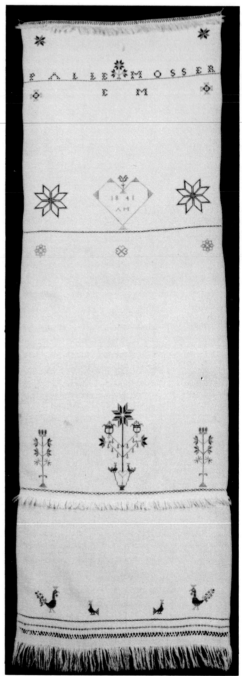

FIGURE 184 *Hanna Brenneisen, 1799.*
Lancaster county. Balanced plain weave
linen fabric; red and blue cotton, brown
and cream silk cross stitch; white linen
darning stitch in drawn thread panel. See
Figures 204, 320. 61-3/8" x 12¾".[711]

FIGURE 185 *Palle Mosser, EM, 1841* .... Balanced plain
weave linen fabric; red, dark red, blue, and gray-green
cotton cross and herringbone stitches and needleweaving; self and applied plain fringe. See Figure 297. 51¼"
x 16½".[59]

FIGURE 186 *Eliza Fretz, 1846.* Balanced plain weave cotton fabric; red cotton and brown silk cross stitch; applied white cotton mill-made fringe. See Figure 86 for similar designs and placement. 44¼" x 15½".[129]

113

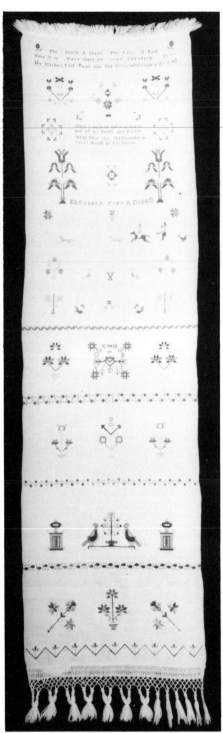

FIGURE 187 *Elisabeth Frey, 1843* .... Lancaster county. Balanced plain weave linen fabric; red cotton and red, dark yellow, light yellow, green, pink and blue wool cross stitch; applied mill-made plain and knotted fringes. See Figures 24, 473, Plate 29. 62¾'' x 16¼''.[466] Courtesy, Dr. and Mrs. Donald M. Herr.

FIGURE 188 *Iudith Martin.* Lancaster county. Alternate bands of balanced plain weave and huckaback linen fabric; red and blue cotton, red, brown and yellow silk cross stitch; self plain fringes. See Figure 13. 51½'' x 19½''.[1031] Courtesy, Clarke E. Hess.

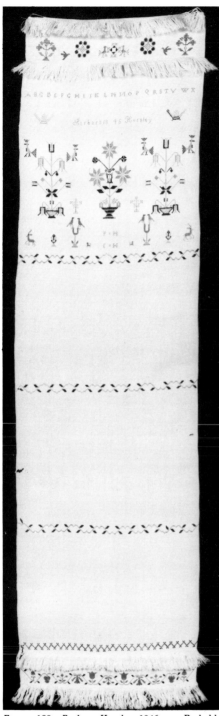

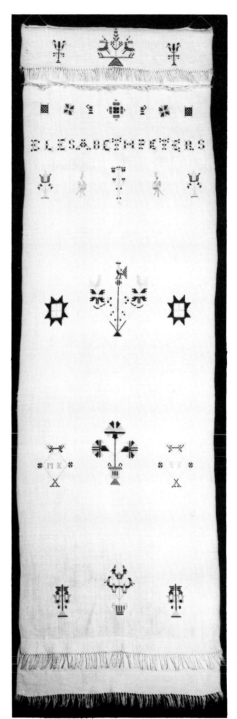

FIGURE 189 *Barbara Hernley, 1846 . . . .* Probably Lancaster county. Balanced plain weave linen fabric; red and blue cotton cross stitch; self and applied plain fringes. See Figure 283. 61″ x 16½″.[1257] Courtesy, Mary Ann McIlnay.

FIGURE 190 *Elesabeth Peters.* Balanced plain weave linen fabric; red and blue cotton, gold and brown silk cross stitch; self and applied plain fringes. 64″ x 19½″.[333]

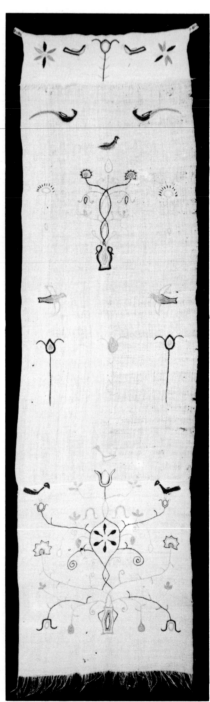

FIGURE 191 *Fiahna Landis, 1835. Manheim township, Lancaster county* . . . . Balanced plain weave cotton fabric; multicolor wool chain stitch designs; red cotton and brown silk cross stitch inscription; applied mill-made white cotton fringe. See Figure 233. 62¼'' x 18¼''.[1324] Courtesy, Collection of Paul and Rita Flack.

FIGURE 192 Balanced plain weave linen fabric; red, dark blue, light blue cotton and yellow silk chain stitch; self plain fringes. See Figure 230. 60'' x 16¼''.[1319]

FIGURE 193 *Barbara Leaman, Barbara Huber, 1846.* Balanced plain weave linen fabric; multicolor wool chain stitch; zigzag hemstitching; applied mill-made knotted fringe; self plain fringe. The large bird and flower motifs in the upper panel were taken from the printed *Taufscheine* of the 1840s. 62" x 16¾".[1263] Courtesy Mary Ann McIlnay.

FIGURE 194 *Fanny Hess, 1843.* Balanced plain weave cotton fabric; yellow, red, pink, olive green, and black wool chain stitch; applied mill-made white cotton fringes. See Figures 268, 361. 62" x 18½".[1312]

FIGURE 195 *Clinton Ebersole, 1888.* Lebanon county. Balanced plain weave linen fabric; red cotton cross stitch; applied fringes. 45¾" x 18½".[638]

118

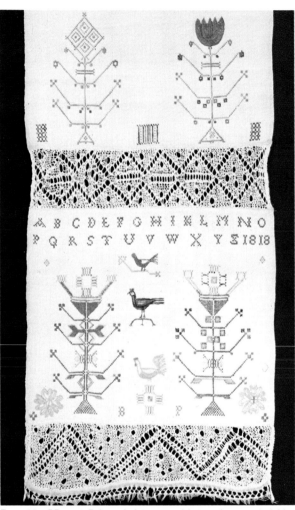

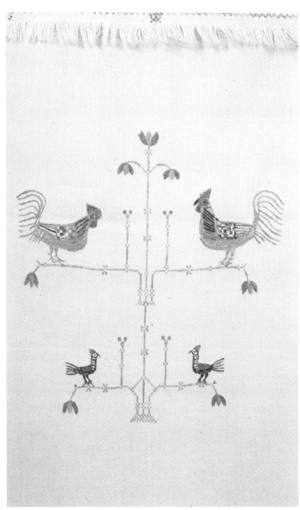

PLATE 25 *BP, 1818*. Balanced plain weave fabric; red cotton, dark blue and light blue linen cross, chain, and outline stitches; white linen hand knit lace insertion. See Figures 501, 502, Plate 26. W. 15¾".[289]

PLATE 26 Balanced plain weave linen fabric; red cotton, dark blue and light blue linen cross, chain and outline stitches. Design: L. 14¾"; W. 11".[289]

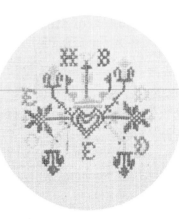

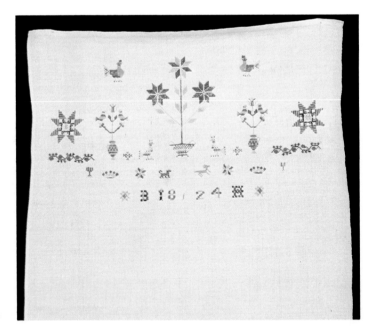

PLATE 27   (top left) *eaeGle*. Balanced plain weave linen fabric, wool cross stitch.[18] Courtesy, Dr. and Mrs. Donald M. Herr.

PLATE 28   (top right) Balanced plain weave linen fabric; red and blue cotton, brown and yellow silk cross stitch.[776]

PLATE 29   (above) Hunting scene. Balanced plain weave linen fabric, red cotton, light yellow, dark yellow, green, blue and pink wool cross stitch.[466] Courtesy, Dr. and Mrs. Donald M. Herr.

PLATE 30   (right) *BH, 1842*. Balanced plain weave linen fabric; red, dark blue, light blue cotton; gold and brown silk cross stitch. W. 16¾".[1070]

PLATE 31   (Left, page 121) *CL, 1801*. Balanced plain weave linen fabric; silk cross and chain stitch; self and applied plain fringes. See Figure 94. 54½" x 15½".[428] Courtesy, Hershey Museum of American Life.

PLATE 32   (right, page 121) *KB* Balanced plain weave linen fabric; cotton cross stitch; cotton darning stitch in drawn thread panels; self plain fringes. 64" x 15½".[1364]

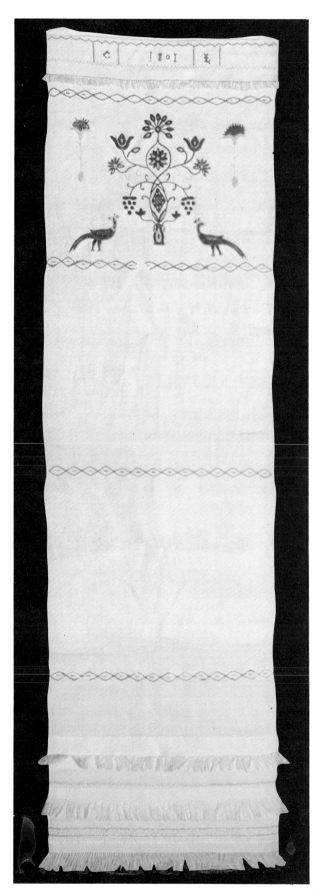

121

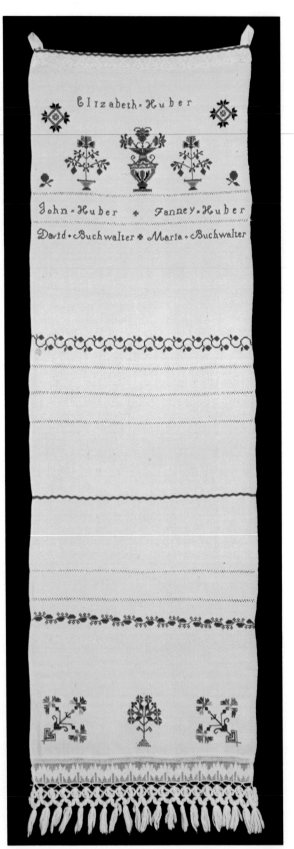

PLATE 33 *Elizabeth Huber* . . . . Balanced plain weave linen fabric; wool cross stitch; applied mill-made lace and rick rack braid; applied cotton mill-made fringe. 58" x 17".[778]

When i am dead and in my grave
And all my bones are rotten
Remember me when this you see
Least i should be for gotten C×D

PLATE 34 *Abraham Diener, 1857 . . . .* Lancaster county.
Balanced plain weave linen fabric; red cotton, green, pink,
yellow, red-orange, wine red, olive green, gold, and gray-
blue wool cross, straight and herringbone stitches; applied
cotton mill-made plain fringes. 50'' x 19''.[212] Courtesy, Mennonite Heritage Center, Souderton.

PLATE 35 *Barbara, BG, 1810*. Balanced plain weave linen fabric; red cotton, brown silk cross and running stitches; red cotton and white linen darning stitch in drawn thread panels; self plain fringes. 61'' x 17-1/8''.[24]

PLATE 36 *Sara Yorty, 1831.* Lebanon county. Balanced plain weave linen fabric; cotton cross stitch, cotton darning stitch in drawn thread panels; self and applied plain fringes. 63" x 19¼".[264] Courtesy, Dr. and Mrs. Donald M. Herr.

125

PLATE 37 *Barbara Bamberger, 1833* .... Lebanon county. Balanced
plain weave linen fabric; red and blue cotton, yellow and brown silk
cross and straight stitches; needleweaving; self and applied plain fringes.
See Figure 88. 60" x 15¾".[465] Courtesy, Dr. and Mrs. Donald M. Herr.

126

PLATE 38 *Susana Heller, 1826 ....* Quakertown area, Bucks county.
Balanced plain weave linen fabric; silk cross and eyelet stitches; cotton
darning stitch on drawn thread panels; knit cotton lace; applied plain
fringe. 54'' x 14½''.[334]

PLATE 39 *CH, 1818*. Lancaster county. Balanced plain weave linen fabric; red cotton, white, aqua, brown, and yellow silk straight, satin, seeding, chain, outline, and running stitches and French knots; cotton darning stitch on drawn thread panels; self plain fringe. See Plate 2. W. 16-1/8''.[285]

PLATE 40 *Christina Lenz, 1817.* Balanced plain weave linen fabric; cotton cross and running stitches; cotton darning stitch on drawn thread panel; self and applied plain fringes. 71" x 17-1/8".[109]

129

PLATE 41 *Susana Steinweg, 1848.* Balanced plain weave
linen fabric; red, dark blue, light blue cotton, black and
gold silk cross and chain stitches, self and applied plain
fringes. 57'' x 17-3/8''.[102]

130

PLATE 42 *Barbara Landisen, 1846.* Balanced plain weave linen fabric; red, dark blue, light blue cotton, dark brown and gold silk cross and chain stitches; self and applied plain fringes. 60" x 17".[641]

PLATE 43 *Barbara Mark*. Balanced plain weave linen fabric; cotton cross stitch; self plain fringe. See Figure 179. W. 16½".[1313]

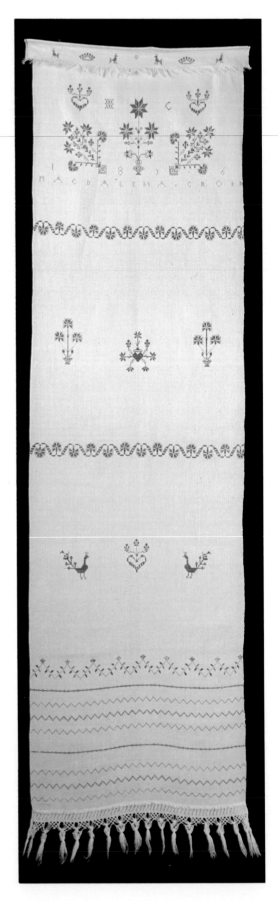

PLATE 44 *Macdalena Crobb, 1836*. Balanced plain weave linen fabric; cotton cross stitch; self and applied plain and mill-made cotton fringes. 62½" x 17".[642]

D. SELECTION POSSIBILITIES

The size of a design was a prominent factor when choosing which counted thread motif to use. Height, width, and stitch size were carefully calculated, but could be easily adjusted to fill space requirements. Each cross stitch was usually counted and sewn over two warp threads wide by two weft threads high; however, the overall size of the design could be increased 50 percent by enlarging the stitch size to three threads. Motifs on towels were seldom sewn with cross stitches larger than four threads because the designs became too big.[118,119] On the other hand, this large stitch was suitable to use on very fine weave linen fabric because it enlarged the design to a more practical size. This emphasizes once again the importance of a correlation between the woven towel fabric, embroidery thread, and stitch size.

Combinations of various sizes of counted stitches were used, perhaps as an attempt to achieve a small degree of realism. A flower, for instance, was embroidered with a four thread cross stitch, but the birds on the flower were sewn with cross stitches just two threads high. The finished bird, therefore, was smaller and perhaps more in the proportion the seamstress wanted.[231]

Size adjustments of this type were not encountered in drawn thread designs because the large thread grid is not as flexible as woven fabric.

Because it was the grid spaces that were counted and not the fabric threads, there were certain design limitations in drawn thread work not experienced in cross stitch or free-form embroidery. Height more than width determined if a particular motif could be used although single wide-design elements or composite designs could seldom be considered. Conspicuously absent is the cartouche surrounding the name or date, alphabets, numerals and inscriptions.

Most count thread designs were built in units of uneven numbers. For instance, one, three, five, and seven stitches per row made a triangular form from which a floral stem could easily be started from the top single stitch. If the same three-cornered form was composed of rows with two, four, six and eight stitches, the center threads from which to start a floral stem straddled the upper two cross stitches instead of being directly above it. This necessitated careful counting. [Figure 393.]

It is seldom that we find entire cross stitch motifs developed from an even numbering system. At times some of the larger more complex designs were composed of both even and odd units. Design construction of this type is not quickly recognized by towel viewers, but it becomes immediately apparent when drafting the designs onto paper. It allowed some needed versatility.

The same thing occurred in drawn thread stitchery, but odd and even numbering was not generally mixed within one design as in cross stitch. Designs built on the even numbers indicated that certain threads were wrapped instead of having the thread fill grid holes or spaces. Lidia Dundor embroidered a woman on her thread panel composed of even numbered rows of stitches. This wrapping thread was particularly noticeable at her waist and on the top of her head. In each spot the single thread between the two filled grid spaces was wrapped with embroidery thread which made the woman appear to have a wasp waist and one hair sprouting from her head.[703]

MF attempted unsuccessfully to build a Greek cross on a drawn thread grid of even units of two stitches. Its distorted shape was almost unrecognizable.[704] In another instance, Hedded Meier and Rayel Ziegler, 1827, seem to have conducted an experiment by embroidering three identical drawn thread eight pointed star designs on a one, two, and three unit numbering system. The differences were further accented by a wrapping of red cotton around the central threads inside the stars.[718] [Figure 127]

It was helpful to understand this basic construction of count thread design elements before picking up needle and thread or attempting to personalize a favorite design. It allowed certain freedoms yet imposed restrictions.

Drawn or traced free-style designs, devoid of count thread boundaries allowed for a more realistic expression with needle and thread. Stylized flowers, hearts, birds, and birds in trees and flowers were sewn more often than were hand-drawn animals, buildings, crowns, diamonds, deer, circles, or crosses.

The size of these hand-drawn figures was easily adapted to the need at hand. It was not limited by thread or grid count per inch. The number of free-form designs per towel, however, was considerably less than count thread motifs.

Size determined where a design fit, but the basic choice of colors and ultimate color arrangement within a cross stitch design could disguise the most fundamental design element. Such color changes allowed embroiderers to use the same primary motif as a friend or relative had, yet imposed certain individuality upon it. At first the motif's common formations escape the eye. Elizabeth Dillier combined the principles of color variation and changed stitch size to embroider her towel full of the same design, but in small, medium, and large proportions.[231]

The use of color as a disguise did not occur in the almost all-white field of drawn thread embroidery. Its colorations have been thoroughly discussed under embroidery technique.

Free-form designs, on the other hand, were embroidered in colorful cotton,[74,85,253] silk,[285] or wool[75,316] often in contrast to other embroidery on the same towel. In this case color was not a mask. Color teamed with design and stitch variations provided accented diversions to a traditional needle art form.

We have divided count thread, drawn thread, and free-form designs into broad, general classifications. In each major grouping the count thread designs are discussed first, followed by drawn thread and then free-form motifs. This listing is not meant to be exhaustive, but to put into perspective the design selections originally made particularly those sewn with cross stitch. Many of the motifs were used on samplers and household textiles, but their use there has not been cited in the text.

Alphabets and Numerals

Alphabets were cross stitched onto towels much the way they were sewn on samplers, but not with such frequency. The basic first step in reading and writing involved learning the alphabet. The primers used in the parochial schools called themselves *ABC und Namen Bücher* (ABC and name books) because they showed the alphabet and used it in names of animals and things and in tables of given names for people. *Fraktur Vorschriften* also gave the "ABCs" in several forms. Individual formations of letters were open to personal interpretation within the confines of style.

The block-type letter sewn most frequently descends from European tradition and can be likened to some forms of writing seen on Pennsylvania German *Fraktur* in that the primary downward stroke was broken or fractured at mid-point. This breaking point was sometimes accented by thread color. When the letters were used to spell a name or write a text the colors chosen usually tied into the overall color theme rather than drew attention to the lettering itself. Colors sewn into alphabets often alternated with every letter or every three or four letters, but occasionally the alphabet was sewn in just one shade.

Alphabets sewn in this block letter formation were found on a small percentage of towels dating from 1806[1232] to 1876.[341] The English letter "J" was omitted until about 1827[606] after which it was generally included. Most are complete alphabets, but A to E,[566] A to P,[1232] A to F,[1180] and J to Z[390] were sewn on some towels. Some listed two Ns[1278] and two Ws[339,341] and Maria Dillier stitched one and a half alphabets.[606] Her first alphabet had a "J", but her half alphabet omitted it. Elisabet Staufer, 1827, put two alphabets on her towel[1285] as did Nancy/Anna Lang. The one was at the very top of the towel followed by "Anna Lang" and the second was made with much larger letters and preceded "Nancy Lang."[269] Another Elisabeth Stauffer sewed three alphabets on her towel, but arranged them on the right and left sides in vertical columns.[962] [Figure 177]

The geometric formation of the block letter invited choice in size; the most common was seven stitches high. It was used extensively throughout the decorated towel era and was also the size and style letter most often stitched on household and agricultural linens when hand-sewn identification was necessary.

A second and popular enlargement of this block upper case letter was composed of seven square units with each square measuring two by two cross stitches. This produced a letter that extended fourteen stitches from top to bottom. Still geometric in shape, this block letter was widely used, but it required more space.

Only a few towels in this study contained alphabets made with this large letter, among them several undated,[44,265] one dated 1816,[269] and one dated 1839.[467] More

often these letters were used for spelling a name, for the first letter of a name, or for initials.

There were instances of this block letter expanded to even greater heights by making the square units three by three or four by four cross stitches in which case the letters were twenty-one or twenty-eight stitches high.[114,265,269,365,369,473] [Figure 196] In 1833 AW stitched an unusual alphabet with the letters A to D in this large format of fourteen stitches. She completed the alphabet with an increasing stitch size of four threads instead of the usual two. She kept the letters the same size, but used one-fourth the stitches.[310]

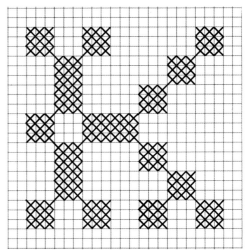

FIGURE 196 The block letter was enlarged by increasing the size of each unit from a four stitch square to a six stitch square.[150]

Lower case alphabets on towels were composed of letters based on the Caslon typeface. They were not really a geometric block or smooth script formation, but individual attempts in executing small curved lines with cross stitch. The lower case letters remain basically unchanged regardless of the style upper case alphabet or letter with which they were used. A complete lower case alphabet was found on only a few towels in this study with dates 1825,[231] 1843,[1224] 1849,[63] and 1854.[706] They each contain the English letter "J". [Figure 180a; Plate 7]

When an upper case and lower case alphabet appeared together on one towel as they did on the 1825 Elisabeth Dillier towel each alphabet was sewn in its entirety.[231] Upper and lower case letters were not mixed. The upper case was usually sewn first followed by the lower case alphabet. (A definite correlation between needlemade letters and those drawn with pen and ink can be seen on an anonymous hand drawn *Fraktur*, circa 1810. There, the letters were blocked out as embroidery patterns rather than in a writing style. [Figure 197] Weiser and Heaney, II, 540).

The impact of the 1844 Reading almanac and Carl F. Egelmann's 1831 copybook on young embroiderers has already been discussed. It should be pointed out, however, that in 1831 both of Egelmann's printed block style alphabets, the English letter "J" is conspicuously ab-

FIGURE 197 Anonymous artist. Drawing. Southeastern Pennsylvania, ca.1810. Hand-drawn, lettered and colored on laid paper with plow watermark. 25.2 x 19.6 cm. Courtesy, The Free Library of Philadelphia 1082.

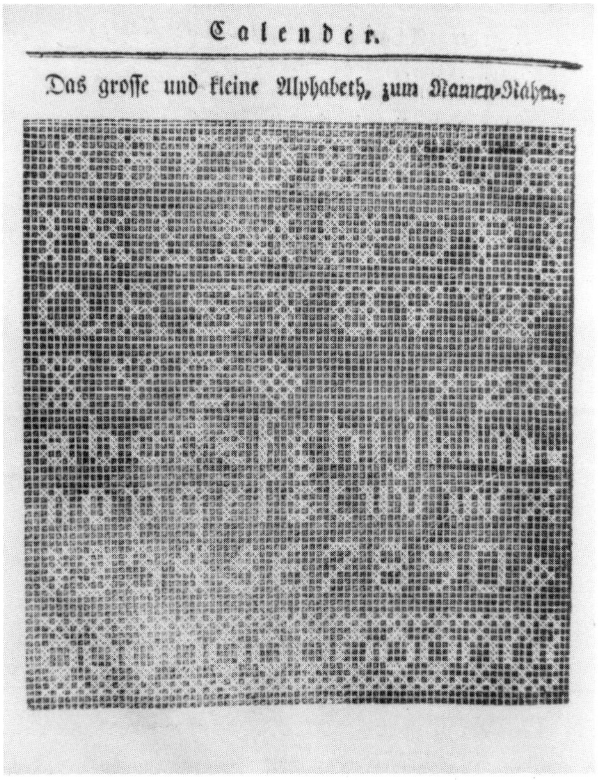

sent. But, he included the long "S". By 1844, his block lettered alphabet in the almanac, on the other hand, did have the "J". [Figure 198]

These two publications appeared during the peak years of decorating hand towels and found a ready market throughout the Dutch country. They were also published about the same time that script-type letters began to gain popularity, although Egelmann did not take them into consideration.

After 1830[336] script lettering gradually became a fashionable choice for embroidering initials, the first letter in a name, an entire name, or as accents in inscriptions otherwise sewn in block letters. Formations of script letters more closely resembled a hand written signature whereas the embroidered block letter bore likeness to the printed typeface. They were a welcome change to the world of embroidered lettering, but were necessarily large because of their cross stitched curves and flourishes. Chrestena Bauman in 1841[69] and Anna Bender in 1837[1098] made towels with a complete embroidered script alphabet. [Figure 199]

Numerals were cross stitched in a block geometric formation in similar fashion to block letters. They were expanded in height from the basic seven stitches to fourteen stitches and, like lower case letters, showed great variety in execution. More irregularity could be seen in embroidered numbers than in most other designs because of the difficulty in forming the curved, rounded edges with blocks of cross stitch.

FIGURE 198 A page from the 1844 almanac printed by Carl F. Egelmann in Reading. L. 8¼"; W. 6½".

FIGURE 199.[69]

135

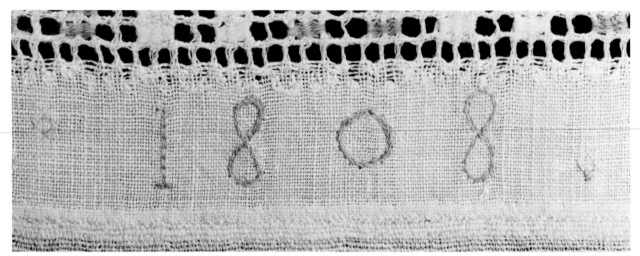

FIGURE 200 The date was sewn in red cotton chain stitch. Just below is a butt seam often used to join two hemmed edges.[104] Courtesy, Sally and Pete Riffle.

Maria Bichslern compensated for this logistical problem by embroidering the year 1808 in red cotton chain stitch.[104] [Figure 200] Others used the outline stitch to sew their obviously hand drawn numbers.[66,217,320] But, Sara Speicherin still made a backward six when she embroidered 1826.[189]

Listing the numbers did not occur as commonly on towels as the alphabet did. Elisabeth Rinker in 1848 put the numerals one to zero just after the alphabet at the top of the towel;[319] EF AF, 1842, put her alphabet and numerals one to eleven on the bottom panel.[4] [Figure 12] In both instances numerals were placed together with an alphabet and did not stand alone.

An interesting and unusual method of recording numerals as well as listing in English the months of the year was sewn on the 1850 Emanuel J. Minnich towel. The embroiderer stitched a large chained circle with twelve cross stitched spokes radiating from a central square. Beginning at center top going in a clockwise direction were the embroidered abbreviations for the months of the year under which were the numerals one through twelve. The towel had to be rotated to be read.[18] [Figure 201]

Alphabets and series of numerals were not part of the drawn thread or free-form embroidery tradition. To date we have not seen any towels with a hand drawn alphabet or set of numerals, nor have we seen an alphabet darned on a thread grid. They were reserved for cross stitch.

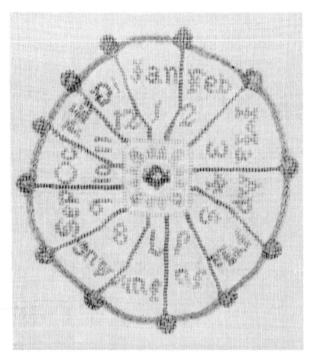

FIGURE 201 Gold, dark pink, and light yellow wool cross and chain stitches. The motif is about nine inches in diameter.[18] Courtesy, Dr. and Mrs. Donald M. Herr.

136

FIGURE 202 A row of red and blue cotton cross stitched dogs and cat.

Animals

Animals form an entertaining category of designs. The animal world was imminent in the life of Pennsylvania German children, both as a textbook and for pleasure. The perky family dog always had his tail curled over his back no matter what other conformations his body might have. There are short and long necks, bodies and legs. Some dogs had a stubby snout and their ears stood at attention. Others are more relaxed with their ears laid back on their head. Each embroidered dog has its own personality, just like the real thing![377,437,569] [Figures 202-204, 218]

Other animals on towels are less common than dogs. The cat is distinguished in cross stitch from the dog by a longer curled tail, two pointed ears, and a straight stitch for the nose.[340] [Figure 205] Larger cats, namely the lion, occur on towels dated 1799,[76] 1822,[87] and 1838.[830]

FIGURE 203 Brown silk cross stitch dog.[1110]

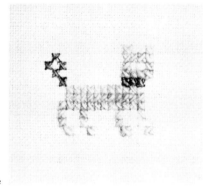

FIGURE 205 (right) A red cotton cross stitch house cat with a blue cotton tail, legs and collar.[340]

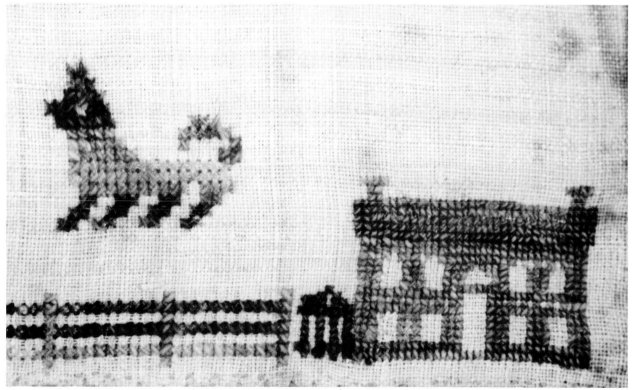

FIGURE 204 This red and blue cotton cross stitched house, gate, three rail fence and dog were part of a yardscape scene at the bottom of a 1799 towel. See Figure 184.[711]

137

Figure 206[830]

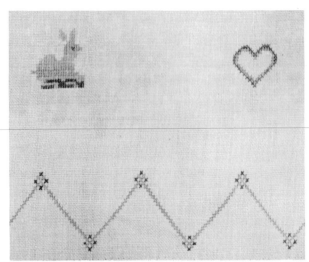

FIGURE 207 A blue eyed red cotton cross stitched rabbit resting on a blue and red base.[620] Courtesy, North Museum of Franklin and Marshall College, Lancaster.

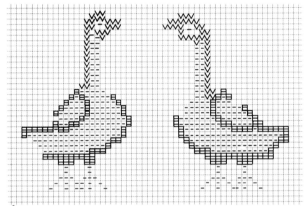

Figure 208[770]

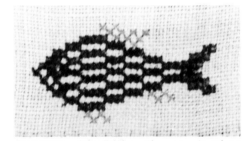

FIGURE 209a A small fish motif was sewn in red cotton and brown silk cross stitch by Anna Carle, 1825.[756]

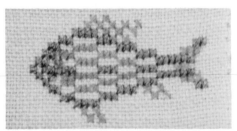

FIGURE 209b A nearly identical fish was embroidered by Frances Charles in 1832. Red cotton and brown silk cross stitch.[1110]

The 1799 version resembled an oversized house cat whereas the 1822 and the 1838 lion were almost identical to and apparently copied from heraldry. [Figures 206, 181, 464, 466]

Two long-eared rabbits were cross stitched on towels, one in 1837[197] and the other dated 1841.[620] [Figure 207] Susanna Herr sewed what appeared to be a pair of long-necked geese on her towel in 1843.[770] [Figure 208] Another pair of geese appeared at the center of the 1832 Daniel Harr towel,[83] and on a Susanna Herr, 1827 towel.[951] Fish were also stitched, one in 1825,[756] one in 1832,[1110] and another in 1848.[755] [Figure 209] Horses were not prevalent in cross stitch embroidery; they did gallop in a hunt[466,755] or pull a carriage,[357,590,792,1196,1208] however.[Figures 174, 415; Plate 29]

The stag was always depicted with large antlers spread from his head in varied formations. His four feet were either firmly planted on the ground,[76,150] or he was running,[15,189] or he was standing on his back legs with his two front feet raised preparing to jump.[141] [Figures 210, 211, 329]

A more composite design was created when a pair of facing deer were sewn to the right and left of a tree-like motif.[333] In one instance the tree had a bird resting on the top branches,[933] [Figure 212] and on another towel the two harts were placed under a large crown rather than a tree.[340] [Figure 115]

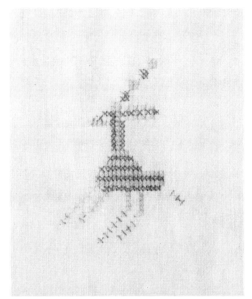

FIGURE 210 Embroidered deer have as much personality as all other animals. Red cotton and brown silk cross stitch.[430] Courtesy, Hershey Museum of American Life.

FIGURE 212 Two facing deer under an evergreen tree with a bird above. Red cotton cross stitch.[933]

FIGURE 211 Heart, deer and crown motifs cross stitched in red cotton and brown silk.[1110]

Drawn thread embroidery did not host many animals. The household dog was occasionally portrayed with the same frisky tail and mixed body conformations as seen in cross stitched versions.[287,624] [Figures 213, 129, 134] Frany Fretz, 1833, included many dogs and roosters in her drawn panel.[1176] Heddy Oxenfort, 1839, embroidered an animal on a thread grid which is a toss up between a dog and a ram. It was probably a curved horn and not ears on top of the head and his short tail extended straight out and was not curved.[691] [Figure 214] Running or leaping deer also are to be found on drawn grids, [Figure 124] but are almost never placed with a tree or flower.[120,571]

Some young girls embroidered free-form animals such as a turkey,[797] [Figure 215] a small horse,[491,495,1283] [Figures 216, 18] a cow,[769] a goose, and a guinea fowl (or is it another turkey?).[769] Generally speaking dogs were not hand drawn onto towels, but HM, 1835, used a nine inch tall space at the top of her towel in which to show a pair of free-shaped dogs situated inside a three-sided row of flowers.[793] A hand drawn deer, with fawn-like spots on his body, was sewn in a jumping position having been copied from a broadside printed by the Baumans at Ephrata in the early nineteenth century.[253,758] The deer was an uncommon motif in free-form embroidery. [Figures 83, 18, 133] A large spotted rabbit closely resembled in size and shape the form often associated with tin cookie cutters.[322] [Figure 558] Still other free-form animals defied recognition. One of these had the head and ears of a horse, two legs that rested on a triangular-shaped base, and a long neck that branched into rooster-like tail feathers. Perhaps this was free embroidery's adaptation of the Dutchman's *Elbedritsch!*[322] [Figure 558]

Birds were, by far, the most popular members of the animal kingdom to be embroidered onto towels. See below.

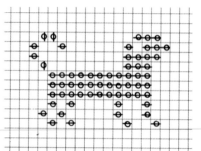

FIGURE 213[624]

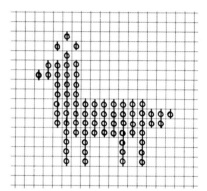

FIGURE 214 A drawn thread animal that could be a dog or a ram.[691]

FIGURE 216 A chain stitched tan and black wool horse.[552] Courtesy, Mr. and Mrs. Richard F. Smith.

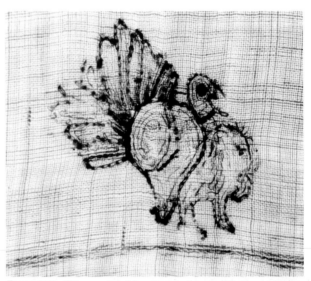

FIGURE 215 This very faded free-form turkey motif had to be backlit to be photographed. The turkey's body, wings, legs, head and tail feathers were embroidered with red cotton chain stitch. The lines inside were sewn in red cotton running stitch, but the eye was stitched in blue cotton. L. 3''; W. 3¼''.[797]

140

Architecture

The Pennsylvania German farmhouse is the only farmstead building embroidered on towels, perhaps because it was the woman's domain.

The earliest incidence found occurs in 1799 when two girls each made towels with houses on them. Catarina Kemper embroidered what might be called a front yard scene across the bottom panel. A house with a fruit tree behind it is stitched on both the right and left sides. Two dogs and a deer are between the house, and a length of post and rail yard fence stands in the foreground.[76] Catarina embroidered two houses of different architecture. The smaller is a story-and-a-half house with center door and one window to each side. It was sewn with a flat perspective of the gable end showing one downstairs window and two gable chimneys. [Figure 217] The larger dwelling is a center hall Federal house. It has two full stories, eight front windows and a front door with transom. Thus, there are four houses sewn on this towel in two locations.

Hanna Brenneisen also embroidered the identical Federal house on her towel in 1799. She sewed two houses too, one on the right and one on the left side at the bottom of the towel. Extending from the corner of each house toward the center is a gate and lengths of post and three-rail fence. Alongside each house, but inside

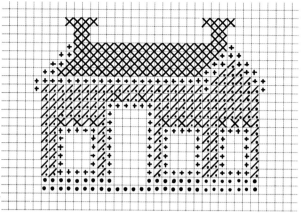

FIGURE 217[76]

the fence, she placed two dogs; in the center a very large floral arrangement.[711] These girls were neighbors and shared this house design. [Figure 204]

Susannah Barnhard sewed on her towel what could be identified as a house under construction or perhaps one of half-timber construction. Its stick-like appearance delineates partitioned areas inside the outer walls of the house and not the usual door and windows. The angled corner bracing for half-timbering is missing however.[1266] [Figure 218]

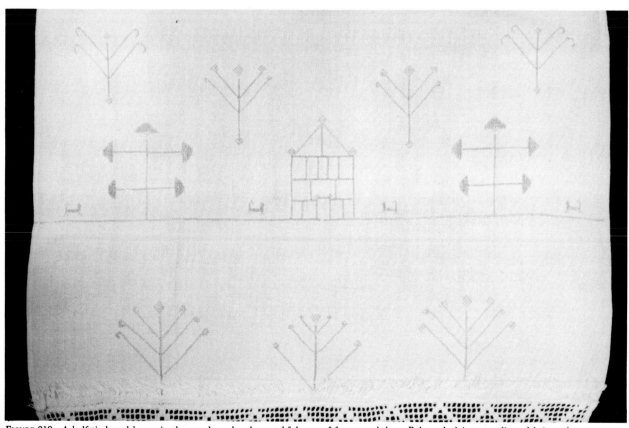

FIGURE 218 A half timbered house in the woods under the watchful care of four guard dogs. Balanced plain weave linen fabric; red cotton cross stitch.[1266]

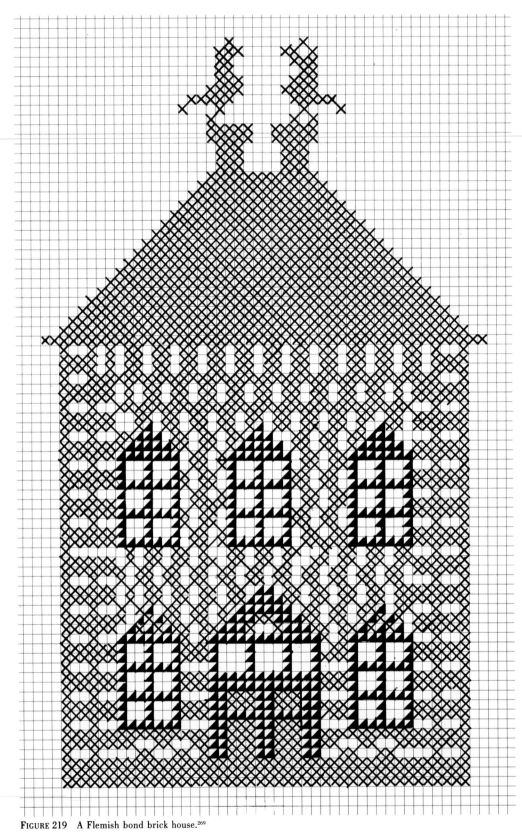

FIGURE 219   A Flemish bond brick house.[269]

By 1816 Nancy/Anna Lang embroidered one large red brick English Georgian mansion with stitched fancy brick work, large windows, paneled front door, and roof with double chimneys on which a bird is perched, as if to complete its elegance.[269] [Figure 219]

The two houses Hedded Meier and Rayel Ziegler embroidered in 1827 are not much more than a gable end view of a story-and-a-half cabin. They have a heavy roof-line and what may be a small window.[718] [Figure 127]

A large house sewn on the 1833 Barbara Bamberger towel appears to have been copied from a printed broadside advertising the public sale of real estate. Four steps lead up to the front door located between the first and second of three downstairs windows; there are four windows on the second floor. There are also two gable chimneys and a very narrow, flat perspective of the gable end of the house.[465] [Figure 88; Plate 37]

Catherine Ebersole, 1848, positioned her house at the top of the towel just above her name. The walls and roof line are silhouetted and not filled in solid. It has a center hall with one window on each side of the door. The window sash are delineated with backstitch. There are two embroidered roof lines, probably an attempt to sew architectural perspective. The house also has two gable chimneys. [Figure 220] Catherine embroidered a tree on each side of the house to put it in a more natural setting.[753] Anna Ebersole, probably a relative, also included a similar house on her 1847 towel.[1144] [Figure 221]

One cannot help but be amused when looking at the Nolt family register towel to see two small buildings that are like a house more than a barn or church. They have no obvious doors or windows, but rows of what could be fancy brick work. Perhaps this represented the Nolt family homestead from which sprang all those people listed on the register.[106] [Figure 175]

The house that MD embroidered on a drawn thread panel in 1835 has a central front door with benches sewn to the right and left. There are two windows on the first floor, four windows on the second story, and two attic windows. There is also a central chimney. She placed one of these houses on the right and left sides of the panel with a tree of birds and two dogs between them. It is symmetrical, but the design placement also has a touch of realism just as in cross stitch panels with houses and yardscapes.[287] [Figure 222]

Drawn thread panels were the area on a towel where another type of architecture was expressed with needle and thread, the architectural-type chest. "The chest with a lift-top lid remained the most important item of storage furniture in the rural homes of southeastern Pennsylvania." (Fabian, 26) "That such chests were considered personal pieces of property can be readily sensed by observing the number which bear the names or initials of the original owners . . . it appears that the chests were acquired in the early or mid-teenage years or at the time of marriage." (Fabian, 28) Molded or reeded pilasters with arched top panels on the early chests seem to have been copied onto thread grids by several towel makers.[1171] One grid is dated 1809 above and between the

FIGURE 220 Centered at the top of the towel was this house motif with name, date, and wreath inside a box. Red cotton cross stitch.[753]

FIGURE 221 Red and blue cotton cross stitch house.[1144]

FIGURE 222 A yardscape with identical houses (with benches by the front door), a tree, dogs, and birds with fanned tails sewn in white cotton darning stitch. The applied fringe, one inch long, is linen threads that were inserted with a needle through both the hem and each grid space and tied in place. See Figure 552. 6½″ x 12½″.[287]

arched panels much as it might have been placed on a chest.[307] [Figures 223, 224]

HA CA drew in free-hand a central hall house with gates and post and rail fence extending from each front corner. A fruit tree grows to the right and left of the house behind the fence in the side yard. The outline is the primary stitch depicting the house, roof, windows, door, panes of glass, gates, posts, rails, tree trunk, and branches. Satin stitched fruit in the tree and herringbone on the roof add reality to the scene.[125] [Figure 132]

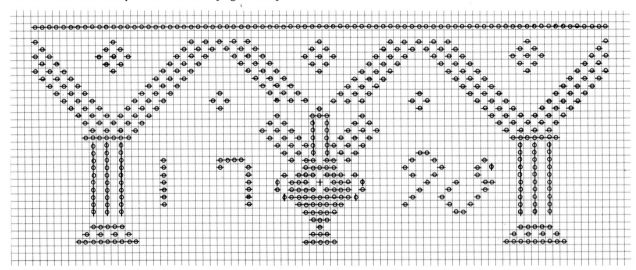

FIGURE 223 Designs resembling reeded pilasters and arched panels on a chest are embroidered in white cotton darning stitch on a drawn thread panel.[195]

144

FIGURE 224 Another drawn thread panel with white cotton motifs similar to those found on painted chests.[1171]

Birds

Fowl of one sort or another occur over and over in numerous arrangements and combinations. Many of these are perched on flowers or trees. Others stand alone such as eagles, peacocks, roosters, and a variety of songbirds and other barnyard fowl. Domesticated fowl were women's work; songbirds were *Feggel*, a model of worship, as hymn and *Fraktur* texts remind us; and all birds were captivating for their own beauty and capacity to fly.

Birds in flowers and trees

Peacocks,[234,545] roosters,[756] a turkey,[467] a guinea fowl,[717] and numerous song birds roost, perch, or nest in roses, carnations, tulips, heart and star-shaped flowers, and other perennials. Conifers[141,620] and even an oak tree[580] provide sanctuary for these fowl as well. [Figures 225-228]

Stylized combinations of birds, trees, and flowers achieved great popularity and variety. They range from a flock of six or eight birds alighted on one spray of flowers to one lone wild bird standing on a tulip. [Figure 225] Perhaps it was a needle and thread attempt to show perspective when birds were embroidered onto tops of flowers balanced on their tail with their bills pointing up.[233]

Flowers and trees with resting birds were embroidered on drawn thread panels, but their large size prohibited a more widespread use of the design. More birds are in flowers than trees and the shapes of the birds resemble songbirds more than roosters or peacocks. [Figures 229, 137] Tail feathers were distinguished. Most were fanned,[25,194,571,608] others drooped,[29,291,379] [Figure 219] and some bird's tails had an upward curve.[287,407]

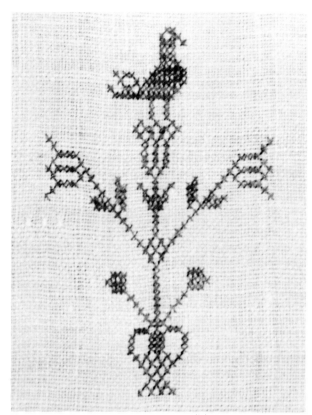

FIGURE 225 Bird on tulip motif embroidered in red cotton cross stitch.[68] Courtesy, Clarke E. Hess.

FIGURE 226 A bird perched on top a tree sewn in red cotton cross stitch.[217] Courtesy, Mennonite Heritage Center, Souderton.

145

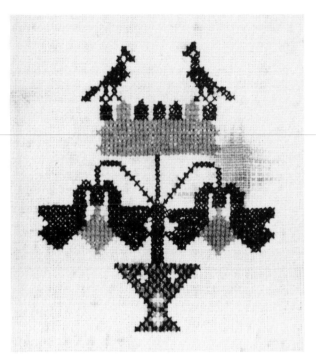

FIGURE 227 A pair of birds resting on a red and blue cotton cross stitched flower.[197] Courtesy, Clarke E. Hess.

FIGURE 228 Birds resembling guinea fowl resting on tree branches. Red cotton cross stitch.[717] Courtesy, Sally and Pete Riffle.

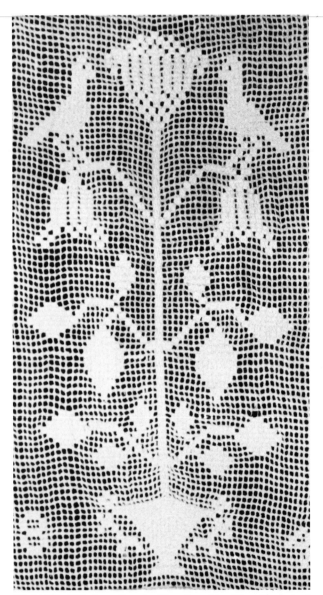

FIGURE 229 This drawn thread grid was bound in white cotton instead of linen thread, and the tulip with birds design, almost thirteen inches high, was embroidered in fine white cotton darning stitch.[291]

146

MD, 1835, embroidered four drawn thread panels with an assortment of flowers with nesting birds; however, the songbirds bore a remarkable likeness to the dogs embroidered on the same panels. Body and leg conformations were almost identical. One bird had a full round tail curved over its back like a puppy and another bird's fanned-out tailfeathers were positioned on top of its back and not to the rear of the body. [Figure 222] On the same towel two birds appear to walk up the stem or tree trunk; perhaps they were woodpeckers or nuthatches![287] [Figure 552]

Birds singing in the tree tops or on opened flowers were often executed in free-style embroidery. MR, 1819, chain stitched a stylized flower on top of which was a large bird flapping his wings.[709] [Figure 266] The bird nestled in amid flowers and large leaves [Figure 268] on the Iacob Hess, 1835, towel was more peaceful.[556] This motif was executed in polychromed wools[552,556] and red and blue cotton.[43,608,709,718] More elaborate versions appeared on the all-white towel variants.[71,548] [Figure 559]

Sara Schitzin, 1819, executed an all-red peacock with large tail stop a diamond shaped flower by combining cross stitch and an irregular chain stitch. The overall height of the original design is 8¼ inches.[268] [Figure 461] Hedded Meier and Rayel Ziegler, 1827, made an even larger and more intricate flower with bird motif that is more than twelve inches tall. It utilizes the chain, buttonhole, outline, satin, counted and ad lib cross stitches in red and blue embroidery cotton with a soft twist.[718] [Figure 127]

An urn sprouting tulips with a bird appeared on several towels.[510,699] They all had enough similarities to have been copied from a single source available to a wide audience rather than to have been developed within a single or double family unit. The urn generally had two handles and the stems rose and crisscrossed to form the upper tulip that supported a single bird. Other decorative flowers and tulips branched from the main stem. [Figures 230,94; Plate 23]

Eagles

The eagle on embroidered towels was copied from surrounding patriotic objects such as contemporary coins.[620] One eagle stood erect with one large arched wing silhouetted alongside his body.[620] [Figure 231] Elizabeth Gotschal,[111] [Plate 18] Eliza Fretz,[1291] [Figure 186], Franey Kulp,[1265] [Figure 86] and Rebecca Minnich[18] [Plate 27] on the other hand, cross stitched the symbolic and mighty spread-winged eagle imitated from the United States seal. (A similar version was also pictured on the front cover of Johann Ritter's Reading almanacs). It had a striped body and tail and clutched flowers in its talons. Rebecca placed the word *eagle* directly under the bird, and Eliza stitched two rows of stars and a crown over the eagle's head. Mariah Getz sewed a more realistic spread-winged eagle with his feet resting on an octagonal cartouche encircling the embroidered letter E.[604]

Women who wished to announce their national loyalty, but could not devote the space these large birds require, devised a small cross stitch spread-winged eagle with

FIGURE 230 A balanced plain weave linen fabric; red, dark blue, light blue cotton and yellow silk chain stitch. This design is 16½ inches high. A flat felled seam joins two pieces of towel fabric near the top of the motif. See Figure 192. L. 19" from fringe to seam; W. 16¼ ".[1319]

FIGURE 231 A more realistic-type flower motif and a bird with raised wing holding a branch in his claws embroidered in red cotton cross stitch.[1238]

147

fanned-out tail feathers.[15,744] Symbols of patriotism were gradually added to the folk tradition of towel decorating. [Figure 232]

AK embroidered on a thread grid a spread-winged eagle with feathers rising from the top of his head. It is 13½ inches tall, one of the largest drawn motifs. The design consists of an eagle standing on a series of diamond and triangular shapes in which are crosses and a large heart. Hanging from the right and left points of the diamond are crosses. It is a more complex motif than normally found in drawn thread embroidery.[412] [Figure 142]

Sophia Elizabeth G. Witmer, 1860, outlined a small spread-winged eagle and filled the body and wings with colored wool chain stitch to make one of the few free-form eagles found on towels.[593] [Figure 233]

Peacocks

Peacocks abound in Pennsylvania German needlework just as they do in other forms of Pennsylvania Dutch folk art. They were found in the barnyards of the Pennsylvania countryside, appreciated for their beauty and their alertness, but also served as a moral warning about pride.

This stately bird was distinguished in count thread needlework by the plumage on his head and his large open or closed fancy tail feathers. The less attractive pea hen was seldom sewn.

Small renditions of the peacock enabled the design to fit in most places, but his only distinction was the feathers on his head.[59,243,255,333] [Figure 234] Occasionally he had a waddle under his beak.[1112] [Figure 185] Elsewise he resembled other birds. Larger versions enabled the embroiderer to stripe his body with color and develop his impressive tail.

A number of persons sewed a long, closed, but variegated tail as if it were dragging on the ground[560] [Figures 235-237] while other women positioned the widespread tail directly behind the bird showing off his fanned feathers and ocellated spots.[67,68,86,191,366] [Figures 238-240] The strutting peacock looked even more proud with his stretched-out tail projecting far above his head.[67,197,355,361] [Figures 241-244]

FIGURE 233 A balanced plain weave cotton fabric; multicolor wool chain stitch. See Figure 191.[1324] Courtesy, Collection of Paul and Rita Flack

FIGURE 234 This red and blue cotton striped cross stitch bird has one foot raised, an opened wing, and a crown on top of his head.[67] Courtesy, Clarke E. Hess.

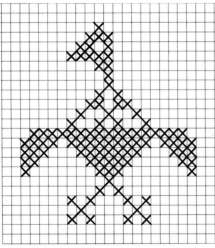

FIGURE 232[744]

148

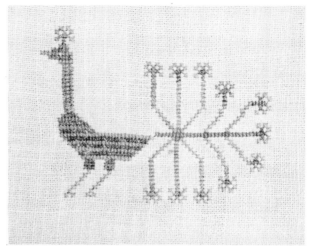

FIGURE 235 A pair of red and blue cotton cross stitched peacocks with closed tail feathers. The tails are not identical.[197] Courtesy, Clarke E. Hess.

FIGURE 238 This motif is worked in alternating rows of red and blue cotton cross stitch.[191]

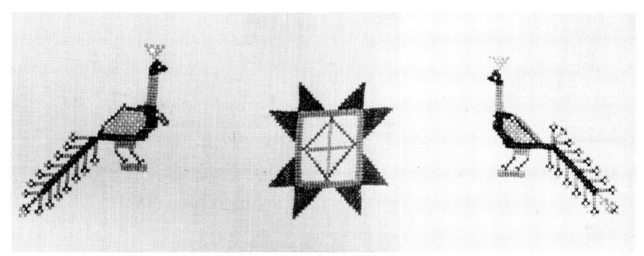

FIGURES 236, 237 Red and blue cotton cross stitched peacock (left) and pea hen (right). See Plates 13, 14.[1335]

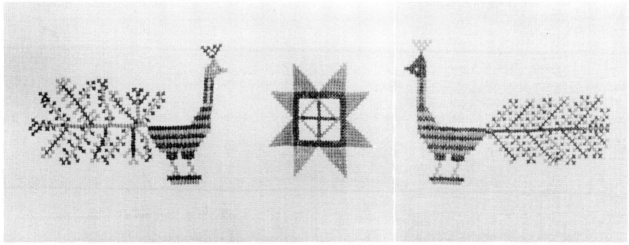

FIGURES 239, 240 Red and blue cotton cross stitched peacock (left) and pea hen (right). See Plates 13, 14.[1335]

FIGURE 241 Red and blue cotton cross stitched peacock with open tail.[67] Courtesy, Clarke E. Hess.

FIGURE 243 A red and blue cotton cross stitched peacock complete with blue eye.[311]

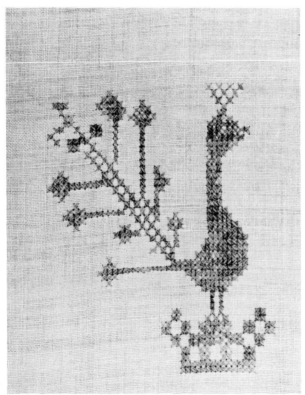

FIGURE 242 Peacock on crown; red cotton cross stitch.[608]

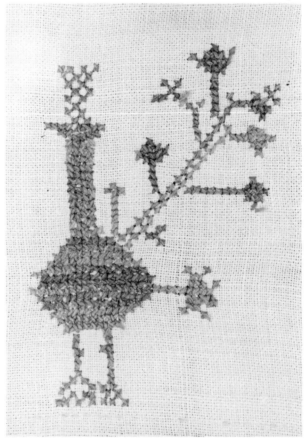

FIGURE 244 Some peacocks have more personality than others! Red cotton cross stitch.[270]

FIGURE 245 A red and blue cotton cross stitch peacock inside a pen-of-sorts with a pair of facing deer. The border at the bottom of the pen extends the full width of the towel.[731] Courtesy, Sally and Pete Riffle.

In 1853 a young peacock was cross stitched inside a pen of sorts on the BC EC towel. Young because his head feathering was small, his tail was an immature length, and he had gangling legs. The square enclosure was probably outside because it had flowers vining up the sides, and two stags stood with front feet raised on each upper corner. Even young peacocks did not fit inside a typical birdcage, but required a large specially built pen if they were to be confined. On the other hand, this square form may have represented a bower, arbor, or leafy retreat from the heat of summer's sun. The original intent and significance of this one-of-a-kind motif is beyond confirmation.[731] [Figure 245]

FIGURE 246 A pair of white cotton peacocks embroidered with the darning stitch in a horizontal direction.[55]

FIGURE 247 Balanced plain weave cotton fabric; red, white, black and yellow wool chain stitch.[552] Courtesy, Mr. and Mrs. Richard F. Smith.

The same peacock motif with fancy, but less complex, tail designs was embroidered on drawn thread panels in pairs[55] [Figures 246, 156, 157; Plate 3] or alone.[105,287] [Plate 4] They occurred as often as the unidentified song birds. The direction of the darning stitch offered subtle contrasts in the birds' feathering.

Peacocks were not seen in free embroidery as often as song birds. CF[491] and SF[510] outlined the profile of a peacock dragging his long tail and the only distinguishing feature on some other hand drawn, chain stitched birds was the plumage on top of their heads.[289] [Figure 247]

Roosters

The rooster is seen least often on towels. He can be distinguished in needlework from other fowl by his raised, irregular tail feathers. His head, beak, and body assumed assorted positions and roosters were embroidered in all colors, shapes, and sizes.[68,83,150,217] [Figures 248-250] Catharina Weidman copied in 1838 the large rooster, with intricate feathering detail, on the back cover of an ABC book which was no small task.[1047] [Figures 90,91] Mariah Getz decided to sew a hen instead.[604] Embroidered roosters did not show as wide a variety in execution as did other birds. [Figures 251,321]

Roosters in drawn thread embroidery were identical to those sewn in cross stitch. One interesting example, sewn on a leno panel by RS in 1835, portrayed a facing rooster and hen.[50] [Figures 252, 34]

Stylized roosters are not always easy to identify unless they have the traditional raised irregular tail feathers. We admit our difficulty in interpreting the hand-drawn hand-sewn work of others. BP in 1818 drew an unmistakable rooster and embroidered him with patterned combinations of chain, outline, and ad lib cross stitches to denote striped feathers and a variegated wing. He had a high arched tail with long feathering, a large hooked beak, a big glassy eye, a tall comb, round waddle, and threatening spurs on his heels.[289] [Plate 26] MR, 1817, executed a simpler rooster with a single row of chain stitch, but she didn't forget his zigzag tail feathers, comb, and waddle.[709] [Figure 253]

FIGURE 248 Red cotton cross stitch rooster on balanced plain weave linen fabric.[1110]

FIGURE 249 A red cotton cross stitch rooster.[217] Courtesy, Mennonite Heritage Center, Souderton.

FIGURE 251 Balanced plain weave linen fabric; red and blue cotton cross stitch. See Figures 7, 171.[1151]

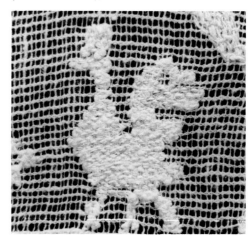

FIGURE 252 White cotton darning stitch rooster embroidered on a leno woven grid.[50]

FIGURE 250 A red cotton cross stitch basket with handles holding assorted blue and red cotton flowers and a red cotton rooster with blue legs and feet.[222]

FIGURE 253 Light blue linen and white cotton outline and chain stitch with a red cotton comb and waddle. He had no eye or feet. L. 1¼''; W. 2''.[289]

FIGURE 254 (left) A red cotton cross stitch bird.[1110]

FIGURE 255 (right) A red cotton cross stitched bird that seems to resemble a guinea fowl.[717] Courtesy, Sally and Pete Riffle.

FIGURE 256 (below right) A peacock turned *Elbedritsch*.[271]

Songbirds and barnyard fowl

Songbirds are quite numerous throughout towel needlework. General warblers, [Figure 254] tamed birds that are tied or in a cage, [Figures 261, 262] a robin, a guinea fowl, [Figures 255, 228] a goose, [Figure 208, Plates 32, 45] a "Butter Ball" turkey, [Figure 77] and the proverbial *Elbedritsch* are all to be found. [Figure 256]

A generic description of these fowl would classify them as a small species usually sewn at rest, not in flight, with their wings at times outlined with color or by stitch variation.[232,233,606] Color, although it was unrealistic, was an effective means to demonstrate variegation and stripes in the body of the bird, or to set apart the head and legs. [Figure 257]

Profiles exhibit a straight or hooked beak, long and short necks, a round eye, and one or two legs with claws. The birds' tails were often the most distinguishable characteristic for it appeared that embroiderers attempted to differentiate various birds by their tails. Fanned-out

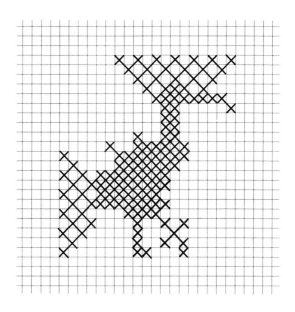

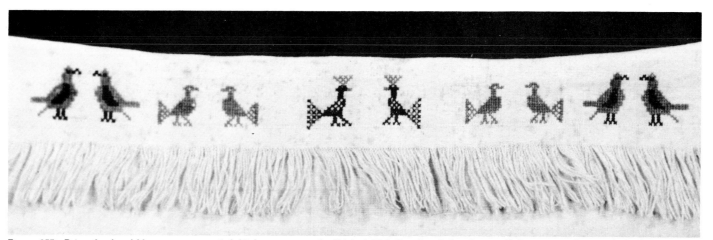

FIGURE 257 Pairs of red and blue cotton cross stitch birds sewn across the 2½ inch high flap. A weft thread was pulled to create a line on which all the feet were placed.[197] Courtesy, Clarke E. Hess.

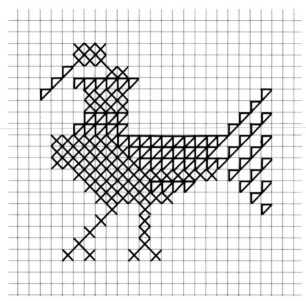

FIGURE 258[281]

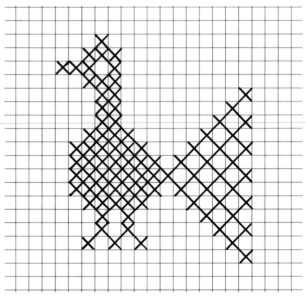

FIGURE 260[15]

tail feathers were easy to sew,[15,246,281] [Figure 258] but so were those that dragged on the ground,[232,325,606] [Figure 259] or extended in a straight line.[18] Other tails were shaped and thus took on a more realistic form.[933] One wonders if the small bird with a curved up-going tail might be mythical.[404,445,624]

Innovative attempts to form perspective with needle and thread brought about engaging results especially on something as small as a bird. Elizabeth Longenecker sewed a front view of a bird, but a side angle of the head and tail. He appears to be walking toward the viewer,

but into a headwind.[15] [Figure 260] Salome Kriebel attempted to capture a realistic stance by embroidering a bird twisting its neck to look over its shoulder.[164]

Colorful wild songbirds were once tamed and cared for as family pets by members of farm households. Some birds were tied by the foot as on the 1827 Catarina Walborn towel,[358] [Figure 261] while other chirpers were kept in the kitchen inside a handmade birdcage.[443,454] [Figure 262] Most embroidered birds were of the wild sort and not so restrained, but appeared to be running, walking, flying,[1257] [Figure 189] standing, or perching in pairs [Figures 263-265] or one by one.

One can hardly refrain from identifying Maria Dillier as an early nineteenth century birdwatcher. She cross stitched thirty-eight birds in and around flower trees as the main feature on her towel.[606] Elizabeth Erb[426] and Rachel Lefever,[394] on the other hand, perched their birds atop a chevron border. [Plate 7] Small, medium, and large birds of a feather were sewn together, other fledglings sang alone.

Songbirds were an equally strong design in drawn thread and free-form embroidery. Drawn thread birds bore likeness to those executed in cross stitch. They had opened wings,[29] spread-out tail feathers,[177,368] curved

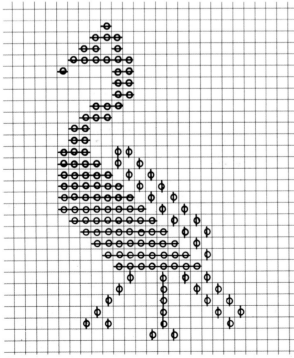

FIGURE 259[307]

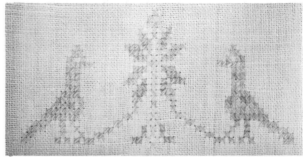

FIGURE 261 A pair of tame birds tied to a flower. Red cotton cross stitch.[358] Courtesy, The Henry Francis duPont Winterthur Museum.

154

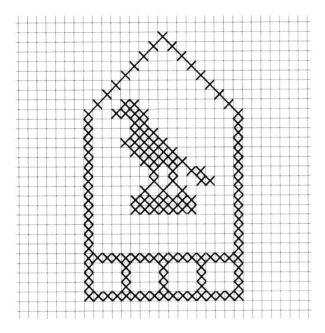

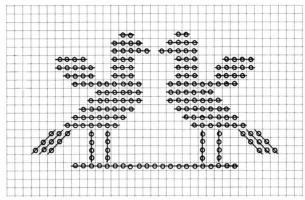

FIGURE 264[29]

FIGURE 262 (left)[454]

FIGURE 263 (below) A pair of birds each with a wing and a small feather on the head. Red cotton cross stitch.[933]

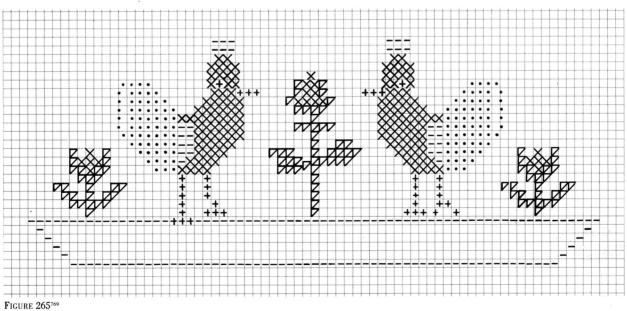

FIGURE 265[769]

necks,[307] shaped beaks,[307] and all other semblances to those in cross stitch. The direction of the darning stitch in the all-white thread embroidery gave direction to the bird's feathers. [Figures 125, 140, 151-154, 58]

Most birds were a practical and workable size to embroider on a thread grid so sensible needleworkers profited by incorporating many birds into their drawn panels. One seamstress embroidered twenty different birds throughout three drawn panels.[690]

Back, chain, and outline were serviceable stitches for sewing birds. They opened a myriad of doors for creative free embroiderers who seized the opportunity. Women sewed birds in every imaginable size, position, and color. Some warblers were amazingly life-like, others more stylized. [Figures 76, 215]

MR, 1817, chain stitched four birds with flapping wings and opened squawking bills. The feathers on the breast and wing were even set upright![709] [Figure 266] Others were more serene like the bird looking over his shoulder[718] or the love birds with beaks touching.[510]

One of these birds sat on a short branch,[289] a spray of flowers,[732] [Figure 267] a large leaf,[316] [Figure 268] or the uneven ground.[709] A number of the girls used a back or chain stitch[268,312] to outline the profile of the bird and then filled the body with rows or groupings of ad lib,

FIGURE 267 Free-form bird and flower design of the type often seen on *Fraktur*. It was embroidered on the upper corners of a three inch high flap in red and blue cotton outline, satin and straight stitches. L. 2"; W. 3¼".[732] Courtesy, Sally and Pete Riffle.

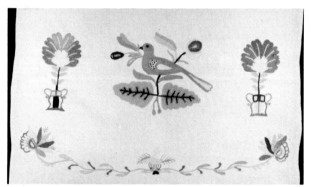

FIGURE 268 Balanced plain weave cotton fabric; pink, red, yellow, olive green, and black wool chain stitch. See Figure 194. W. 18½".[1312]

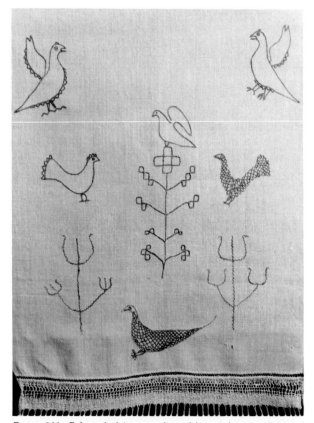

FIGURE 266 Balanced plain weave linen fabric; red cotton chain and threaded straight stitches. Motifs embroidered not quite in mirror-image. The flower with bird design in the center is nine inches high. See Figure 76. W.17".[709] Courtesy, Sally and Pete Riffle.

FIGURE 269 Free-form bird embroidered with chain, star eyelet, straight, seed, and cross stitches. 3¾" x 3¾".[268]

156

FIGURE 270 Red and blue cotton cross and chain stitch birds and shaded numbers in the date.

uncounted cross stitches to denote the wings, body, and tail feathers. [Figure 269] Others used the more typical free embroidery satin,[732] or outline[153] stitches to achieve the same effect. [Figure 270]

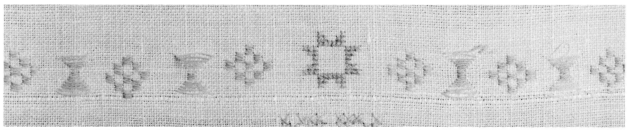

FIGURE 271 Balanced plain weave linen fabric; red cotton cross and satin stitch border. Note that a weft thread was pulled to mark the fabric where to place the border.[194] Courtesy, Sally and Pete Riffle.

Borders

Borders on a towel define space and accent areas. They were created and developed fulfilling the most elaborate imaginations. Not only were colors and design elements combined, but stitchery techniques were also blended. Straight, cross, satin, herringbone, or eyelet stitches, and backstitching, interlaced hemstitching, or drawn thread work are but a few processes that were effectively intermixed.[194,541] [Figures 271, 39, 51, 78]

Woven borders, already mentioned, were spaced by the weaver and as such were an integral part of the towel fabric. Embroidered and drawn thread borders, or applied fringes in single, double, or triple rows, on the other hand, were all placed at the discretion of the towel maker. Construction and types of fringes will be discussed later, but plain or elaborate fringes were important border elements as were the embroidered or drawn thread ones.

The simplest horizontal border was made by removing just one weft thread from the towel material to create a line or base from which to count threads. This enabled the embroiderer to place designs, letters in a name, lines in an inscription; it helped keep the border itself in a straight line. It served a practical utilitarian purpose, but was not very decorative. [Figure 257]

Embroidered edgings could be enlarged to a medium or large height by simply increasing the cross stitch size from the usual two by two threads to four[119] or eight[309] threads. Another technique used by Anna Kinig in 1862 was to remove every other weft thread inside a given area which gave the fabric a loose open weave.[117] Counting threads and embroidering cross stitch on such material produced a larger stitch which in turn formed a much higher border with the same numer of stitches.

Border size could also be regulated by rescaling a given design. A three stitch high zigzag border could easily be expanded any desired distance, for instance. [Figures 272-278]

Using embroidered borders did not necessarily indicate that the resulting paneled area was to be sewn with additional designs. Some borders were so large they served as both a border and panel decoration. Borders alone could create the towel's main attraction.[523] [Figure 279; Plate 44]

This attraction was intensified if borders were created by combining many of the familiar cross stitch designs

157

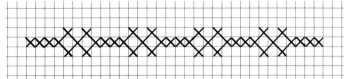

FIGURE 272[344]

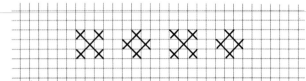

FIGURE 273[553]

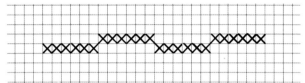

FIGURE 274[64]

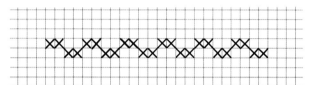

FIGURE 275[18] Courtesy, Dr. and Mrs. Donald M. Herr.

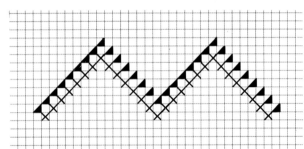

FIGURE 276[83]

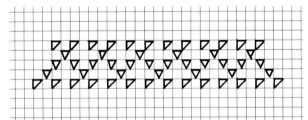

FIGURE 277[540]

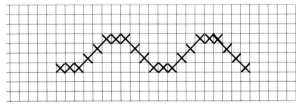

FIGURE 278[243]

FIGURE 279 The second and third of four borders on one towel in red and blue cross stitch.[264] Courtesy, Dr. and Mrs. Donald M. Herr.

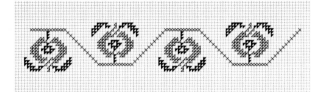

FIGURE 280[313]

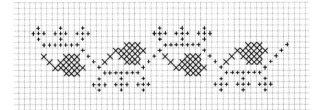

FIGURE 281[191]

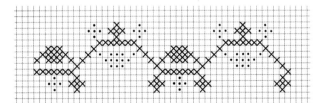

FIGURE 282[624]

FIGURE 283 Balanced plain weave linen fabric; red and blue cotton cross stitch; self and applied plain fringes. See Figure 189. W. 16½".[1257]

FIGURE 284 Red and blue cotton cross stitch border. See Figure 168 for top of towel.[1279]

158

FIGURE 285 Two different borders embroidered in red and blue cotton cross stitch. The upper applied plain fringe is 2½ inches long; the bottom applied plain fringe is three inches long. 11½" x 18".[258]

previously discussed. There were edgings with tulips, roses, and carnations in bud,[624] or in full bloom,[63,313,429] borders with birds,[63,288] stars,[191] leaves,[258] or with vines, crowns and flower.[191] [Figures 280-283]

There were also the more geometric borders composed of units of blocks or squares,[58] crosses,[232,340] diamonds,[25,76,541] chained,[18,429] or zigzag patterns,[18,24,104] [Plate 36] plus combinations of all of the above! [Figure 284]

The Carl F. Egelmann printed cross stitch borders were copied with almost as much frequency as his designs.[15,196] They offered still another distinctive type of border design. [Figures 118, 119]

There were two general types of embroidered borders; those just discussed that extended across the full width of the towel and those that turned corners and continued in a vertical direction. Many of the same design elements were used in each border type with some restrictions in borders with a definite top side.

Simple vertical borders were most often seen as an edging on the narrow top flap or at the periphery of an inscription.[18,65,231,258] [Figure 7] When they enclosed an entire towel, however, the border appeared as a frame around the picture which would ultimately hang on the door. Meri Weinholt embroidered in chain stitch a blue wavy line with red leaves,[467] [Figure 165] and Elesebeth

Horte sewed a red cross stitch zigzag pattern to frame her towel.[706] [Figure 180a]

On the other hand, Anna Lemin ran a wide cross stitch floral border down each side of only the bottom half of her towel.[590] Catharina Gerwer[39] and Lydia Clayton[258] reduced the vertical side borders even further by embroidering them on just the bottom panel. Lydia's vertical border is a plain uncomplicated zigzag that abuts a straight line of stitchery. [Figure 285] Catharina Gerwer, however, created a vertical zigzag border with a double row of straight stitches two threads high that are sewn on each warp thread going on the diagonal. No wonder she did not continue it on all four sides.

Combining a horizontal and vertical border was more easily said than done. Space was needed when turning a corner, but because of the size of the pattern repeat it wasn't always possible to turn the border at the appropriate place. The corner was an obvious trouble spot that needed precise calculations, preferably before sewing commenced, especially when embroidering high and intricate borders. [Figures 286-291] This probably accounted for the fact that horizontal and vertical borders on towels seldom match. At the corner one design stopped and another began.

159

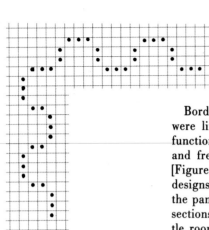
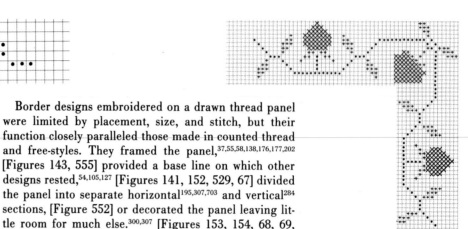

Border designs embroidered on a drawn thread panel were limited by placement, size, and stitch, but their function closely paralleled those made in counted thread and free-styles. They framed the panel,[37,55,58,138,176,177,202] [Figures 143, 555] provided a base line on which other designs rested,[54,105,127] [Figures 141, 152, 529, 67] divided the panel into separate horizontal[195,307,703] and vertical[284] sections, [Figure 552] or decorated the panel leaving little room for much else.[300,307] [Figures 153, 154, 68, 69, 99]

Drawn thread borders that turned corners within a thread panel were necessarily small.[334,359] Often the top and bottom were one design and the side borders another.[347,427] [Figure 135] Other variations included drawn panels with bottom and side borders combined,[135] [Figure 124] top and side borders only,[120] [Figure 136] a single top border,[45,92] a top and bottom border with nothing at the sides,[93,97] [Figures 130, 142, 154a] and panels with just a right and left side border.[136]

The zigzag[28,55,129,331,361,387] and diamond[54,282,284] designs were easiest to use on the thread grid. Borders of crosses,[76] touching hearts,[280] [Figure 292] alternate crowns, stars, and crosses,[374] [Figure 53] rotating hearts and flowers,[249] and those with facing birds,[334] or a name and year were more decorative and specialized.

Some of the wider drawn thread borders had intricate patterning similar to configurations in hand-knotted and commercially produced fringes.[285,392] [Figure 524] These often occurred as horizontal borders throughout the towel rather than as a functional component within a drawn panel. This second type of drawn thread border found on the towel and not in the grid more often utilized hemstitching and some of its variations as previously discussed. [Figure 48] But, simpler designs such as a row of small crosses were also used.

Free hand embroidered borders were plain or fancy, large or small, and were sewn with one or several different stitches. [Figures 293, 39] They too divided the surface of the towel into horizontal units, held the top flap in place,[44] and framed inscriptions or the entire towel. Some of the examples included straight or zigzag[415] rows of chain stitch [Figures 294, 49] and interlocked rows of half circles, sewn in outline stitch, whose form could have been easily guided by tracing the base of a water glass.[125] [Figures 95, 96] Still other borders involve four chain stitched tulips stretched out across the towel,[692] [Figure 295] and others that combine free and counted embroidery stitches.

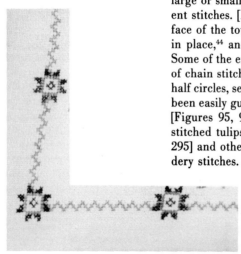

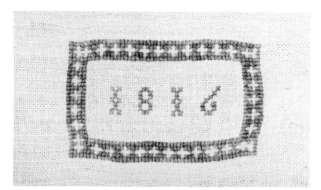

FIGURE 290 A border with crosses that turned corners and enclosed the date 1816. Red cotton cross stitch.[625] Courtesy, North Museum of Franklin and Marshall College, Lancaster.

FIGURE 293 Free-form grapes and grapevine border combined with count thread cross stitch embroidery. Red and blue cotton satin, cross chain, and straight stitches.[1125]

FIGURE 286 (upper left)[464]

FIGURE 287 (upper right)[150]

FIGURE 288 (lower left) A red and blue cotton cross stitch border with stars that turned a corner around an embroidered text.[191]

FIGURE 289 (lower right) A pink wool border that turned corners around an inscription.[18] Courtesy, Dr. and Mrs. Donald M. Herr.

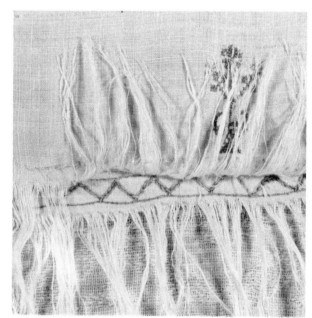

FIGURE 294 One cannot be sure why this embroidered border was placed under the fringe. It is red cotton and blue silk chain stitch and three-eighth inches high with five-eighth inches between the points. It was applied between the linen self-fringe and a pattern weave cotton panel.[271]

FIGURE 291 A simple red cotton cross stitched border that easily turned corners.[625] Courtesy, North Museulm of Franklin and Marshall College, Lancaster.

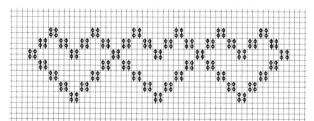

FIGURE 292[280]

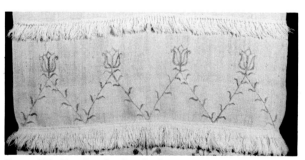

FIGURE 295 Free-form border of red cotton chain stitched tulips 4½ inches high; self plain fringe above bound into groups and applied plain mill-made white cotton fringe below.[692] Courtesy, Sally and Pete Riffle.

Cartouches

A cartouche or similar element was sometimes used to emphasize a name, initials, date, or text. A cross stitch octagonal cartouche with leaves and flowers called attention on one towel to the fact that, "My Parents are George and Matty Meck 1841."[620] [Figure 296] This was a design easily enlarged to fit any combination of words or verses, which fact accounts for its popularity. The heart motif was also expanded[468] as the Fanny Nissley towel shows.[574] [Figure 103] It was very wide and enclosed a long statement.

Susanna Heller embroidered what was probably the most elaborate framework for texts. She surrounded each of seven verses with a cross stitched box from which all kinds of flowers and birds rise. These original designs were arranged symmetrically, but because of this unusual presentation, the towel, at first glance, appears atypical.[334] [Plate 38] Texts generally had less pretentious borders.

Names, initials, and dates required less space to embroider than did poems or verses of hymns. Therefore, they were set apart in hearts, hearts with flowers, [Figure 297] squares, [Figure 298] blocks, rectangles with straight or zigzag edges, wreathes of flowers, diamonds, octagons, [Figures 299, 300] flowers, floral sprays, stars, and oval shapes. A single design placed between initials or in the midst of the name was less conspicuous.

Drawn thread grids were too coarse to be practical for recording texts, although grid space was reserved for initials, the year, and an occasional name without a cartouche. The cartouche motif is almost unknown in drawn thread embroidery because of its large size. [Figure 141]

In free-form embroidery towel makers had more options and fewer space restrictions than with counted thread techniques. Most young girls, however, refrained from elaborate free-style dressings around their handwritten name or initials. They chose instead to sign the towel in cross stitch and embroider the towel with free-form designs. Signatures and decorations were usually kept separate.

CF sewed her monogram inside a hand drawn circular cartouche design,[491] the initials HA CA were stitched in the centers of two overlapping hearts,[125] [Figure 132] and Margrit Hueszlerin is spelled on two lines within a single heart motif.[249] The heart seemed to be the favored hand drawn design, if any was used.

Individuality characterized this group of motifs more than any one design, shape, or combination of motifs.

FIGURE 296 A wreath of red and blue cotton cross stitched flowers and leaves surrounding an inscription.[620] Courtesy, North Museum of Franklin and Marshall College, Lancaster.

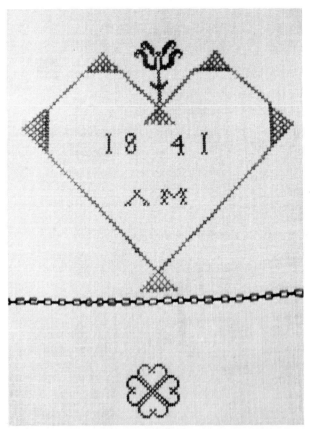

FIGURE 297 Balanced plain weave linen fabric; light red and dark red cotton cross stitch. See Figure 185.[59]

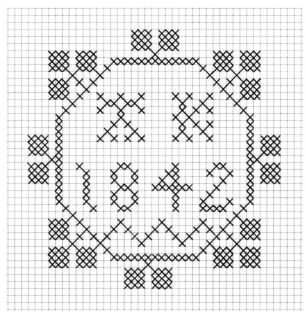

FIGURE 298[476]

FIGURES 299, 300 Two identical motifs were necessary to embroider the initials and year F[anny] M[oyer] 1854. Red cotton cross stitch.[343]

Circles

Circular figures appeared as embroidery designs. These ring-like motifs enclosed other smaller cross stitched designs such as stars, crosses, diamonds, and flowers, or they encircled a monogram, inscription, name, or date. [Figures 301, 302]

These uses of the circle were not generally seen in drawn thread embroidery, but CF enclosed her initials with a hand drawn circle with scalloped edges that resembles a cookie cutter. Perhaps that was her pattern.[491]

The two Carl F. Egelmann circular designs had their own distinct appearance. One disc-like element has small open cross-shaped areas inside a thread-filled circular shape,[196] and the second contains three circles and a

Greek cross.[258] [Figure 118] Many attempts were made to sew Egelmann's circles, but few met with great success. Perfect roundness was difficult to execute in cross stitch because threads were counted and stitches were sewn in short straight rows in an attempt to form the illusion of a curved line. That this was confusing is evident from examining the finished designs. [Figures 12, 119, 180a; Plate 37]

Darning circular shapes on a thread grid was just as difficult as embroidering them on linen material. Occasionally small circles were made[315,370] that resemble the numeral zero. Larger circles often contained concentric rings.[292] Egelmann's design of a Greek cross surrounded by a circular border was attempted on a drawn grid, but with meager success.[291]

163

There was more success embroidering circular designs that had eight sides,[426,] finely scalloped edges,[437] or large points[87] which were developed more from sewing staggered straight lines than attempting curved ones. Wreaths of flowers seen on later dated towels often appear more round because the leaves and blossoms camouflage the eight sides on which the circle was built.[362] [Figure 220]

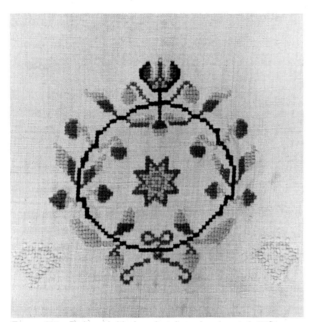

FIGURE 301   Red, gold, black and pink wool cross stitch.[437] Courtesy, The State Museum, Pennsylvania Historical and Museum Commission 34.129.18.

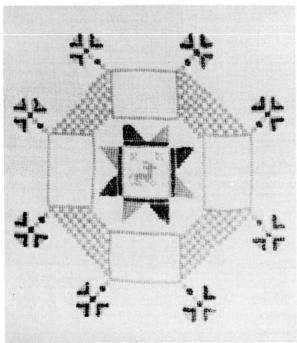

FIGURE 302   Red and blue cotton cross stitch on a balanced plain "fine" weave linen towel. It is a large design, approximately five inches across.[194] Courtesy, Sally and Pete Riffle.

Crosses

The cross by definition is "any figure or mark formed by the intersection of two straight lines." "A common heraldic bearing representing the Christian emblem or some variation of it."

The embroidered cross motifs followed the basic forms of the Greek, St. Andrew's, and Maltese cross. Simple arrangements of the Fourchée cross[86,157,233,264] and the Pomée cross[37] were encountered infrequently, and the only time a Latin cross was seen was when it was sewn atop a crown.[231,606] [Figure 303] The absence of the traditional western Latin cross, except on crowns, seems to suggest that this motif had a decorative, rather than religious significance.

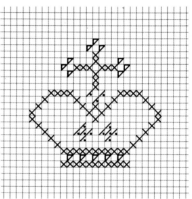

FIGURE 303[231]

The swastika, a symbol or ornament in the form of a Greek cross with the ends of the arms bent at right angles, was likewise not a popular cross design sewn on towels. A whirling swastika was sewn in a free-style, not cross stitch, on the 1827 Cadarina Kuns towel. It bears more semblance to graceful barn decorations than to rigid crossed lines seen in needlework.[864] A small drawn thread St. Andrew's cross assumes a swastika-like appearance on one towel by the alternate direction of the darning stitch with which it was made.[571] Another woman created a more stylized swastika by sewing bent loops at the ends of the crossed lines.[126]

The cross stitch pattern of the Maltese cross permitted expansion in size and embellishment so that the girls took advantage of this opportunity. It was a familiar design having been a favorite motif for barn swallow-holes. [Figures 304, 305] In 1833, LAK enlarged and

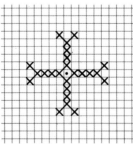

FIGURE 304[233]

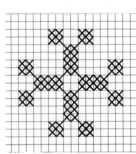

FIGURE 305[86]

embellished a drawn thread Maltese to include a St. Andrew's cross.[28] The basic form of the Maltese cross was generally unembellished in drawn thread embroidery. It was a small size and used often. An irregular red and blue Maltese cross was executed in chain and straight stitches in the upper right and left corner of a free-embroidered panel.[489] This is the only free-form Maltese cross recorded to date.

In their simplest construction the Greek and St. Andrew's crosses were made of just five cross stitches. From that elementary form units of stitches were compiled and the size and complexity of the cross motif mushroomed into countless, kaleidoscopic configurations. Many motifs retained the original cross form despite added intricacies. Other designs married and their progeny bore traits of both the Greek and St. Andrew's cross. Flowers, angled lines, squares, diamonds, and other geometric shapes were added to these crosses by some young women as if to gild the lily. [Figures 306-312]

Plain and fancy crosses were spaced throughout drawn thread panels many times. One motif was repeated over and over, [Figure 64] open areas were filled with a variety of cross formations; sometimes one large cross motif was the focal point within the panel. [Figure 57] The Greek and St. Andrew's basic cross patterns were embellished as much as the thread grid allowed, and rows of the St. Andrew's cross were easily adapted to borders.[14]

Three towel makers found the satin to be a convenient stitch to formulate a Greek cross. Lea Stolsfusz embroidered a small cross with open center in each upper corner of her free-embroidered towel.[722] [Plate 21] Maria Bollingern[488] and Abeth Ditze[451] made larger versions of the same open-centered Greek cross by counting threads before sewing. Each unit of Maria's cross is eight threads and Abeth's is ten threads in length. This is another instance of the adaptability of the satin stitch from free-form to count thread. These are a few of the unusual non-cross stitched cross designs.

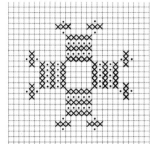

FIGURE 306[65]

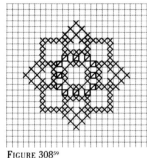

FIGURE 308[59]

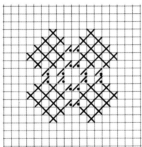

FIGURE 310[102]

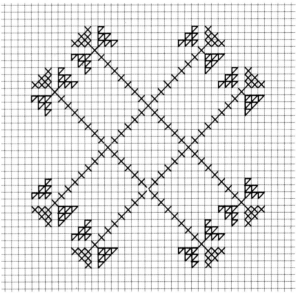

FIGURE 312[604]

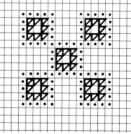

FIGURE 311[571]

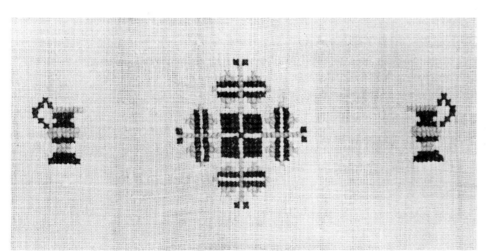

FIGURE 309 A pair of tankards and a cross motif are centered in the upper panel of the towel. Red and blue cotton cross stitch.[333]

165

Crowns

This directory would be incomplete without a discussion of crowns. This design element was easily changed to fulfill creative desires or meet size requirements. Small, medium, and large crowns that fit hundreds of descriptions were embroidered.

Some crowns were composed of square units[312] others had three knobs, [Figure 313] five knobs, [Plate 16] or a center point. The larger more elaborate crowns supported flowers[420] [Figure 314] or a bird,[47,69] [Figures 315-317, 242] In fact, MK embroidered a crown with three birds.[364] A round crown, complete with Latin cross centered above it, is found on several towels.[231,606] [Figure 303; Plate 45]

This same crown was depicted on a drawn thread panel in 1810 by Catharina B. Weidman. This was also the tallest drawn thread crown recorded. It measured twenty-seven grid spaces high.[379] The widest crown, twenty-four spaces across, was made by Marei Ewerle and was a round crown design, but without cross.[29] [Figure 318] Drawn thread crown motifs of small size are seldom seen.

Crowns have not been seen or recorded in free-form embroidery.

Although crowns occur frequently on Pennsylvania German samplers, they were not utilized as often on towels. On one towel there is a text from Revelation 2:10, "Be thou faithful until death and I will give thee the crown of life." One crown is among the motifs on the towel.[715] [Figure 178] This widely-quoted text also occurs on *Fraktur*, in connection with crown drawings, and was frequently used in confirmation and funeral sermons. It probably explains some of the popularity of the crown motif in Pennsylvania German folk art and, to the extent that these motifs have any meaning, defines the purpose of the crown. Compare the discussion of hearts and religious motifs below.

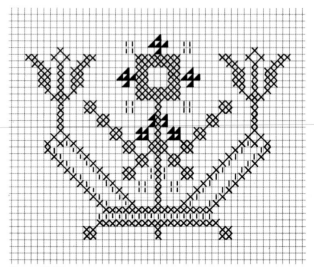

FIGURE 314[420]

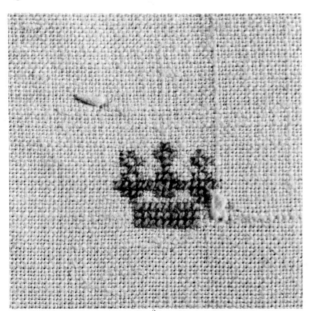

FIGURE 313   A red cotton cross stitch crown with three knobs.[217] Courtesy, Mennonite Heritage Center, Souderton.

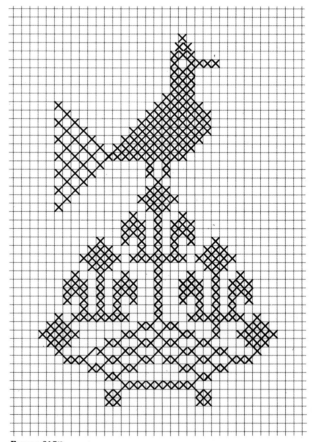

FIGURE 315[69]

Figure 316[234]

167

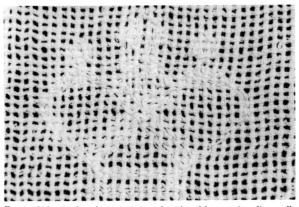

FIGURE 316a Birds and flowers on three crowns. Red and blue cotton cross stitch.[150]

FIGURE 318 A white linen crown embroidered by weaving diagonally over and under the grid threads.[29]

FIGURE 317 Two birds on a crown in red cotton and brown silk cross stitch. The red cotton needlewoven borders below were made by weaving over and under two and three warp yarns.[756]

Dates and names

Numbers that are cross stitched on towels generally state a date of birth, death, a commemorative occasion, or the time of towel embroidery. More than half of the towels in this study were dated. We found a towel marked for every year from 1793 to 1850 except for 1802, 1803, and 1805.

The embroidered year on a towel indicated when it was made. Some women said so with needle and thread. *Ienner 1820 Veronica Rutt.* (January 1820 Veronica Rutt).[697] *Ienner 1820.* (January 1820)[1156] *Hedded Meier hots gemacht Im Iahr 1827.* (Hedded Meier made it in the year 1827).[718] [Figure 127] *Hornung 1828.* (February 1828).[1133] *Ihm Iayr 1828.* (In the year 1828).[1338] *Im Iahr 1833.* (In the year 1833).[1212] *Im Iar 1838.* (In the year 1838).[1202] *Ihm Iar 1841.* (In the year 1841).[1194] *This towl I made in the year 1846.*[901] *Ienner 1847.* (January, 1847).[1144] *Maria B. Kreiders work done 1859.*[803]

Others specified even more by embroidering the exact day, month, and year the towel was completed. *She marked this towel done the 2th day of October AD 1848 Anna Frey.*[755] *Chrestena Bauman In the year of Our Lord May 3, 1841.*[69] *Den 15 Merz 1854 Elesebeth Horte.* (March 15, 1854 Elesebeth Horte).[706] [Figure 180a] *SS Dieses hand duch ghoret mier Sara Schitzin gmacht den 8 Merz 1819 Sara Schit.* (SS This hand towel belongs to me Sara Schitz made 8 March 1819).[268] [Figure 461]

Arranged by month, the dates reveal a clear pattern.

January 2, 1841[856]
January 6, 1838[88]
January 24, 1849[18]
January 24, 1830
March 2, 1839[1059]
March 3, 1842[944]

March 4, 1839[1151]
March 8, 1819[268]
March 14, 1850[675]
March 15, 1854[706]
March 18, 1853[362]
March 19, 1838[283]
April 30, 1865[592]
May 2, 1821[609]
May 3, 1841[69]
May 4, 1837[574]
May 6, 1833[1280]
May 22, 1838[15]
August 24, 25, 1842[1054]
August 28, 1852[602]
September 5, 1842[4]
September 27, 1795[886]
October 2, 1848[755]
October 4, 1843[466]
October 20, 1819[408]
November 3, 1840[394]
December 3, 1838[196]

FIGURE 319 *Elizabeth Alderfer, 1834* . . . . Montgomery county. Balanced plain weave linen fabric; red and blue cotton cross stitch. Note that the large numerals and the initials EAD were sewn with a single row of red and a single row of blue cotton. The one-quarter inch wide and one inch long linen hanging tabs were sewn 1-5/8 inches from the side edge not at the corner of the towel.[519] Courtesy, Albert and Elizabeth Gamon.

These dates readily indicated that fancy stitchery was not done during the busy harvest season, and seldom in the flax spinning season of November and December. Appropriate almanac checks revealed the towels were finished any day of the week including Sunday. According to one reference at least one woman made and worked on her towels on special religious holidays. In the 1884 Centennial celebration of Montgomery county in Norristown the following were exhibited. "Four towels, spun and worked by Mary Zieber, on the three holidays of the year, second Christmas, second Easter, and second Whitsuntide; over 100 years old." (Bean, Appendix XXVIII)

Some young women recorded their age with needle and thread. Birth dates were sometimes coupled with the time of embroidering the towel in the form of a short inscription. *Elizabeth Alderfer is geboren den 6 Iune im Iahr 1815.* (Elizabeth Alderfer was born 6 June in the year 1815).[519] [Figure 319] *Ich Fronica Krebelin bin geboren im Jahr Christi 1803 den 20 October 1819.* (I Fronica Krebelin was born in the year 1803 The 20 October 1819).[408] *Mary Witmer is born in the the year 1835 January 18 [?].*[440] *Fanney Whitmer is born in the year 1833 August the 28 1852 End.*[802] This documentation provides the age of the girl who did all this sewing and aids in determining which of the many Elizabeth Alderfers and Fronica Krebelins made the towel.

When two different dates appeared on the same towel one was often at the top and the other sewn near the bottom edge or in the drawn thread work. [Figure 124] These dates could have indicated the length of time needed to make the towel or more specifically when each section of the towel was completed. Some examples are

Catharina Bolinger 1841 CB 1836;[238] *Salome Gerberin 1811, 1818;*[450] *Emanuel J. Minnich 1850 1849;*[18] [Plate 11] *Anna Brubacher 1837* in cross stitch and *AB 1841* in drawn thread work;[701] *MST 1834* in cross stitch and *1833* in drawn thread work.[449]

Designs were sewn in various sizes to embellish and accent the embroidered year especially if the date was not included in an inscription or with the name. The year was incorporated into floral motifs by placing two digits of the year to the right and left of the central stem or vase. The first two digits were also positioned inside the design on the left side of the towel and the last two digits to the right inside a duplicate design with the name or small motifs between them. Other times the year and the towel maker's initials were placed in a single round or oblong floral cartouche or an enlarged heart design. [Figure 297, 300]

Hanna Brenneisen used a circle of four hearts with flowers in which to put the year 1799. It was one of a few particular circular motifs that occasionally enclosed the date, and it was always sewn in a central spot on the towel.[711] [Figure 320]

Names were also significant. The names that appear most often are those of the original owner and presumably the maker. A signature indicated a certain self-approval, pride in her own hand work. It identified her work for her family and future generations. Historians today welcome these names as authentication of a Pennsylvania Dutch folk tradition.

The upper areas of the towel were preferred for the placement of the name. The spelling was often spaced to extend the entire width of the towel using block, script,

FIGURE 320 Balanced plain weave linen fabric; red and blue cotton and brown silk cross stitch. See Figure 184.[711]

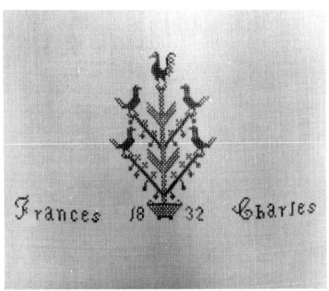

FIGURE 321 Name embroidered with script upper and lower case letters. Red cotton, brown silk cross stitch.[1110]

upper or lower case letters, or any combination thereof. Small diamond, cross, crown, or flower designs often accompany the spelling in an effort to lengthen or balance the line of writing. [Figures 321, 322, 28] Deborah Heebner, 1827,[347] and Susanna Heebner,[482] embroidered their full name with script upper case letters. The task was even more complicated because this sewing was done on a pattern woven towel—no small accomplishment!

FIGURE 322 A border of diamonds in which the letters of the name Catarina Hege were placed. The flap measures 2¾ inches high and the ends were sewn to the towel edge to hold it in place. The white linen hanging tab was three-eighth inches wide and 1½ inches long.[545] Courtesy, Pennsylvania Farm Museum of Landis Valley, Lancaster.

Names were generally spelled with cross stitched block letters, but women used both English and Pennsylvania High German spelling which accounts for the feminine suffix *in* placed at the end of surnames. *Christina Hessin* (Hess),[392] *Salome Barthin* (Barth),[475] *Susanna Milerin* (Miller),[1096] *Elisabeth Biemersderferin* (Biemersderfer),[872] *Cadarin Deiblerlin* (Deibler),[421] *Elisabet Eberlin* (Eberly),[496] *Anna Erhardin* (Erhard),[707] *Salome Gerberin* (Gerber),[450] *Maria Dienerin* (Diener),[237] *Anna Ruttin* (Rutt),[404] *Susanna Walbin* (Walb),[273] [Figure 130] and *Margaret Hueszlerin* (Hueszler)[249] are a few examples.

Pennsylvania High German spelling is also evidenced in the use of the letter *I* in names and not the letter *J*. *Iudit Gehman*,[1] *Iohannes Leise*,[480] *Iohannes Witmeyer*,[288] [Figure 463] *Iacob Graf*,[553] *Iacob Hess*,[556] *Beniamin Kinig*,[186] [Figure 468] and *Iudith Martin*.[490] [Figure 188]

The German language education of *Elizabeth D. Landes*[222] and *ES 1809*[745] is evident in sewn signatures. Elizabeth used a block letter formation for cross stitching the letters of her name in a German *Fraktur* typeface. She also used English letters. [Figure 323] *ES* sewed her initials in chain stitch also in the *Fraktur* typeface. In 1846 Barbara Landisen also chain stitched her name in the thick and thin letters of the German *Fraktur* typeface.[641] [Plate 42] On another towel Christina Hess outlined her initials in stem stitch and then filled them with chain stitch.[285] After Christina Hessin finished embroidering her initials in this fashion she went one step further and executed two fanciful designs in a tiny running stitch that are reminiscent of a printed tailpiece. [Plate 39] The girls also included their name or initials using more conventional letter styles.

In rare instances the Pennsylvania High German handwriting is illustrated on towels. Writing German script with pen and ink involves complicated structured letter formations with long sweeping curves, loops, and circles. How much more difficult it was to embroider such let-

FIGURE 323   On the top line Elizabeth D. Landes cross stitched her name in red and blue cotton block letters. On the second line she embroidered her name in German *Fraktur* typeface, also in red and blue cotton cross stitch.[222]

ters! Knowledge in needlework other than just cross stitch was required. It was this lack of knowledge rather than lack of skill that prevented most young Pennsylvania Dutch girls from sewing their name and inscriptions in their native language script. Two towels contain script executed with a high degree of proficiency, Anna Herr, 1816,[468] [Figure 324] and Christina Hessin, 1815.[392] [Plate 46]

FIGURE 324   Red cotton, aqua silk outline, straight, satin, cross, and seed stitches. The cross stitched heart contains the initials AH, the name Anna Herr sewn in German script, and the year 1816. See Figure 149. 9½" x 14".[468] Courtesy, Dr. and Mrs. Donald M. Herr.

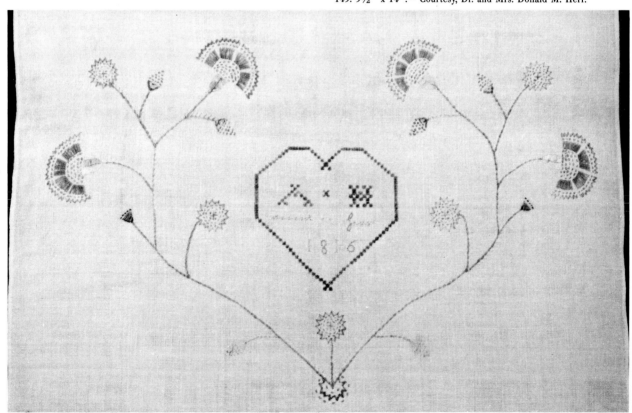

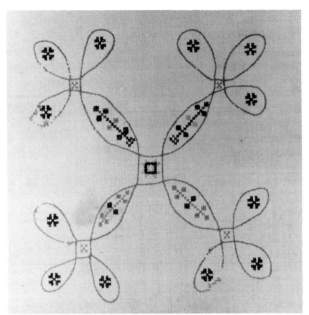

FIGURE 325   Red and dark blue cross and chain stitch.

The tailpiece was a printed ornament at the bottom of a page or at the end of a chapter some of which took on calligraphic formations. [Figures 325, 167] Eliza Fretz, 1846,[1291] [Figure 186] and Faney Kulp, 1861,[1265] appear to have copied one of these large swirling designs and placed it in the center of the towel surrounded by more traditional symmetrical cross stitch motifs. Elizabeth Hunschberger, however, copied in 1849 a more geometric-shaped tailpiece composed of diamonds and triangles and placed it directly under her name and date.[1116]

The printed word continued to fascinate adventuresome young embroiderers. The embroidered names and initials of Maria Heebner,[461] Catharine Kratz, 1838,[1247] [Plate 24] and Henry Kiefer, 1858,[693] [Figure 162] were obviously inspired by printed Roman type and no longer the German script or block letters.

Towel makers were young unmarried girls; in most instances it was maiden names that were sewn on towels. Rebecca Gerhard, born 1820, died 1875, made and dated a towel 1844 which was the same year she married Abraham Schultz. [Figure 557] She put her maiden initials on the towel.[279] So did others: Elisabeth Alderfer, 1853, who married Jacob H. Allebach,[171] Mary Reist, 1851, who married John Henry Boltz,[234] and Sarah Kriebel who married Abraham Dresher in 1852.[402]

Regina Heebner Schultz was one of the exceptions. She afixed her married name *Regina Schultz* to her 1830 towel after her marriage to the Rev. John Schultz.[261]

A sufficient number of towels bear men's names that the relationship of men to decorative towels must be considered. These towels have no features distinguishing them from other towels except the name. Sisters, mothers, sweethearts, or new wives were the likely persons to embroider a hand towel for a man. Whoever did so often sewed her name or initials alongside his name. *Catharine Gerber Iacob Gerber 1814 Maria Gerber*,[1361] *Jacob Schitz*

ES,[135] [Figure 124] *David Herr Susann Herr*,[103] [Figure 144] *Henry Hottenstein CH*,[1088] *Henry Rinker Sarah Stahr*,[677] *Banjamin and Eva Reichert*,[1148] *Willmina Hetwig Iohannes Leise*,[480] *Emanuel J. Minnich* and his sister *Rebecca J. Minnich*.[18] [Plate 11]

Only a man's name appeared on some towels: *Iohannes Witmeyer*,[288] [Figure 463] *Jacob Stouffer*,[849] *David Lehman*,[324] *Iacob Graf*,[553] *Iacob Hess*,[556] *George Hoke*,[559] [Figure 135] *Daniel Harr*,[83] *Christian Neff*,[185] *Henry Kiefer*,[693] [Figure 162] *Ioseph Lang*,[724] *John D. Sensenig*,[831] *Abraham Petersheim*,[1057] *Eli Zug*,[1014] [Plate 20] *Daniel Buch*,[1064] *Henry Buch*,[904] *Peter Rutt*,[1156] *Michael Mezer*,[1250] and *Benjamin Steman*.[1143]

Names or initials appeared at any place on the surface of the towel, top, middle, bottom, or in between. Names were sometimes included within a longer text or in conjunction with an alphabet, but more often they stood alone *Maria Kurtzin*,[619] *Crisdna Kepner*,[407] or with a date *Hanna Kressman 1827*,[615] *Anea Musselman 1822*.[537] The name and initials could be sewn on the towel several times in separate places and it is not at all unusual to see the same initials or year in the drawn thread work. In both initials and full names a mark of punctuation, usually an "X" could be added to separate syllables. Thus one Elisabeth Alderfer put *E x AD* on her towel, separating first and last names.[519] [Figure 319]

In most instances women worked no more than their initials in drawn thread embroidery such as *BG*,[24] *CH*,[91] or *ES*.[198] [Figures 124, 126, 131] Others included the date: *LAK 1833*,[28] *18 RS 35*,[50] [Figure 34] *CB 1836*,[238] *ANG 1797*,[387] or *SM 1814*[384] sewn with a backward letter *S*.

If the year was sewn on the thread grid by itself such as *1809*,[307] or *1845*,[280] [Figure 139] the girl's name or initials were most likely cross stitched on the main towel fabric. A young lady we know only as *CA* darned her initials inside a heart motif, unusual in drawn thread work.[300] [Figure 141]

If the grid panel was large enough, and the name short enough, the entire name was spelled out, sometimes including the year. [Figure 326] *Deborah Heebner 1825*,[347] *Elisabeth Diehl*,[25] [Plate 49] *Sarah Landes*,[177] and *Susana Kriebl 1825*.[348] This, of course, might have taken two lines depending on the size of the thread grid and the length of the name. Hannah Ziegler, on the other hand, not only placed her name vertically on the thread grid, but began the spelling at the bottom of the panel instead of at the top. She also placed the individual letters upside down, rightside up, or sideways, all of which made her name difficult to read.[765] [Figure 327]

Embroidered and drawn thread initials also appeared separately, together, or with the full name. *Anna Histand 1814 AH* was sewn in cross stitch and the *AH* initials were also in the drawn thread panel.[89] *Salome Merki* worked her name in cross stitch and later included her initials *SM* in the drawn thread panel.[323] Susanna Kauffman sewed only *SK* on her towel,[260] and Sara Merki placed her drawn thread initials in a vertical position with the *S* above the *M* instead of on the left side.[363]

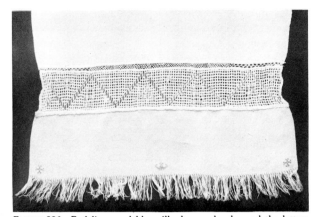

FIGURE 326 Red linen and blue silk chevron border and the letters B a e r embroidered with the darning stitch on the drawn thread grid.[422] Courtesy, Hershey Museum of American Life.

FIGURE 327 *Hanna Ziegler.* White linen darning stitch on a fine two by two thread drawn thread grid which is unevenly bound. 8" x 13-5/8".[765]

Initials appear as a single pair such as *MB* for Maria Berc,[369] or *SS* for Sarah Schultz.[230] [Figure 143] Double pairs of initials also occur such as *MAR HO* for Maria Hostetter,[581] [Figure 150] or *LID BAC* for Lydia Bachman.[719] Other times it was uncertain what two or more sets of intials represent such as *EK 1845 SI.*[746]

Later towel owners and family descendants sometimes added their initials and date as their mark of ownership as did *Elisabeth Leatherman 1841 CW Lizzie H Detweiler 1898.*[445] On another towel *Susana Berge* is sewn in cross stitch, but the initials *EGW* for Elizabeth Garges Wasser are embroidered in outline stitch in script letters elsewhere on the same towel.[256] Other examples of changed ownership include *Anna Beiler 1845 AS MS 1869,*[447] *Benjamin Steman 1838 Lizzie Stehman 1899,*[1143] *Maria Dienerin 1843 MI 1869,*[237] *Beniamin Kinig 1862 1927,*[186] [Figure 468] and a name tape with *CM Cusler* sewn on the back of the *Palle Mosser* towel.[59]

Amish women particularly liked to work additional designs and names into towels their mothers, grandmothers or great-grandmothers had begun. Barbara Beiler's name appears on a towel dated 1836, together with the initials ML. Almost a century later Savilla Fisher added her name in 1928.[1146] *Rebecca Lentz 1853, Sarah Lapp, Rebecca Smoker, 1903,* and *Sarah Beiler 1928* all had a hand in embroidering one towel.[1362] Another reads *M S Was Grandfathers Moses Smoker Died October 7 1876 aged 49 years Then Fathers Eli A Smoker Died September 18, 1932 Age 65 years Now Mary B. Smoker 1934.*[942] The entire family of Jacob and Mary (Stoltzfus) Blank are named on their towel.[971] Amish homes frequently have handlettered or stitched family lists hanging on the wall. *Lea Beiler, Sarah Yoder 1852* were members of the Amish community in the Big Valley in Mifflin county,[972] as was Sarah Renno—or *Sere,* as she spelled it.[787] Mattie Nisley began a towel in 1815, marking the year and her initials. She married Abraham King and their daughter *Freni Kinig* added her name *IMI AHR 1839.* She mar-

ried Andrew Diener, and their daughter Frany, who married Joel Zook added *F K Z* and *1893* to the towel. Finally their daughter Anna D. Zook added *A Z 1917.*[973] [Figure 166] *Cadharina Stolzfusz* began work on a towel without dating it. Her husband's granddaughter *Anna Stoltzfusz,* or Nancy as she was also known, added some work prior to her marriage in 1849. Their granddaughter Mary Lapp added some embroidery in 1896 and her daughter *Fannie King* completed it with twentieth century flourish in 1948.[969] [Figure 167] Amish women enjoyed making towels, which are often treasured by their descendants. One of the seamstresses in the Amish community, Barbara Ebersol, made Fraktur bookplates for many persons. On some of them she drew designs blocked for cross-stitch embroiderers. She is probably the BE who made a towel for Catharina Ebersol.[1258]

Possession of the towel subsequent to the maker was, at times, suggested by the presence of a second name hand written in black ink directly on the towel fabric. An example of this is a towel with the initials *MBH* sewn in cross stitch and the name *WS Sands* written in ink across the upper right corner.[187] A second example has a text embroidered near the middle of the towel, *MB 1844 Martha Brubaker is my name [e]arth is my dwelling place heaven is my station Christ is my salvation ....* Directly underneath this is a lengthy hand written poem in black ink, *Susan B. Harnish is my name the grass is green the rose is red here stand my name when I am dead ....*[437]

Copper name plates were also used to stamp a name in ink onto a towel. Two towels in point are ones on which the girl added her married name, but frequent laundering has left the ink badly faded. On one towel the initials *MS* were sewn in cross stitch, but the name *Mary S Heitner* was stamped in black ink directly under the initials.[49] *Sarah Young 1837* was embroidered two times at the bottom of the towel and the faded ink stamp that reads *Sara Moyer* is centered at the top edge.[182] [Figure 328]

173

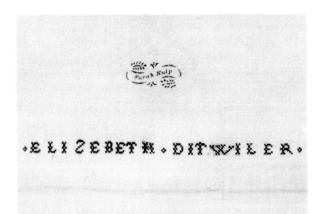

FIGURE 328 Towel owners identified their towels in various ways. Elizebeth Ditwiler cross stitched her name in black silk, whereas Sarah Kulp used a stencil and black ink.[1000]

Dual names or different sets of initials could mean that one woman made a towel for a friend or relative. Examples of this include the towel of *Hedded Meier* and *Rayel Ziegler*[718] [Figure 127] and *RH MS* for Ruth Hoppel who made the towel for Mary Stauffer.[573] [Figure 547] There is one towel with a text that leaves no doubt, *L. Clayton's Needlework for Catharine Dentzler 1856.*[258] [Figure 7] And still other towels were sewn with such varying weights of embroidery thread, different style motifs, and obviously good and poor workmanship that more than one embroiderer is apparent.[465,1197]

It is important to note that all names were not embroidered in cross stitch even if the traditional block lettering was used. The star or star-eyelet stitch was sometimes used to sew initials such as *EW*[157] that were sewn in red singles cotton or the initials *AW* stitched in 1833.[310] [Figure 329] In 1837, Fanny R. Steman used the star stitch to embroider her entire name in upper case block letters. Her only problem was that she sewed *N* backward and *Y* upside down.[197] Double cross stitch, which is similar to the star stitch, was also used on occasion to form fancy initials.[7,442]

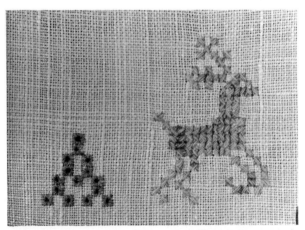

FIGURE 329 The star eyelet stitch was seldom embroidered on towels. Here it was sewn in red cotton to form the initial *A*. The running deer was also cross stitched in red cotton.[310]

The style of drawn thread letters and numerals corresponded directly to those used in cross stitch. The upper case, block-type letters, either seven or fourteen[107] spaces high, were sewn most often. Some script-type and lower case letters were also used.[135,177] Drawn thread numerals show some originality in execution, but were generally more legible than some cross stitched ones. They were counted and made in the same style as in cross stitch.

The outline or stem stitch was a wise choice when sewing names in a free-form style not governed by counted threads. Mary Nes embroidered her name using a red wool outline stitch on a coarse weave linen fabric,[40] whereas Maria Good outlined her hand written name in blue cotton.[219] [Figure 330]

FIGURE 330 *Maria Good.* Blue cotton outline and cross stitch. Note the white linen stitching along the upper folded edge and the unbound self plain fringe beginning to unravel. The flap is four inches high.[219]

The chain stitch was seldom used for embroidering names. [Figure 331] A small letter *K* chained in white cotton was found in the upper left corner of a 1795 towel,[195] and a white linen chain stitch was used to make the letter *C* in the name *Crisdna* on another towel.[407] *Mary Sensenigs*[834] and *John D. Sensenig*[831] each had their name sewn onto their towels in alternating red and blue chain stitched script-type letters.

We do not want to overlook the almost humorous dilemma *Cassa Ramp* had putting her name on her towel. She first sewed her name in seven cross stitch-high letters and the year 1835 across the upper area on the towel. But, she then expanded the letter size to an enormous thirty-six stitch height and in her excitement embroidered her name to read, *Ramp Casran.*[114]

If the placement of a name on the top flap or upper areas of the towel did not provide enough distinction, if the choice of thread color and stitch technique did not furnish sufficient emphasis, a third option was to ornament the name by placing it inside an especially designed cartouche or similar element.

Initials were particularly well suited for this type of adornment. Star,[111,149,319] heart,[79,268,560] and diamond[69,196,624] shaped designs were enlarged to accommodate a single letter or pair of initials. It was then necessary to sew duplicate designs to the right and left, each one enclosing a different initial. [Figure 364 Plates 15, 30]

Small flowers were placed between initials[385,416] or a floral vine arched over[540] or completely encircled them.[571] Initials have also been seen on the vase containing a

FIGURE 331 *Anna Shelly, 1833.* The name and date is embroidered in white cotton chain stitch; the border is brown silk chain stitch.[1316]

flower bouquet.[454] One special octagonal design accommodated both the maker's initials and the year. It was necessary to sew it twice onto the towel with each motif having one initial and two digits of the year as part of its design.[343] [Figures 299, 300]

Diamonds

A diamond is a plane figure formed by four equal straight lines bounding two acute and two obtuse angles. Artistic license was taken by young embroiderers as they cross stitched a myriad of diamond designs onto towels. Conventional diamond shapes were developed from the very small four cross stitch size to ones large enough to encompass stars[32] and floral motifs.[273] Flowers often rise from the four points or birds stood on the tapered ends just as they perched on most anything. A diamond's geometric proportions permitted talented needleworkers great freedom in exercising their creativity. [Figures 332, 333a]

Diamonds were another practical design for drawn thread grids. Their dimensions were easily altered to accommodate any size grid and its basic formation adapted to decorative changes.

Drawn thread diamond designs had open,[235,331] [Figure 334] closed,[194,281,412,712] [Figures 335, 336] or decorative centers.[14,257,305,335] Others gave rise to flowers.[53] [Figure 65]

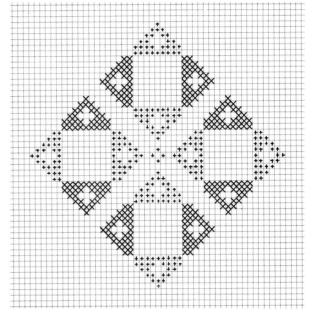

FIGURE 333[450]

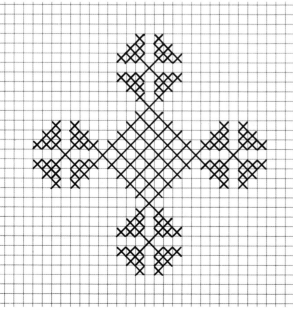

FIGURE 332[268]

FIGURE 333a Balanced plain weave linen fabric; red and blue cotton cross stitch. See Figure 130.[273]

175

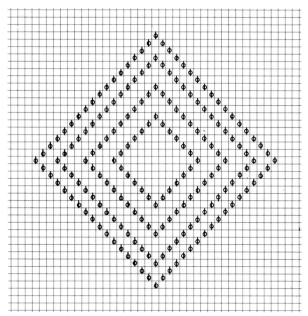

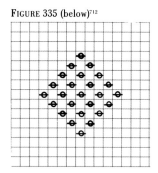

FIGURE 336 White cotton darning stitch. 14" x 15½".[94]

The points of two small diamonds were symmetrically positioned to form a double diamond[337] or four little diamonds were arranged to form one larger diamond motif.[305]

Alternate rows of diamonds filled entire drawn thread panels.[66,299] This created open areas in which to embroider smaller diamonds, squares, hearts, crosses, and flowers. On other towels the centers of the diamond remain open resulting in a cross-hatched effect.[124]

Susanna Schenckin, 1816, arranged short, straight stitches in a diamond pattern less than one inch across. Three rows of these diamonds were then placed between two cross stitch chains to form a wide border.[429] A more elongated diamond was made by Fronica Kriebelin by placing a running-type stitch over numbers of threads and then going under one thread and continuing over an uncounted group of threads. This diamond was about one-half inch high and had points every 1-5/8 inches. Diamond points touched and effected a horizontal border.[408]

Sara Schitz, 1819, embroidered five different diamonds throughout her towel. Each one was composed of four symmetrically arranged small diamonds. Four of these diamonds were cross stitched, but the fifth one was made with a counted straight-type stitch. Each staggered straight stitch was four threads long with the stitch above beginning in the middle of the stitch below.[268] [Figure 461] This appears to be a technique used more in canvas work than in counted thread or free-embroidery even though the straight stitch was used interchangeably between counted and uncounted needlework.

The geometric shape of the diamond design was better suited to counted thread embroidery than to traced or hand drawn techniques.

Flowers

"The arts of needlework and gardening have existed side by side for centuries, drawing a unique and special inspiration from each other." (Beck) The garden was the woman's province on the farmstead and in it she propagated an abundance of ornamentals and flowers in addition to food needed to feed the family. The grape hyacinth, prince's feather, dahlia, aster, petunia, tulip, lilies, pinks, violet, poppy, peony, snapdragon, geranium, fuchsia, iris, marigold, hollyhock, roses, columbine, and bleeding heart are but a few examples. "Flowers were and still are a must for the Pennsylvania Dutch housewife." (Keyser, 10)

Flowers were as numerous in all forms of Pennsylvania German needlework as they were in native gardens and house yards. Hand towels are ablaze with their presence. Most cross stitch and drawn thread examples had one, [Figure 337] three, [Figure 338] or five flowers growing from sometimes single, sometimes multiple stems. A large percentage appeared to emerge from the ground as if depicted flowering out-of doors. [Figures 339, 231] A bouquet or floral arrangement is in a basket, [Figure 340] teapot, [Figure 341] heart, urn, [Figures 342, 343] or stylized container. [Figures 344, 345] Some flowers embellish a decorative border. [Figures 280-283; Plate 7]

Some of the cross stitch and drawn thread floral interpretations are recognizable and identifiable. The tulip will be discussed below. Carnations and roses were others that found favor in both the garden and in embroidery.

176

FIGURE 337   Red cotton and brown silk cross stitch.

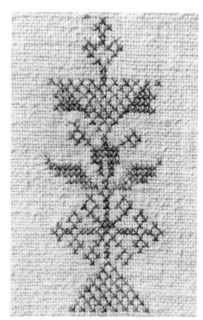

FIGURE 339   Balanced plain weave linen fabric; red cotton cross stitch.[228]

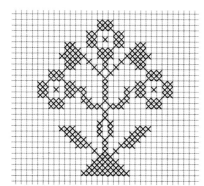

FIGURE 338[201]

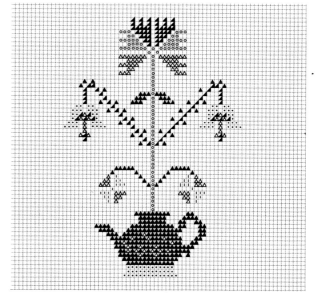

FIGURE 341[234]

FIGURE 340   Balanced plain weave linen fabric; red cotton brown silk cross stitch; self plain fringe. See Figure 169 for top half of towel. W.17¼".[1211]

FIGURE 342 The straight lines on the handles and upper sides of the urn indicate a half a cross stitch or a diagonal straight stitch, not a different color.[261]

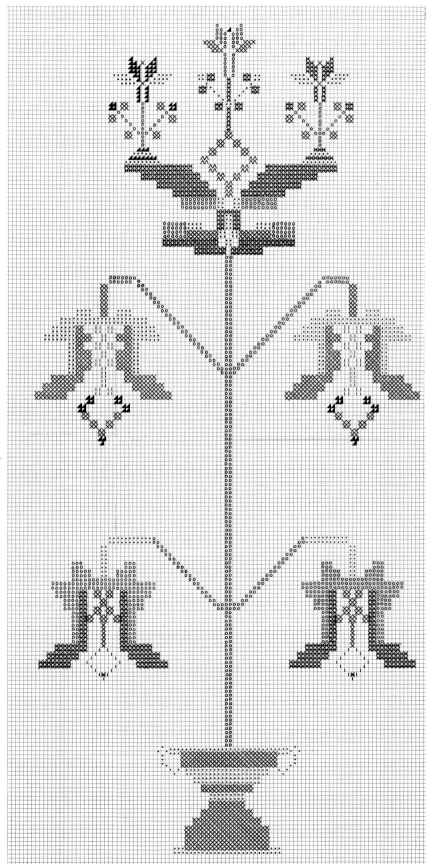

FIGURE 343

179

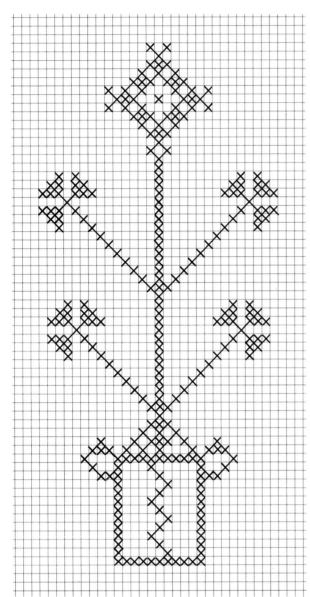

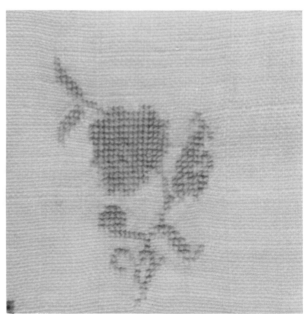

FIGURE 346 A more realistic than geometric rose motif. Red cotton cross stitch.[442] Courtesy, Hershey Museum of American Life.

FIGURE 347 Red and blue cotton, tan and gold silk cross stitch. This single rose with buds and leaves was sewn in each of four imaginary corners around a larger arrangement of roses. See Figures 182, 348.[750]

FIGURE 344 (above)[553]

FIGURE 345 (below)[695]

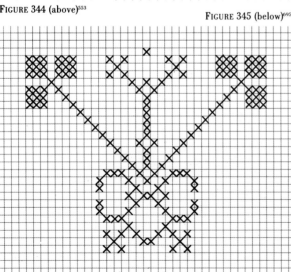

FIGURE 348 Red and blue cotton, tan and gold silk cross stitch. This large arrangement of roses was centered near the bottom of the towel and surrounded with additional roses. See Figure 347, 182.[750]

[Figure 346] Lydia Kurtz was apparently a rose fancier for she embroidered an unusual quantity of roses on her 1846 towel. [Plate 12] All of her designs presented a more natural, lifelike image than usually found. Perhaps a reason for this was that each rose was very finely sewn with brightly colored wools and the finished work resembled needlepoint more than cross stitch.[469] [Figures 347, 348]

Roses in drawn thread embroidery were identified by their round, eight petaled blossom. Some were found in baskets[103] and handled urns,[191] or as a single floweret.[299]

Other flowers can be distinguished by shape. There are star, heart, square, diamond and triangular flowers. Perhaps to the folk mind some of these embroidered figurations represented thistles, fuchsias, stars of Bethlehem, or other well known garden flowers. Or their easily changeable geometric proportions, rather than familiarity, made them desirable for embroidery. Very few were alike. [Figures 349-352]

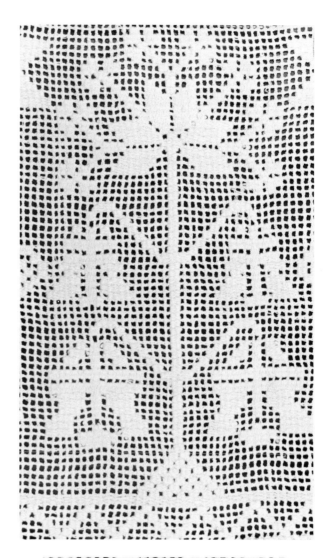

FIGURE 349 One of the largest flowers sewn on a drawn thread grid measures 13¾ inches high. White cotton darning stitch.[35]

FIGURE 350. (upper right) White cotton darning stitch. An almost identical motif was cross stitched on the same towel, but it had a peacock on top and the flower emerged from a crown.[545] Courtesy, Pennsylvania Farm Museum of Landis Valley, Lancaster.

FIGURE 351 (right) A flower in a pitcher sewn in white cotton darning stitch. The applied fringe was white cotton yarns tied into every other grid space and knotted in a diamond pattern for three-quarter inches. The free-falling fringed threads are 2½ inches long.[137]

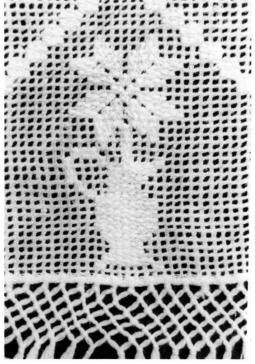

181

FIGURE 352 Free-form flower embroidered on a leno woven panel with units of the darning stitch and a chain stitched curved stem.[50]

There were more star-shaped flowers and carnations than any other kinds. [Figures 353-356] Susanna Kauffman made two towels, one in 1823[259] and the other in 1827,[260] and embroidered the same large grouping of carnations in the drawn thread panel of each towel. Sallme Friederick, 1838,[293] and HSF[93] sewed the same carnation emerging from a heart, and MK, 1842,[201] and Anna Ruttin, 1804,[404] used the identical three carnation flowers in a basket motif. Two additional towels each without name or date have embroidered on their thread panel a large matching carnation and tulip floral arrangement.[202,370] It was interesting to note that Anna Ruttin 1804,[404] MK, 1842,[201] and Esther Niszley, 1821,[609] all embroidered the same floral arrangement on their drawn thread panel. The girls probably lived in the vicinity of Manheim township, Lancaster county and traded and copied this motif at least between the years 1804 and 1842. Flowers continue to produce evidence that needleworkers swapped embroidery designs.

Tulips, discussed below, and carnations were the two primary types of flowers sewn in free-form fashion on decorated towels. [Figure 357] The carnation generally had circular notched edges executed by careful placement of the chain,[718] satin,[732] or straight stitch.[285] One towel maker embroidered in turkey red a clearly defined fuchsia of the type often seen in Victorian transfer embroideries. It was unmistakably a design from the popular culture worked on a folk textile. [Figure 358]

In each type of embroidery seen on Pennsylvania decorated towels, counted thread, drawn thread, and free-form, the abundance of flower motifs was most noticeable. It was, by far, the largest design category of all the embroidery motifs we have recorded. To view these flowers is to walk through a pleasure-garden, a conservatory, a nursery, a kitchen garden. They are instant springtime!

FIGURE 353 A flower and border in red cotton and brown silk cross stitch.[107]

FIGURE 354 An arrangement of what could be acorns with a star flower. Red cotton, cross stitch.[1218]

FIGURE 355   Red cotton, brown silk cross stitch.

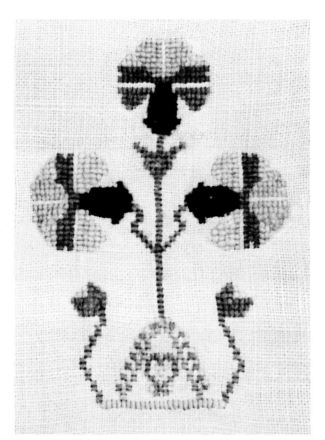

FIGURE 356   Dark blue, gold, yellow, red, and pink wool cross stitch.[18] Courtesy, Dr. and Mrs. Donald M. Herr.

FIGURE 357   Balanced plain weave cotton fabric; multi color chain stitch.

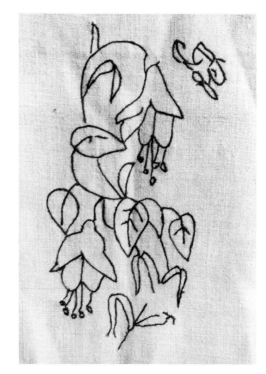

FIGURE 358 (right)   Balanced plain weave linen fabric; red cotton, outline stitch.[447] Courtesy, Goschenhoppen Folklife Museum and Library, Green Lane.

183

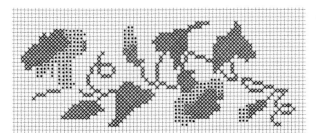

FIGURE 359   Morning glory vine.[3]

FIGURE 360   Balanced plain weave linen fabric; red cotton, outline stitch.[447] Courtesy, Goschenhoppen Folklife Museum and Library, Green Lane.

FIGURE 361   Balanced plain weave cotton fabric; yellow, pink, red, and olive green wool chain stitch. See Figure 194.[1312]

Corner flowers

The term "corner flowers" distinguishes those flowers that originated in a corner and emerged diagonally onto the towel. The decorated towel was divided into paneled areas which in turn created many corners with which the embroiderer had to deal. Flowers placed diagonally in the bottom right and left corner provided a needed stopping point for the movement of design within the panel. Rarely this pair of flowers faced opposite directions or hung down from the upper corners. [Figure 23]

Corner flower designs were variations of the other floral themes. They had one main stem with two branches. Carnations rank first among the flowers that were embroidered on the stem and branches, [Figures 362-364] but roses, star-like flowers, and other *Blumme* are used at the embroiderer's discretion. [Figures 365-370] Greater variety existed in the shape of the containers in which the flowers sat. Square and triangular forms are common; other stems just began as if growing from the corner.

Corner flowers embroidered on drawn thread panels were not found as often as cross stitched examples. They were small and emerged diagonally from the corner of a border[126] or from a square shaped vessel.[933] [Figure 145]

FIGURE 362   Corner flower with one opened blossom and two flower buds. Red cotton, cross stitch.[131]

184

FIGURE 363 Corner flower of carnations. Red and blue cotton cross stitch.[191]

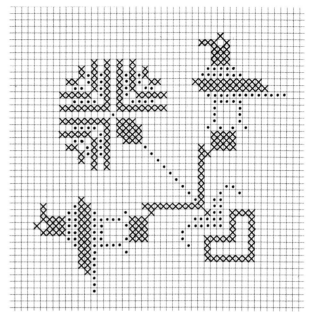

FIGURE 365[732]

FIGURE 366 Red cotton, cross stitch.[196] Courtesy, Clarke E. Hess.

FIGURE 364 (left) Red cotton cross stitch.[196] Courtesy, Clarke E. Hess.

185

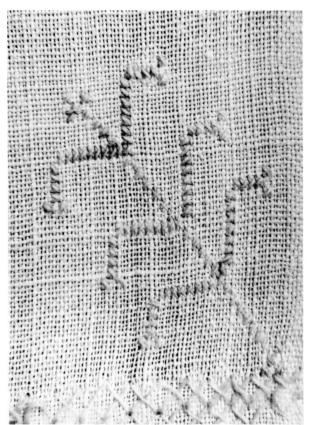

FIGURE 367 One of the simplist corner flower motifs; it appears to grow out of the earth. Red cotton cross stitch.[119]

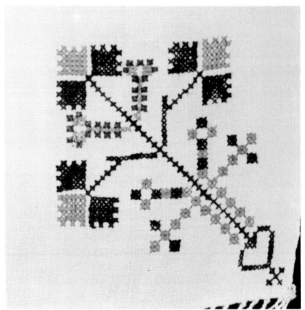

FIGURE 369 Red and blue cotton cross stitch.[559] Courtesy, Mr. and Mrs. Richard F. Smith.

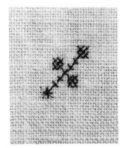

FIGURE 368 One of the smallest corner flowers. Red cotton, cross stitch except at the bottom where the stem springs from a double cross stitch.[132]

FIGURE 370[261]

186

Tulips

If ever there were a national election for an official Pennsylvania Dutch flower, the tulip would surely be the first candidate. Its widespread use in Pennsylvania Dutch folk art is evidence of the remarkable appeal and intrinsic significance of this flower. The impact and vast quantities of tulip motifs in Pennsylvania Dutch needlework is recognized far beyond the borders of the Dutch country. It is one of the loveliest designs found on decorated towels. The tulip was one of the commonest springtime garden flowers in Dutchland.

For these reasons we have separated *tulipa* from all other genus of flowers that embellish towels. The tulip is distinguished in cross stitch needlework by its three large petals. Its buds and opened blossoms were depicted in baskets,[18,365] [Figures 371, 372] a sgraffito urn,[545] a dish,[467] a pitcher,[18] [Figure 373] or on a stand.[547] Single or multiple tulips were arranged with carnations and other flowers, or they were supported only by a leafy foliage. They emerged from single or double hearts,[13,170,273,624] [Figure 374, 36] diamond shapes,[340,366] or the earth.[68,427,546] [Figures 375-382]

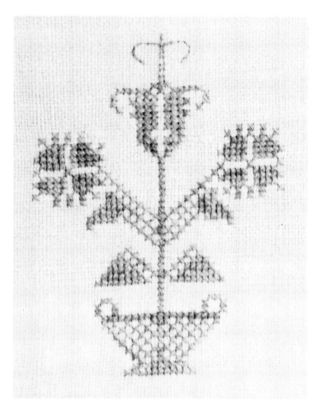

FIGURE 372   Red cotton, cross stitch. Each backstitch above the tulip is two threads long.[708] Courtesy, Sally and Pete Riffle.

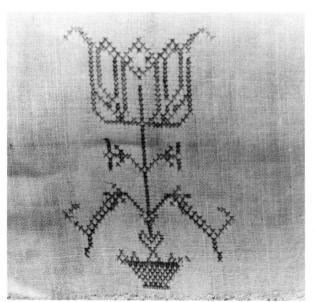

FIGURE 371   Red and blue cotton, cross stitch.[62]

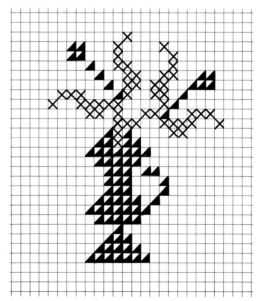

FIGURE 373[18]   Courtesy, Dr. and Mrs. Donald M. Herr.

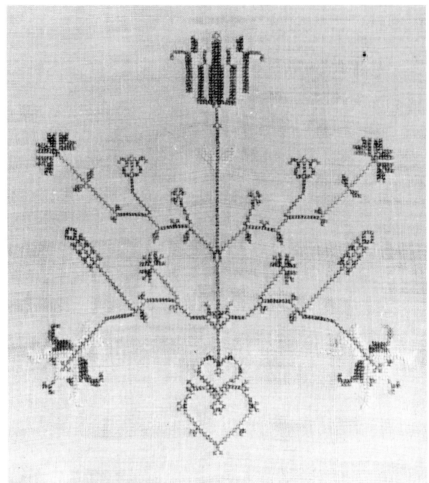

FIGURE 374   Red and blue cotton, cross stitch. See Figure 130.[273]

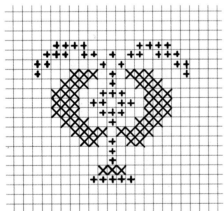

FIGURE 375[427]

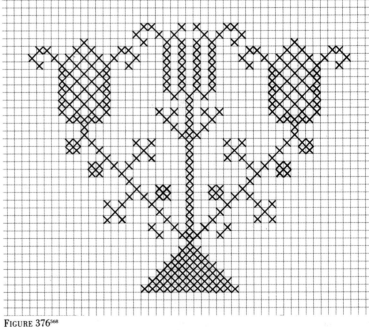

FIGURE 376[568]

188

FIGURE 377   Red cotton, cross stitch.[746] Courtesy, Sally and Pete Riffle.

FIGURE 378   Red and blue cotton cross stitch.

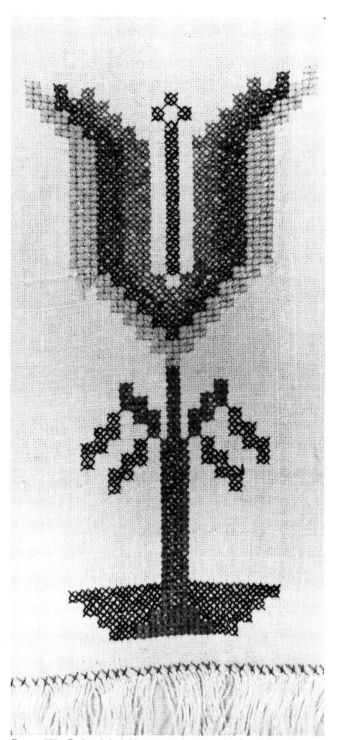

FIGURE 379   Red and dark blue cotton, brown and yellow silk cross stitch; self plain fringe. See Figure 180.[1275]

189

FIGURE 380   Red cotton cross stitch.[1278]

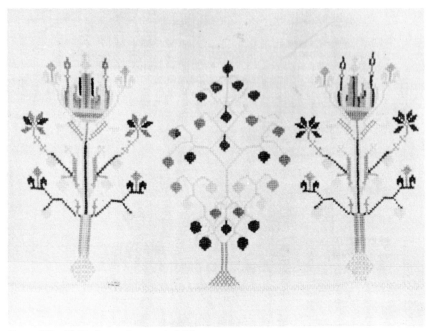

FIGURE 382   Multicolor wool cross stitch.[1264]

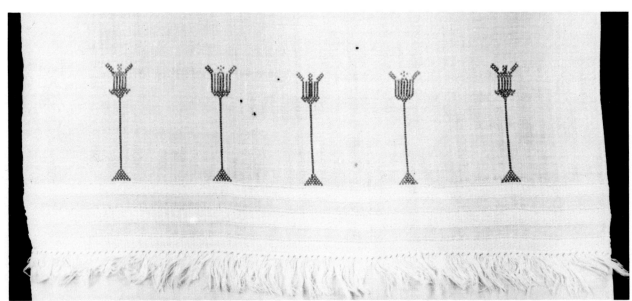

FIGURE 381   Red cotton cross stitch. Pattern woven bands in white linen; self plain fringe.[1278]

FIGURE 383   White cotton darning stitch. Threads were knotted into every grid space before falling into a 3½ inch long fringe. 5¼" x 14½".[98]

For an instant women appear to have gone on a rampage of *tulipomania*. Prolific and divergent depictions of tulips were staggering. Four young ladies however, step forward with a common tulip motif to remind us gently of tradition.

Elisabeth Dor[n]bach, 1821,[282] Sara Lauch, 1824,[311] Susanna Miller, 1840,[254] and Mary Hershey, 1845,[68] within a twenty-four year span, each embroidered the identical cross stitch tulip on their towels. The major difference was the container that held the three tulips and two star flowers. Elisabeth and Susanna sewed a single handled pitcher while Sara and Mary chose a double handled urn. Elisabeth's towel, dated 1821, was sewn in red cotton and brown silk which was a typical color combination of the earlier period of decorating towels. Susanna and Mary used all red and Sara chose red with dark and light blue, all more representative of a later date.

Some drawn thread tulip buds and blossoms are shown as in nature. [Figure 383, 60] Others are in receptacles such as a star,[187] a heart, [277,412,440] [Figure 384] a diamond, [136] a basket,[103] a crown,[92,249] an urn,[35,418,545] [Figure 64] and a pitcher.[417]

Elizabeth Fry, 1818,[61] Elizabeth Yocum, 1852,[123] and other towel makers[92] embroidered only the tulip flower on a short stem. On the other hand, many mature tulip plants were shown emerging from the earth.[6,98,240,249,404] Elisabeth Diehl embroidered the same opened tulip and

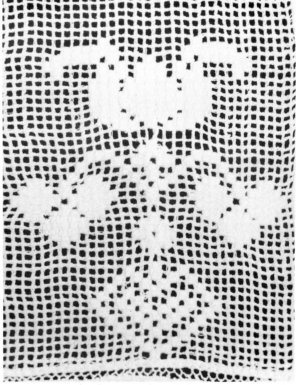

FIGURE 384   White cotton darning stitch except on the stem. The stitches did not interlock in the center which created an eyelet effect.[277]

191

four tulip buds on the drawn thread panel as she did in satin stitch on the woven towel fabric.[25] Parallels between cross stitch and drawn thread tulips are often apparent.[571] [Plate 49]

Tulips were the favorite hand drawn flower and they took on assorted sizes, shapes, and embroidery stitches. [Figures 385, 386; Plate 21] Petals and leaves were outlined and filled with satin,[461,722] chain,[43,356,509,745] and threaded straight stitch.[709] BP, 1818, combined counted thread and free-form embroidery by placing a chain stitch tulip atop a large branched and leafed stem sewn in cross stitch.[289] Tulips emerging from a heart are on a gracefully curved stem that extends the full width of the towel. The initials SB and date 1812 are carefully placed inside this large motif.[1219]

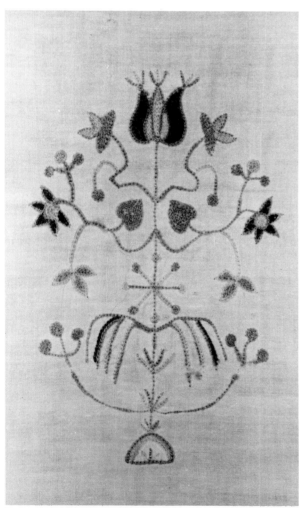

FIGURE 385 Multicolor wool, chain stitch.

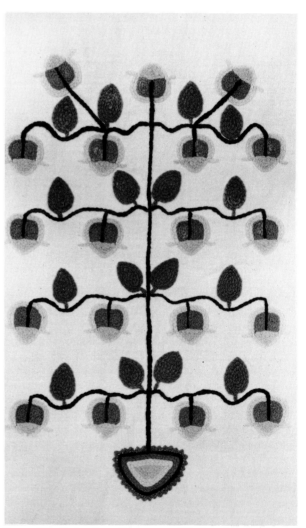

FIGURE 386 Red, yellow, olive green, and black wool chain stitch. 11" x 8".[552] Courtesy, Mr. and Mrs. Richard F. Smith

Hearts

The heart was the core and "noble heart" of the distinctive OEHBDDE design (see p. 205) and also a shape conducive to embodying names, dates, and epigraphs. This symbol was an intrinsic and individual representative of towel tradition. Beyond its elementary form, the embroidered heart developed as the support and sustainer of flowers, [Figure 36] birds, and crown motifs. [Figure 27]

Little individual hearts were filled with stitchery,[18,351,440] while others remained open[243,247,436] or had partially opened and decorative centers.[365] Some contained initials. [Plate 37] A single or double row of stitchery[426] or blocked units of cross stitches[68,107,114] formed round, pointed, elongated, or irregularly shaped heart designs.

Small and medium sized heart motifs were commonly placed symmetrically within a paneled area, but combinations of hearts were put together making one large motif which highlighted a panel. Catarina Hege illustrated this in a small way, for she sewed one heart directly above another to make one design unit.[545] The concept of using two hearts together was enlarged to even greater proportions by Mary Reist who arranged the two hearts back to back and added three elaborately flowered stems emerging from each heart and one extending from each side where the hearts are joined.[234] [Figure 387]

Four hearts were aligned in a circular pattern to form a type of small flower.[59,106,246] [Figure 388] Lea Iungst magnified the ring of four small hearts by embroidering and arranging four larger hearts with their apex to the center. A stem and three carnations emerged from each of the four hearts to construct an almost square overall form.[66] [Figure 389] A similar circular arrangement of four hearts was also used as a vehicle in which to record a year.[1,711] [Figure 320]

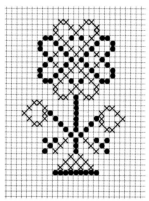

FIGURE 388[106]

FIGURE 387 Red and blue cotton cross stitch.[562] Courtesy, Mr. and Mrs. Richard F. Smith.

FIGURE 389 Red and blue cotton cross stitch.[66]

Heart shapes were sewn at the end of branches on a tree as if they were flower buds. The uppermost heart on the tree, however, was topped with a crown.[150] [Figure 390] It was the single heart motif, and not a grouping of two or four hearts, that supported large and small regal crowns. [Figures 391, 392] Each heart and each crown design was personalized before integration into one motif. Variations abound.

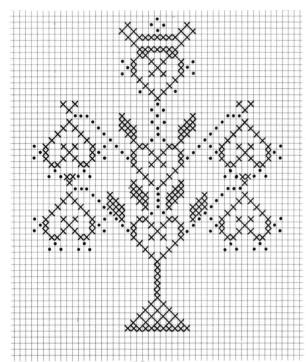

FIGURE 390[171]

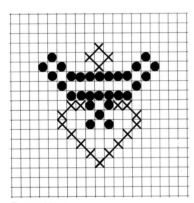

FIGURE 391[106]

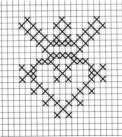

FIGURE 392[331]

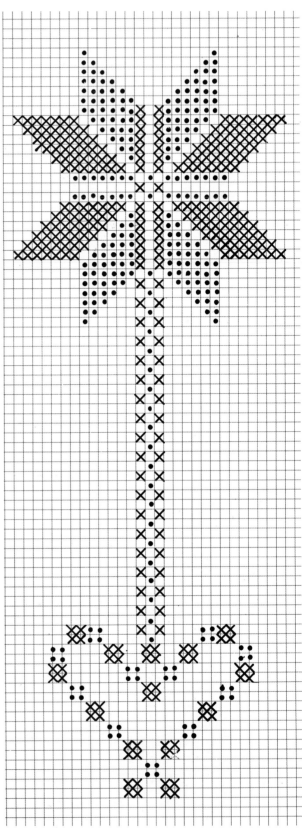

FIGURE 393[580]

194

Hearts were embedded in flowers,[18] or they gave rise to a small single bud,[56] one open bloom,[580] [Figure 393] or a multiple stemmed bouquet.[62,150,230] [Figures 394, 395] In fact, Maria Knece, 1822, embroidered an eleven inch high floral bouquet that stemmed from a heart.[1199] Anna Anganey put four small birds roosting in the flowers,[479] but often two birds alight on each lobe of the heart if no flowers are present.[135,562] Sara Speicherin combined birds and a small heart with crown by placing the crowned heart between the beaks of two small erect birds.[189] [Figure 396]

Heart designs in drawn thread did not occur as frequently as hearts in cross stitch. They seldom contained names, initials, and years, nor were they aligned in circular formations or grouped as flower trees. They were however, sewn with open,[137,307] [Figure 397] closed,[14] or decorative centers.[138,200] [Figure 398] One design was composed of three hearts inside one another.[1129] Drawn thread hearts gave rise to flowers,[126,273] [Figures 60, 384] crowns,[427,609] and one appeared to have a Latin cross between the two lobes.[332]

Individually sewn free-style hearts such as the two small chain stitched hearts sewn by one towel maker are uncommon.[384] Free-form hearts more often encompassed a name or initials, but even that is not typical. [Figure 132]

FIGURE 394   Red cotton and brown silk cross stitch.[230]

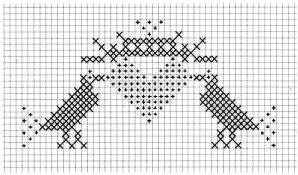

FIGURE 396.[189]

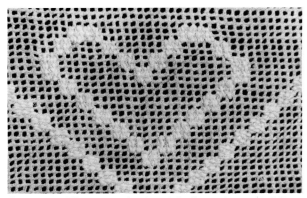

FIGURE 397   White cotton darning stitch all sewn in a vertical direction. The three by three thread grid is smaller than ones usually found.[137]

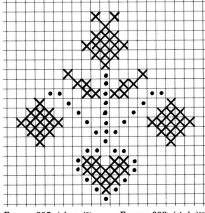

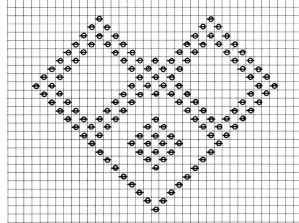

FIGURE 395. (above)[76]   FIGURE 398. (right)[307]

195

Household articles

Immediate surroundings inspired some cross stitch designs. The stretcher-base table and ladder back chair were favorite pieces of household furniture sewn onto towels.[269,553,574,803] The embroiderer set the table with a decanter of red wine, two filled wine glasses, and then placed a ladder back chair at each end of the table as if waiting for guests to arrive. [Figure 399] This grouping of furniture was usually embroidered as a unit and seldom sewn individually although single chairs [Figure 400] and a small bench-like table without chairs have been seen occasionally.[1208] [Figure 401]

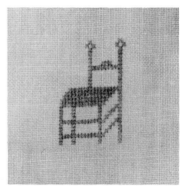

FIGURE 400   Red cotton cross stitch chair.

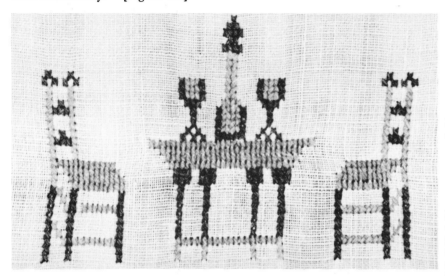

FIGURE 399 (left)   Red and blue cotton cross stitch.[574]

FIGURE 401 (below)   Interior scene that includes a table with wine decanter and wine glasses, two ladder back chairs, and two ladies each wearing a hat with up-turned brim and carrying a tulip. Red cotton cross stitch.[1208]

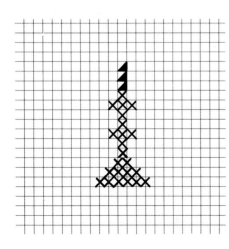

FIGURE 402. (left)   [269]

FIGURE 403 (right)   Red and blue cotton cross stitch. See Figure 182.[750]

Catarina Kemper probably used her family's tea table in 1799 as a model for a towel design. She was able to depict the "birdcage" underneath it, the bulbous turnings on the center leg, and three feet. She then placed on the table top a seven-armed candelabra which was as large as the table.[76]

In addition to these pieces of furniture, small ordinary objects such as a candlestick with candle,[269] [Figure 402] scissors,[452,750] [Figure 403] an hour glass,[119] wooden pump,[1271] [Figure 404] an empty wine glass,[201,288] flagon with lid,[5,24,116] [Figure 405; Plate 35] pitcher,[333,361] and coffee pot[1283] [Figures 406,18] were all preserved with needle and thread.

Wide and narrow empty baskets with footed [620] or flat bases,[368] or baskets with one large handle reaching over the entire top[620] or with one smaller handle at each side[368] were everyday objects easily copied in cross stitch. Stitch placement and color combinations suggest that some baskets were extraordinary. [Figure 407]

Pennsylvania Dutch women have long been known for their love of flowers so it was natural for them to embroider a basketful of roses onto a towel. That tells us, among other things, another use for the basket. The roses and green foliage are depicted in either a primitive style[111,134,254] [Plate 16] or in more realistic fashion with color shading worked into each blossom.[345] Magdalene Dienner, 1859, embroidered her red roses with a yellow center reminiscent of the *Rosa gallica* 'Officinalis' so popular throughout the Dutch country at that time.[286]

It was these same small household articles that were depicted in drawn thread and free-form embroidery: pitcher,[62,491] flagon,[16] key,[624] [Figure 408] a pair of candlesticks together with a pair of wick trimmers,[1256] [Figure 504] and wine glasses.[24,299,311,373] [Figure 504] An empty basket or one filled with flowers was not often embroidered on a drawn thread grid or sewn in a free-style. ER in 1828 embroidered a two handled basket on a drawn thread grid—perhaps her sewing basket.[355]

After the Egelmann copybook appeared in 1831 with designs "For Marking On Linen" ladies began to include his urn on their towels. This design, copied from this printed source, was certainly not drafted from the original vessel.[4] [Figures 7, 222]

FIGURE 405 Red cotton cross stitch.[116]

FIGURE 406 Coffee pot. Black and tan silk cross and chain stitches. Borders of zigzag hemstitching, chain stitch and threaded straight stitch. See Figure 18.[1283]

FIGURE 407 Red and blue cotton cross stitch. The top border was sewn in red cotton chain stitch.[102]

FIGURE 404 The wooden pump with spout and up-turned iron handle.[1271]

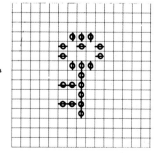

FIGURE 408.[624]

197

Human figures

Human figures—men, women and children—are a relatively uncommon motif on towels. Men and women appear together in pairs with their empty arms extended, placed on the hip, or holding hands,[796] [Figure 409] but women alone were portrayed more frequently.[72,142,144,248] [Figures 410-412, 77]

One towel maker depicted a lady standing under an arched bower.[367] Lydia Pepley sewed a woman wearing a large hat with up-turned brim who had one arm resting on her hip. The other arm was extended and held a crown.[792] This same design was sewn on another towel, but the woman wearing the large hat held a tulip, not a crown.[1208] [Figure 401] Margaret Kresman, 1827, embroidered two women pointing to flowers placed between them.[588] Women were also occasionally positioned atop a blooming flower in a more symbolic placement than in a life-like situation.[264,467,685,1313] [Figure 165; Plates 36,43] Men were more often depicted in cross stitch than in drawn thread or free-form embroidery. They stood straight and stiff as if posing for their portrait.[466,755] [Figure 413]

Embroidered people wore the clothing of the day such as knee breeches,[443,796,1195] coat,[111] [Plate 16] hat,[111] hat with an upright Indian-like feather projecting from the crown,[554] [Figure 414] gowns,[467] and caps[467] all of which did not detract from the fascinating proportions of their bodies. Earrings and fingers were even accented by thread color or embroidery stitch.[467] [Figure 77]

People were embroidered on towels as part of a dra-

FIGURE 409   The man's hat is sewn in gold silk and both faces are in white linen. His eyes are gold silk, hers blue cotton. Each has a red mouth. His head is outlined in gold silk and her head in dark blue cotton. The woman's entire outfit is embroidered in red cotton and she has dark blue stockings and shoes. The man's clothing, however, consists of a red cotton long sleeved shirt with a light blue cotton vertical stripe down the bosom, dark blue cotton knee breeches, light blue cotton stockings and dark blue cotton shoes with heels. All cross stitch.[796]

FIGURE 410   Red cotton cross stitch.[58]

FIGURE 411   Red and blue cotton cross stitch. See Figure 143.[1314]

matic event. One wonders at the drama that must have taken place to inspire sisters Elisabeth[466] and Anna[755] Frey each to devote an entire panel on their towel to a hunting scene, containing two cross stitched huntsmen, one blowing a horn, astride galloping steeds following a pack of dogs chasing a stag and chicken-like bird. [Plate 29] Human figures also occur in the Adam and Eve[111] [Plate 16] and Joshua and Caleb [620,1208] motifs. [Figures 427,428]

Another unusual or action-filled design unit that included embroidered people was the tall and narrow stately four-wheeled carriage pulled by a team of horses complete with doubletrees and harness. Two birds perched on the roof and a pendant-of-sorts hung from the ceiling inside. A driver stood in front with reins, a watchful footman was at the rear, and inside the carriage sat a gentleman smoking a pipe! This motif seems to

FIGURE 413 Red and blue cotton cross stitch.[620] Courtesy, North Museum of Franklin and Marshall College, Lancaster.

FIGURE 412 Red cotton cross stitch.[706] Courtesy, Sally and Pete Riffle.

FIGURE 414.[554]

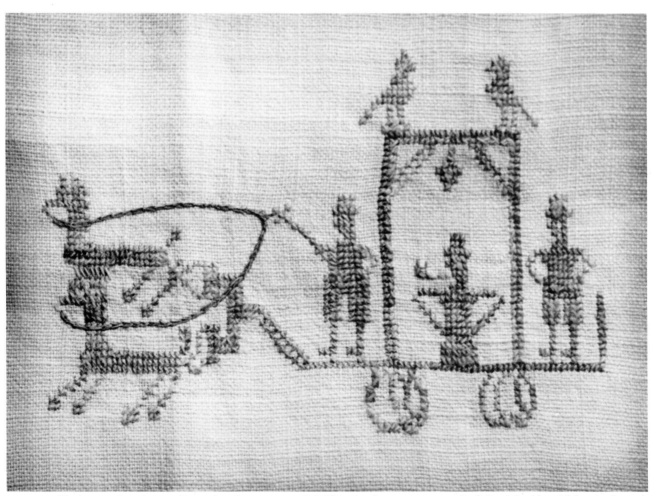

FIGURE 415 The horse and carriage motif sewn in red cotton cross stitch. The reins, however, were sewn in chain stitch with a tightly twisted two ply blue cotton. Short straight stitches denote the pipe.[792] Courtesy, Collection of Renfrew Museum, Waynesboro. Photographer Dan Arthur, Waynesboro.

have received little or no personalization for it appears to be almost identical on all the towels. Color is the only variation.[357,590,792,1196,1208] It has appeared on towels dated from 1808[1196] to 1827.[1208] [Figures 415, 30, 174]

In 1827, Susanna Herr cross stitched a wreath of flowers and two angels with wings, one positioned on each side of the wreath.[951] Eva Lani embroidered what appear to be winged angels on her drawn thread grid,[1178] but angels, with or without a garland of flowers, were seldom seen on Pennsylvania towels.

If human figures were darned onto the drawn thread grid it was most likely that of the woman who stood by herself with her hands on her hips.[837] [Figure 153] On one towel, however, she was carrying a branch of flowers,[29] [Figure 140, 61] and on other towels she was standing on top of an opened flower blossom.[370,510] One lady, without legs or feet, carried a bird and urn; some women were armless;[1150] some were rotund;[1256] most were slender.

Distinguishing features that were sewn into the woman's garb included tucks or a woven border at the hemline of the petticoat,[62,139] and an apron.[566] Vertical stripes and cross-shaped decorations in the petticoat plus a crown on top of her head gave one woman a queenly appearance.[195] [Figure 67] Body and facial features such as the woman's eyes, nose, mouth, and breasts were sometimes accented with color, additional stitch, or empty grid space. [Figure 416] One embroidered lady appears to smile at the viewer.[194,1117,1220] [Figure 417] MAIGI embroidered a short armed woman who wore a red and white dress, red shoes, and had red eyes.[815] Women were often sewn in pairs, but one towel maker had six women in one panel.[1286] Men were seen on drawn thread grids even less than in cross stitch. [Figure 418] ML darned a man with two outstretched arms positioned between two women, each of whom was reaching towards him.[587]

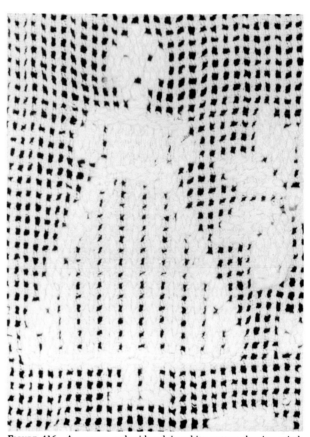

FIGURE 416 A woman embroidered in white cotton darning stitch whose eyes, mouth, and striped petticoat were denoted by the absence of stitches.[1182]

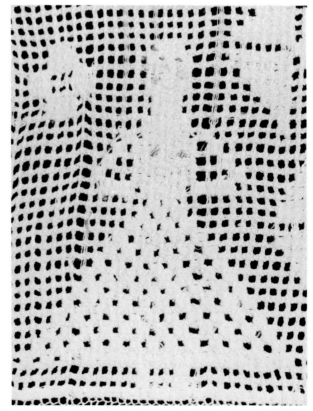

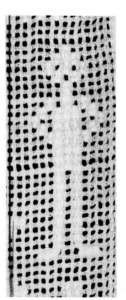

FIGURE 417 (right) White cotton darning stitch. Red cotton straight stitches were sewn on top of the darning stitches to indicate face and body features.[194] Courtesy, Sally and Pete Riffle.

FIGURE 418 (left) White cotton darning stitch.

A person outlined and embroidered in free-form occurs less often than versions sewn in cross stitch or drawn thread. The few people recorded to date were members of a panel of symmetrically arranged free-form designs. Two women, sewn in red cotton, stood on each side of a tree with bird on top. Their arms were folded across their chest and they were filled solid with spiral rows of chain stitch.[495]

Pattern woven textile motifs

Both cross stitch and drawn thread designs were copied from pattern woven textiles. The weaving tradition of the Pennsylvania Germans was a discipline with roots reaching back at least as far as the embroidery of textiles. The weavers had certain motifs which they recognized by name, among others *Ballen, Stern, Rosen, Kreutz, Hertz, Ross mit vier Augen, Gens Augen*. Some of these motifs appear on the decorated towels in either

cross stitch or drawn thread work, just as patterns from the Jacquard coverlets do. [Figures 419, 420]

The rose which Anna Gehman did in her drawn panel is identical to those found on both double cloth and damask twill coverlets.[420] The cross stitch rose with its surrounding circles on Barbara Ellenberger's 1827 towel could have been lifted from a twenty shaft coverlet.[266] [Figures 421, 422]

Motifs appear to have been copied from Jacquard coverlets in a slightly later period.[1267] [Figure 423] In 1846, Rabacka Hiestand used a design which was used by Solomon Kuder on his coverlets in the 1840s.[116] [Figures 424, 425] Susanna Miller of Annville township, Lebanon county, in 1840, used commonly found coverlet border motifs on her towel—the eagle, and a flower stalk along with a center star motif.[254] Susana Rock used another border member, the fruit tree, and colored it with a blue trunk and red branches, just as it would have appeared on a Jacquard coverlet.[561] [Figure 426]

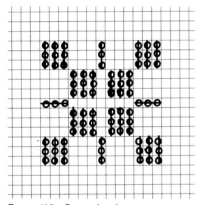

FIGURE 419 Cross taken from pattern woven fabric design on towel dated 1826.[334]

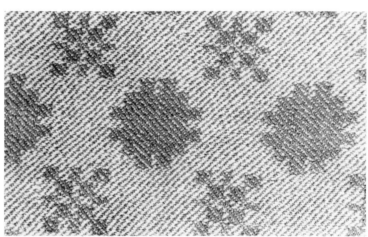

FIGURE 420 Coverlet. Double faced twill with balls and crosses in blue and yellow wool. Southeastern Pennsylvania c. 1820.

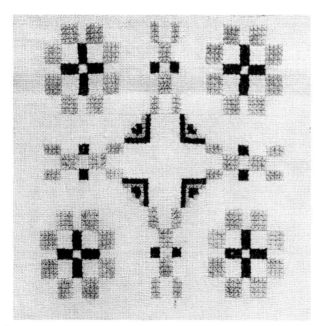

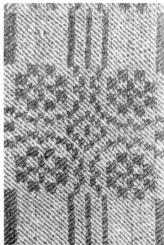

FIGURE 421 (left) Red and blue cotton cross stitch rose design copied from a coverlet pattern.[266] Courtesy, Abby Aldrich Rockefeller Folk Art Center, Williamsburg, Virginia.

FIGURE 422 (above) Coverlet. Double faced twill roses in red and blue wool. c.1830 Southeastern Pennsylvania.

201

FIGURE 423 Red cotton cross stitched designs that were probably copied from woven coverlets.[254]

FIGURES 424, 425 A pattern woven on a Jacquard coverlet by Solomon Kuder, weaver in Lehigh county, was copied in cross stitch almost thread for thread onto a balanced plain weave cotton towel dated 1846. On the coverlet the design was red, blue, and green wool with white cotton ground. On the towel it was embroidered in red cotton.[116]

FIGURE 426 Red and blue cotton cross stitch.[561] Courtesy, Mr. and Mrs. Richard F. Smith.

Religious motifs

Bible stories illustrated with needle and thread are among the rarest designs sewn on Pennsylvania towels. This type of needlework is more closely associated with European embroidery than with anything sewn by the Pennsylvania Germans. Only a few examples have been found to date.

The first Bible story presented on a decorated towel is that of Adam and Eve (Genesis 3). Elisabeth Gotschal, 1825, illustrated Adam and Eve after the fall; they are both fully clothed including shoes and hat! They stand on either side of the tree with the forbidden fruit and serpent. Eve holds an apple in her right hand and if there were any doubt about identification the letter *A* is embroidered over Adam's head and the letter *E* over Eve's.[111] [Plate 16]

Catharine Over, 1827,[1208] and Catharine Meck, in 1841,[620] embroidered the two spies returning from the land of Canaan bearing a cluster of grapes on a staff between them. (Numbers 13, 14). It is a single unit cross stitch design placed by itself and is not part of a larger scene. The Catherine Meck towel also has inscriptions sewn in both English and Pennsylvania High German, but it is the English wording that assured the towel's Pennsylvania origin. [Figures 427, 428] SD went one step further and embroidered Joshua and Caleb in her drawn thread panel.[1210] [Figure 429]

Occasionally there is an object embroidered on a towel which looks like a monstrance, the container to hold a consecrated host for processions in the Roman Catholic religion. Since there were very few Catholics among the Pennsylvania Germans, this is probably an example of a motif which was added without its meaning.[1285] [Figures 430, 431, 177]

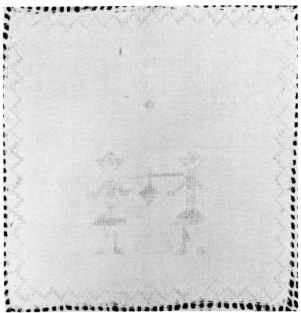

FIGURE 428   Joshua and Caleb. Red cotton cross stitch.[1208]

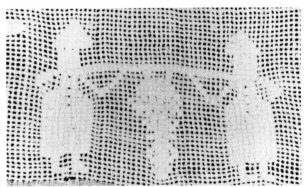

FIGURE 429   Joshua and Caleb. White cotton darning stitch.[1210]

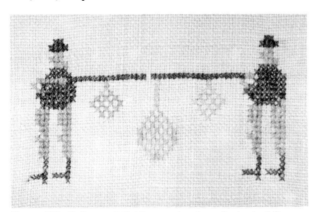

FIGURE 427   Joshua and Caleb returning from the land of Canaan. Red and blue cotton cross stitch.[620] Courtesy, North Museum of Franklin and Marshall College, Lancaster.

FIGURE 430   Green and gold silk cross stitch.[1285]

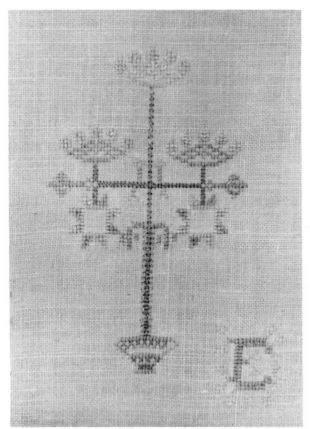

FIGURE 431 Green and gold silk cross stitch.[1285]

FIGURE 432 Red cotton and brown silk cross stitch. Top border is red cotton herringbone and white linen stitching. See Figure 146.[1261]

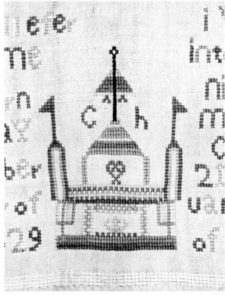

FIGURE 433 Dark red, cream, gold, pink, red, and mauve wool cross stitch.[611]

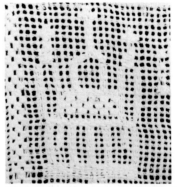

FIGURE 434 White cotton darning stitch.[1055]

Five towels, one dated 1799,[1261] [Figure 432] one 1827,[1317] [Plate 45] another 1847,[611] and two without dates[926,1055] have a motif that may have been intended to be the city gate of the heavenly Jerusalem, [Figure 434] a theme compatible with the religious mentality of the Pennsylvania Germans, or an altar, an ornate table with a cross and two candles. An altar scene does stand on Susanna Killefer's towel on which she records her first communion. In that instance the letters CH occur right over it. Do they mean church, or perhaps Christ?[611] [Figure 433] The altar motifs seem to have candle flames sometimes and even a tabernacle, the little cupboard in Roman Catholic altars for retaining consecrated hosts after the Mass. Another form of altar which is clearly a table with baroque legs, two candles and a cross in the center is probably related to these motifs.[1038] [Figure 435] Such altars were not to be found in the Protestant churches in the Dutch country when towels were being made, so that this too, may be a motif without clear intention.

The same Elisabeth Gotschal who sewed Adam and Eve on her towel also cross stitched a heart with crown design to the right and left of center. The heart was elaborated with flowers at the sides and top and included the initials RH. Although one cannot be certain, these initials may stand for *reines Herz* (pure heart). We know they are not the initials of her husband Peter Metz.[111] [Plate 19]

204

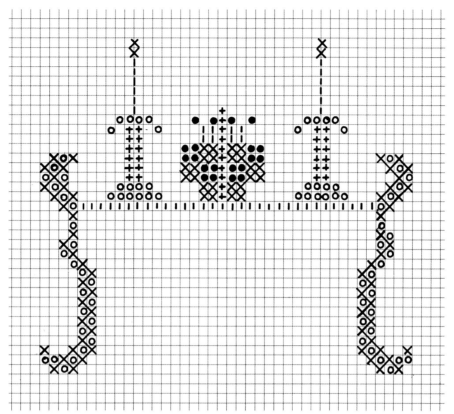

FIGURE 435.[1038]

The design that stands above all others among religious symbols and provokes comment most often features a heart in the center, a crown above, and branches with flowers of sorts extending from the heart. Surrounding the whole in either a clockwise or counterclockwise direction are the initials OEHBDDE. Each initial, in this case, represents a major syllable in the words, *O Edel Herz Bedenk Dein End* (O noble heart, consider your end). There is interest in the design itself and all its variations and in the religious admonition that surrounds it. [Figure 436; Plates 17, 28]

In 1946 Frances Lichten first published the design with the initials and what she felt their meaning was. (Lichten, 56)

Lichten was correct. The initials OEHBDDE are for the epigram that is the first line of a couplet that may be from a hymn: *O edel Herz bedenk dein End, Wer weist wie nah der Lauf vollend* (O noble heart, consider your end; who knows how soon the course is run).

The earliest example known of the entire couplet is dated 1794 on a piece of *Fraktur* from the Goschenhoppen area in Montgomery county. (Garvan, 313) A 1791 *Fraktur* from the same area, now in the Schwenkfelder Library, bears only the first line, the one whose initials occur on *Fraktur*. [Figure 437] Since the initials occur for the first time on towels after 1799 we are unable to say whether the saying came to Pennsylvania with the design (which seems unlikely) or was added to it here. As early as 1827 there was an example of this design's use without the OEHBDDE initials.[266] In fact there are

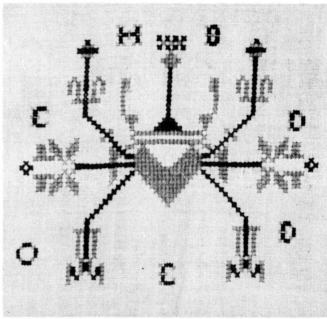

FIGURE 436   Red and dark blue cotton cross stitch.[102]

205

many such examples showing the absence of initials throughout the remainder of the decorated towel era. Using only the design and omitting the initials may indicate that the maker's religious beliefs did not agree with them or that she did not understand the symbolism and its significance.

This particular cross stitch heart design was used as early as 1611 on a sampler in the Netherlands. (Meulenbelt-Nieuwbrug, 18) Most likely it was used before that date in other areas of Europe. Dutch samplers include many examples of this design, alike but different. Most European examples contain a rather large heart, elaborate in its execution. Likewise, the crown above it is often as big or bigger than the heart and it too is somewhat detailed. Interestingly enough there are instances when flowers replace the large crown. The branches with flowers extend from the heart in either a straight or diagonal direction whereas on Pennsylvania towels the branches usually extend diagonally and are a bit longer. It is important to note that the initials OEHBDDE were not used alone or with any design on any of the European pieces examined to date and that the motif has not been seen on any European decorated towels. The design has been seen only on European samplers, and then never with the initials. It is known in Canada, chiefly among Mennonites in Ontario who appear to have taken the design with them from Pennsylvania.

In Pennsylvania, the design together with the initials appeared on towels as early as 1799.[711] Plainer and simpler than its European counterpart, it was usually executed in cross stitch and it was used on other household textiles as well.

The OEHBDDE design was not frequently used in drawn thread embroidery, but a few examples have been found. The first in our records was made in 1813 by BH and it includes the initials that rotate in a counterclockwise direction.[357] Esther Fuchsin also included the design with initials in her drawn thread grid, but her towel is undated.[1119] [Figure 438] Maria A. Stewer, 1823, embroidered hers without the initials, however, which took less space on the thread grid.[822] Another was made by CB in 1831 and is one of a set of two such designs on the same towel. Neither the cross stitch or drawn thread version has the initials.[58] [Figures 439, 125] Another example appeared on an undated towel, but it too lacks the initials.[240]

The design includes four basic elements as mentioned above: the heart, the crown, [Figure 440] the branches with flowers, and the initials. While most of the Pennsylvania Dutch women who chose to include this motif on their towel used these same four components, these ladies made subtle changes rather than merely duplicating another's work.

Differences such as the length of stems or branches, the kind of flowers seen above and below the heart, the size and shape of the heart, and what appeared on top of the heart such as a crown, a pot of flowers, [Figure 441] or in one case of a small bird, [Figure 442] all add variety to this one motif. Elisabeth Berlet put the heart

FIGURE 437   Anonymous artist. Bookmark. Southeastern Pennsylvania, 1810. Hand-drawn, lettered and colored on laid paper. 9.2 x 6.6 cm Courtesy, Free Library of Philadelphia [613]

FIGURE 438   White cotton darning stitch.[1119]

206

FIGURE 439   Red cotton cross stitch.[58]

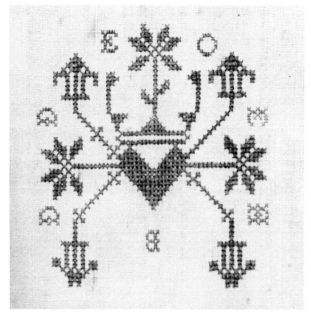

FIGURE 441   Red cotton cross stitch.[196] Courtesy, Clarke E. Hess.

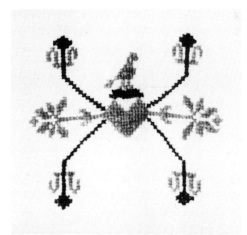

FIGURE 442   Red and blue cotton cross stitch.[569]

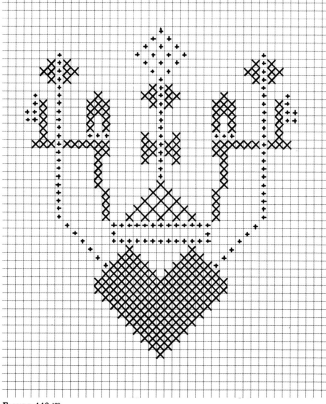

FIGURE 440.[189]

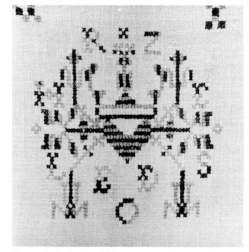

FIGURE 443   Red and blue cotton cross stitch. See Figure 158.[1259]

with flowers into a vase.[409] Further, two towels show the addition of four stars on the outer edge of the design.[327,466] Some women misplaced, added to, or deleted from the initials,[191,1278,1259] such as the woman who sewed RZ at the top, ES to the right, EDO at the bottom, and IH to the left.[1259] [Figure 443] Perhaps they had another saying in mind. Perhaps they were confused. Perhaps they did not know the initials' meaning. One towel has the four initials on one line and the last three on another.[968] And then there are those women who have the entire motif duplicated one above the other[962] [Figure 177] or side by side,[1133] or upside down.[63,1133] [Figure 157]

The central heart provided opportunity for creativity for the embroiderer. Sometimes the heart was stitched solid with one or two colors forming an outer border or stripes. [Plate 17] Other times there were open areas inside the heart; [Plate 28] many hearts were merely a silhouette or outline. Whether round, pointed, or elongated, each heart had extending from it three branches to the left and three branches to the right. The branches often have leaves and it is from these six stems that flowers appear. The tulip is most common and is usually in full bloom, seldom in bud. On two towels dating from the 1840s on which this design is used, an upside down tulip hangs from the point of the heart.[62,68] The addition of this extra flower was not commonly seen. [Figure 444]

Directly on top of the heart rests the crown or a stylization thereof. Often those towels with an earlier date have a more recognizable crown while others seem to have had only the base and side pieces to the crown with a flower in the center. This flower could have been a tulip like the other six flowers, but more often it was a carnation or a small, colorful, non-descript variety of blossom. The side pieces of the crown varied from short and plain to moderately high and elaborate. The base remained as a double or single line on which to rest the pot of flowers[191] or bird.[569] The demise of the full scale crown could indicate a change in folk cultural traditions, a shift in religious attitudes, or matter of personal choice between flowers or a crown. It could also signify the embroiderer's lack of knowledge of the motif's meaning.

Usually when this design was used the initials OEHBDDE were placed inside the configuration itself or just around the outer edge forming a circular effect. The first letter *O* appeared in any position on the circle, so to speak, and thus began the sentence in a clockwise or counterclockwise direction. Frequently the letters are placed in an upright readable position, but often the towel has to be rotated in the direction of the sequence of the initials lest they appear upside down or sideways.[63,191,196,596] [Figure 108] On one towel the letter *B* was eliminated and the year 1828 embroidered in its place.[355] On still another towel the maker's initials were included as part of the design, but in the script-type letter.[135] The only initial Rayel Ziegler sewed with the design was an *R* centered at the bottom under the heart,[718] [Figure 127] but Fanny Meyer used *FM*.[830] [Figure 187] Almost without exception, the letters OEHBDDE were embroidered in upper case block letters. One of the few exceptions is

FIGURE 444   Red cotton cross stitch.[68] Courtesy, Clarke E. Hess.

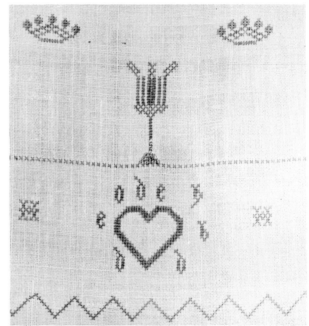

FIGURE 445   Red cotton cross stitch.[1278]

Elizabeth Hershey, 1845,who sewed *odehbdde* in lower case.[1278] [Figure 445]

The most revealing of these designs was executed by women such as Maria Kurtzin,[619] Hannah Sauder, 1846,[1348] and Catharina Sauder, 1855,[1347] who stitched the letters *EEDL HERTZ* inside this heart and flower motif. They arranged *EEDL*(noble) over the top half of the motif to read left to right and the word *HERTZ* (heart) under the bottom half reading left to right. The last letter *Z* is at the center bottom. [Figure 446,469,470] A towel made in Ontario is even more specific. It reads *O EDEL HERTZ BE DEI EN.*

The question arises whether a denominational preference emerges from the use of the design with or without initials. We submit the following list of names and dates found to date on the towels on which this design element was found. They represent about 8 percent of the total number of towels. The last names clearly indicate a variety of religious backgrounds, and if there are more Mennonite names than from any other church, there are also many more Mennonite towels than there are examples made by girls of other churches. However,

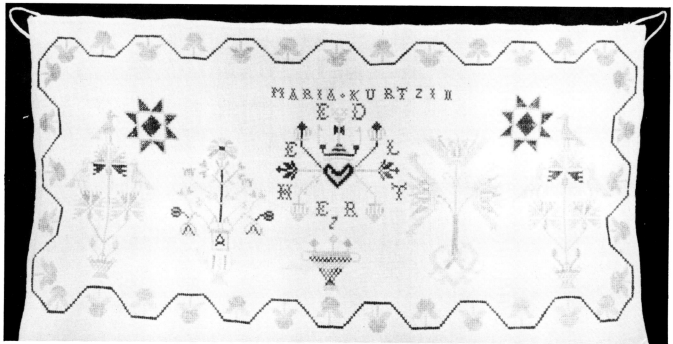

FIGURE 446   Top panel of the towel in which the *O edel Hertz* motif appears with the words *EDEL HERTZ* spelled out. Red, dark blue, light blue cotton and brown silk cross stitch.[619] Courtesy, North Museum of Franklin and Marshall College, Lancaster.

about three-quarters of the towels with the *O edel Hertz* motif were made by girls with names of Mennonite background. Interestingly the motif has been found on only one Schwenkfelder towel, but there is a Schwenkfelder sampler dated 1792 which has it. Susanna Hübner, a Schwenkfelder *Fraktur* artist, in 1807-1808 put the full couplet or just the first half of it inside hearts on at least six religious text *Fraktur* done in Montgomery county. (Weiser-Heaney, I,275)

SA HA n.d.

Bachman, Nancy 1834
Bamberger, Barbara 1833
Bamberger, Barbara 1825
Bauman, Chrestena 1841
Beard, Elizabeth L. 1835
Benner, Maria 1829
Berc, Maria 1822
Berlet, Elisabeth 1821
Beyer, Margret 1840
Biemersderffer, Elisabeth 1820
Booser, Elizabeth 1843
Borgholder, Elisabeth 1831
Brenneisen, Hanna 1799
Brenneman, Lydia n.d.
Brower, Elizabeth 1813
Buckwalter, Fiann n.d.
Buckwalter, Fiann 1856
Buckwalter, Mary 1864
Buckwalter, Litty 1853
Burckhart, Maria n.d.
CB, 1831 (drawn work)
EB, 847 [for Elizabeth Buchwalter]

Carpenter, Mary 1837
Cassel, Mary 1828
Crobb, Macdalena 1836

Dornbach, Elisabet 1814

Ebersole, Catherine 1848
Eby, Ann 1852 (drawn work)

Frankenfield, Elizabeth 1820
Fretz, Eliza 1846
Fretz, Eliza 1848
Fretz, Mary 1846
Frey, Elisabeth 1843
Fuchsin, Esther n.d. (drawn work)

Gantzi, Magdalena 1821
Gotschal, Elisabeth 1825
Greybill, Nency 1839
Gross, Magdalena 1829
Barbara BG, 1810

Harr, Daniel 1832
Hege, Catarina n.d.
Herr, Elizabeth 1846
Herr, Susanna 1843
Hershey, Elizabeth 1845
Hershey, Mary 1845
Hiethwole, Anna 1826
Hockman, Ann n.d.
Horst, Anna n.d.
Huwer, Anna 1848
BH, 1813 (drawn work)
IH, CH, HH, FH, CH, AH n.d.

209

MH n.d.
CH n.d.

Kauffman, Elizabeth 1834
Kintz, Catarina 1809
Kratz, Catharine 1838
Kreiber, Esther 1835
Kreiders, Maria B. 1859
Kreiter, C n.d.
Kurtzin, Maria n.d.
MK n.d.

Lapp, Catharina 1857
Lapp, Leah [?] 85 [?]
Lehmanin, Barbara 1828
Lehn, Barbara n.d.
Lemin, Anna 1818
Lesch, Maria 1828
Lutz, Ledya 1829

Martin, Judith n.d.
Meier, Hedded 1827
Metzler, Maria 1819
Meyer, Anna 1846
Meyer, Fanny 1838
Meyer, Mary 1821
Meyer, Barbara 1835
Miller, Meri 1831
SAHM n.d.

Nissly, Mary 1841
Niszly, Esther 1821
Nolt, Maria n.d.

Reist, Elizabeth 1846
Ritter, Maria n.d.
ER 1828

Sauder, Catharina 1855
Sauder, Hannah 1846
Sauder, Esther n.d.
Schitz, Jacob 1839, 1840
Schneider, Catharina 1828
Schyffer, Elisabeth 1836
Schyffer, Feronica 1839
Staman, Anna 1839
Stamm, Mary 1845
Staufer, Elisabet n.d.
Stauffer, Elisabeth 1821
Steinweg, Susana 1848
Steman, Fanny 1838
Stewer, Maria A. 1823

Walp, Hannah 1829
Weaver, Nancy 1836
Weidman Catharina 1838
Weinholt, Rebecke 1847
Wenger, Fayanna 1842
Witmer, Mary 1849
AW 1833
LW n.d.
MW n.d. (drawn work)

Young, Maria 1838

Ziegler, Rayel 1827

Generally speaking the motif was a popular one and quite durable. It survived transplantation from Europe and its use in Pennsylvania spanned the entire decorated towel era. Its execution knew no regional or denominational boundaries for it can be found wherever decorated towels were made. Placement on the towel varied from top to bottom to center. The design was put where it best fit with surrounding motifs; there was no common placement for it that we observed.

While the basic design form was used throughout the Dutch country there were variations on the theme. One of the simplest versions is a plain unadorned heart motif divided into thirds with the letters OEH embroidered inside.[1144] [Figure 447] Elizabeth Hershey, 1845, also used a small heart without crown, stems or flowers, but she encircled the heart with the initials *odehbdde*.[1278] [Figure 445]

Larger variations included a towel on which an eight pointed star is the focal point, not the heart. The star is surrounded by four horizontal-vertical square crosses and by four diagonally made crosses. Surrounding the whole were the initials *OADHBDDA*. If we consider the possibility that *Edel* could also have been spelled with an *A* instead of an *E* and that an *A* could have been used to spell *End*, we may conclude that this set of initials represent the same epigram as the more typical OEHBDDE. In this design there are no branches with flowers nor is there any semblance of a crown. The design is completely symmetrical and it is the placement of the initials that gives it status and direction. It is worked in all-red cotton floss and appeared on an 1829 linen towel made by Hannah Walp originally from the Richland area in Bucks county.[274] [Figure 448]

Another large version features a small cross inside a square from which four hearts emerge. Each heart was topped with three flowers and two buds. Around the design are the initials *OEDHBDDE* with the *ED* and not just the *E* representing *Edel*. (The motif had considerable popularity in Canada. The longer spelling OEDHBDDE is common there). There is not one, but four hearts included in this motif, but no crown. It was made in 1829 by Maria Benner also from Richland in Bucks county.[596] It is interesting to note that these two designs were made in the same year by two girls who were related by marriage.

A completely different arrangement of the four basic features of the design can be found on Elisabet Staufer's towel, 1827.[1285] A heart at the bottom gives rise to three flowers the center one of which bears an oval. Another heart is in the center of the oval and a crown sits on top of it. [Figure 449]

At any rate, saying and design do fit together, although perhaps not precisely as the design's originators intended. The design may originally have been a representation of the purity of Christ or of the Virgin Mary; but clearly the pietistic Pennsylvania Germans saw in it a representation of a "noble heart" which had learned the lesson to be learned from pondering one's demise, a heart which now was "awakened" to true faith and service to God. Thus, the heart supports a crown: "Be faithful unto death and I will give you the crown of life." (Revelation 2:10)

How long and how widely the motif was understood by those who stitched it into their towels is beyond answer. The evidence seems to suggest the possibility that within several decades of its first appearance, the initials were ignored, or confused, or the design was altered essentially, as if any connection between initials and design were now lost. Granted the extreme conservatism of the people who produced these embroidered documents, it is altogether conceivable that portions of the ensemble survived after its intention had been scuttled.

FIGURE 447   Red cotton cross stitch.[1144]

FIGURE 448   Red cotton cross stitch.[274]

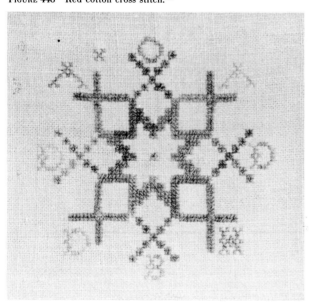

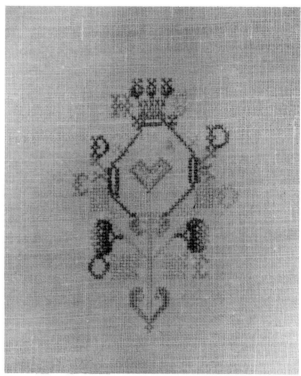

FIGURE 449   Multicolor silk cross stitch.[1285]

211

Squares

Squares were not used much by themselves as a design element on towels, a surprising fact, because their shape lends them so well to cross stitch.

Solid,[18] striped,[1] and open centered squares [271] were usually small, but the most widely used embroidered square was made of just four cross stitches. This small square was spaced between words and designs or used by itself; more frequently it was combined into borders, letters, and geometric designs.

Some squared designs had embellishments on the outer edges that converted them into cross-type designs.[8,408] And still others were enlarged with intricacies that conformed to square shape.[268,550] [Figures 450-452]

The drawn thread square is also not often found on towels. Small squares of solid stitchery[296,609] or slightly larger ones with alternate open spaces[198] were placed at random on several thread panels. Abeth Ditze[451] exercised a little more creativity by first making a square-shaped thread grid. Inside she embroidered seven alternating squares that formed a checkerboard.

Embroidered free-form decorative squares were also not prevalent on towels.

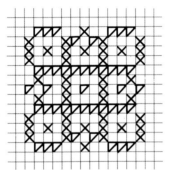

FIGURE 450 (above)[450]

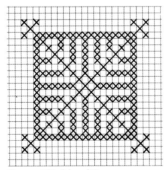

FIGURE 451. (above)[268]

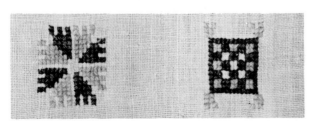

FIGURE 452   Red and dark blue cotton cross stitch.[333]

Stars

Eight pointed stars are one of the largest groups in the catalog of towel designs. (Four pointed stars have been seen only on samplers to date). The eight pointed variety has been found on a needleworked picture, a lady's pocket, pillow cases, a wedding handkerchief, a tablecloth, a feedbag, a blanket, and numerous samplers throughout the Dutch country. But, it was first and foremost a decorated towel motif. If only one design had to be chosen to represent the decorated towel tradition it would be the eight pointed star.

As with most cross stitch designs sizes of stars varied to meet the need at hand. This size was governed by two dimensions: the number of stitches in the length of each point by the number of tapered rows of stitches per point. The smallest star was two by two. A larger star has points that are fifteen stitches long and thirteen rows wide. The ordinary points measure three by four stitches, four by five, and the most common four by six. The more elongated ones are nine by three, eleven by four, ten by three, and eleven by three. The largest star recorded to date was not measured by cross stitches, but in inches. It is 8¾ inches wide and 10¼ inches high.[1344] [Figure 453]

Stars were either embroidered with hollow centers[16,132] or filled with stitchery,[4,199] or with a square,[87,467] a star,[120,238] [Figures 454, 455] a cross,[131,547] [Figure 456] a diamond,[310,604] [Figures 457, 231] or an angled line inside the center or eight points.[59,620] If large enough, the star contained initials[111] or a vase of flowers.[133]

Embellishments surrounding the outer edges of the star formed by diagonal stemmed flowers are scarce.[265,339,366] Generally stars contained additional decorative elements. Five stars were arranged in a St. Andrew's cross formation by Lea Iungst,[66] but perhaps the most significant combination of cross and star was the

FIGURE 453   A large brown silk star with red cotton birds holding a brown silk branch in its mouth. Cross stitch.[1344]

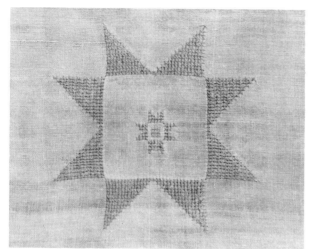

FIGURE 454   Red cotton cross stitch.[120]

FIGURE 455   Borders with stars. Red cotton cross stitch.[1225]

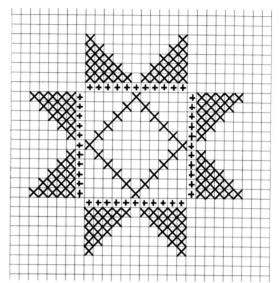

FIGURE 457.[199]

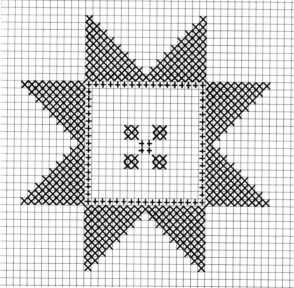

FIGURE 456.[547]

FIGURE 458   Red cotton cross stitch.[1191]

eight pointed star with a single[420] or double[116] cross in each point. One towel had a large star motif surrounded by eight smaller stars,[1191] [Figure 458] but an even more elaborate star was depicted by a woman who placed a small deer inside an eight pointed star. Surrounding the star is a wide bordered octagonal cartouche with flowers growing from each of the eight points.[194] [Figure 302]

213

FIGURE 459.[201]

214

Elizabeth Dillier adopted the star motif as the main feature for her towel by embroidering a grand total of fifty red and blue eight-pointed stars. They are identical in design, but not in color. This towel is a testimony to the priority of the star as a towel motif.[232] [Figure 176]

Embroidered drawn thread stars closely resembled those sewn in cross stitch in their counted thread formation and decorative centers. [Figures 131, 139] They were easily adapted to any size thread grid. Small,[293] medium,[45] and large sized[120,276] stars were plain[135,298] [Figure 58] or elaborate.[202,293] They stood alone as a single design[178] [Figures 124, 125] or as several arranged in group formation.[202] [Figure 127]

Medium or large size stars were sometimes encircled by smaller designs worked in between the points. MD, 1835, embroidered four small hearts,[287] Lisabet Moser, 1847, sewed four Greek crosses,[120] but Sallme Friederick, 1838, arranged eight smaller stars around a large central star.[293]

Only occasionally did drawn thread stars give rise to flowers,[187] a bird,[98] star flower,[448,449] [Figure 139] or diagonally stemmed flowers.[202,276] Extra decorative qualities frequently placed within the star itself were internal borders,[449] diverse crosses,[24,55,137] a circle,[202] initials,[332] [Figure 460] a rose,[338] squares,[35] a dog,[449] [Figure 139] small stars,[293] or diamonds.[16]

Iudit Gehman, 1827,[1] and AM, 1818,[417] each sewed a nearly identical star with a diamond in the center on their drawn thread panels. These were examples of the positive and negative imagery previously discussed. (p. 50) AM filled the center diamond figure with stitchery, whereas Iudit filled the grid background and left the diamond shape open and devoid of embroidery.

Marei Ewerle sewed many of the designs on her thread grid using a weaving over and under technique for the full length of the design. This single pass with the needle and thread created a narrow outline of the design. The star made in this manner appears airier and lighter than those embroidered in a more common manner.[29] [Figure 140]

HWB, 1839,[320] and another towel maker[235] each embroidered a four pointed star on a thread grid. This unusual star was found on samplers more than on decorated hand towels and it is quite unusual in drawn thread embroidery.

With the single exception of flowers, stars were the most frequently found design on drawn thread grids.

Flawless, accurate eight pointed stars were easier to depict by counting threads than by drawing them free hand. Perhaps this is why stars were not as prevalent in free-form hand towel embroidery. The versatility of satin stitch allowed embroiderers to sew small and large stars[718] more easily than chain[797] stitches did. One young woman, however, appears to have used a cookie cutter, quilt pattern, or similar device to trace six, eight, and sixteen pointed stars before embroidering them with the outline stitch.[125] [Figure 132] Free-form stars were usually medium to large sized, but did not occur frequently.

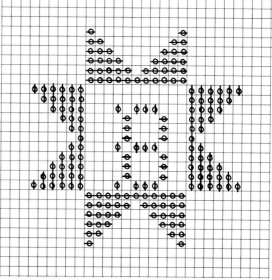

FIGURE 460.[332]

215

Texts

Texts embroidered on towels contain more information than the maker's name or a date. They include the Pennsylvania German name for this piece of needlework, lines used in popular autograph books, phrases and sets of initials that identify the towel's maker/owner and members of the family, statements of why a towel was made, proverbs or sayings known in the folk culture, commemorative words, poetry, lyrics of a folk song or hymns, phrases inspired by the Bible or quotations from it, and single word comments.

Placing a long or short text on the towel required forethought and careful planning for it was almost impossible to insert as an afterthought. Texts required large amounts of space and they needed to be balanced with appropriate designs in order to "fit" and not be ill-proportioned.

Most texts extended in sentence form from left to right. Some verses were arranged in a square or rectangular formation enclosed with an embroidered border. Meri Weinholt turned her verse into a border by beginning to sew it along the left side, turning the corner and continuing across the top of the towel and then sewing down the right side making it necessary to rotate the towel when reading it, *Das Han Duch Hapic Meri Weinholt Genet Im Iahr 1839* (The hand towel I Meri Weinholt sewed in the year 1839).[467] [Figure 165]

Words were spelled with block letters in either Pennsylvania High German or in English with a heavy Dutch accent. The girls who made these towels received little schooling; their words showed a wide variety of spelling, capitalization, and word arrangement.

English texts sometimes include contractions of such words as "we will" or "they will" complete with an embroidered apostrophe.[442] Examples can be seen in the work of Rebecca Minnich who sewed, ". . . when these few years of pain are past we'll meet around the Throne at last. . . ."[18] [Plate 11] A *th* was embroidered, at times above the line of writing, before or after a specific date to make 14 May to read *14th May.*[466] [Figure 28] Other punctuation mark-type sewing included a small *X* used as a period between words, at the end of a line, or after abbreviated words such as *Mrs.*[1151] or *a.d. 1839.*[1059] [Figure 171]

Pennsylvania High German words spelled phonetically or from memory made their translation a special challenge. Attempts were occasionally made with needle and thread to indicate sound values. An inscription sewn by Sara Schitz read, *SS Dieses hand duch ghoret mier Sara Schitzin gmacht den 8 Merz 1819 Sara Schit* (This hand towel belongs to me Sara Schitz made 8 March 1819).[268] The original needleworked spelling included a small backstitched letter *e* which is actually the sound value of the umlaut, placed over the letter *o* in the word *ghoret* properly spelled *gehoeret.* Esther König was another who indicated an umlaut by cross stitching a small square above the letter *o* in her last name.[1094] [Figure 461]

One group of texts explains why we call this piece of needlework a decorated hand towel. Meri Weinholt em-

broidered *Das Han Duc,*[467] [Figure 165] Sara Schitz sewed *Dieses hand duch,*[268] [Figure 461] Maria Burckhart sewed *Hand Tuch,*[1309] Elizabeth Longenecker marked her *towel,*[15] Litty Buckwalter,[362] Fanny Steman,[196] Elisabeth Frey,[466] and Fiann Buchwalter[592] all stitched the English word *towel* in their inscriptions, Fanny[574] and Mary[856] Nissley both embroidered *hand toul,* Mary Landis *made this hand toul,*[936] Maria Minnich has both *towl* and *toll* on her towel,[1054] [Figure 476] and a towel for Anna Brubacker has on it *This towl was mad[e] by . . .*[1059] all of which yields the simple term *hand towel.* Sarah Eby in 1854 embroidered the letters *HA ND TO WL* into the four points of a star motif so that they may be read clockwise.[975] [Figure 462]

FIGURE 461 *Sara Schitz* Red cotton chain, straight, running and cross stitches. The center flower with peacock is fifteen inches high and fourteen inches wide. The bird's feet are four threads above the flower. Note the tiny running stitch umlaut above the letter *o* in the word *Ghoret.* W. 15½".[268]

A second category of texts consists of four distinct rhymed compositions. These well known verses were written in autograph books, sewn on English and Pennsylvania German samplers, (Krueger, 23, 24, 438, 507) or written as a personal sentiment to accompany the gift of a handmade drawing. (Weiser and Heaney, II, 646) They read as follows. (Some of the variations we found are included in parenthesis).

[a.] *The grass is green*
   The rose is red
   Here is my name
   When I am dead

[b.] *When I am dead*
   And in my grave
   And all my bones are rotten
   When (If) this you see
   Remember me
   Or else (At last, Unless, Lest, Let all the rest)
   I shall be forgotten [Plates 34, 37]

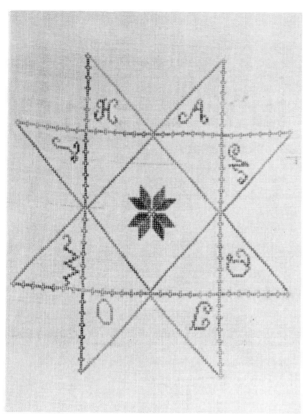

FIGURE 462 Red cotton and gold silk cross stitch.[975] Courtesy, Clarke E. Hess.

[c.] *The rose is red*
The leaves are green
The days are (time is) past
Which (Where) I have seen
(Remember me) [Figure 28]

[d.]   *is my name and*
heaven is my station
       is my dwelling place
And Christ is my salvation (sustation)

The last poem allowed the girls to cite anything from a country to state, county, or township as their dwelling place. Fanny[574] and Mary[856] Nissley both recorded *Rapho township Lancaster County and state of Pennsylvania* on their towels. *Manor township lancaster county state of Pennsylvania* was the residence of Anna Brubacker.[1059] Anna A. Kreider sewed *Pequa town is my Dwelling Plasn*,[1030] and Fiahna Landis was from *Manheim township*.[1324] Catharine[539] and Maria[464] Leaman, and Rachel LeFever[394] all stated that *Lampeter* was their dwelling place. Anna Staman lived in *Warwick township Lancaster County*.[191] Anna Brubacher was from *Elizabeth township Lancaster county, state of Pennsylvania*,[701] and Anna Frey dwelled in *Pennsylvania*,[755] but Elizabeth Kauffman[442] and Elizabeth L. Beard[1189] were from *America!* Mary Hershey in 1841 sewed *West Hempfield Township* across the flap of her towel. Underneath she repeated that her dwelling place was not only West Hempfield, but also *North America*.[1333]

As many as three of these verses were sewn on one towel with the sentence order sometimes reversed or revised. Most were embroidered in English, but Magdalena Diener worked hers in Pennsylvania High German, *Das gras ist grin die rose ist roth hier steth mein namen nach meinem tod MD* (The grass is green the rose is red here is my name when I am dead MD).[286] Catharine[539] and Maria[464] Leaman embroidered these poems in English, but when you read them there is little doubt of the girl's Pennsylvania Dutch background. *... the rose is ret the leavs are grean the day are past witch I have sean when I am dead an in mi grave and when mi bones are all roten...*

Original ideas, biblical thoughts, or other phrases were occasionally combined with these verses such as *Marth[a] Brubaker is my name [e]arth is my dwelling place Heaven is my station I wright with my hand and penn my daughter attent unto my wisdom and bow thine ear to my understanding....*[437] *Anny Conrad is my name and so it shall remain Warwick is my station heaven is my dwelling place....*[283] [Figure 28] *West Hempfield Township Mary Hershey is my name North America is my station mh West Hempfield is my dwelling Place and Christ is my salvation Now be the Gospel banner.*[1333] *The grass is green The rose is red Here is my name when I am dead Fiann Buckwalter She marked this towel done the 30 day of April.*[592] Two girls stitched the same sentiment. *Catharine Derr hand and thread Here is my name when i am dead....*[664] *Alithbeth Ebersole hand and thread here is my name when i am dead....*[591]

Abbreviated formations of these four poems retained the original concepts of remembering a name after death or identifying a place of residence. Several examples of the condensed versions included the words: *This towl I made for sake of the when this you see remember me 1847 JS* sewn on the Jacob Stouffer towel.[849] *Maria B. Kreider work done 1859 This work of mine my friends may have When I am in my silent gra[v]e Look on this work then you shall see How kind my parents where to me.*[803] This same verse was used by Mary Mast *This work of mine my friends may have when i am in my silent gr[a]ve Look on this work and then you see how [ki]nd my parents ware to me.*[1301] *Susanna Miller 1840 Anvill Township Lebanon County Pennsylvania SM.*[254] *Elisabeth Damy my hand and nwedle Christopher Damy Catharine Damy AD 1836 CS*[560] and *Mary Magdalena Damy My Hand and Nwedle 1836 Christopher Damy Catharine Damy 1836.*[1335] [Plates 13, 14]

Spaced across the entire width of Iohannes Witmeyer's towel were the initials *Pe To La Co Pe Is* which we have taken to mean Pequea Township, Lancaster County, Pennsylvania.[288] [Figure 463] MK, 1842, put *MT L C P* across the bottom of her towel which we have also taken to mean Manor or Manheim Township, Lancaster County, Pennsylvania.[201] The letters were sewn there without anything else to assist in deciphering their meaning.

Salome Kriebel at age twenty years sewed in red cotton across the bottom of one of her towels the following verses. *Bey aller deiner Freud und lust bedenke das du*

217

FIGURE 463 *Iohannes Witmeyer, 1848. Pe To La Co Pe Ia* [Pequa township, Lancaster county, Pennsylvania]. Balanced plain weave linen fabric; red, dark blue, light blue and brown cotton, and brown silk cross stitch; self plain fringe. W. 19¼".[288]

sterben must SK Wohl dem der taeglich sterben kan der trift im tod das leben an 1843 Salome Kriebel geboren den 16 ten Ianuary 1823 (In all your happiness and joy remember that you must die. It is well for him who can die daily. He will meet life in death 1843 Salome Kriebel born 16 January 1823).[453]

Sets of hand sewn initials with a common last letter compose a group of texts found on towels. Family registers take several forms. The shortened versions listed family members by first and last initials such as are on the following towels. *Franey Kulp JK BK AK JK FK EK 1861.*[1265] *Mary Stamm 1845 IK AK I Stamm 1845 E. Stamm Is Es as es Ms Ls ms Is Is ds as ss.*[361] *Barbara Bamberger 1833 AB Pb Fb 1835 MB Ab EB MB John Krall is Born the 6 11 October 1839 EB MB BA.*[465] *Susana Der Anna Der HD ED SD.*[1350] *Esther Kreiber GK EK MK BK FK GK EK EK AK AK GK CK.*[1367] *Maria B. Kreider JK AK MK DK JK AK EK 1859.*[803] *1837 MG Mary Carpenter MC Ig FW MG HG MG EG SG.*[56] *Julianna Longenecker JL EL SL JL GL JL 1831.*[90] *Maria Young 1838 JY MY SY MY MY CY AY LY SY LY RY SM CM CM FY EY MY.*[798] The unusual combination of initials that are on the 1825 Elisabeth Gotschal towel may well represent married couples who were Elisabeth's

friends or relatives. *1825 EG DACH IFDG HBHH IAEB SWSA IKSF CAEH ISCG ILEC HICK IHHK IOBG HIGG IHCH ILSB EG HFMH AHMN RH.*[111] [Plate 15]

A complete family register listed all of the individual members of a family with or without dates of birth or death. Such a large quantity of embroidered information required considerable space and dominated a towel's ornamentation. A good example of this is a towel made in 1839 by Magdalena Schyfer (1819-1902) who married Daniel Buch. The Schaeffer family were New Mennonites who lived in West Earl township, Lancaster county, near Farmersville. Of the girls only Magdalena married. The others remained on the farm with their father and did such heavy men's work that the local boys chanted a couplet about them long after they were dead.

Des Schaeffers Meed, des Schaeffers Meed
Die fohre die Mischt, der Schaeffer schprayed

(Schaeffer's girls, Schaeffer's girls
They haul the manure, Schaeffer spreads it).

[Related by Harry F. Stauffer of
Farmersville to A.G. Keyser]

Magdalena's genealogical towel lists first and last names with birthyears: *Isaac 1789 Schyfer Feronica 1794 Schyfer Lydia 1815 Schyfer Benjamin 1817 Schyfer Martha 1819 Schyfer Fenny 1821 Schyfer Elisabeth 1825 Schyfer Esther 1830 Schyfer Isaac 1831 Schyfer.*[7]

Members of the family still own additional pieces of workmanship by these girls: a towel made by Magdalena (a name the Pennsylvania Dutch anglicized to Martha);[1106] [Figure 464] a towel presumed made by Martha for Daniel Buch dated 1843;[1064] a sampler with the name of Feronica or Fanny (1821-1893);[1107] a towel made by or for *Fenny* dated 1838;[1063] [Figure 465] a towel made by or for *Feronica* in 1839;[1060] [Figure 466] a towel made by or for Betsy (1825-1865) marked *BS* and *Elisabeth Schyfer 1836*[1061] [Figure 467] Interestingly no towel for Esther (Hettie) (1830-   ) or Lydia (1815-1892) survives. Family tradition says that Hettie was an asthmatic who had to sit on a chair (and passed her time by smoking).

The Jacob Blank towel records the names of all the children of Jacob and Mary Blank. *Jacob Blank he yos born the 20 march September the 8 1857 Mary Blank She was born The 2 decemr The 1st october David Blank he was born The 20 novemr the 2 october Fanny Blank she was born 23 november aPril the 8 1858 Mary Blank was born aug the 11th 1858* was all sewn on the left side of the towel. *John Blank he was born the 27 July the 5 m october Nancy Blank she was Born the 25 december Sary Blank She was born the 29 december 13 october F K* was sewn on the right side of the towel.[971] This family was Old Order Amish and resided in Lancaster county. Jacob (March 28, 1816 - February 28, 1893) and Mary Stoltzfus Blank (September 2, 1819 - April 1, 1893) had the following children: Fannie (November 23, 1839 - January 29, 1902); David S. (November 20, 1841 - December 13, 1926); John S. (July 27, 1844 - December 19, 1918); Nancy (December 25, 1848 - February 22, 1925); Sarah

(December 29, 1850 - March 8, 1924); Mary (August 11, 1858 - November 24, 1925); Mary Blank and Jacob Blank whose names appear on the towel, but not in the Fisher genealogy. They apparently died at a young age. The initials *FK* are probably the towel maker's initials and the date *April the 8, 1858* when the towel was completed. The birth of Mary Blank on August 11, 1858 was added later by a different worker. (Fisher, 2988)

Nine lines of sewing across the top of the towel were required to record the Nolt family tree. *Maria Nolt 1890 JN 1795 age 74 B8 HN 1801 age 61 11 24 HC 1809 age 39 1 11 MC 1816 age 41 0 29 Daniel Nolt 1835 Elizabeth Nolt 1840 JCN 1860 MN 1862 SN 1864 HCN 1865 age 60 1 EN 1867 age 42 11 RN 1870 LN 1870 MN 1872 AN 1873 DCN 1876 age 08 11 Step Father JZ 1810 age 76 4 27.* The persons living at the time the towel was made are stitched in red, those with an age, and therefore dead, in gray.[106] [Figure 175]

A member of the Weidman family which attended Emanuel Lutheran Church at Brickerville made a similar genealogical towel. Catharina B [arbara] Weidman listed herself first in 1838 and then launched into her family: *peter weidman* [her father]; *christina weidman* [her mother, probably nee Schnürer born June 4, 1783]; *george weidman* [her siblings follow, born August 28, 1806]; *susanna weidman* [born February 19, 1809]; *daniel weidman* [born July 11, 1811]; *joseph weidman* [born December 17, 1813]; *catharina weidman* [born December 4, 1817, the seamstress]; *margaret weidman* [born September 10, 1819]; *peter weidman* [born January 17, 1822]; *emanuel weidman* [born October 6, 1825]; *israel weidman* [possibly a nephew, Daniel's son, born February 28, 1836]; *elisabeth weidman* [possibly a niece]; *my andy catharina sees* [Catharine Weidman married Balthaser Sees or Süs]; *my andy elisabeth yundt* [Elisabeth Weidman married Georg Jundt]; *my hand lydia sally maria weidman* [possibly other nieces]; *mardaw* [Martha] *1838.* The towel was made when Catharine was twenty-one years old.[1047] (Records of Emanuel Lutheran Church, Brickerville)

Two sisters, Maria[464] and Catharine B.[539] Leaman continued the practice by embroidering the names of their parents *Abraham and Barbara Leaman* as well as their maternal grandparents *David and Maria Buckwalter.* Catharine Meck simply sewed *My parents are George and Matty Meck.*[620] Maria B. Kreider embroidered in cross stitch *My Parents are John and Anna Kreider there parents Jacob and Maria Baslar Daniel and Anna Kreider.*[803] Anna A. Kreider simply put *My Parents Are George and Maria Kreider.*[1030]

Sara Kinig embroidered a towel the year following the death of her parents, Benjamin and Lidia Kinig. She spelled out in Pennsylvania High German both of their names with birth and death dates and arranged the information into two inscription areas alongside each other. It is interesting to note that both parents and three of their children all died in 1861. The towel reads, *DK CK Beniamin Kinig war geboren den 28 iuni 1806 und starb den 16 iuni 1861 Lidia Kinig war geboren den 28 October 1814 und starb den 25 April 1861 SK Sara Kinig*

1862 SE 1927 (DC CK Beniamin Kinig was born on 28 June 1806 and died on 16 June 1861 Lidia Kinig was born on 28 October 1814 and died on 25 April 1861 SK Sara Kinig 1862 SE 1927).[186] (Fisher, 151) [Figure 468]

Hannah Sauder, 1846,[1348] and Catharina Sauder, 1855[1347] embroidered nearly identical towels with the following inscriptions: *Iacob Sauder is gestorben den 1 August im ihar 1842 und sein alter war 64 ihar 8 monat und 12 tag* (Jacob Sauder died 1 August in the year 1842 and his age was 64 years 8 months 12 days). *Maria Sauder ist gestorben den 8 April im iahr 1843 und ihr alter war 24 iahr 7 monat und 7 tag* (Maria Sauder died 8 April in the year 1843 and her age was 24 years 7 months and 7 days). [Figures 269, 270]

The most useful texts, from a folk cultural point-of-view, are words which describe decorating hand towels as a leisured and relaxed pastime. Three young women chose to sew this phrase on their towel. *Maria Berc So kan ich die Zeit ertreiben 1822* (Maria Berc Thus I can pass time 1822).[369] *Elizabeth Booser is my name 1843 So kan ich meine zeit ferdrei[v]en* (Elizabeth Booser is my name 1843 This is the way I pass my time).[62] (See jacket) *Sara Mokaweh So Kan Ic Zeit Vertreiwen 1820* (Sara Mokaweh Thus I pass time 1820.)[728]

Other texts seem to be one-of-a-kind. In 1826 Anna Schneider stitched a verse on her towel that is incised on some pottery plates. *Ich lib was rein ist wan schon nicht mein ist und mein nicht werdern kan so hab ich do.* . . . The threads are missing from the last several letters, but when translated it reads, "I love what is pure even though it is not mine and cannot be mine, even so [I have joy in it]."[199] (Garvan, 182)

Eighteen year old Susan Killefer commemorated with needle and thread the date of her confirmation and first communion. Her towel, dated 1847, was made the year after her first communion; the inscription reads, *Susan C. Killefer is my name I was born the 30 day of September in the year of our Lord 1829 I was received into the communion of the German reformed church on the 21 day of february in the year of our Lord 1846.*[611]

Catharina Lapp, 1857, embroidered *Sweet Home* underneath a house motif[968] and Elisabeth Ebersohl sewed *SUHMEHBG* which we admittedly do not understand.[1248] Mary Funk, 1819, memorialized her father's death by sewing on her towel, *This Is The Text of my Father's Funeral Psalms The 23d C 4 Verse.* It is embroidered in black silk.[1341] [Figure 472]

Susana Heller, who lived in the Quakertown area of Bucks county, devoted her entire towel to the execution of a poem, the lines of which were embroidered inside box-like borders on which rest flowers and trees with birds. These unusual designs filled the towel, having been placed in seven individual locations. The embroidery was worked in cross and star-eyelet stitch in gold and dark brown silk and a large drawn thread panel contained crosses, hearts, stars, crowns, and her initials *SH*. At the top edge is a row of hand knit white cotton lace. The texts were written in both English and Pennsylvania High German. Curiously it includes the English word *sampler*

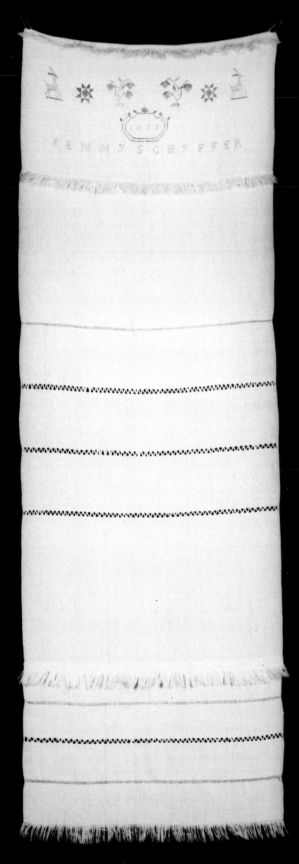

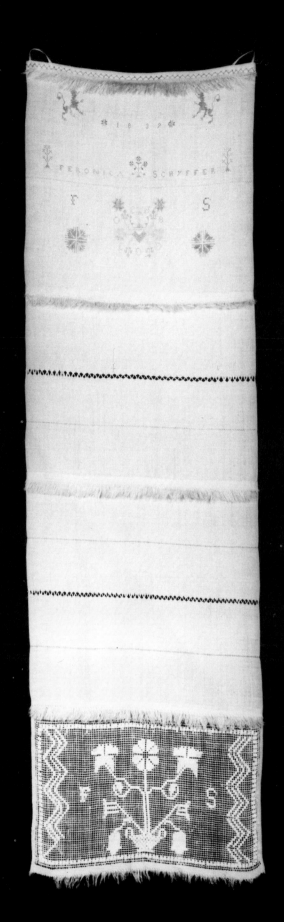

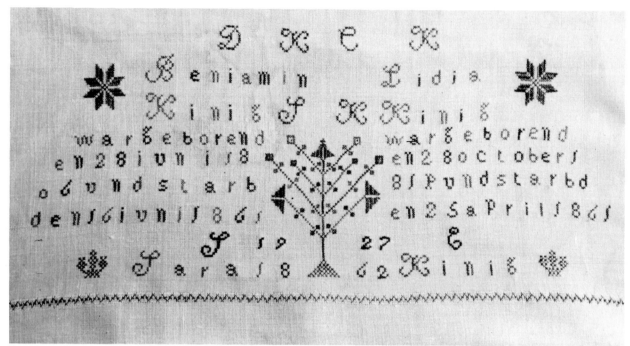

FIGURE 468 *Beniamin Kinig, Lidia Kinig ....* Lancaster county. Red and blue cotton cross stitch.[186]

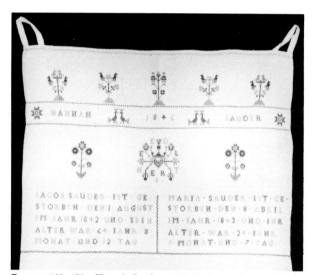 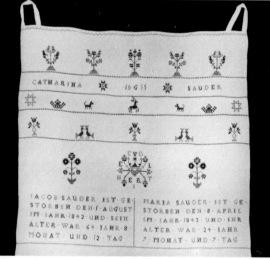

FIGURES 469, 470 *Hannah Sauder, 1846; Catharina Sauder, 1855 ....* Two towels, made nine years apart and almost identical, with the same inscription recording the deaths of Jacob and Maria Sauder. Red and blue cotton cross stitch.[1347,1348]

FIGURE 464 (p. 220 left) *Magdalena Schyffer, 1835.* West Earl township, Lancaster county. Balanced plain weave linen fabric; red and blue cotton cross stitch; white cotton darning stitch in drawn thread panel; self and applied plain fringes; zigzag hemstitched border one-half inch high. 56" x 18¾".[1106]

FIGURE 465 (p. 220 right) *Fenny Schyffer, 1838.* West Earl Township, Lancaster county. Balanced plain weave linen fabric; red and blue cotton cross stitch; self and applied plain fringes; zigzag hemstitched borders three-eighth inches high. 57½" x 19¼".[1063]

FIGURE 466 (p. 221 left) *Feronica Schyffer, 1839.* West Earl township, Lancaster county. Balanced plain weave linen fabric; red and blue cotton cross stitch; white linen darning stitch in drawn thread panel; self and applied plain fringes; zigzag hemstitched borders one-half inch high. 62½" x 18½".[1060]

FIGURE 467 (p. 221 right) *Elisabeth Schyffer, 1834 ....* West Earl township, Lancaster county. Balanced plain weave linen fabric; red and blue cotton cross and star eyelet stitch; white cotton darning stitch in drawn thread panel; self and applied plain fringes; zigzag hemstitched borders one-half inch high. 58½" x 18".[1061]

FIGURE 471 *E B 1799* The towel was probably made in Pennsylvania before being taken to the Kitchener area, Ontario, Canada. Balanced plain weave linen fabric; red cotton and brown silk cross stitch; applied knotted fringe.[1403] 40½" x 14". Courtesy, Doon Pioneer Village, Kitchener, Ontario.

and not *towel*. Size and construction definitely mark this piece of needlework as a decorated towel, but perhaps Susana considered it to be a sampling of her expertise with needle and thread. The words read, *Ihman Iar An 1826 This sampler belongs to me Susana Heller Kein lieb und treli auf erden is als nur bey dir herr Iesu Chris*

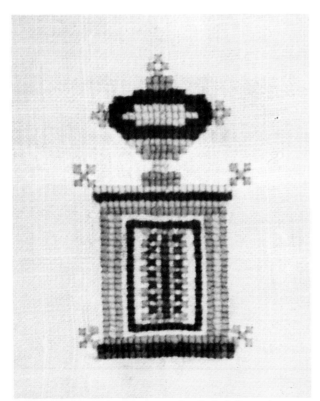

FIGURE 473 A mourning urn on top of a plinth similar to those seen on mourning pictures. See Figure 187. Multicolor wool cross stitch.[466] Courtesy, Dr. and Mrs. Donald M. Herr.

FIGURE 472 *Mary Funk, 1819 . . . .* Black silk cross stitch.[1341]

Susana Heller Nicht scham dich rath ich aller meis Der dich das lehrt was du nicht weis wer et Was kan den halt man werth den un geschickten nimand begehrt SH (In the year 1826 This sampler belongs to me Susana Heller No love and truth on earth is as yours Lord Jesus Christ Susana Heller Do not be ashamed I counsel you most of all That someone teaches you what you do not know Whoever is skilled is considered worthy The unskilled no one craves SH).[334] [Plate 38]

Maria Young worked in the 19 teen year of her *[age in]* March 1838 a towel with an English language folk song and the initials of seventeen members of her family.
I Just dropt in to See You all and ax You how you do
I'll sing You a song it is not very long
itts about my Long tail blue
Just look at my long tail blue
o how do you like my blue
ill sin you a song it is not very long
itts about my long tail blue
Some niggars they have but one coat but I you [. . . .][98]
[Figure 474]

Other texts were inspired by or quoted from the Bible. Julianna Longenecker referred to the sentiments in St. James, chapter three when she embroidered, *glick selig ist dermensch zu nennen der seine zunge zemen kan* (Fortunate is the person who can bridle his tongue).[90]

A towel marked *MF IF* has the following inscriptions from the King James version of the Bible sewn in two upper-middle panels.
Fear none of those things which thou shalt
suffer behold the devil shall cast some of you
into Prison that ye may be tried and ye shall
have tribulation ten days be thou Faithful unto
death and I will give thee a crown of life.
[Revelation 2:10]
And I heard a loud voice saying in heaven now
is come Salvation and strength and the kingdom
of our god and the power of his Christ for the
accuser of our brethren is cast down which ac
cused them before our god day and night.
[Revelation 12:10]

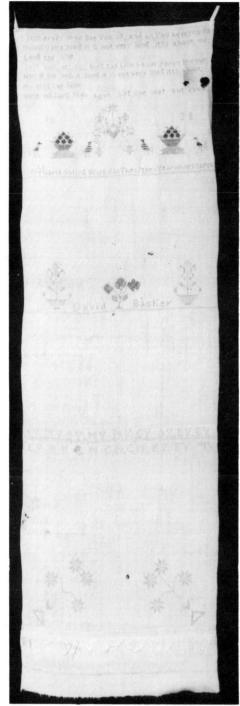

FIGURE 474 *Maria Young, 1838 ....* Balanced plain weave linen fabric; red cotton, light and dark gold silk cross stitch; self and applied plain fringes. 61″ x 18¼″.[798]

It is significant that a crown can be found among other motifs on this towel.[715] [Figure 178]

Another has this quotation of John 1:49a, *Nathanael answered and saith unto him Rabbi thou art the son of God.*[964]

A woman identified only as *AF* from Montgomery county was inspired by the standared German evening or New Year's hymn known as *Abermal ein Tag/Jahr verflossen.* She embroidered the first half of the first verse on the top and middle sections of her towel. The upper area reads, *A faber mahl ein Iahr ein tag ver floss sen na heyzu der ewigk eit wieein peilwirt.* And in the middle panel she sewed, *abge schosensover gehet meizeit* (Once again a year/day is past, closer to eternity as an arrow is shot thus my time is fleeting).

The full stanza was used by most Pennsylvania Germans and could be sung at family evening devotions using the words, the end of the *day* or the end of the *year,* whichever was appropriate. When *AF* sewed this verse, however, she failed to make the distinction between day and year and used both terms just as the hymnal does. Her spelling of both hymns indicates that she did not attend school very long or that she embroidered the words from memory.[601] [Figure 475]

FIGURE 475 *A F...* Red cotton cross stitch inscriptions; red and white cotton darning stitch on drawn thread panels.[601] Courtesy, Albert and Elizabeth Gamon.

224

At the bottom of the towel AF also embroidered the first line from still another hymn entitled, *Ach wie betrübt sind fromme seelen.* But she spelled it, *Achwiebetrvbt sind from eselen ew AF* (Oh how troubled are the virtuous souls AF).

The first line of a German hymn *Ich weis ein blumlein hubschund fein* (I know a little flower, pretty and fine) occurs on the towel Christina Borkholder made in 1844. It is in a heart which has a little flower perched on top of it.[1042]

Catharine Meck in 1841 apparently sewed this German hymn from memory for her words are spelled phonetically. *Nun lasst uns gahn trattan met sengan und met batan zum harrn dar unsarm laban beshea har kraft gagaban. Wer gahn dahen und wandarn fon genam eahr sum andarn wer laban und gadahan fom altan bes sum naman.*

([1.] Now let us go and walk
with singing and praying
To the Lord who until now
gave strength to our lives.

[2.] We go along and wander
from one year to the next
We live and prosper
from the old to the
new [year.])

This new year's hymn, written by Paul Gerhard, was used by most Pennsylvania German religions, including the Lancaster county Mennonites with whom Catharine Meck was probably affiliated.[620]

Maria Scheirich, 1827, put the first and fourth verses of the hymn *Meine Zufriedenheit steht in vergnuglich keit* at the bottom of her towel. *Meine zu iriedenheit steht in fergniglich keit vas ich nicht endern kan nihm ich gedultig an* (My contentment rests in fulfillment; what I cannot change I accept patiently). *Hoffnung lasz fir und fir bleiben dein schifepanier sieht es heut stirmisch drein morgen wirds stille sein* (Allow hope to be your ship's banner for ever and ever. If it looks stormy today tomorrow it will be still).[1225]

Anna Huber, 1836 embroidered this hymn on her towel. *Wie sicher lebt der mensch der staub sein leben ist ein fallent laub und dennoch schmeikelt er sich gern der tag des totes sey noch fern* (How securely man made of dust lives. His life is a fallen leaf, and yet he deceives himself about it gladly. The day of death is still quite far off).[1016]

Similarly, Elisabeth Rohrer embroidered these two lengthy verses, one underneath the other.

There is an hour when i must die
Nor do i know how soon twill come
How many children young as i
Are called by death to hear their doom.

Let me improve the hours i have
Before the day of grace is fled
There no repentance in the grave
Nor pardon offe[red] to the
[d]ead

This sentiment reflects the large number of children who died and the way society used that fact to keep children's conduct and religion from becoming untoward.[544]

Maria Minnich also sewed verses from nineteenth century hymns on her 1842 towel arranged in two long columns, one to the right and one to the left. *Farewell dear friends i must be gone i have no home or stay with you ill take my staff and travel on till i a better world do view Chorus. - Farewell Farewell farewell my loving friend farewell Farewell young Cnverts of the cros Oh labor hard for Christ and heavn Youve counted all things here but dross Fight on the crown will soon be givn Farewell & c Farewell poor Careless sinners too It grieves my heart to leave you here Eternal vengeance waits for you turn and find salvation near o turn o turn o turn and find salvation near.* On the right side of the towel this is embroidered: *Hosanna to the Prince of light That clothed himself in clay Entered the iron gates of death and tore their bars away Death is no more the King of dread since christ our lord arose he took the tyrants sting away and spoiled our hellish foes See how the conquror mounts aloft And to his Father flies with scars of honnor in his flesh And triumph in his eyes There our exalted Saviour reigns And scatter blessing down our Jesus fills the right hand seat of the celestial throne.*[1054] [Figures 476, 477]

The most elaborate examples of embroidered texts are found on two towels made by Rebecca J. Minnich. The first was a standard sized towel that she made for her brother Emanuel with eight different inscriptions.[18] [Plate 11] The second example was a miniature towel she embroidered for her five year old sister Catharine Halannah. It has five separate verses.[575] [Plate 48]

They begin at the top with the name and date. *Emanuel J. Minnich his Towel January The 24 And In The Year Of Our Lord A D 1850.* And on the other, *Catharine Halanah Minnich Her Towel March the 14th In The Year of our Lord A D 1850.*

Following this on Emanuel's towel are two verses positioned to the right and left of center. The one on the left is titled, *The Goldenrule* and was taken from Matthew 22:37,38. It reads, *Love God with all your soul and strength with all your heart and mind.* To the right is the verse entitled *Remember This* which says, *We soon shall Hear him say Ye blessed Children Come.* Underneath the name and date on Catharine's towel is just one verse, *Within thy courts one single Day Tis better to attend than Lord In any other Place A Thousand Days to Spend.*

Both towels have this classic well-known phrase embroidered in the center panel. On one is *Emanuel J. Minnich is my name and heaven is my Station and Lancaster county is my Dwelling place And Christ is my Salvation and when I am dead And in my Grave and all my bones are rotten if this You see Remember me or els I must begotten and Fore ever A men.* On the other towel Rebecca embroidered, *Catharine Halanah Minnich is my name and heaven is my station and Lancaster County*

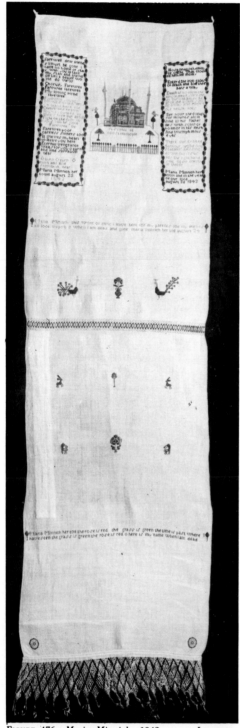

FIGURE 476 *Maria Minnich, 1842 ....* Lancaster County. Balanced plain weave linen fabric; red and blue cotton and blue, green, yellow and grey wool cross stitch; knotted linen fringes. 60" x 16 5/8".[1054] Courtesy, Dr. and Mrs. Donald M. Herr.

is my dwelling place and Christ is my salvation And when I am dead an in my grave and all my bones are rotten If this you see remember me or else I must be fore gotten and forever Amen.

FIGURE 477 Balanced plain weave linen fabric; blue, green, yellow and grey wool cross stitch.[1054] Courtesy, Dr. and Mrs. Donald M. Herr.

Directly beneath this poem on Catharine's towel is a type of presentation text sewn within a circular wreath of thirteen roses. *This ring Is round it has No end when I Look on this ring Then I can see How kind my sister was to me Rebecca J. Minnich.* There were two verses sewn to the right and left of center at this same position on Emanuel's towel that say, *In this vain world of sin And pain we only meet to Part again but when we Reach the heavnly shore We then shall meet to Part no more A men. The hope that we shall See That day Should chase our Present griefs away when These few years of pain are Past We'll meet around The Throne at Last A men.*

Centered under these two poems are Rebecca's words of presentation to Emanuel in which she reminded him of all the hours of sewing she did for him. *Rebecca J. Minnich her work when You look on this Towel then Remember Me think on the Time what I Spend for You to See Emanul J Minnich.* The last inscription on Catharine's towel says, *And We soon shall hear Him say Ye Blessed Children come. He soon Will call us hence away And take his wanderers Home.*

A complete alphabet including the English letter *J* and *AD 1849* extended across the bottom edge of Emanuel's towel. There is none sewn on Catharine's towel.

The last texts come from Fanney and Barbara. Fanney Whitmer stitched the word *END* following the dates of her birth and the completion of her towel.[802] Barbara Lehman also spelled out the word *ENDE* on the bottom left corner of her towel. On the opposite right bottom corner is embroidered a mirror image of the word which appears as *ƎⱭИƎ*. Both girls apparently decided that this one sewn word concluded that piece of needlework. [Figures 478, 479]

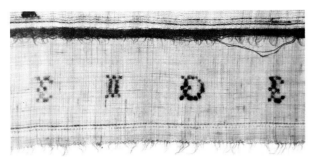

FIGURES 478, 479 The word *Ende* was sewn on the left side at the bottom of the towel and mirror-image letters were embroidered on the right side. Red cotton cross stitch. Back lit.[797]

Trees

Both deciduous and coniferous trees were embroidered on towels. Already in 1799 one appeared on a towel near a house to complete an almost realistic setting.[76] The combination of tree and house appealed to only a small number of embroiderers;[76,125,753] [Figures 132, 218; Plate 37] others used the tree as a central motif in the panel.[606] The size of some trees was easily expanded or contracted to enable this design to be sewn on many panels in mirror image.[16,76,231,764] [Figure 480]

The evergreen tree, easily recognized by shape, not color, is seen most often on towels.[797] Deciduous trees, on the other hand, offered more divergence. [Figures 79, 84, 85, 226, 382] If we allow our imaginations free rein

we can distinguish between a chestnut, red oak, and twenty ounce pippin! Elizabeth Leatherman sewed a tree that resembles a weeping willow.[157] A cross stitched stylized tree-flower combination was preferred to realism by most young embroiderers.

Of all drawn thread work trees evergreens were made most often. Only a few other trees were easily recognized.[27,55,298,518] Some were planted in the earth and other trees rose from an urn. It is difficult to determine whether certain drawn work motifs were intended to be trees.

A fruit tree was hand drawn in each side yard of a house embroidered by HA CA. The tree was taller than the house and had satin stitched fruit embroidered on it leafless branches.[125] [Figure 132] Other free-form trees had a central trunk with curved branches.[322] [Figure 481] Many more flowers than trees were hand drawn.

FIGURE 480 Red cotton and brown silk cross stitch[359] Courtesy, The Henry Francis duPont Winterthur Museum.

FIGURE 481 Tan and brown silk chain and cross stitches; border of threaded straight stitch.[1283]

227

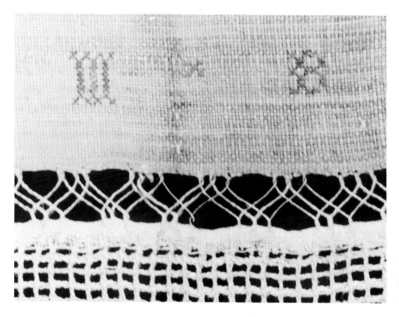

FIGURE 483   The cretan insertion stitch was sewn in groups of three, one-half inch high, to attach the selvage edge of the towel to the hemmed edge of the drawn thread panel.[98]

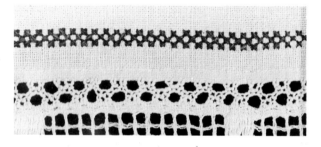

FIGURE 484   A white cotton needlelace, one-quarter inch high, was made as a buttonholed half-bar type insertion and placed between the towel and drawn thread panel. Dark blue cotton cross stitch border.[280]

FIGURE 485   White linen buttonholed bars.

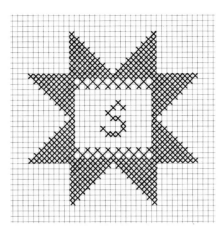

Finishing

There were as many options for finishing the towel as there were for making and decorating it. The methods used to sew the separate towel units together into one single length could be as plain or as intricate as the young woman desired or had the ability to make.

As previously discussed the butt, flat felled, overlapped, and overcast seams were the primary method of joining towel sections (p. 23). On many occasions, however, the joinings were more decorative than an ordinary seam.

A. LACES

Lace is a fine openwork fabric of five main types: bobbin lace made by twisting threads; knitted lace formed by looping with knitting needles; knotting threads with sewing needle; a mixed technique of bobbin and needle lace combined; and mechanically made mesh. Pennsylvania Dutch lacemakers preferred making needle lace with a sewing needle or knitting lace with knitting needles. The making of both these forms of lace required the use of readily available implements in the household sewing basket.

Needle Lace

"Needle lace is composed of an almost infinite variety of lace-like embroidery stitches made with a needle and useful for filling any shaped space. . . . They are attached only at the perimeter of the design thus forming an open net similar to knitting or crochet. The difference between needle lace and the more familiar surface embroidery is that needle lace is not attached to the background at every stitch." (Nordfors, 9)

A single continuous thread was used for needle lace which technically made it a form of sewing as opposed to laces made with groups of many separate threads that are all fixed at one end. (Emery, 56) The stitches were worked in rows, each row forming a base for the next and if the length of the thread be misjudged there were ways of starting a second which cannot be detected in the finished work.

Needlemade laces were made on Pennsylvania towels throughout the decorated towel era, but not much after 1850. Most examples were seen on towels dating between 1820 and 1830. They can be from one-quarter[137,280,690] to seven-eighths inches high[299] and were almost always sewn in very finely spun two-ply white linen threads. Pennsylvania German made needle lace was generally handled as insertions in that it joined together two finished edges. [Figures 484-495, 15]

While we cannot be certain of the precise preparatory techniques used in the nineteenth century, it is reasonable to assume that the two hemmed edges (unless a selvage was used) to be joined were basted or pinned to a third underlying paper or material an equal distance apart. The original spacing is so even and the stitch size so regular on the old towels that it is doubtful that the two separate towel pieces were hand-held without benefit of underbracing while creating and attaching the insertion to two edges. The lace was stitched to the towel edges at the same time it was being made. It was a one step process. The backing was removed when the lace was finished.

The stitches used to make needle lace were those with more independence that were sewn and used alone and did not rely on a background for attachment. These independent or detached stitches were further subdivided into looped filling stitches, edging stitches, and insertion stitches. None of the edging stitches have been seen on towels, but the insertion stitches and combinations of looped stitches were seen. (The reader is referred to The Embroiderer's Guild of America, Inc., 6 East 45th Street, New York, N.Y. 10017. Books such as Jill Nordfors, *Needle Lace and Needle Weaving*, 1974, and Th. de Dillmont *Encyclopedia of Needlework* are helpful for pattern directions to make needlemade laces. What follows are simple basic explanations of primary stitches used to make this lace).

Insertion stitches

The cretan stitch, seen most often, was a basic and simply executed insertion needle lace stitch not to be confused with the counted thread embroidery stitch with the same name. It is worked either vertically from top to bottom or horizontally left to right. The stitches can be spaced singly or in groups, far apart or close together, twisted or plain. The plain cretan stitches on old towels were singly spaced far apart and not twisted.[254,273,288,430] Elizebeth Barndt, however, sewed the cretan in groups of three stitches across the insertion instead of single stitch spacing.[188] (Nordfors, 68) [Figure 483]

Twisted insertion, sometimes called faggoting, is similar to the cretan stitch, but is worked diagonally back and forth over the open space. Each time a stitch is taken, the needle goes behind the finished edge; each time a twist is made, the needle goes behind the finished stitch. (Nordfors, 66, 67) It generally filled an area on towels between one-eighth[37,933] and one-quarter inch high.[317] Hedded Meier and Rayel Ziegler used the twisted insertion stitch and embroidered two rows of it, joined in the center, as a border across the width of the towel. No threads were removed. It was not an insertion, just decorative.[718]

The buttonhole stitch and half-bar insertion are other needle lace techniques that were used without fabric backing. The stitch uses a horizontal thread to join the two finished edges of the towel, but it is only half covered with buttonhole stitches. (Nordfors, 64)

These are three of the detached insertion stitches that we have been able to identify as part of Pennsylvania decorated towel tradition. There are many towels with unfamiliar stitchery that could well be personal interpretations of the buttonhole, Italian-buttonhole, knotted, plaited, or laced insertion stitches.

Looped filling stitches

Looped filling stitches as well as "Insertion stitches decoratively join two pieces of fabric by filling a narrow space between the finished edges with detached stitches." (Nordfors, 62) The purpose is the same, the stitches differ. These looped filling stitches are constructed with a single thread in which rows of loops worked back and forth form their own net or mesh.

The basic detached buttonhole is a simple loop stitch that has multitudinous variations. "It can be worked close together or far apart, singly or in groups, in one direction or in both directions, in rows or in a circle. It may be knotted or plain, close and textured, or open and lacy." (Nordfors, 36) It was this basic stitch that was used for most of the intricate needle lace seen on old decorated towels. (Nordfors, 37) [Figures 484-495]

Needle lace used to attach components of towels to each other, all worked in bleached two ply homespun linen sewing thread. (Figures 486-90)

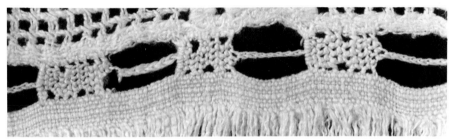

FIGURE 486   Three-eighth inches high.[299]

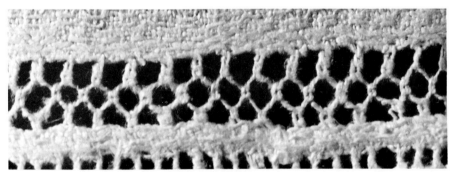

. FIGURE 487   Three-eighth inches high.[307]

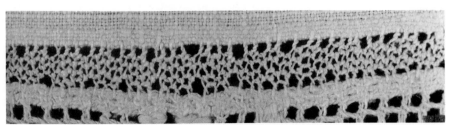

FIGURE 488   Three-eighth inches high.[299]

230

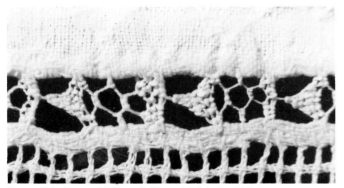

FIGURE 489   From a 1794 towel. Three-eighth-inches high.[35]

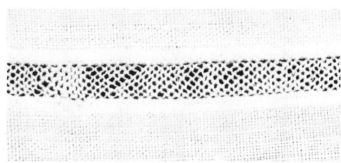

FIGURE 492

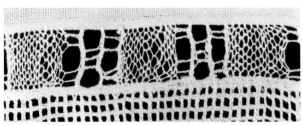

FIGURE 490   Seven-eighth inches high.[299]

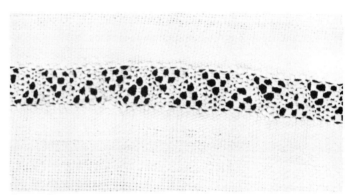

FIGURE 493

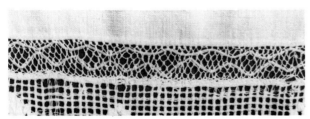

FIGURE 491   Threaded needlelace, three-quarter inches high, with unbleached linen threads through it.[335]

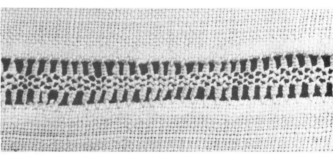

FIGURE 494

FIGURES 492, 493, 494, 495   Four needlelace patterns used on the same
1826 towel. They are three-eighth to one-half inches high and were all
made with white linen sewing thread.[189]

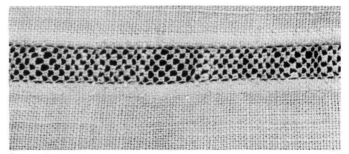

FIGURE 495

The following directions are for a simple needle lace insertion copied from an undated towel.[1293] This stitch is executed simply by doing the buttonhole stitch both backwards and forwards, i.e., from left to right and from right to left.

To begin, be sure the sides of both pieces of fabric have a one-eighth inch hem, folded under twice. Hold the two pieces of fabric sideways, thereby executing the stitches from top to bottom.

There needs to be a reinforcing bar in order to stabilize the width of the space to be filled and prevent stretching. In order to accomplish this, pass the needle and thread back and forth across the top of the opening (from A to B to C to D) until there are two threads across the opening. Cover these two threads with the buttonhole stitch working from right to left (E to F). Upon reaching the left side (F), pass the needle and thread approximately one-eighth inch down the foldline and emerge at G. Moving from left to right, continue executing the buttonhole stitch by hooking into the previous row leaving a loop between every other two sets of stitches to which the next row (working right to left) will hook into.

Continue this back and forth procedure until you reach the bottom of the opening, at which time another reinforcing bar is to be stitched in a similar manner as at the beginning. [Figures 496, 497]

Definite open and intricate designs were worked into the needle lace insertions with no two examples alike. If these lace insertion patterns originally had Pennsylvania Dutch names, they have escaped us. Directions for their replication have also been lost; one must copy from the original lace.

Such delicate work has survived best if the towel maker sewed reinforcing buttonholed threads at each end of the insertion area. [Figure 498] If this was not done the great majority of the needle lace stitches have started to pull loose.

A rare example of detached needle lace can be seen, not as an insertion, but as the decorative center on a small flower at the bottom of a towel made by Catarina. An open lacey mesh of buttonholed blue cotton threads filled the central area attached only on the perimeter.[732] [Figure 499] (When stitches are used to cover an area without being attached except along the borders they are described generically as detached. They are in a sense used to construct a separate fabric. It is possible to work this framework on top of fabric or to fill in opened areas).

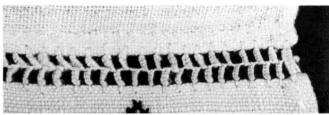

FIGURE 498   Linen needlelace one-quarter inch high. A buttonholed bar was placed at the end of the insertion as reinforcement.[290]

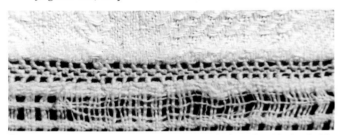

FIGURE 496   Linen needlelace one-quarter inch high made with the double net stitch.[1293]

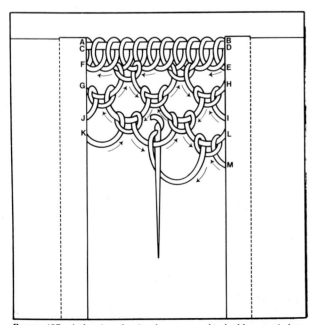

FIGURE 497   A drawing showing how to use the double net stitch to make needlelace.[1293]

FIGURE 499   The center of the right red cotton satin stitch flower is filled with dark blue cotton detached needlelace. The lace is attached only at the outer edges and can be lifted off the towel fabric in the center; three-quarter inches in diameter.[732] Courtesy, Sally and Pete Riffle.

Needle laces have a strong European background some of which was incorporated into decorated towel tradition. Small amounts of needle lace were inserted in the front opening of men's white linen shirts, but to the best of our knowledge needle lace was not put on other clothing. It was reserved for towels and an occasional sampler. [Figure 98] It is a traditional needle art form no longer practiced in the Dutch country.

Knitted lace

"Making lace is a 'constructional' use of stitches, that is, they are stitches used to construct a fabric as opposed to 'accessory' stitches that are taken through a fabric with a thread and needle by a process known as 'sewing.' " (Emery, 232)

Knitting consists of loops or stitches that are connected together in unbroken continuity to produce a very elastic fabric. Knitted lace was formed on knitting needles in a size correlative to two-ply white cotton[95] and handspun bleached or natural linen thread. Diverse interlacing of the knitting threads produced contrasting stitches. Using 'overs' created open patternings. We are not aware of any nineteenth century printed or hand written knitting instructions relevant to decorated towel tradition.

There were only several instances when knitted lace was used as an insertion and those towels were dated from 1818[289] to 1840.[1179] The elastic qualities of anything knit made it impractical as a joining despite its decorative attributes. Once an insertion was knit it needed to be hand sewn to the towel units so that two steps were necessary in applying this towel finish. [Figure 66]

One example of a knit insertion was made in white linen with a chevron pattern. It measured 1½ inches high.[122] This design was copied and directions to knit this insertion follow. [Figure 500] A facsimile can be produced by using 0 gauge needles and threads the size of #8 Pearl Cotton.

Cast on 25 stitches and knit 2 rows.
Row   3 - knit 2 - yarn over - knit 2 together - yarn over - knit 2 together - knit rest of row.
Row   4 - purl - do this every other row.
Row   5 - knit 3 - yarn over - knit 2 together - yarn over - knit 2 together - knit rest of row.
Row   6 - purl.
Row   7 - knit 4 - yarn over - knit 2 together - yarn over - knit 2 together - knit rest of row.
Row   8 - purl.
Row   9 - knit 5 - yarn over - knit 2 together - yarn over - knit 2 together - knit rest of row.
Row 10 - purl.

Continue in this pattern having one more stitch before yarn over on every other row. Always purl on way back to starting edge. Do this until two stitches from the other edge on second yarn over including knit together. Then reverse pattern or yarn over row to two stitches on starting edge and start all over for the length of piece.

Another towel, made in 1818, had three separate knitted white linen insertions. The one on the top flap was 1¾ inches high, and those throughout the towel are 3½ and 3¾ inches high.[289] [Figures 501, 502] The largest

FIGURE 501   Handknit linen lace insertion, 3½ inches high, on a towel dated 1818. It is one of three knit insertions on this towel. See Plate 25.[289]

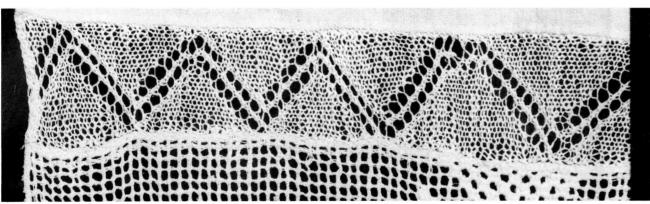

FIGURE 500   Knitted lace insertion, 1½ inches high with chevron pattern; white linen.[122]

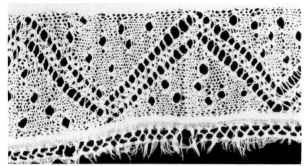

FIGURE 502 Handknit linen lace, 3¾ inches high, sewn along the bottom edge of an 1818 towel. Just below is a one-quarter inch high piece of linen fabric which had every four warp yarns wrapped together in a zigzag fashion, three-eighth inches high similar to zigzag hemstitching. See Figure 501, Plate 25.[289]

knit insertion found to date was 5¾ inches wide and it was inserted vertically down the center of the towel. Near the bottom it was met by another horizontally inlaid knit insertion which was 2-5/8 inches high. Together they formed an inverted "T" shape on the towel. This lace was knit with two-ply natural color linen thread. [Figure 503]

It was more usual to find hand knit lace sewn to the top or bottom of the towel as an edging.[4,95,156,217,334,336,344,1108,1148,1226] [Figure 12] Here the lace was allowed to hang free and display its own beauty.

SFB had a two inch high hand knitted lace bottom edging with a gently scalloped edge[95] whereas Elisabeth Fried, 1845, knitted a 5¼ inch high lace with deep scallops.[156] CM, 1828, combined her hand knit lace with tassels.[215]

Knitted additions to towels were not common and were probably innovative rather than traditional. Knitting seemed to be better suited to caps, mittens, gloves, and stockings than to decorated towels.

Crochet

"In crochet loops are interworked not only vertically with those in the previous row, as in knitting, but laterally as well—with others in the same row. It is basically a kind of chaining. A simple progressive chaining of the element forms the first row and each successive row is a similar chaining which progresses horizontally and interworks vertically and horizontally at the same time." (Emery, 43)

Crochet is an effective kind of fancywork that can be applied to many requirements. It was made with a little bone, steel, or wood hook and a large variety of threads from fine round ones to special crochet cotton and knotting cotton.

Crocheted edgings on decorated hand towels are not common and often times were additions made by later towel owners. The edgings, made in various patterns, are usually crocheted with white or ecru colored cotton yarns and are hand sewn to the top[1140] or bottom[1185] of the towel. In one instance a drawn thread panel, no longer attached to a towel, had a crocheted edging sewn to the top and both side edges while a wider decorative panel crossed the bottom.[1256] [Figure 504]

Bobbin lace

Bobbin or pillow lace is made with a group of many separate threads whose handling is facilitated by the use of individual bobbins and special shaped pillow. The separate threads of bobbin lace are fixed at one end and weighted by the bobbins at the other. The construction of bobbin lace illustrates a highly refined and elaborately developed use of threads that have a common starting point.

FIGURE 503 (left) *Barbara Bugern, 1800.* Balanced plain weave linen fabric; silk cross stitch; red, dark blue, light blue, and white cotton darning stitch in drawn thread panel; linen knitted lace insertions; blue and white linen knotted fringe. See Figure 518. 60" x 18½".[315]

234

FIGURE 504 This drawn thread grid was removed from its original towel and even though worn was valued enough to have warranted a new cotton crocheted border in the last quarter of the nineteenth century. The panel includes some unusual motifs worked in the white cotton darning stitch, among them the wick trimmers and candle sticks. 18½" x 16¼".[1256]

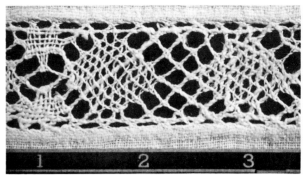

FIGURE 505 Handmade bobbin lace insertion made with a light and heavy weight two ply linen.[814]

The implements needed include a cushion or pillow on which the lace pattern is mounted, many bobbins, a thread winder, patterns of which the designs have been transferred to a card with certain parts pricked out, a pricker which is a long metal holder for a coarse sewing needle used to prick the holes in the card for the pins, and the pins. They must be long, round, headed, coarse or fine, and be of brass so as not to rust.

Making the lace requires twisting, crossing, and passing movements. Principal parts of the pattern are worked with close passings like the net or lattice ground or linen ground which figures are then connected with open work-type stitches. Sometimes little picots are worked along the edge to indicate where to attach the work to the finished piece.

Bobbin lace, as it appeared on towels, was generally white in color. Catharine Moyer in 1898 used white cotton,[214] [Figure 183] but most girls used linen thread. SV MI combined a heavy and light weight linen thread in her bobbin lace.[814] [Figure 505] She used the bobbin lace as an insertion, three-quarters of an inch high, to connect a drawn thread panel to the towel. Catharine Moyer, on the other hand, inserted the inch high piece of lace at the very top of her towel. It was separated from the hanging tabs by only a narrow hem in which case the lace supported the weight of the entire towel. (Two tablecloths have patterned bobbin lace insertion identical to the SV MI towel. One tablecloth has the name Anna G. Herr and the second has the initials and date, SA SK 1841. (Gehret and Keyser, 1976, pl. 93) These three Penn-

sylvania German textiles with identical bobbin lace suggest the possibility of a professional lacemaker and/or seamstress who was making and selling bobbin lace by the yard to private customers or to the local store).

Bobbin lace making equipment and the lace itself played only a minor role in the Pennsylvania German folk culture or hand towel tradition despite the examples just given. Not only do lace making tools and supplies seldom, if ever, appear in estate inventories, but the near absence of bobbin lace on Pennsylvania German needlework is obvious.

B. POINTS AND RICK RACK

A chevron or zigzag edging effect was created by a process of twice folding small squares of white cotton fabric into a triangular shape.[247,274,279,402,983,1000,1206,1321] By first folding opposite corners together and then folding opposite corners together again two sides of the triangle became folds and the third side, or base of the triangle, contained all the raw edges. (Roan, Gehret, 33. This was an edge finish sometimes used on quilts, pillowcases, and petticoats as well as on decorated hand towels in areas east of the Schuylkill river). The individual triangles were placed side by side across the back of the top or bottom edge of the towel with the raw edges sewn evenly in place. A narrow strip of fabric or tape was then slip stitched on top of these raw edges as a finishing. The sizes of the sawtooth-like points varied from one-quarter to one inch high and from one-half to three inches wide at the bottom edge. [Figure 506]

Elisabet Rosenberger, 1822,[983] MR RT, 1823,[247] Hannah Walp, 1829,[274] and Sarah Fretz, 1846[1206] positioned these points across the towel's top edge. Rebecca Gerhard,[279] Sarah Kriebel,[402] and Elizebeth Ditwiler[1000] utilized the white cotton fabric points as either a decorative insertion [Figure 80] or as an insertion connecting the towel to the bottom fringe. [Figure 507] RS[927] went one step further by folding points from white cotton fabric that contained a woven red stripe. Each point was folded so the red stripe appeared in the same location on the triangle. Therefore, not only the shape, but the stripe of color added interest to this edging. [Figure 133]

There was also a hand-folded tape or fabric edging that was used, similar in appearance to rick rack braid.

FIGURE 506 The front and reverse sides of the nine-sixteenth inches high white cotton folded fabric points sewn to the top edge of the linen towel. The same white cotton tape, three-eighth inches wide, used for the hanging tabs was used to cover the cut edges of the fabric points on the back of the towel.[99]

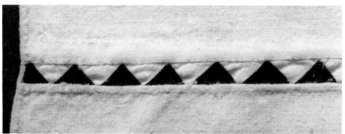

FIGURE 507 Folded white cotton fabric points, three-eighth inches high and one point per inch, used as an insertion.[1000]

FIGURE 508 Plain weave white cotton mill-made tape folded into points and used as an insertion between the selvage edge of the towel and hemmed edge of the drawn thread panel.[1182]

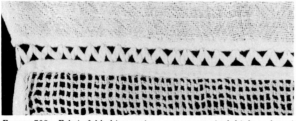

FIGURE 509 Fabric folded into points, one-quarter inch high, and used as an insertion. Note also the fabric binding on the thread grid which strengthened and helped maintain shape.[291]

A length of white cotton twill or plain weave mill-made tape, [Figure 508] or a long length of linen or cotton fabric with raw edges turned in, was folded on itself zigzag fashion to make a continuous series of alternate up and down points. LK, 1847,[291] used a hand-folded white cotton fabric edging of this type, [Figure 509] whereas Catharine Ann Fretz, 1846,[325] and another towel maker[1182] folded a white cotton twill tape into points.

Points made in this fashion could be attached to the towel in one of two ways. If used as an insertion, the top and bottom points were sewn to the towel units being joined. If used only as an edging, the folded series of points were placed along the towel's hemmed edge with only the top half of the points visible. The lower half of the points was then covered with a separate strip of tape or fabric to minimize damage during laundering.

Rick rack (ric rac) comes under the general heading of a mill-made flat braid. It became a popular household trim after the decorated hand towel tradition peaked. Sallie L. Halteman, 1896,[1011] however, was one of the few girls[1190] who used commercially manufactured white cotton rick rack both as a top edging and as insertion on her towel. Elizabeth Huber sewed a row of green cotton rick rack braid across the top edge as well as another row across the middle of the towel. [Plate 33]

The distinct appearance of fabric and tape points or rick rack was not often encountered.

C. FRINGES

By definition fringes are an ornamental bordering that can be made of any thread, hanging loose from the edge. (Clabburn, 113) Fringed borders were often a decorative feature on embroidered towels especially when three[32] or four[200] rows of fringe were grouped or spaced throughout the towel. It was a natural trimming, not a joining, and there were many ways of making it.

Self fringe

The simplest and most often made fringes were those produced by unravelling the warp or weft threads of the towel material. We have termed this a self fringe because it originated in the towel material itself and was not a separate addition.[3,62] This fringe occurred at the bottom and top edges of the towel, never at the sides.

Self plain fringe

The term self plain fringe indicated not only a short fringe that originated in the towel fabric, but that these fringed threads hung free and loose in a plain fashion. They might have been bound into groups, but they were not knotted or interwoven in any way.

Most self fringes of this type were overcast in some way to prevent further unravelling and unnecessary thread loss during laundering. Examples of un-bound fringe show the surrounding woven towel material to be loosened and weak.[6,45] [Figure 330] Overcasting was done after the unravelling procedure and usually consisted of diagonal stitches sewn two[44] to four[51] threads deep into the woven material. These plain overcasting stitches were generally sewn in white linen,[44] but if red cotton,[42] [Figure 510] blue cotton,[51] or blue and red yarns were threaded together in one needle[5] another element of color, accent and design were added to the towel.

Stitches other than the normally used overcasting stitch bound the small self plain fringe. In 1824, Barbara Kuns embroidered a red cotton inverted V-shaped stitch with two passes of the needle.[64] Elisabeth Gut, 1817, bound the self fringe with what appears to be a combination of back and straight stitch—not a blanket stitch.[294] On still another towel a red cotton and black silk crosshatching type work was used.[103]

The buttonhole stitch was employed to bind fringe by several persons.[1,96] Fanny[250] and Mary[440] Witmer laid two red cotton threads side by side just above the fringed threads and couched or tied them in place with small diagonal stitches which held the fringe in place as well as couched the long laid threads. [Figure 511]

A more complicated binding procedure on the Iohannes Witmeyer towel combined drawn thread work with the simple self plain fringe. Weft threads were cut and removed within a three-quarter inch high space, four weft threads were then left in place to bind or hold the fringed warp ends. The fringe was bound in red cotton over those remaining four weft threads with a simple diagonal overcasting stitch that amazingly has not pulled out.[288]

Binding self fringed threads into groups was a tedious, time consuming job. Some used what appeared to be looped chain stitches,[62,68] but Elisabeth Peters[333] sewed a dark brown silk blanket-type stitch to bind the fringe into groups of ten warp yarns. AH in 1816,[468] and Maria Kreider[692] embroidered small red cotton cross stitches for this group binding. One patient towel maker segregated the towel fringe into groups of three yarns, a smaller than normal calibration.[296] The binding and grouping of self plain fringed threads was a one-step process when done in this fashion. The finished appearance, however, was determined by the coarseness or fineness of the thread groups and the stitch separating them. [Figure 512]

Whether the self plain fringe was simply overcast or intricately grouped and bound the short fringed threads were allowed to hang unentangled. They extended from one-half[32] to three inches,[15,184] but most self fringes are one inch long. This length kept tangling and matting to a minimum.

Self knotted fringe

Self knotted fringes were not made so quickly and easily as the short plain ones. Knotting was a way of interworking free hanging threads into a fabric by knotting threads around adjacent threads first to one side then the other to produce an ornamental fringe of knotted threads. They ranged from coarse to very fine, heavy to delicate and used knots and combinations of knots. (Emery, 65)

Knotted fringes were decorative embellishments on hand towels from 1794 through 1855; however, their use and execution peaked between 1815 and 1825. As with

FIGURE 510 Self plain fringe, 1½ inches long, bound with red cotton thread, but not before one woven thread began to unravel.[42]

FIGURE 511 Couched red cotton threads bound the fringe and added color to the one inch high flap. The two thread long stitching just below the top fold helped to hold the flap in place.[67]

FIGURE 512 Plain fringe 2½ inches long, bound into groups of yarns to prevent fraying. White cotton darning stitch on drawn thread panel; red cotton needleweaving and cross stitch; threaded needlelace. See Figure 491. 9½" x 15¼".[335]

many of the decorative details, knotted fringes were used on the Pennsylvania towels' Germanic antecedents. (Meyer-Heisig, Abbildung 31, 49, 55)

Knotted fringes were as long as eight inches[317] including the patterned knots and the free-hanging fringe. It was typical to see twelve threads tied into a group and then be pattern knotted into smaller series of threads for a length of five inches.[45] [Figures 513-515, 41, 42, 47, 48]

A towel dated 1794 is one of the earliest examples of this "fine" work.[317] It must be remembered that the fine weave linen used to make the towels was made of finely spun yarns which in turn produced tiny knots and intricate lacy patterns. Most have a diamond or chevron design knotted into them whose pattern similarities are obvious in some drawn thread borders on the same towel.[97,99,188]

Self knotted fringes that originated in the towel fabric were most often made at the lower edge of the towel which permitted the knotted designs to hang and be seen below the surface of the towel and its embroidery. In 1820, however, LZ knotted every six warp yarns together for a distance of three inches to make two rows of knots across the upper face of her towel.[344]

FIGURE 514   The diamond design in the 2¾ inch long knotted fringe appears to be related to the diamond motifs in the drawn thread panel. White linen darning stitch on drawn thread panel. 15½" x 16".[305]

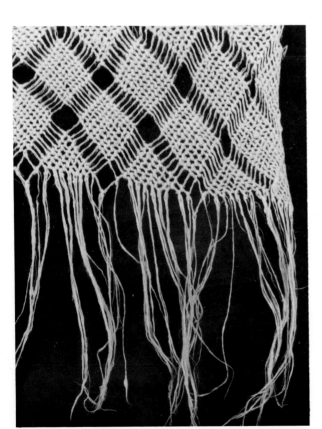

FIGURE 513   A large diamond design was knotted into 2¾ inches; the free hanging fringe is four inches long. On a towel dated 1810.[271]

Skill in knotting fringes appeared to go hand in hand with mastery of embroidery and proficiency in needle laces. Most fringes were knotted in two or more rows. Typical examples include those made with square knots. The fringe was divided into groups of four threads. The outer two threads were tied around the inner two threads, or filler threads, using a square knot. After knotting for the desired distance two threads were taken to the right and two threads taken to the left to be joined with two threads from another group and the process was repeated.[132] In other instances the overhand knot was used to make a fish scale pattern.[139] Another pattern was developed by tying an overhand knot three times right over left, right over left, right over left using equal numbers of threads.[39] The half hitch was another of the knots used. On one towel the fringe was divided into groups of six threads. Working with strands of three the towel maker made three half hitches, separated the threads in half and tied three more half hitches. The third or uneven thread was tied into every other row so the threads stayed the same length.[140] [Figures 516, 517]

FIGURE 515 *1795* Red cotton and white linen darning and Greek cross filling stitches. Knotted linen fringe in diamond pattern three inches long; free hanging fringe four inches long. See Figure 67. 21¼'' x 17- 5/8''.[195]

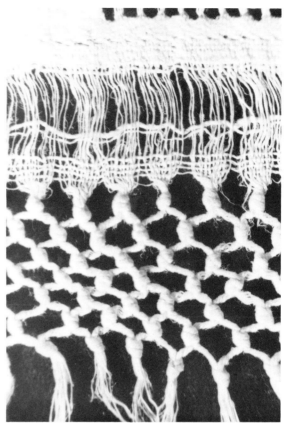

FIGURE 516 Knotted fringe formed by tying the frayed warp yarns in overhand knots.[39]

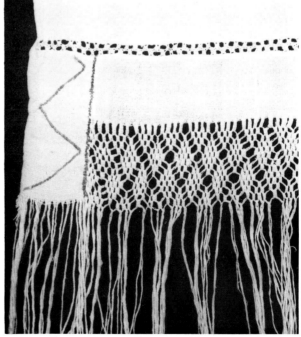

FIGURE 517 Knotted fringe. The overhand knot was used in twice tying equal numbers of threads right over left to form a fish scale pattern.[139]

Applied fringe

Fringes that were made separately and sewn or tied onto the towel we term as an applied fringe. They were narrow or wide, plain or knotted, hand or machine made. They were useful as borders or edge finishes and could be repeated any place on a balanced plain weave[83] or pattern woven towel[84] with as much frequency as the woman had fringe to do so. Lydia Bachman, in 1831, sewed twelve rows of fringe as the featured decoration on her hand towel. Only a few small embroidered designs accompany her name.[719]

Applied plain fringe

One of the most uncomplicated applied plain fringes used a piece of folded balanced plain weave linen material the width of the towel. The folded edge was ultimately sewn to the towel, but first the two cut edges were unravelled the same desired distance. They were then bound together as the fringed threads were overcast.[66,257,701] [Figure 485] It was usually attached to the bottom rather than the top edge of the towel[43] and, of course, this fringe was thicker and had more body because it was double. The amount of woven fabric left unravelled at the top of the fringe varied as much as one inch and the two vertical ends were generally sewn closed.

A narrow, single piece of balanced plain weave linen material was also used to make small plain fringes.[63] Once the fringe was made and bound it was most often attached to the wrong side of the towel underneath an existing self fringe, or it was sewn directly on top of a hem.[283] [Figure 27]

When it was applied to the towel the raw edge on the fringed fabric was folded under so no cut edges were visible, and then it was sewn into place. When the second attached piece of fringed material was no more than three inches, the fringe fell directly below the first creating two fringed borders. If it was distantly spaced it added another panel to the towel. [Plate 7] Ana Thuma made three fringes in this manner and attached them first to each other and then to the towel. She then hemmed the fringes together with the sides of the towel rather than hemming each separate unit individually as is usually done. This produced a bulky side hem.[520]

Most fringes are all-white; however, one resourceful woman unravelled a piece of blue and white vertically striped linen fabric into a knotted fringe. It, of course, retained its striping and therefore added built-in color.[315] [Figure 518]

Applied plain fringes of this type were easily and quickly made with little cost to the towel maker. Short, applied plain fringes were important border elements when they were sewn in one or multiple rows throughout the length of the towel. Here their decorative value was greater than that of a towel finish.

Applied knotted fringe

Applied knotted fringes were usually attached to the towel by tying counted numbers of linen threads into each, every other, or every third grid hole in the drawn thread panel and anchoring them with a weaver's-type

FIGURE 518 The applied blue and white linen fringe on this 1800 towel had a two inch long knotted pattern with seven inches of free-falling threads. It was made of fabric woven with a blue and white stripe warp. All the lace on this towel was knit with unbleached two ply linen yarns. Red, dark blue, light blue, and white cotton darning stitch on drawn thread panel. See Figure 503. 10¼" x 18½".[315]

knot. These fringes were white linen[127,446] or white cotton[137] and hand-knotted into chevron designs before falling into a three[49] or four[259] inch fringe. [Figures 519, 520, 383]

Color was introduced to applied knotted fringes by women such as Susana Rock who tied red, white and blue cotton threads across the bottom of the drawn thread panel.[561] [Plate 22] Elisabeth Erb's two towels, one dated 1811[42] and the other 1812,[427] each have tufts of red cotton inserted into the three rows of white linen fringe. [Figures 5,6]

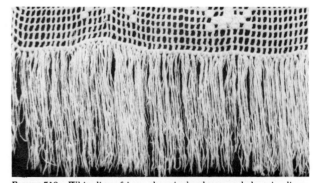

FIGURE 519 White linen fringe, three inches long, made by tying linen threads into each grid hole and knotting them in place.[49]

FIGURE 520 Another applied fringe in which linen threads were tied into every other grid space and then decoratively knotted together before falling into a three inch long fringe.[127]

FIGURE 521 The applied fringe along the bottom edge was made of linen threads inserted into every other grid space and loosely knotted into groups of three. White cotton darning stitch on the one piece drawn thread panel. See Figure 552. 18" x 12½".[287]

If fringes to be knotted were not attached to the towel by tying threads into the grid panel they were individually sewn on the top[287,369] or bottom [273,350] hem before being knotted for one or two rows [369] or left to hang freely.[287] [Figure 521]

Applied knotted fringes resulted from painstaking hours of counting and knotting fringed threads. Making it from fabric other than the towel provided the option for finer or coarser threads thereby producing a smaller or larger knotted design.

Applied braided fringe

Braiding instead of knotting fringe was performed by several young ladies. Susanna Walbin sewed groups of four white linen threads into the bottom hem spaced by the thread grid holes above them in the drawn panel. She divided and braided groups of three threads together for 1¼ inches before allowing the fringe to fall. There is a loop at the end of each braid to finish it.[273]

Braiding, however, was more often combined with knotted fringe as an accompanying element, not as a major decorative procedure. Maria Krausin braided together every three warp yarns across the width of her towel. This braid was three-eighths of an inch in length. The threads were then re-grouped into 4½ inches of knotted work after which they were braided for another 1¾ inches. A tiny knot secured the end of each braid.[339]

MK braided together, as in braiding hair, every three warp yarns that fell from a diamond patterned knotted fringe. Each braid was tied with a knot.[366] [Figure 522]

Fringe on the MR, 1817, towel does not appear to be knotted, but made by a combination of twisting and braiding warp yarns. The process was stopped by winding a thread around each braided strand as a rubber band around a pigtail.[709] Catherine Bitting knotted a chevron pattern in the bottom fringe on her towel. The end of every individual fringed thread contained a knot.[486]

Making plain, knotted, and braided fringes required patience and certain deftness to manipulate many fine threads. It was another instance in which young girls proved their skill.

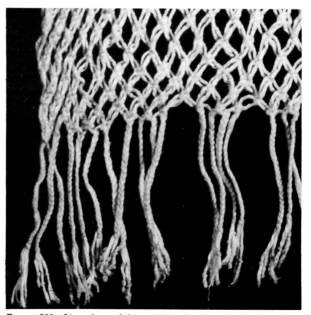

FIGURE 522 Linen knotted fringe 4½ inches long; braided ends 1¾ inches long with a knot at the end. See Plate 8.[339]

Applied commercially made fringe

The widespread use of white cotton machine-made fringe began about 1825. By 1850 this purchased fringe replaced the traditional drawn thread panel at the bottom of the towel.

In addition to its placement along the lower edge, purchased fringe was at times sewn at the upper area of the towel in place of the flap.[69] [Figure 28] Some towel makers applied this fringe throughout the towel as decorative borders[71,75] and in one instance a machine-made fringe with tassels was sewn on both side edges of a drawn thread panel as well as across the bottom. This is one of the few examples of fringe attached to side edges of a decorated towel.[51]

Commercially produced fringe had a narrow footing or braid along its upper edge with which to fasten it securely to the towel. The fringe was from one-half[4] to seven inches wide[171] which measurement included existing tassels. [Figure 523]

Its decorative qualities exceeded what could be made by hand. Some had a gauze-like mesh, others had series of roped loops, many had tassels. The cost to purchase this fringe was not prohibitive as its extensive use suggests. Its application to the towel saved the young woman many hours of hand knotting and its machined appearance was prestigious and well liked. [Figures 524-527]

FIGURE 524　A mill-made white cotton fringe, 5½ inches long, with a chevron pattern similar to the design embroidered in the drawn thread panel just above it. The location of the three-eighth inch high needle-lace, also with chevron design, is unusual. This towel dates 1794.[35]

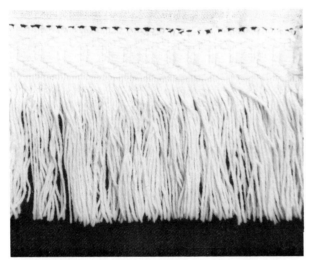

FIGURE 523　A mill-made white cotton fringe, 2½ inches long, attached to the bottom edge of an 1846 towel by sewing through the picots on the heading of the fringe.[150]

242

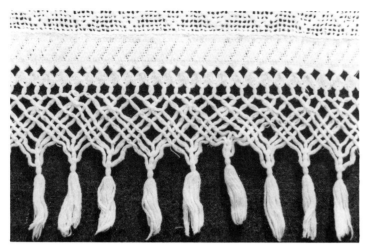

FIGURE 525   A white cotton mill-made fringe five inches long on a towel dated 1833.[28]

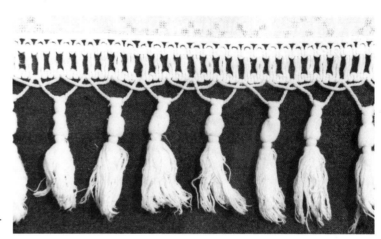

FIGURE 526   Mill-made white cotton fringe/braid with tassels on an 1835 towel.[114]

FIGURE 527   White cotton mill-made fringe with ropes and tassels, five inches long, on a towel dated 1842.[115]

D. TASSELS

Small plain tassels that ornament decorated towels were handmade without accessories such as a wooden ball mold. They are almost always made with white linen threads and seldom exceed 2¾ inches in length.[467,690] An exception in coloration were the red wool tassels applied by AGS on what appears to be an early towel although it has no embroidered date.[374] Mery en Groff wrapped the white linen tassels with red cotton producing a two color tassel.[1179]

Tassels were not a popular towel finish. Fewer than twenty towels were found that include handmade tassels, and only four were dated: 1822,[553] 1831,[1179] 1834,[1150] and 1839.[467]

Most of the towels with tassels had a large amount of drawn thread embroidery on them. Close examination revealed a crimp in the threads of the tassels indicating the threads were formerly woven in fabric, but were removed when making a drawn thread panel. There are few towels without drawn thread work that had handmade tassels attached to them.[1150] [Figure 528]

Two towel makers attached white linen tassels across the lower edge of their towels.[373,547] Some were sewn directly into the hem[373] whereas others were fastened in every fourth grid hole of the drawn panel.

It was more usual to place handmade tassels on the side edges of the towel.[621,1086] After all, the top and bottom were commonly trimmed with hand knotted or purchased fringes. Meri Weinholt, 1839, affixed a white linen side tassel near each bottom corner.[467] [Figure 165] On the Iacob Graf, 1822, towel, however, there are four side tassels, two on the right and two on the left edges.[553] The upper pair is located about twenty-one inches from the top of the towel, and the remaining two tassels are sewn between the drawn thread panel and bottom decorative fringe. Each tassel is two inches long and was joined to the towel by a one inch shank of buttonholed threads. It was not butted against the hem as usual, but was given a cord from which to hang.

Abeth Ditze evenly spaced four white linen tassels along each side edge of her towel. Another woman applied seven tassels to the right and seven to the left hems for a total of fourteen.[284] Some women made extensive use of tassels; one used fifty,[1336] [Figure 529] another fifty-two,[690] [Figure 530] another sixty six,[1284] and still another seventy-four tassels.[1292] Half the total number of these tassels were sewn to each side of the towel. There were none along either the top or bottom edges. The purpose of these tassels was certainly more decorative than functional.

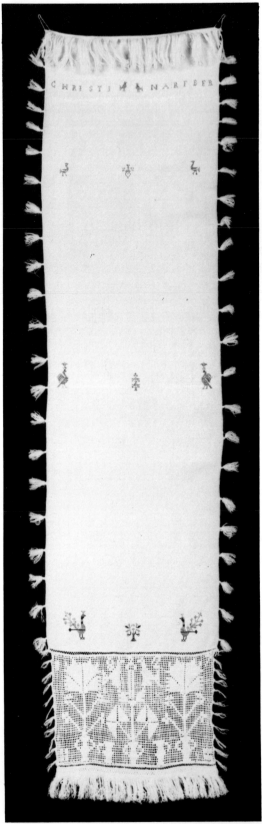

FIGURE 528 *Christina Reber, 1827.* Balanced plain weave linen fabric; red cotton cross stitch; white cotton darning stitch on drawn thread panel; self and applied plain fringes; white linen tassels. The tassels and applied side fringe were made from the fabric yarns withdrawn to make the bottom drawn thread grid. 56¾ x 13¼''.[1284] Courtesy, Mary Ann McIlnay.

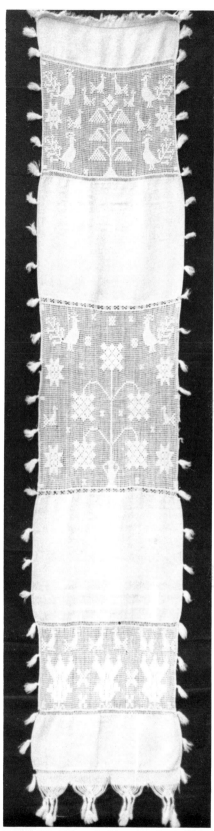

FIGURE 529 Here too the side tassels were bound groups of drawn yarns. Balanced plain weave linen fabric; white cotton darning stitch in drawn thread panels; white linen tassels; self plain fringe; applied mill-made white cotton fringe. See Figure 530 for similar motifs. 73'' x 14¾''.[1336]

FIGURE 530 Balanced plain weave linen fabric; white cotton darning stitch on drawn thread panels; white linen tassels; self plain fringe; applied mill-made white cotton fringe. See Figure 529 for towel with similar motifs. 73½'' x 14-5/8''.[690] Courtesy, Sally and Pete Riffle.

E. HANGING TABS

A final, but important, finishing component in towel construction was the two tabs with which the towel was hung and displayed. They were affixed to the towel in each upper corner and appeared in as great a variety as did other aspects of hand towel decoration.

The length of the loops was determined in part by the size of the wooden peg, nailhead, or metal knob on which the towel hung. Tabs ranged from short three-eighth inch buttonholed loops[4,109,120] to 4½ inch long tapes.[99] This is the measurement from the towel edge to the tab fold. The width of the tab was governed by the material from which it was made more than by where or how the towel was hung.

Hanging tabs fall into two general categories: those that were purchased, and those that were homemade. Far more towels have store bought cotton twill or other commercially made tapes than tabs of domestic manufacture. One towel had a small brass ring sewn to each upper corner,[269] and another had silk ribbon which was probably not the best choice of tab materials.[285] [Plate 39] White cotton twill tape three-eighths to one-half inch wide was used most often. [Figure 531]

Homemade tabs were fashioned in numerous manners thereby adding one more decorative facet to an already personalized needlemade medium. A few examples of handmade tabs include: a strand of linen threads buttonholed together;[4,25,47,129] [Figures 532, 533, 25] handwoven linen and cotton tapes in natural,[31] bleached,[29,257] red white and blue,[1113] or multicolor;[54,284,329] [Figures 534, 535] twisted or plied linen yarns;[85] a three strand braid;[703] [Figure 536] plain or pattern woven cloth folded and sewn into a tape;[139,421] [Figure 537] four-ply white linen yarns occasionally knotted together;[512] and loosely twisted white cotton yarns with tassels at the top.[85] It appears towel makers made loops however they could with whatever materials were at hand. [Figure 538]

Hanging tabs were usually limited to the upper two corners. Each girl seems to have had her own idea, however, of how and where they should be attached to best enable the towel to hang straight and even. The methods of attaching them are as varied as the loops themselves.

Most often the looped tab is placed perpendicular to the top edge of the towel with its two ends, one on top of the other, sewn to the back of the towel. [Figures 539,540] In some cases, however, the ends of the loop were one to 1½ inches apart.[131] [Figure 541] Tabs that were sewn to the side-top resembled ears more than hanging loops.[232,250] Some loops go around the outside corner with one end of the tab fastened to the side and the other end attached to the top corner of the towel.[509] Others are sewn directly into the corner and extend diagonally.[421] [Figure 542] Loops were placed on the side edges with nothing along the upper area,[509,1220] some tabs were sewn flat along the back of the upper edge to conceal them,[542] and still others were stitched along the top, but were sewn 1½ inches from the corner toward the center.[398] [Figure 543; Plate 24]

Endeavors were made to hang and stretch the top of the towel with an even, gentle tension to prevent sagging in the middle and stop the top edge from rolling forward. CB, 1831, added a third centered loop,[58] [Figure 167; Plate 48] and Reg [ina] K Schultz, 1824, hand sewed a casing across the top of the towel in which to insert a rod before hanging. The casing appears original, not a later addition, but this is not at all usual.[262]

Down to the very last detail, decorated towels combined tradition with individualized expressions.

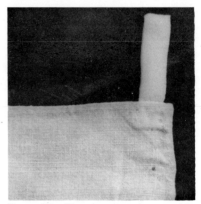

FIGURE 531   Many hanging tabs were white cotton mill-made twill tape. 1¾" x ½".[38]

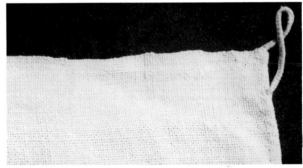

FIGURE 532   White linen buttonholed hanging tab sewn from the top corner to the side edge. L. 5/8".[602]

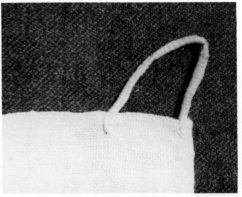

FIGURE 533   White linen buttonholed hanging tab attached to the top on the reverse side of the towel. L. ¾".[132]

246

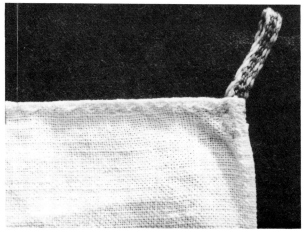

FIGURE 534　Hand woven white and brown linen and blue cotton tape. L. ¾''; W. 1/8''.[37]

FIGURE 537　White cotton fabric (not tape) hanging tab. L. 1½''; W. 3/8''.[133]

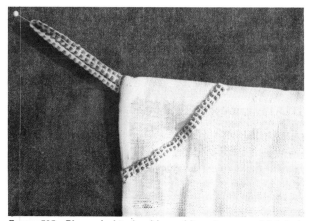

FIGURE 535　Blue and white hand loomed linen tape, one-eighth inch wide, used for both the hanging tab and as reinforcement across the upper corner. The tab is 1¾ inches long and the piece of tape sewn diagonally on the towel is three inches long and has both cut edges turned under. They did not extend to the back of the towel.[54]

FIGURE 538　Mill-made white cotton braid used as a hanging tab. L. 1''.[114]

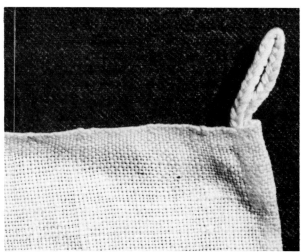

FIGURE 536　A hanging tab made by braiding linen threads.

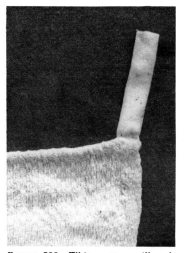

FIGURE 539　White cotton mill-made tape folded in half lengthwise and then sewn to the towel in a loop. L. 1¾''; W. ¾''.[28]

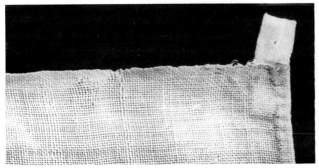

FIGURE 540   Plain weave white cotton mill-made tape. L. ½''; W. 3/8''.

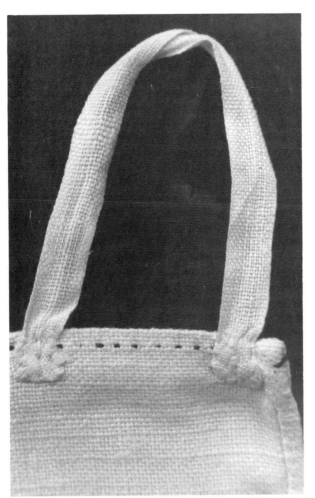

FIGURE 541   The cut edges of hanging tabs were turned under and sewn to the towel with tiny stitches. This mill-made white linen tape was one-quarter inch wide and 1¾ inches long and the ends were spaced one inch apart. A dark blue cotton running stitch was sewn across the top edge through the double thickness of flap and towel fabric to help keep the flap in place.[697] Courtesy, Sally and Pete Riffle.

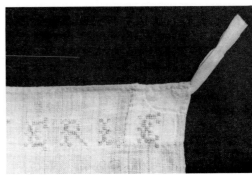

FIGURE 542   A white cotton patch that indicates not only the stress the upper corners were under when the towel was stretched and hung on the door, but also shows that even a worn towel was valued enough to repair and continue displaying it.[29]

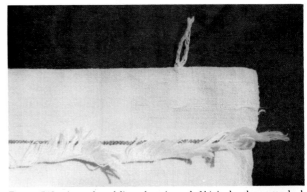

FIGURE 543   A crocheted linen hanging tab 1½ inches long attached to the towel 1¾ inches from the edge of the towel.[39]

248

Variants

We have now examined the most prevalent framework of decorated towel construction which involves choices: choices of towel fabric and assembly, embroidery colors and stitchery techniques, design patterns and placement, and decorative finishes.

Four small groups of ornamented towels contrast in some notable way to those other representatives of this folk custom. These are towels that are: 1) block printed;[9,81,1106,1326] 2) miniature size;[392,573,575,637,698,827,842,1317,1318] 3) all-drawn thread embroidery;[124,621,1207] and 4) all-white stitchery.[25,71,279,322,402,461,518,548,932]

These specific towels offer even more divergence than those special ones already cited for their excellence in stitchery, unique designs, and significant motif arrangement. These unconventional towel types may be yet one more expression of individual creativity; they may also be completely independent phases of the decorated towel tradition of the Pennsylvania Germans which never became generally popular.

A. BLOCK PRINT TOWELS

Not much is known about the Pennsylvania Dutch block printing tradition or the technological processes needed to produce a decorated towel of this type, but they may be direct descendants of the printed towels made in Swabia and Saxony in the mid eighteenth century. (Meyer-Heisig, Abbildung 80,81,87)

The few old block printed textiles still in existence seem to have originated during the first half of the nineteenth century in Pennsylvania. Block printed fabrics of any kind, however, were not usual in the Pennsylvania German household although more tablecloths and table scarves are found than are bed coverings and decorated hand towels. (The York County Historical Society, York, Pa., and the William Penn Memorial Museum, Harrisburg, Pa. have in their collections some block printed Pennsylvania textiles).

Block printed designs embellish only a few Pennsylvania Dutch hand towels. The first towel is made of a plain balanced weave cotton fabric that measures fifteen inches wide by 52¼ inches long. It boasts large blue, green, and red circle designs, birds, deer and various borders. A white cotton machine-made fringe is attached along the lower edge.[9]

A second towel is printed in red and blue on a pattern weave cotton fabric. It is 15½ inches wide and 45½ inches long. The towel has a printed border along all four sides. Swags and flowers cover the upper area with a whirling swastiska-type design directly below. There is a large circular floral motif printed near the lower edge that is surrounded by other kinds of flowers.[81] [Figure 544]

Birds and flowers were the basic theme printed on another balanced plain weave cotton towel. This one is seventeen inches wide and fifty-four inches long which includes twelve inches of mill-made fringe. Although the colors are faded, a printed border on four sides of the towel can still be seen.[1106] [Figure 545]

A young woman embroidered her initials CH in red cotton cross stitch inside the center of a large printed sunburst design at the top of her towel. The rest of the towel has birds with leaves in their bills, spotted deer, flowers, leaves, and small geometric crosses printed in red and green on the balanced plain weave cotton towel. The designs also include a border along the four edges. It measures 16 ³/₈ inches wide and 46½ inches long and has a two inch long mill-made fringe sewn across the bottom.[1326]

All of the towels were printed on cotton fabric. None of them had a top flap or drawn thread embroidery; block printed motifs were the only ornamentation. Only one towel bore the initials of the original owner and none were dated. Some of the printed designs were identical and were probably printed by the same printer.

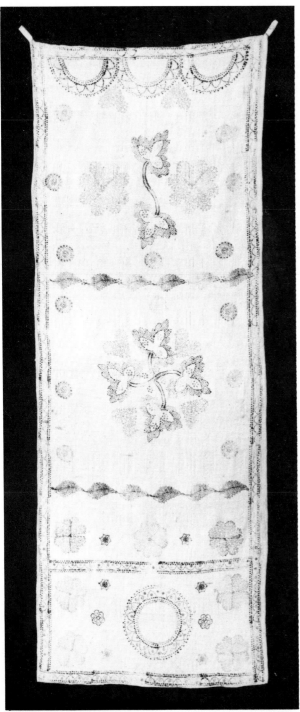

FIGURE 544 The designs are printed in red and blue on this eight harness pattern cotton fabric towel. 45½" x 15½".[81] Courtesy, Mary Ann McIlnay.

FIGURE 545 Balanced plain weave cotton fabric; designs printed in blue, green, orange-red, and mustard yellow. 54" x 17".[1106] Courtesy, Dr. and Mrs. Donald M. Herr.

B. MINIATURE TOWELS

Decorated towels in miniature hold a special fascination. All that is true of larger towels in terms of fabric, construction, embroidery threads, colors, choice of designs, and fancy needlework also applies to these small ones.

Of the known small scale decorated towels two were made for girls aged five and twelve years. Can we dare to think that other miniature examples of needle expertise were made and given to youngsters as a plaything? Or, perhaps, as an extra-special gift?

The smallest towel resembles a book mark more than a towel for it is 2 5/8 inches wide and 8¼ inches long. It is made of homespun linen fabric. The bottom fringe, now cut off, would have made its original length slightly greater. Unfortunately it is without name, initials, date, or family history, but it does include many of the features found on the larger towels. There are tiny thread loops for hanging, four needlewoven borders in red and blue cotton, and four small red and blue cross stitched designs of a heart with flowers, a single flower and a cross. To indicate the top flap a tuck one-sixteenth of an inch high was taken five-eighths of an inch below the top selvage edge and was sewn in place with a single row of blue cotton backstitch.[827] [Figure 546]

Another small towel measures six inches wide by 12½ inches long. It was made in 1825, according to family tradition, by Ruth Hoppel, a family friend, for Mary Stauffer when Mary was just twelve years old. Both of their initials RH and MS and the year 1825 were embroidered near the top. The linen towel has a top flap with fringe, tabs for hanging, and several rows of fringe at the lower edge. Star, heart, and deer designs were cross stitched in red and blue cotton and brown silk, but there is no drawn thread embroidery.[573] [Figure 547]

The colorful little towel, dated 1827, is full of symmetrical motifs that include crowns, hearts, flowers, and altar or heavenly Jerusalem design, a pair of geese with two goslings, and a set of numerals one to nine all sewn in multicolor silk. Spaced across the top and bottom edges are five thread buttons, some of dark blue cotton and some of yellow silk. The linen towel measures 5 7/8 inches wide and fifteen inches long. There is no flap or drawn thread work, but the top and bottom edges each have an inch long self-plain fringe bound into groups of threads. The hanging loops are one inch and 1 1/8 inches long and are made of a very fine linen tape.[1317] [Plate 45]

Circumstances surrounding the making of the little towel marked Christina Hessin are unknown. It is 8¾ inches wide by twenty-three inches long with fringes at the top and bottom edges. Her initials CH are sewn in satin stitch inside a large heart motif, but her full name is embroidered in German script across the upper area of the towel in place of a top flap. Needleworked designs at the top of the cotton towel are sewn in red cotton and aqua and gold colored silk. They form a large heart with a free-form vine and flowers under it. The remainder of the towel is devoted to finely executed drawn thread embroidery and other fine stitchery.[392] [Plate 46] (See pp. 10, 58 for a discussion of related towels).

An undated miniature towel had the name Anna G. Herr printed with an ink stamp at the lower edge. The towel has four narrow drawn thread borders one-half to 1½ inches high spaced throughout its length, and an embroidered border of needleweaving and herringbone stitch as its major ornamentations. White linen, red cotton, and black, green, blue, and pink silk were the colors needlewoven through these drawn thread areas and sewn together with the herringbone stitchery.

This linen towel, almost the same size as Christina Hess's, is 9 1/8 inches wide by 22½ inches long, including the lower fringe. Stitched into the self plain fringe along the bottom edge at each outer corner were two clusters of black silk threads. The top flap, which is an inch wide, was accented by a small plain fringe. There are no loops for hanging the towel.[637] [Plate 47]

Another small towel without name or date is also almost the same size. It measures 9¼ inches wide and 22½ inches long which includes the bottom self-knotted fringe. It was made of white cotton fabric with red and dark and light blue cross stitch embroidery. The three flower designs in the top panel are not symmetrical, but the central star and diamond motifs in the second panel are balanced. Large cross stitched chevron borders occupy two additional panels on the towel, another panel supported one flower design, and the last panel is empty. The self fringe across the lower edge is two inches long; it is neatly knotted into a diamond pattern.[698] [Figure 548]

A little linen towel with the initials BR is ten inches wide and 18½ inches long. It was made with two pieces of fabric, has a top flap three-quarters of an inch high with one inch of self fringe; one linen tape tab for hanging remains. There are seven different red cotton and brown silk cross stitch designs, mostly flowers, arranged throughout the towel plus three M-shaped figures which were embroidered through the double thickness of the flap and towel fabric. No date or examples of drawn thread embroidery were sewn on this towel.[842] [Figure 549]

There are also towels which are a bit larger than the smallest ones, but are not large enough to fit into the full-size towel category. The linen towel made by Sara Spengler is 12¼ inches wide and twenty-three inches long. There is no flap or drawn panel, but there are rows of zigzag hemstitching, needlewoven borders, the alphabet, and nine different motifs sewn in red cotton and brown silk. Two rows of plain fringe were sewn to the bottom edge and small buttonholed thread loops for hanging extend from the side edge of each top corner. It is not dated, but family tradition states it was made circa 1835.[1318] [Figure 550]

Rebecca J. Minnich made a small towel as a gift for her five year old sister Catharine Halanah Minnich, March 14, 1850. It is just 11 1/8 inches wide and twenty-eight inches long. Ten different designs are cross stitched

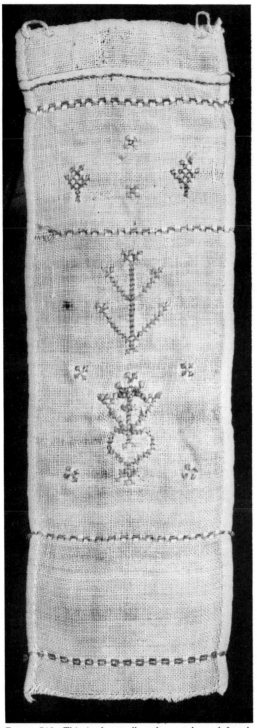

FIGURE 547   R[uth] H[opple], M[ary] S[tauffer], 1825. Balanced plain weave linen fabric; red and blue cotton and brown silk cross stitch; self and applied plain fringes. 12½" x 6".[573]

FIGURE 546   This is the smallest decorated towel found. Balanced plain weave linen fabric; red and blue cotton cross stitch and needleweaving. 8¼" x 2-5/8".[827]

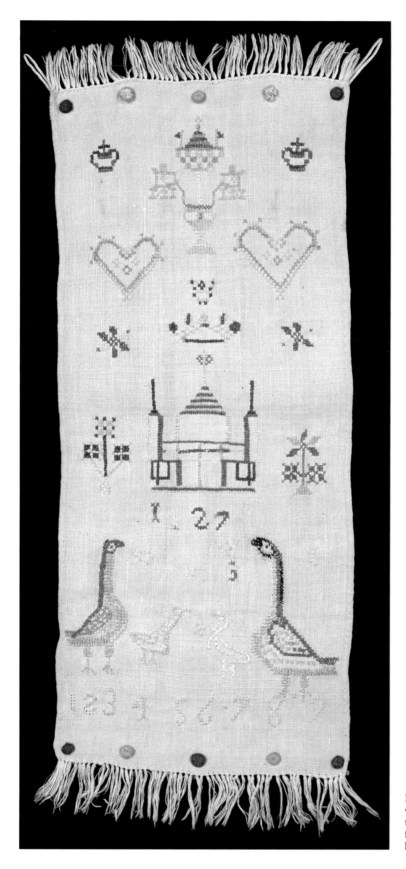

PLATE 45 *1827* .... Balanced plain
weave linen fabric; red, blue and tan cotton, multicolor silk cross stitch; self plain
fringes; yellow and blue cotton thread
buttons. Miniature size. 15" x 5-7/8".[1317]

253

FIGURE 549   *BR.* Balanced plain weave linen fabric; red cotton and brown silk cross stitch; self and applied plain fringes. 18½'' x 10''.[842] Courtesy, Albert and Elizabeth Gamon.

FIGURE 548   Balanced plain weave cotton fabric; red, dark blue, and light blue cotton cross stitch; self knotted fringe. 22½'' x 9¼''.[698] Courtesy, Sally and Pete Riffle.

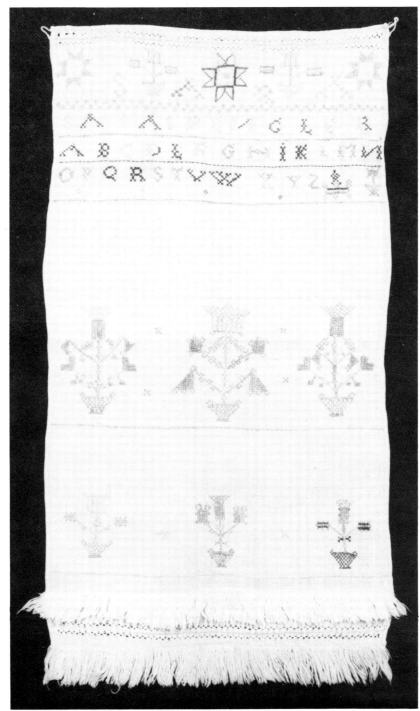

FIGURE 550 *Sara Spengler.* York county. Balanced plain weave linen fabric; red cotton and brown silk cross stitch and needleweaving; zigzag hemstitching; applied plain fringes. 23" x 12¼".[1318]

PLATE 46 *Christina Hessin, CH, 1815.* Lancaster county. Balanced plain weave cotton fabric; red cotton, aqua and gold silk outline, seed, straight, chain and satin stitches; cotton darning stitch on drawn thread panels; applied plain fringes; applied cotton fabric with red, brown and white woven stripes. Miniature size. 23½'' x 8¾''.[392] Courtesy, The Henry Francis duPont Winterthur Museum.

Catharine Halanah Minnich Her Towel &
March The 1 th & In the Year Of Our Lord
A D 1850

Within thy courts one single
Day T is better to attend than
Lord In any other Place A
Thousand Days to Spend

Catharine Halanah Minnich is my
Name And Heaven is my Station
And Lancaster County Is my
Dewlling Place And Christ Is my
Salvation And When I am dead And in
My Grave and all my bones are rotten
If this You see Remember me or else I
Must be Foregotten And Fore ever
Amen

This ring
Is round it has
No end when I
Look on this ring
Then I can see
How kind my Sist
er was to me
Rebecca M
innich

And We soon shall hear
Him say Ye Blessed
Children come We soon
Will call us hence away
And take his wand'rers
Home

PLATE 47   *Anna G. Herr.* Lancaster county. Balanced plain weave linen fabric; red cotton, brown, blue, olive green, and peach silk cross and herringbone stitches; needleweaving; self and applied plain fringes. Brown silk tassels attached at each bottom corner. Miniature size. 22½" x 9-1/8".[637]

PLATE 48   *Catharine Halanah Minnich, 1850 . . . .* Lancaster county. Balanced plain weave linen fabric; wool cross stitch; self plain fringes. 28-1/8" x 11-1/8".[575] Courtesy, Dr. and Mrs. Donald M. Herr.

257

in twenty-three separate places in finely spun multicolored wool onto the finely woven linen towel fabric. In addition, the towel carries five individual inscriptions. There is a top flap with self fringe, small twisted cords for hanging, and a fringe across the lower edge. This one is the largest and most elaborate of the miniature towels studied.[575] [Plate 48] (See pp. 225-226 for a discussion of related towels).

C. WHITE TOWELS

White towels can be classified in at least two categories, drawn thread and surface embroidered. The drawn thread category can be further subdivided into those towels which were worked on a full length grid and those which were worked as self drawn work. Also in this category are those all-white towels which have a large panel of either balanced plain weave or pattern weave with a drawn panel or panels somewhere in their length. The surface embroidered towels can be grouped by design placement, stitch technique and color.

Drawn thread towels

All-drawn thread embroidered towels have warp and weft threads removed to make the entire towel on a drawn grid with no balanced plain weave material included. Their appearance is far from typical. Only a few examples came to our attention and one is marked SK, 1843.[1207]

The first all-drawn thread towel has a white linen ground and white cotton designs. It is 14¼ inches wide and 36¾ inches long and along the bottom edge are fragments of what might have been tassels or an applied fringe. The top and bottom edges were bound with an applied piece of three-eighth inch wide fabric which provided strength and rigidity for hanging the towel. Each side had a one-quarter inch hem of the self-pulled thread material. The entire one-piece towel was embroidered with horizontal rows of alternating chevrons that presented an overall geometric pattern.[124]

A second all-drawn thread towel has been seen by photograph only. It consisted of three large drawn thread panels that appear to have been joined in some way, possibly with needlelace. Each panel had its own arrangement of typical designs including vases of flowers, stars, and a quantity of bird motifs. A single row of machine-made fringe was sewn across the bottom of the towel. The hemmed sides have many tassels attached to them that appear to be spaced about every two inches for the full length of the towel.[621] (Photograph of towel in exhibit at Historical Society of York County, 1976).

SK, 1843, made her all-drawn thread towel with two pieces of joined fabric each of which contain large floral designs. It is 15½ inches wide and fifty-seven inches long and the designs were embroidered in white cotton.[1207] [Figure 551]

Without any linen fabric, all-drawn towels have a lacey, delicate appearance whose designs were shown to best advantage when hanging on a painted red, blue, or yellow door.

FIGURE 551 *SK, 1843.* An unusual towel made entirely of drawn thread fabric. 57" x 15½".[1207] Courtesy Mary Ann McIlnay.

258

FIGURE 552 *MD, 1835*. Balanced plain weave linen fabric; white cotton darning stitch in drawn thread panels. Only the date is sewn in red cotton cross stitch. Self and applied plain and knotted fringes. 64" x 12½".[287]

The all-white towels that include alternate panels of drawn thread embroidery with woven fabric are more sturdy than those all-drawn thread ones. The separate panels are often attached with fancy insertions; one towel has seven different needlelace patterns used to connect towel units together.[1336] [Figures 552,553] Other towels contain self-drawn thread panels making insertion work unnecessary.[1337] All -white towels of this type were made more often than those with an all-drawn thread grid, but not as often as those with colored embroidery threads.

Surface white embroidery

In general, the term whitework refers to any embroidery worked in white thread on a white ground. (Clabburn, 282) There are "open" and "closed" types. In the "closed" form of whitework the stitches are worked upon the fabric in the same manner as in flat embroidery. The whitework that appears on Pennsylvania German decorated handtowels is of the "closed" variety. That is all the designs were embroidered in white thread on white towel fabric as in flat embroidery. No decorative holes were cut and bound as in the "open" form of whitework.

All-white surfaced embroidered towels bear dates from 1827[548] to 1860[322] and with the exception of color and design placement were similar to other towels. The towels were all standard size and were made of either pattern woven or balanced plain weave, cotton or linen, or cotton batiste-type fabric. Towel construction included the typical hems, seams, and insertions, top flap, fringes, drawn thread panels, and tabs for hanging. The embroidery thread varied in weight and type, and the stitches were bold or delicate as required by the towel fabric. Whitework runs the full range of needlework quality; some is quite fine and others are less impressive.

We have further classified these towels by their design placement. Six of the towels originated in Montgomery county Schwenkfelder families and have a single white decorative panel at the lower edge.[279,322,461,518,548,1315] In the second variation the towel surface is dominated by just one large, white floral motif that extends from the top to the bottom. They too were embroidered by Schwenkfelders.[71,402,932] The third type involves embroidery that is placed only on the outer edges of the towel.[929] The fourth and last subdivision by design placement is one in which all the white designs were arranged symmetrically throughout the towel according to more traditional practice.[25]

Towels whose whitework embroidery was limited to a single panel include an undated towel made by Maria Heebner. On this example a plain weave panel attached to the bottom of a pattern woven towel contains three tulips nine inches high sewn in white satin stitch. The center tulip stems from a scalloped circular design while the two remaining tulips emerged from a star. It appears that after the satin stitches were completed Maria superimposed added chain, outline, and short straight stitches to give further detail to the tulip petals and leaves.[461]

PLATE 49 *Elisabeth Diehl.* Manheim township, Lancaster county. Balanced plain weave linen fabric; linen satin stitch; cotton darning stitch on drawn thread panel; self plain and knotted fringes. 60'' x 15½''.[25]

FIGURE 553 Balanced plain weave linen fabric; white cotton darning stitch in drawn thread panels; applied plain fringe. 66" x 18-5/8".[725] Courtesy, Sally and Pete Riffle.

FIGURE 554 *MF* Balanced plain weave linen fabric; red cotton cross stitch initials; white cotton darning stitch in drawn thread panels; applied plain fringe. Drawn thread and fabric squares measure three inches. 60¼" x 14¾".[704] Courtesy, Sally and Pete Riffle.

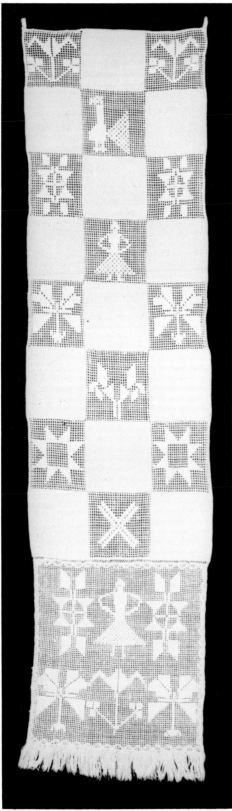

FIGURE 555   Balanced plain weave linen fabric; white cotton darning stitch in drawn thread panels; applied plain fringe. 55" x 13¾".[1337]

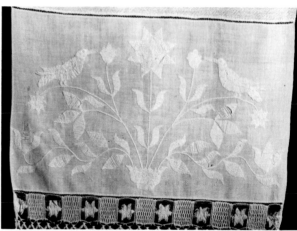

FIGURE 556   *Maria Heebner.* Montgomery county. Pattern woven linen towel; balanced plain weave cotton panel; white cotton satin and chain stitch; red cotton cross stitch name. 11¼" x 19-1/8".[1315]

Maria Heebner of Worcester township, Montgomery county, married William A. Schultz, October 18, 1859. The year of her marriage helps to date this towel between 1855 and 1860. Maria was a folk artist who portrayed flowers, fruits, and birds in her painting book. (Lichten, 222). It seems reasonable to assume that the tulip designs sewn on her towel were drawn by her and not copied from a printed source.

There is another all-white towel also with the name Maria Heebner cross stitched on it with remarkable simiarities to the towel just described. This pattern woven linen towel has a balanced plain weave cotton panel attached to the bottom which contains a basket of flowers whose stems extend the full width and height of the panel. They are sewn in white cotton satin and chain stitch.[1315] [Figure 556]

A stylized flower, possibly hand drawn, was the center attraction on another whiteworked towel that was originally from Upper Hanover township, Montgomery county. The solitary heart, eight inches tall, gives rise to three flowers; the motif was embroidered at the bottom of the towel just above the attached drawn thread panel. This lone design is primarily in white cotton satin stitch with the flower stems embroidered in the outline stitch. The satin stitched heart has an inside and outside border of French knots and the center of each flower is sprinkled with French knots. Above this motif are two large separate flowers which seem to be an enlargement of those coming from the heart. They were made in the same manner.[518]

Some of the most intricate and elaborate whitework was embroidered by Rebecca Gerhard in 1844, the same year she married Abraham Schultz, from Upper Hanover township, Montgomery county. Her white cotton embroidery appears on a balanced plain weave cotton panel, 7 3/8 inches high, that was sewn to the bottom of a patterned towel. The 6½ inch high free-form design

FIGURE 557 R[ebecca] G[erhard], 1844. Upper Hanover township, Montgomery county. Balanced plain weave cotton panel attached to a pattern weave linen towel with three-eighth inch high white cotton folded fabric points; white cotton satin, back, stem, and straight stitches and French knots. The initials, year and small motif were sewn in gold silk. 7-3/8'' x 18-1/8''.[279]

emerged from a central pineapple-type motif and extends the full width of the towel in mirror image. Many of the figures are connected in some way. Flowers and birds are recognizable and the other designs are ornate oval and circular shapes. The fine precise sewing includes the back, outline, satin, and straight stitch and numerous French knots. Her initials and the year were embroidered in very small gold silk chain stitches. The complexity of the overall design and the deftness of the embroidery exemplifies unusual needlework skills. The white coloration showed her expertise to good advantage.[279] [Figure 557]

MW 1827, embroidered some more sophisticated whitework not usually encountered in Pennsylvania folk embroidery near the bottom of her towel. With needle and white cotton embroidery thread she created a large, single, centralized, free-form flower with bird design that is about 10½ inches high and twelve inches wide. Instead of merely outlining the various design shapes, as was done on most of the towels described above, MW filled the bird and each of the five different flowers with various stitch combinations utilizing the chain, outline, satin, lazy daisy, star eyelet, and French knots. The design was so well planned and executed one cannot help wonder if MW purchased this embroidery pattern, received special needlework schooling, was a professional seamstress, or had the towel made for her by a professional embroiderer.[548]

In direct contrast to this elegant whitework is a towel dated 1860 which has an eleven inch high white embroidered panel full of large stylistic animals. A big spotted rabbit runs through a woods of six trees with hanging branches while two primitive birds watch from above. The rabbit, birds, and trees were all outlined in white cotton chain stitch. None was filled solid with stitchery. There were five elongated oval shapes sewn across the bottom, and the date, 1860, was stitched at center top. The panel depicts a realistic scene rather than a symmetrical arrangement. It is an artistic expression in free-form embroidery.[322] [Figure 558]

In the second division of whitework design placement there are towels embroidered with one large motif only. It appears that Maria Masteller, 1848, might have used a compass to form the one large and two small flowers sewn on her linen towel. The flowers are on a central stem with branches and leaves that rise from a flat heart. This large design is embroidered in white cotton stem stitch. However, her name and the date inside the heart are sewn with red cotton stem stitch. The letters in her name are similar to the printed German typeface and include the long "S" in Masteller. The upper case letter "M" as well as the long "S" are sewn with thick and thin lines just as a scrivener would have made them. The linen towel measures 16 ³/₈ inches wide and fifty-four inches long, and this single design dominates the entire surface of the towel.[932]

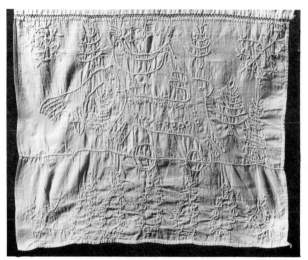

FIGURE 558 *1860* Balanced plain weave cotton panel; white cotton chain and satin stitches. The spotted rabbit is four inches high and six inches wide. 11-1/8" x 15-1/8".[322]

Regina Kriebel who lived in Hereford township, Berks county,[71] and Sarah Kriebel from Worcester township, Montgomery county,[402] each made a fine weave cotton towel and embroidered on it one long, free-style flower motif that extended the full length of the undated towel. The flowers were worked in single rows of white cotton chain stitch. Regina's 30½ inch tall flower rose from the earth and Sarah's twenty-seven inch high flower from a heart. Inside the heart were flowers and leaves on stems bent to the curvature of the heart shape. Sarah's towel was made of sheer cotton batiste-type material and her embroidery was worked in a chain-like stitch. [Figures 559, 560]

The girls' work differed at the bottom of the towel where a drawn thread panel was often attached. Regina embroidered another flower design with a small bird perched on a tulip 13¾ inches high, and Sarah attached fancy, commercially made fringes. Although Regina and Sarah were not closely related and lived at opposite ends of the Schwenkfelder settlement area, their unusual towels bear a remarkable resemblance. Surely they felt the pressures and influences of English speaking neighbors. But then, many of the Schwenkfelder decorated hand towels, as previously stated, were distinctive.

The third type of whitework design placement involves a towel whose floral motifs were sewn across the top and bottom edges and along each side leaving the center and middle area of the towel open and free of design. This white cotton towel without name or date was embroidered with an unusual variety of stitches: the satin, stem, chain, lazy daisy stitches, and a modified buttonhole stitch plus the French knot and bullion knot/stitch. The designs on each side edge are alike; however, the top and bottom rows each have their own set of motifs. The top is edged with a row of bullion stitched loops and the bottom of the towel has applied commercially-made fringe sewn to it. The towel is from the Bethlehem area and its embroidery may have been influenced by the Moravian needlework schools there.[929] [Figure 561]

FIGURE 559 *Regina Kriebel.* Montgomery county. Balanced plain weave cotton fabric; red cotton cross stitch name; white cotton chain stitch; white cotton applied mill-made fringe; white cotton mill-made lace insertion one-half inch high. 55" x 15¼".[71]

264

FIGURE 560 *Sarah Kriebel.* Montgomery county. Balanced plain weave cotton batiste-type fabric; Red cotton chain and back stitch in name; white cotton chain and satin stitch in design; white cotton fabric folded points one inch high; white cotton mill-made applied fringe three inches long. 38½" x 16".[402]

The fourth segment of whitework design placement closely parallels the other towels discussed in chapters two to four. It is illustrated by a towel made by Elisabeth Diehl whose name, but no date, was sewn in her drawn thread panel. She embroidered designs on two separate towel panels in a fine, white linen thread in counted satin stitch blocks of unequal size. Strict counting and sewing of these blocks required stitching on a one to one thread ratio. For every warp and weft thread in the woven material one pass of the needle was needed. Individual blocks were perhaps six threads long by four threads wide and were sewn with the embroiderey threads in a horizontal or vertical direction. Altering both the size and the direction of the stitches in each embroidered block or groups of blocks creates contrast and interest in the design. Count thread embroidery of this order was especially critical and demanding.

FIGURE 561 Balanced plain weave cotton fabric; white cotton satin, stem, chain, lazy daisy, buttonhole stitches and French knot and bullion knot; white cotton mill-made applied fringe. 36" x 15¼".[929]

It was this type of embroidery and white linen coloration that prevailed in all the designs on this towel. Two large tulips stand to each side of a central flower with six resting birds. Across the top of the towel is a horizontal four inch high diamond border also made with counted satin stitch blocks of unequal size. The towel construction, design patterning, and design arrangement were otherwise traditional. It had a top flap, buttonholed loops for hanging it, a typical drawn thread panel, and self knotted fringe along the bottom edge.[25] [Plate 49]

FIGURE 562 *HCB, 1728.* Balanced plain weave linen fabric; white linen couching-type stitch. For an example of what appears to be a Pennsylvania relative of this European towel see Figures 559, 560. Lace: 7¼''; towel: 111-7/8'' x 19¼''. Courtesy, Swiss National Museum, Zurich.

266

APPENDIXES

Appendix I
Charts

The information on these charts was taken from the sheets compiled on each towel containing a date. Detailed sheets were prepared on about 580 towels up to and including number 835. Because of the time limitations most of the towels from numbers 836 to 1424 were studied less intensely. If a feature seldom seen or not previously recorded was found on one of these towels, then a more detailed look was given that particular towel.

	1780-9	1790-4	1795-9	1800-4	1805-9	1810-4	1815-9	1820-4	1825-9	1830-4	1835-9	1840-4	1845-9	1850-4	1855-9	1860-4	1865-9	1870-4	1875-80
Number of Dated Towels	2	3	13	4	7	19	21	38	39	42	49	34	43	17	12	5	1	0	2
Stitch Types																			
Cross	3	1	8	4	5	18	18	33	35	36	45	28	37	15	12	3	1		2
Herringbone	1		2	2	1	1	7	9	6	6	10	7	3	3	2	1			
Chain	1		2	1	4	2	5	5	5	3	3	4	9	2	1	2			
Running	1				1	2	2		3	2	4	2							
Satin			2	1	2		4		4			3				1			
Straight				1			5	2		2	1		2		1				
Back						1		1	4	3	3	1	1						
Outline							2		2	1	3	3					1		
Hemstitch							1	1				3							
Lazy Daisy							1	1	1				1						
Blanket							1	1				1							
Seeding							1				1	1							
Stitching								3	2		2								
French knots								1	1										
Interlaced hemstitch								1				1							
Eyelet									3	2	2		1						
Button couching									1										
Buttonhole									1										
Threaded herringbone												1		1					
Embroidery Thread Fiber and Color																			
Red cotton	2		1	1		2	5	12	7	11	16	14	9	2	1		1		
Red and blue cotton		1	2	1	3	1	4	8	11	12	15	7	13	4	4	2			
Red cotton and brown silk			3		1	7	4	4	2	2	3	1	2						
Red and blue cotton, brown silk						1	1		3		3		1						
Red cotton and yellow silk								2	1	2	2								
Red and blue cotton, yellow silk				1				1	1	2	2		1	1					
Red cotton and polychrome wool												4		1					
Red and blue cotton, polychrome wool											1		1	3					
Polychrome wool										1	1	1	10	4	5	2			
Polychrome cotton										2		2	2						
White Work on Towels																			
Drawn work		2	10	3	5	12	13	15	18	16	16	9	12	1					
Knotted fringe		1	3	1	2	2	6	4	4	6	3	2	4		2				
Mill made fringe		1				1		4	5	7	13	15	10	4	1	2			
Needle lace		1				1	1	3	2	4	2		4	1					
Needle weaving			1		1		1	2	4		1		1	1					

Appendix II

The following is a complete list of all the towels included in this study. Towels are arranged by the number assigned them. Numbers skipped represent towels without any inscriptions, towels which are European or Canadian, and items such as tablecloths, sheets, samplers and clothing and other embroidered items not in the purview of this study. The list is included here not only as the primary bibliography, but so users may compare illustrations or references in the text to the list. The names of persons here are included in the index. Ownership is given for towels in public collections; any others are in the possession of collectors or the families in which they were made. All research materials, including statements of ownership of towels in private hands, will be filed with the Schwenkfelder Library, Pennsburg, and will be opened to qualified researchers at the discretion of the authors and the Pennsylvania German Society.

1. 1827/ IUDIT GEHMAN
2. S A S
3. Catharine Harnish [Figure 359]
4. A B C D E F G H I J K L M N O P Q R S T U V W X Y Z/ 1 2 3 4 5 6 7 8 9 0 11 September 5 1842/ E F/ A F [Thought to be from a Folmer family, Montgomery co. G H; Figure 12]
5. B A B E/ ELIS SCHW/ 1828/ ELISABETH [From Manheim, Lancaster co.; Heimatstelle Pfalz, Kaiserslautern, West Germany]
6. C L/ 1778 [The date 1778 is not contemporary to the towel.]
7. 1839/ M S/ ISAAC 1789 SCHYFER/ FERONICA 1794 SCHYFER/ LYDIA 1815 SCHYFER/ BENIAMIN 1817 SCHYFER/ MARTHA 1819 SCHYFER/ FENNY 1821 SCHYFER/ ELISABETH 1825 SCHYFER/ ESTHER 1830 SCHYFER/ ISAAC 1831 SCHYFER. [Winterthur 57.111; Swan (1976), p.23; Swank, p.227; cf. 1060, 1061,1063, 1064, 1106]
8. MARIA/ SCHNE/ BELI/ 1813 [Winterthur G69.1148]
9. [Winterthur 66.679]
14. 1799/ I A H O
15. E L/ When I am dead and in my grave And all my bones are Rotten When/ This you See remember me Lest I Should Be forgotten Elizebeth Lo/ ngenecker is my name And Heaven is my Salvation Pennsylvania [sic] / is my dwelling Place And Christ is my sustation E L She Marked/ This Towel Done The 22 Day of MAY A D 1838 [Philadelphia Show Catalogue 1976, p.54; cf. 90, 671; Figure 260]
16. 1830/ MARKREDA W EW/ ER/ E H I B L B
17. ESTER SHEF FEY
18. Emanuel J. Minnich his Towel/ January The 24/ And In The Year Of Our/ Lord A D 1850 / The Goldenrule/ Love God with/ All your soul and/ Strength with all/ Your heart and mind/ Remember This/ We soon shall/ Hear him say/ Ye blessed/ Children Come/ Emanuel J Minnich is my name and Heaven is my/ Station And Lancaster county is my Dewlling [sic] place/ And Christ is my Salvation and when I am dead/ And in my Grave and all my bones are rotten if this/ You see Remember me or els [sic] I must begotten and/ Fore ever A men In this vain world of sin/ And pain we only meet to/ Part again but when we/ Reach the heavenly shore/ We then shall meet to Part no more A men/ The hope that we shall See/ That day Should chase our/ Present griefs away when/ These few years of pain are/ Past We'll meet around/ The Throne at Last A men/ Rebecca J Minnich her work when/ You look on this Towel then Remember/ Me think on the Time what I Spend for/ You to See Emanul [sic] J Minnich/ A B C D E F G H I J K L M N O P Q R S T U V W X Y Z & A D 1849 [Emanuel J. Minnich was born January 19, 1827, son of John (1800-1882) and Barbara Johnson (1806-1876) Minnich. His older sister made this towel for him; she was Rebecca J. Minnich who was born September 4, 1824, died August 8, 1885, age 60 years, 11 months, 4 days. She never married. They were two of twelve children. This information is from the Minnich family Bible. Emanuel's marriage and death are not recorded there. cf. 575, 1054; Figures 201, 275, 289, 356, 373; Plates 11, 27]
24. BAR BA RA/ 1810/ OEHBDDE/ B G [Figures 68,69; Plate 35]

25. ELISABETH DIEHL [From Manheim, Lancaster co.; Gehret and Keyser (1976), pl.47; Plate 49]
28. LAK/ LAK 1833 [Figures 525, 539]
29. MAREI EWERLE [Mary Eberly] [Figures 51, 61, 140, 264, 318, 542]
31. C N
32. 1823/ M B
33. M K
35. 9 D H 4 [Figures 349, 489, 524]
36. L[ydia] T[yson] [From Montgomery co.; cf. 132]
37. SALOME FIERLINGI [Figure 534]
38. F R [Figure 531]
39. CATHARINA GERWER [Figures 516, 543]
40. Mary Nes [or Nolt]
42. B M   B K M [Figures 17, 510]
44. A B C D E F G H I K L M N O P R
45. M D H
46. 1837/ BARBARA ROSENBARY
47. Christina 1836 Swarts [Figures 19, 45,]
48. L M [Figure 57]
49. M S [Figure 519]
50. 18 R S 35 [In drawn thread panel.] [Figures 33, 34, 252, 352]
51. A E S
53. C m R [Figure 65]
55. B S [In drawn thread panel.] [Figures 21, 246]
56. MC/ M C/ MARY CARPENTER 1837/ I G F W [?] M C H C M C [?] / E N E C E C S C/ OEHBDDE [Probably from Lancaster co. Maria Carpenter (1816-1858), nee Gabel, made this towel after her marriage to Henry Carpenter (1809-1848). The various initials are for her parents, his parents, and their siblings in all probability. cf. 106]
57. F F
58. C 1831 B/ OEHBDDE [Figures 125, 410, 439]
59. PALLE MOSSER/ E M/ 1841/ A M [Name tape sewn to a back bottom corner reads, "C.M. Cusler" Figures 185, 297, 308]
60. LYDIA/ KEMPER/ 18 49 [Figure 343]
61. OAHB/ ELIZABETH FRY 1818 [Figure 62]
62. ODEHBDDE/ Elizabeth Booser/ IS my name/ 1843/ SO KAN ICH MEINE ZEIT FERDREI VEN [This is the way I pass my time.] [From the neighborhood of Elizabethtown, Lancaster co.; Figure 371, cover]
63. MARY WITMER/ 1849/ OEHBDDE/ a b c d e f g h i j k l m/ n o p q r s t u v w x y z [cf. 67, 250, 440, 802; Figure 108; Plate 7]
64. BARBARA KUNS 1824 [Allentown, Pennsylvania Folk Art, p.71.; Figure 274]
65. LIDIA BAUMAN/ 1834 [Figure 23]
66. LEA IUNGST/ J G Z 1830 [A paper sewn to the towel says Lea Iungst was the mother of John G. Ziegler. Figures 93, 389]
67. FANNEY WHITMER/ 1854 [cf. 63, 440; and 250, 802; Figures 106, 234, 241, 511]
68. Mary Hershey/ 1845/ OEHBDDE [From Manheim, Lancaster co.; Figures 225, 444]
69. N F B/ CHRE/ STENA/ BAUMAN/ A B C D E F G/ H I J K L M N/ O P Q R S T/ U V W X Y Z/ IN THE YEAR/ OF OUR LORD/ MAY 3 1841/ C B/ OEHBDDE [Figures 199, 315]

71. Regina Kriebel [Regina Kriebel was born in the Hereford area of Berks co. October 7, 1831; died October 13, 1888; married Andrew K. Kriebel (1829-1878). They lived in Towamencin twp., Montgomery co. She was the daughter of Israel and Sarah Schultz Kriebel. Figure 559]
74. 1833/ REBECA BOLLINGER [HSYC 59-214]
75. Anna Byler/ 1861
76. 17 99/ CATARINA KEMPER [A John Kemper is on the 1790 and 1800 census of Earl twp., Lancaster co., residents, very near Conrad Brenneisen (cf. 711), whose daughter Hanna made a towel quite similar to Catarina Kemper's. Figures 217, 395]
79. S B A B 1776 [The date does not appear to be original to the towel.]
83. DanIEL Harr 1832/ OEHBDDE [LHF Figure 276]
84. 18 B G 54
85. MAGDALENA MEIER/ 1822
86. BARBARA RESH A B [Figure 305]
87. 1 A 8 2 M 2
88. A B C D E F G H I J/ ELIZA BOWMAN January 6/ 1838
89. 1814/ AH/ ANNA HISTAND/ [In cross stitch.] A H [In drawn thread panel.]
90. JULIANNA LONGENECKER J L E L GLICK SELIG IST/ DERMEN SCH ZU NENNEN DER SEINE ZUNGE SEMEN KAN/ [Fortunate is the person who can bridle his tongue.] 1831 S L J L G L J L [cf. 15, 671]
91. C H/ OED/ [In cross stitch.] C H [In drawn thread panel.]
93. H S F [Thought to be from a Fryer family from Sassamansville, Montgomery co.]
94. SALOMA ALBRECHT/ 1827 [Salome Albrecht was the eldest daughter of Michael Albrecht and Susanna Kurz. She was born May 23, 1807; married John Schweisfort. In November, 1826, she began weaving in her father's shop. From Sassamansville, Montgomery co. Figure 336]
95. S F B
97. E E [Figures 10, 47,]
98. M[ary] B[ean] [nee Moyer; thought to be from Hilltown twp., Bucks co.; Figures 383, 483]
101. ELIZEBETH BARNDT [Purchased in Trumboursville, Bucks co. cf. 188, 1147]
102. 18 48/ S U S A N A S/ T E I N W E G/ S S/ OEHBDDE/ [Figures 26, 310, 407, 436; Plate 41]
103. SUSAN/ NAHE/ RR 1813/ DAVID/ HERR/ 1813/ C H [A David Herr (born 1789, son of Christian and Anna Hostetter Herr) married Susan Shenk (born 1792). Their first child was born in 1812. They may be the couple for whom this towel was made. From Lancaster co. Herr Genealogy, 225; Figure 144]
104. MARIA BICHSLERN/ 1808 [Figures 75, 200]
105. L B
106. MARIA NOLT 1890/ JN 1795 age 74 b8/ HN 1801 age 61 11 24/ HC 1809 age 39 1 11/ MC 1816 age 41 0 29/ DANIEL NOLT 1835/ ELISABETH NOLT 1840/ JCN 1860 MN 1862/ SN 1864 HCN 1865 age 60 1/ EN 1867 age 42 11/ RN 1870 LN 1870/ MN 1872 AN 1873 DCN 1876/ age 08 11 Step Father/ JZ 1810 age 76 4 27/ OEHBDDE [This towel was made by Lydia Nolt - LN - for Maria Nolt in 1890. It hung on the inside of Maria's guest room. The initials are: JN - John Nolt (1795-1869); HN - his wife; HC - Henry Carpenter (1809-1848) and MC Maria Gabel Carpenter (1816-1858) - his wife's parents named Carpenter, the four grandparents of Lydia and Maria; Daniel Nolt and Elizabeth Nolt, the parents of Lydia and Maria; JCN - John Carpenter Nolt; MN - Magdalena Nolt, m. Good; SN - Susanna Nolt m. Sauder; HCN - Henry Carpenter Nolt; EN Elizabeth Nolt; RN - Rebecca Nolt, m. Daniel Zimmerman; LN - Lydia Nolt (who made the towel), single; MN - Maria Nolt (for whom it was made), m. Daniel Martin; AN - Anna Nolt, m. Benjamin Weaver; DCN - Daniel Carpenter Nolt; JZ - John Zimmerman (1810-1886) who married widow Maria Carpenter. From Lancaster co. This information from Lydia N. Martin, Blue Ball, Pa., who inherited the towel. cf. 56; Figures 175, 388, 391]
107. MK/ MK [Figure 353]
109. CRI STI NA LEN/ Z/ 1817 [Date under towel flap, Figure 73; Plate 40]
111. 1825/ ELISABETH GOTSCHAL/ RH OEHBDDE RH/ DACH IFDG IAEB SWAS/ IKSF CAEH ISCG ILEC HICK/ IHHK IDBG HIGG IHCH ILSB EG/ HFHN AHMN/ [The sets of double initials may refer to married friends.] E 1825 G [Elisabeth Gotschal m. Peter Metz, 1827; their daughter Rebecca m. Jacob Stover, 1860; their daughter Lizzie Stover m. Daniel Johnson, 1892; their daughter Mary Ella married Claude Reinford. The towel is from Lower Salford twp., Montgomery co.; until recently inherited by daughters. Plates 15-19]

112. E[lisabeth] M[etz] 1827 [Towel made after marriage. cf. 111]
114. C Z/ CASSA RAMP/ 1835/ RAMP CASRAN [Figures 526, 538]
115. Susannah Heistand/ 1842 [Figure 527]
116. RABACKA HIESTAND/ 1846 [Figures 405, 425]
117. Anna 1862 Kinig [cf. 186, 1338]
119. ELISABETH EBEN/ [Eby] 18 09 [Figures 54, 367]
120. LISABET MOSER/ 1847/ LISABET MOSER [Figure 454]
123. 1812 ELIZABETH YOCUM
125. H A   C A [Figure 132]
131. L E/ 1812 [cf. 119; Figure 362]
132. 1827/ L [ydia] T [yson] [From Montgomery co.; Figures 368, 533]
133. I C/ 1824 [Figures 37, 537]
134. ANNA KURTZ/ 1834
135. JACOB 18 40 SCHITZ/ JACOB SCHITZ/ OEHBDDE E S/ [In cross stitch.] E S/ I S/ 18 39 [In drawn thread panel.] [Figure 124]
137. C W [In drawn thread panel.] [Figures 351, 397]
140. B E [In drawn thread panel.]
141. LIDIA STEHLER
148. H S/ No 1/ SUSANNA/ 1798
149. S S
150. S A K/ 1846/ S K [Figures 36, 196, 287, 316a, 523]
156. ELISABETH FRIED 1845/ BARBARA FRIED 1849 [GH]
157. E W/ Elisabeth Leatherman/ 1845 [cf. 445. There are also two samplers each with the name Elizabeth Leatherman. The towels and samplers have similar designs.   GH]
169. M H
170. MARY LOUX/ 1851 [Mary Loux married a Hunsberger from Deep Run Mennonite Meeting, Bucks co.]
171. Elizabeth Alderfer/ 1853/ E A [Elizabeth Alderfer, born January 29, 1853; died October 8, 1919; married Jacob H. Alderfer. Both are buried at Salford Mennonite cemetery, Montgomery co. Father was Abraham V. Alderfer, mother Mary F. Moyer. Figure 390]
173. Ann Hockman/ OEHBDDE [From Bucks co. Ann Hockman also embroidered a pair of pillowcases, dated 1836, and a sampler.]
174. B B B/ B M [From a Benner family in Lower Salford twp. Montgomery co.]
175. [From Clymer family in Bucks co.]
176. R R [In drawn thread panel. From Lower Salford twp. Montgomery co.]
177. Sarah Landes [In drawn thread panel. From Lower Salford twp. Montgomery co.]
178. M B/ [In cross stitch.] M[ary] B[auer] [In drawn thread panel.] [Mary Bauer, 1831-1906, married Jacob Mensch, Skippack, Montgomery co.; Figures 25, 126]
179. D. Johnson [In black ink. From Bucks co.]
180. E [lizabeth] K [ulp]/ 1878 [From Lower Salford twp. Montgomery co.]
181. A B [From a Shirk family in Lancaster co.]
182. 1837/ SARAH YOUNG/ SARAH YOUNG [From Lower Salford twp. Montgomery co. The towel is also stamped "Sara Moyer" which could be her married name.]
184. M K
185. CHRISTIAN NEFF/ 1838 [From Lancaster co.]
186. D K C K/ L K/ Beniamin/ Kinig/ war geborend/ en 28 iuni/ 1806 und starb/ den 16 iuni/ 1861 [Benjamin Kinig was born 28 June 1806 and died 16 June 1861.] Lidia/ Kinig/ war geborend/ en 28 October 1/ 1814 und starbd/ en 25 april 1861/ [Lidia Kinig was born 28 October 1814 and died 25 April 1861.] Sara 18 62 Kinig/ S E/ 19 27 [For further information about this family see Fisher #786. cf. 117, 1338; Figure 468]
187. M/ [In cross stitch.] W.S. Sands/ [Written in black ink.] M B H [In cross stitch.]
188. E [lizabeth] B[arndt] [arndt] [cf. 101, 1147]
189. SARA SPEICHERIN/ 1826 [Figures 396, 440, 492-495]
191. Anna Staman is mY name Heaven is mY Station/ Warwick Township Lancaster County is mY Dwelling/ Place Christ is mY Salvation when I am dead and/ in mY grave and all mY bones are Rotten when this/ You see remember me lest I be quite forgotton/ [sic] The rose is red the leaves are green the days are spent/ which I have seen A S 1839/ A OEHBDDE S/ [In cross stitch.] A S [In drawn thread panel.] [Anna Leib Staman (1819-1911) was daughter of Christian Staman (1795-1877) and Catherine Leib (1801-1882). Anna married Jacob L. Hershey (1818-1878). They were Mennonites in Warwick twp., Lancaster co. Anna also made a cross stitch and drawn thread embroidered tablecloth dated 1840. Figures 131, 238, 281, 288, 363]

195. K/ 1795/ [In drawn thread panel.] [Figures 67, 223, 515]
196. The Grass Is Green The Rose Is Red/ Here Is mY Name When I Am Dead Fanny Steman/ She Marked This Towel Done The 3 DaY of December A D 1838 &/ When I am dead and in my grave/ and all mY bones are rotten/ When this you see remember me/ Lest I should be forgotten/ When this you see remember me/ and Heaven is my Salvation/ Pennsylvania is my dwelling place/ and Christ is my sustation/ OEHBDDE [Fanny R. Stehman (1825-1864) was a daughter of John (1793-1829) and Anna Reist (1799-1883) Stehman of Manheim twp., Lancaster co. Fanny married John S. Huber (1820-1911). cf. 197; Figures 364, 366, 411]
197. FANNY R Steman/ 1837 [cf.196; Figures 227, 235, 257]
198. 1825/ [In cross stitch.] E S [In drawn thread panel.]
199. ANNA SCHNEIDER/ ICH LIB WAS REIN IST WAN SCHON NICHT MEIN IST/ UND MEIN NIGHT WERDEN KAN SO HAB ICH DO [Missing.]/ [I love what is pure even though it is not mine and cannot be mine even so (I have the joy of it).] 1826 [Figure 457]
200. FERONICA WITMER [Figure 154]
201. M K/ 1842/ M[anheim] T[ownship] L[ancaster] C[ounty] P[ennsylvania] [Figures 338, 459]
205. M A A/ 18 96
212. C Abraham Dienner 1857 D/ When i [sic] am dead and in my grave/ And all my bones are rotten/ Remember me when this you see/ Least I should be For gotten C D [Abraham Diener, son of Christian and Catharine (King) Diener, was born September 15, 1842, died March 11, 1911. He married a Schick. He also had a sister Catharine. From the Morgantown area, Lancaster co.; cf. 286; MHEP; Plate 34]
214. Catharine Moyer/ 1898 [Thought to be from Bucks co.; MHEP 75-55-1; Figure 183]
215. C M/ 1828 [Thought to be from Bucks co.; MHEP 75-55-2]
216. M M [MHEP 70-60-1]
217. S[arah] A[nn] G[aris]/ 1867 [The date was probably added after towel was made. MHEP 75-136-1; Figures 226, 249, 313]
219. Maria Good/ 18 38 [Figure 330]
222. ELIZABETH D. LANDES 1847/ [In cross stitch in English.] ELIZABETH D LANDES [In cross stitch in German Fraktur letters.] [Figures 250, 323]
223. Barbary Moyer/ 18 57 [She lived in Worcester twp., Montgomery co. and attended Methacton Mennonite Meeting.]
224. M M/ M M/ 1830 [Thought to be from a Moyer family who attended Methacton Mennonite Meeting, Worcester twp., Montgomery co.; cf. 225]
225. M M [Thought to be from a Moyer family who attended Methacton Mennonite Meeting, Worcester twp., Montgomery co.; cf. 224]
228. D[eborah] M[arkley]/ M[ary] R[ittenhouse] [From Montgomery co.] [Figure 339]
229. HANNA 1839 HUEBNER [1810-1879, daughter of Abraham Heebner and Christina Wagner; married Abraham Heebner and lived in Worcester twp., Montgomery co.; Figure 121]
230. SARAH SCHULTZ 1837 [or 1832] [Sarah Schultz was born in 1792 in what is now known as the Peter Wentz farm, Worcester twp., Montgomery co., daughter of Melchior Schultz and Salome Wagner. Sarah Schultz married Rev. David Kriebel and lived across the road in a farmhouse built for them by her parents. Sarah died in 1837. Figure 394]
231. [ELIZABETH] DILLIER HAT DAS GENETH [I]M IAHR I/ 1825/ [Elizabeth Dillier sewed this in the year 1825] a b c d e f g h i j k l m n o p q r s t u v w x y z/ A B C D E F G H I J K L M N O P Q R S T U V W X Y Z [The name "C.M. Cusler" is written in black ink on the name tag sewn to the back of the towel. Thornton Catalogue, January 1977, 313. cf. 232, 606, 660, 687, 1410, 1411; Figure 303]
232. ELIZABETH DILLIER/ 18 32 [Elizabeth also embroidered a pillow case, dated 1834, with thirty four star motifs identical to the fifty star motifs she sewed on this towel. Thornton Catalogue, January 1977, 311; Bishop, p. 318; cf. 231, 606, 660, 687, 1410, 1411; Figure 176]
233. I I [Figure 304]
234. 1851/ MARY REIST/ MARY A B [Mary Reist was from Lebanon co. She married John Henry Boltz. Mary was fourteen years old when she made this towel in 1851 and twenty years when she married. Figures 316, 341]
237. MARIA DIENERIN/ M 1869 I/ 18 43
238. CATHARINA BOLINGER/ 1841 [In cross stitch.] C 18 36 B/ [In drawn thread panel.]
239. Lydia Brenneman/ OEHBDDE
240. M W [In drawn thread panel.]

241. 1831/ LEA STOLSFUSZ [Leah, daughter of John Stoltzfus, Sr. and Veronica King, was born September 2, 1813, and died December 14, 1900. She married Jacob Speicher. cf. 722]
242. 1826/ SUSANA EBY
243. 1846/ ELIZABE/ TH REIST. [BCHS 5671; Figure 278]
244. E [or C] Z [In drawn thread panel.] [BCHS 10349]
245. [BCHS]
246. ELISABEDH SARWER/ 1830. [BCHS 25673]
247. M[ary] R[uth] H T 1823/ M R 17 85. [BCHS 10356]
249. MARGRIT/ [Missing letters] HEUSZ/ LERI/ N
250. A B C D E F G H I K L M N/ O P Q R S T U V W X Y Z/ FANNY WITMER/ 1847 [Gehret and Keyser (1976), pl.42; cf. 63, 67, 440, 802; Figure 105]
251. A E B/ 1847 [In cross stitch.] ANNA M L [In drawn thread panel.] [A hand written note sewn to this towel, "This towel belonged to Amanda Bieber or Beaver and the end on it was worked by Elsie M. Livingood. Amanda was the daughter of Reuben Beaver whose only son was killed at Gettysburg. The whole family has gone."]
253. M[aria Richenbach] S[chultz] [A hand written note attached to the towel, "This towel was probably made by Maria Richenbach Schultz a great grandmother of Homer S. Kriebel. Maria died August 2, 1884 at the age of eighty two years so it can easily be one hundred years old."; Figures 83, 96]
254. S M/ SUSANNA MILLER/ 1840/ ANVILL TOWNSHIP LEBANON COUNTY PENNSYLVAN/ A [sic] [Figures 84, 423]
255. REBECCE WEINHOLT/ 18 47/ OEHBDDE [cf. 467] [Rebecca Weinhold seems to have been the daughter of Peter and Elizabeth (Grill) Weinhold. She was born in 1825. She had an older sister Mary. Since Mary's towel is similar to Rebecca's, it is assumed that sisters made them. This is the only Weinhold family with daughters of these names and the right ages.]
256. E[lizabeth] G[arges] W[asser]/ [From Lower Salford twp. Montgomery co.] SUSANA BERGE [Thought to be from the Spring Mount area in Lower Frederick twp., Montgomery co.]
257. C H B
258. L. CLAYTONS NEEDLEWORK/ FOR CATHARINE DENTZLER 1856 [cf. 1151; Figures 7, 285]
259. S[usann] A K[auffman] / [In cross stitch.] S K 18 27 [In drawn thread panel.] [From the Oley valley in Berks co.; cf. 260]
260. K/ [In cross stitch.] S[usanna] K[auffman]/ 18 23 [In drawn thread panel.] [cf. 259]
261. 18 30/ REGINA SCHULTZ [Figures 342, 370]
262. 18 24/ RE [letters unclear] K SCHULTZ
264. 1831/ SARA YORTY [From the Myerstown area in Lebanon co. Gehret and Keyser (1976), cover. Figures 279; Plate 36]
265. A B C D E F G H I J K L M/ N O P Q R S T U V W X Y Z/ R S/ M I C H I A
266. D.H. Moyer [Hand written in faded black ink under the top flap.] BABARRA E/ 1827/ LLEN BERGE/ OEHBDDE [AARFAC 82.608.1; Figure 421]
267. BARBARA GERBERRIG/ 1819 [Thought to be from Lebanon co.]
268. S S/ DIESES HAND DUCH GHORET/ MIER SARA SCHITZIN GMACHT DEN/ 8 MERZ 1819/ [This towel belongs to me Sara Schitz made 8 March 1819] SARA SCHIT [Figures 16, 269, 332, 451, 461]
269. A B C D E F G H I K L M O P Q R S T U/ V W X Y Z ANNA LANG/ N 1816 L/ A B C D E F G H I K L M/ N O P Q R S T U V W X Y Z/ NANCY LANG/ ANNA LANG [Figures 219, 402]
270. ELIZABETH/ KINDIG/ Z B [cf. 271; Figure 244]
271. ANN KIN/ 18 10/ ELIZABETH/ KINDIG/ K B [cf. 270; Figures 256, 294, 513]
273. SUSANNA WALBIN 1800 [Susanna Walp was the mother of Hannah Walp cf. 274 Figures 130, 333a, 374]
274. HANNAH WALP W/ 1829/ OADHBDDA [Hannah Walp was the daughter of Susanna Walp cf. 273 and was related to Maria Benner, towel 578, by marriage. They were from the Richland-Quakertown area in Bucks co. Figure 448]
275. 17 M[argaret] S[hollenberger] 96 [A note attached to the towel, "Made by Margaret Shollenberger Welker who was Margaret Hollowbush's mother fifth or sixth great grandmother to my grandchildren." cf. 276, 576]
276. M[argareth] W[elker] [She was the daughter of Jacob Welker and wife Margaretha Shollenberger, married Richard Hollowbush of Frederick twp., Montgomery co. and moved to Boyertown, Berks co. She was born July 7, 1805 and died August 29, 1894. cf. 275, 576]
278. S A H B [Thought to be from Beber family near Oley, Berks co.]

279. R[ebecca] G[erhard]/ 1844 [Rebecca Gerhard, 1820-1875, from Upper Hanover twp., Montgomery co. married Abraham Schultz in 1844 the same year she made this towel. Figure 557]
280. MARIA HOCK/ J D S E S/ [In cross stitch.] 1845 [In drawn thread panel.] [Figures 292, 484]
281. B S [Figure 258]
282. ELISABETH DO/ R BAC H[IN] 1821 [Figure 128]
283. Anny Conrad/ Anny Conrad is my name and so it shall remain Warwick/ is my station heaven is my Dwelling Place Christ/ is my Salvation the Rose is Read [sic] the leaves are/ green the days are past wich [sic] I have seen If I am/ Dead and in my grave and all my boons [sic] are Rodden/ [sic] If this you see Remember at me least I shall be/ Forgotten March th 19 A D 1838 [Lancaster co. provenance.; Figure 28]
285. C H/ [In cross stitch in German Fraktur printing.] C H/ [In cross stitch in English.] 1818 [cf. 392, 468 Plates 2, 39]
286. Magdalena Diener/ 1859/ Das gras ist grin/ Die rose ist roth/ Hier steth me in namen/ nach meinem tod M D [The grass is green the rose is red, here is my name, when I am dead. M D] [Magdalena Deiner (August 8, 1841-October 18, 1921) was a daughter of Christian and Catharine (King) Diener. She married Christian Glick. History of the Diener Family, p. 30; cf. 212; Figures 222, 521, 552]
287. 1835/ [In cross stitch.] MD [In drawn thread panel.]
288. IOHANNES WITMEYER/ 1848/ Pe[quea] To[wnship] La[ncaster] Co[unty] Pe[nnsylvan] Ia [Figure 463]
289. A B C D E F G H I K L M N O/ P Q R S T U V W X Y Z 1818/ B P [Figures 253, 501, 502; Plate 26]
290. C S [Figure 498]
291. L K/ 1847 [Both in drawn thread panel.] [Figures 229, 509]
293. SALLME 1838/ FRIEDERICK
294. ELISABETH/ GUT 1817
295. SUSANNA MEIER 1832
297. C B
299. MAGDALENA BRAUN [Figures 486, 488, 490]
300. C A [Figure 141]
301. ELISABETH/ HIMMEL/ B RGE N/ A B C D E F G H/ I K L M N O/ P Q R S T U V W/ W[sic]X Y Z/ E H
302. BARBARA MEYER/ 1835/ OEHBDDE [Figure 46]
305. S T [Figures 334, 514]
306. ELISABETH GRAFF 1818 [Figure 44]
308. L S
309. B R/ 1848
310. A W/ 18 OEHBDDE 33/ A B C D E F G H I K L M/ N O P Q R S T U V W X Y Z [Figure 329]
311. 1824/ 1804/ [Date 1804 under top flap.] SARA LAUCH [Figures 29, 243]
312. LEA KAPP/ 18 40/ A B C D E F G H I J K L M/ N O P Q R S T U V W X Y Z
313. MARY BUCH/ 1841 [Figure 280]
314. ELISABETH/ RINKER/ 1848/ A B C D E F G H I J K L M N O P Q R S T U V W X Y Z/ E R [Family originally from the Saucon area in Lehigh co. Robacker (1973), p. 128; cf. 319]
315. BARBARA BUGERN/ [In cross stitch.] E S/ 1800 [In drawn thread panel.] [Figure 503, 518]
317. 17/ 9 CHRISTINA 4 [In drawn thread panel.]
318. FRONICA GEHMAN 1850
319. ELISABETH/ RINKER/ 1848/ A B C D E F G H I J K L M N O P Q R S T U/ V W X Y Z 1 2 3 4 5 6 7 8 9 0 M NERCH/ D R E R S S [Robacker (1973), p. 128; cf. 314]
320. H W/ 1839 B
321. MARIA RITTER/ OEHBDEEE/ J M M M
322. 1860 [Figure 558]
323. SALOME MERKI/ A B C D E F G H/ I K L M N O P Q/ R S T U V W X Y Z [In cross stitch.] S M [In drawn thread panel.]
324. DAVID 1839 LEHMAN
325. Catharine ann Fretz 1846
326. 18 46/ M N
327. 8 E L 5/ Leah Lapp/ OEHBDDE [Leah, daughter of Michael and Barbara (Stoltzfus) Lapp, was born November 30, 1835, died February 6, 1930, m. 1857 Abraham Petersheim (February 26, 1831-October 27, 1895); cf. 1057, his towel. Fisher, #3606; cf. 328, 946]
328. 1855/ C/ Leah Lapp [cf. 327, 946]
329. E G
331. 1833 H R [Figure 392]
332. M B [In drawn thread panel.] [Figure 460]
333. ELESABETH PETERS/ M K QF [Kauffman Catalogue, 653; Figure 190, 309, 452]
334. IHM/ AN/ IAR/ 1826/ IHM/ AN/ IAR/ 1826/ [In the

year 1826] THIS SAMPLER/ BELONGS TO ME/ SUSANA HELLER/ KEIN LEIB UND TRELI/ AUF ERDEN IS ALS/ NUR BEY DIR HERR/ IESU CHRIS/ [No love and truth is only by you Lord Jesus Christ.] SUSANA HELLER/ NICHT SCHAM/ DICH RATH ICH/ ALLER MEIS/ DER DICH DAS/ LEHRT WAS/ DUNICHT W/ EIS WER ET/ WAS KAN DEN/ hÄLT MAN WE/ RTH DEN UNGE/ SCHICK-TEN NI/ MAND BEGEHRT/ [Don't be ashamed, I counsel you most of all, that someone teaches you what you do not know. Whoever is skilled is considered worthy. The unskilled no one craves.] [In cross stitch.] S H [In drawn thread panel.] [From Quakertown area, Bucks co. Figure 419; Plate 38]
335. MOLLY RYDER/ 1826/ M R/ [In cross stitch.] M R [In drawn thread panel. Figures 491, 512]
336. Sarah Moyer/ 1831 [Or 1851]
338. E L [From Pennsburg, Upper Hanover twp., Montgomery co.]
339. MARIA KRAUSIN/ W W/ A B C D E F G H I K L M N O P Q R S T U V W X Y [Maria Krausin, born July 7, 1815, died April 30, 1893, married William Rex from Heidelberg twp., Lehigh co. probably made towels 340, 935. She was the mother of Roseann Rex (341) and Sarah Ann Rex (934). Figure 522; Plate 8]
340. M K ["MK" is probably for Maria Krauss from Lehigh co. cf. 339, 341, 934, 935; Figures 115, 205; Plate 9]
341. ROSEANN REX WXYZ/ A B C D E F G H I J K L M N O P Q R S T U V/ W 1876 W [Rosa Ann Rex, daughter of William and Maria (Polly) Krauss Rex, was born June 6, 1855 and died March 15, 1927 unmarried, buried at Heidelberg Union Church, Heidelberg twp. Lehigh co.] [cf. 339, 340, 934, 935; Plate 10]
342. S M/ 1843 [From Hereford, Berks co.]
343. F M 1854/ FANNY MOYER [Thought to be from Berks co.; Figures 299, 300]
344. L 1820 S [SL 627.25; Figure 272]
345. S K/ Salome Kriebel [SL cf. 453, 454]
346. DEBORAH/ 18 HEEBNER 27/ D H [SL]
347. DEBORAH HEEBNER [In cross stitch.] DEBORA HEEB-NER 1825 [In drawn thread panel.] [SL]
348. SUSANA KRIEBL 1825 [In drawn thread panel.] [SL; cf. 350]
349. [A paper note sewn to the towel reads, "Grandmother Stauffer made this towel when she was a young girl Grandmother of Annie Bechtel Brunner." SL]
350. SUSAN KRIE[BEL] [SL; cf. 348]
351. Susan Eckerts Towel/ 1857 [From the Mechanicsburg area in Cumberland co. Susan Eckert married a Simmons.]
352. S S [Purchased in Biglerville, Adams co.]
353. M S [Purchased in New Kingston, Cumberland co.]
354. C B
355. E R/ OEH 1828 DDE [Winterthur G69.1147]
356. FRONICA BRANDT [Winterthur 69.1146; Swan (1976), p. 24]
357. B 1813 H/ [In cross stitch.] B OEHBDDE H [In drawn thread panel.] [Winterthur 69.1152]
358. CATARINA WALBORN/ 1827 [Thought to be from Berks or Lebanon co. Winterthur 69.1145; Figure 261]
359. ELISABET RAUCH [Winterthur 69.1150; Swan (1977), p. 133; Figure 480]
360. 18 22/ A M [Winterthur G69.1149]
361. IK AK I STAMM 1845 E STAMM IS ES/ MARY STAMM/ as es ms Ls ms Is ds as ss/ OEHBDDE [Winterthur G69.1158; Swan (1977), p. 125]
362. The Grass is green The Rose is Red Here/ is my name when I am dead Litty Buc/ kwalter She marked this towel Done The 18 day of March/ When I am dead and in my/ Grave and all my bones/ Are Rotten A.D. 1853 When/ This you see Re-member me/ Lest I should Be forgotten/ Litty Buckwalter is my/ Name and heaven is my/ Salvation Pennsylvania/ is my dwelling place/ And christ is my sustation/ L B/ OEHBDDE [Winterthur G69.1168]
363. SARA MERKI/ [In cross stitch.] S S/ M M [In drawn thread panel.] [Winterthur G69.1165]
364. [Name is missing.]/ M OEHBDDE K/ [In cross stitch.] M K [In drawn thread panel.] [Winterthur G69. 1166]
365. HEATTY ENGEL HE/ E E/ A B C D E F G H I J K L M N O P Q R S T U V W X Y Z ESHT/ 1831 [Winterthur G69.1156]
366. M K [Winterthur G69.1164; Swan (1977), p.127; Ames, p.30]
367. [Winterthur G69.1167]
368. MARIA KRAL/ M K [Winterthur G69.1155]
369. MARIA BERC SO KAN ICH D/ IE ZEIT ERTREIBEN/ [This is the way I pass my time.] 1822/ M OEHBDDE B [Winterthur G69. 1159]

370. [Winterthur G69.1153]
371. 1830/ [In cross stitch.] S M/ [In drawn thread panel.] SU-SANNA MIES [In cross stitch.] [Winterthur G69.1163]
372. ELISABETH S[E]N[S]E[N]I[G] [Missing letters can be read from the needle holes from which thread has fallen out.] 1824 [Missing, but needle holes are legible.] [Winterthur G69. 1160]
373. [A]B C D E F G H I K L M N O/ P Q R S T U V W X Y Z [Winterthur G69.1161; Figure 130]
374. A G S [Winterthur G69.1162; Figure 53]
375. ANNA MARIA/ 1816 [Winterthur G69.1151; Figure 129]
376. M H [Winterthur G69.1144]
377. ELISABETH/ MEIER/ E L 1797 [Winterthur 67.759]
378. C S N 1799 G P T [Winterthur 65.2800]
379. CATHARINA/ B WEIDMAN/ 1810 [Winterthur 69.1142 cf.; 844, 1047]
382. M M
383. B[arbara] SB/ [For Shellenberger.] 1823
384. S M/ A S G/ 1814/ [In cross stitch.] S M [In drawn thread panel.]
385. D N[isley]
386. S A OEHBDDE H A [Could be for Anthony since this towel came from an Anthony farm sale in York co.]
387. ANG 1797 [In drawn thread panel.] [Winterthur 67.1472]
388. ELISABETH BLANK/ 1855 [Winterthur]
389. M M 1836/ M M [Winterthur]
390. [sic] J K L M N O P Q R/ S T U V W X Y Z/ Bauman 1838 [Winterthur]
391. C W/ 18 33 [Winterthur]
392. Christina Hessin/ [Sewn in German Script.] C H/ [In English.] 1815 [Winterthur 67.1266; Swan (1976), p.22; Garvan and Hummel, p.190; Swank, p.227; See chapter one for biographical data about Christina Hess. cf. 285, 468 Plate 46]
394. Rachel Lefever is my name And heaven/ is my station Lampeter is my dwelling/ Place And christ [sic] is my Salvation/ When I am dead and in my grave/ And all my bones are rotten When/ this you see remember me Unless/ Im [sic] quite forgotten 1840 November 3 [There were two girls named Rachel Lefever in Lampeter twp., Lancaster co. at the time this towel was made. Rachel, born December 25, 1822; died June 9, 1860; married Samuel Harmon and married John Naylor. Also Rachel born March, 1829; died November 30, 1903; married John Stark.]
396. E
397. 18 36/ F S[kelly]
398. E[lizabeth] D[etweiler]
402. Sarah Kriebel [Sarah Kriebel was born September 30, 1828; died April 29, 1908; married Abraham Dresher, January 13, 1852. She lived on Weber Road, Worcester twp., Montgomery co. Garvan and Hummel, p.190; Figure 560]
404. ANNA RUTTIN/ 1804 [Purchased in Hockerville, Dauphin co.; PHMC 30.32]
405. 1793/ C H [Thought to be from Oley, Berks co.; PHMC 30.39.13]
406. CADARINA/ 1808 [Thought to be from Oley, Berks co.; PHMC 30.39.14]
407. CRISDNA KEPNER/ [In cross stitch.] K C [In drawn thread panel.] [PHMC 35.46.29]
408. 1819/ ICH FRONICA KREBIELIN/ BIN GE BOH REN IM JAHR/ CHRI STI 1803 DEN 20 OC DO BER [I Fronica Krebiel was born in the year 1803 the 20 October] [PHMC 53.15]
409. E B/ [In cross stitch.] ELISABETH BERLET 1821 [In drawn thread panel.] [PHMC 65.40]
410. S[arah] S[ugrist] [Made ca. 1839-40; PHMC 64.56.31; cf. 411]
411. S[arah] S[ugrist] [Made ca. 1840; PHMC 64.56.32; "Pennsylvania German Sampler, Fig. 127; cf. 410]
412. A K [PHMC 65.106.143; Lichten, p. 59; Figure 142]
413. H S/ 1841 [PHMC 65.106.144]
414. H S/ 1841 [PHMC 65.106.145]
415. 17 83/ CB/ AM [PHMC 69.99.1; Figure 4]
416. C S [PHMC 69.99.2]
417. A M/ M M/ 1818 [PHMC 73.98.36]
418. NANCY M DERSTLER/ 1847 [PHMC 73.98.37; cf. 419; Figure 64]
419. ANNA DERSTLER/ 1845 [In cross stitch.] A M D [In drawn thread panel.] [PHMC 73.98.39; cf.418]
420. 1846/ ANA GEHMAN [PHMC N31 22-31-80-5 "Pennsylvania German Sampler," Fig. 126; Figure 314]
421. B D G D/ CADARINA DEIBLERIN [PHMC]
422. 1799/ BARRA BAER HARDIN [In cross stitch.] BA ER [In drawn thread panel.] [HMAL 633; Figure 326]

426. ELISABETHE/ RB/ 18 11 [HMAL; cf.427; Figure 5]
427. ELISAB 1812 ETHERB [HMAL; cf.426; Figure 6, 375]
428. C 1801 L [HMAL; Plate 31]
429. SUSSAN/ NASCHE/ NCKIN/ 1816 [HMAL; cf. 430, 726]
430. 1832/ SUSANA/ SCHEN/ CKIN [HMAL 2898; cf. 429, 726; Figure 210]
431. F H [HMAL]
432. CATHARINA FLORI [HMAL]
433. B A H I/ R B L D [HMAL]
434. CATA LANG [HMAL]
435. E K [HMAL]
437. M B 1844/ Martha Brubaker is my name [e]arth is/ my dwelling place heaven is my station/ Christ is my salvation I wright [sic] with my hand/ and penn [sic] my daughter attent [sic] unto my wisdom/ and how [bow] thine ear to my understanding/ [In cross stitch.] Susan B. Harnish is my name the/ Grass is green the rose is red here/ stand my name when I am dead/ and in my grave and all my / Bones are rotten when this you [Incomplete. Hand written in black ink. PHMC 34.129.18; Figure 301]
440. MARY WITMER/ IS BORN IN TH/ E YEAR 1835 J/ ANUARY 11 18 [Mary Witmer, aged 15, was a member of the household of Christian and Mary Witmer in Mount Joy twp., Lancaster co., in 1850; cf. 63, 67, 250, 802; Figure 109]
441. 1820/ M S [HMAL]
442. E K/ 18 34/ Elisabeth Kauffman/ is my name and heaven is my/ station America is my dwelling place and/ Christ is my salvation/ The rose is red the leaves are green the/ days are past which I have seen When I am/ dead and in my grave and all my bones are/ rotten When these you see remember/ me at last I'll be forgotten/ OEHBDDE [HMAL; Figure 346]
445. CW/ Elizabeth 18 41 Leatherman/ Lizzie H. Detweiler 1898 [GH; cf.157; Figure 40]
446. E A/ [In cross stitch.] 1810/ S K [In drawn thread panel.] [GH]
447. ANNA BEILER/ 1845/ M S/ 1869/ A S [GH; Figures 358, 360]
448. P F/ 1824 [In drawn thread panel.] [GH; cf. 449]
449. M S T/ 1834/ [In cross stitch.] 1833 [In drawn thread panel.] [GH; cf.448; Figure 139]
450. SALOME/ GERBERIN/ 1811/ 1818 [GH; Figures 333, 450]
451. ABETH DITZE [GH]
452. 1851/ 1851/ HANNAH SAUDER [LCHS]
453. Bey aller deiner freud und lust Bedenke das du sterben must SK/ Wohl dem der taeglich sterben kan der trift im tod das leben an 1843/ Salome Kriebel geboren dem 16 ten Ianuary 1823 [In all your happiness and joy remember that you must die. Well to him who can die daily. He will meet life in death 1843. Salome Kriebel born 16 January 1823.] [Salome Kriebel was born January 16, 1823; died November 17, 1891; married Abraham Anders October 21, 1847. Daughter of Melchior Kriebel and Rosina Schultz, she lived in Worcester twp., Montgomery co. Her painted chest has Salome Kriebel, 1843 on the front panel. cf. 345, 454, 456, 457, 476; Figure 111]
454. Salome Kriebel/ 1839/ S K [Salome made a sampler in 1838 with similar motifs as on this towel. Salome's sisters Susanna, [cf.456] Rosina, and sister-in-law Anna [cf.476] sewed like designs on their embroidery. cf. 345, 453; Figures 110, 262]
456. Susanna Kriebel/ 1843 [Susanna Kriebel was born 1836; died 1899; married October 23, 1856 to Abraham H. Kriebel - another line of Kriebel's. Susanna was a younger sister of Salome Kriebel 453, 454; Figure 112]
458. E[lizabeth] C[assel]/ 1834 [From Worcester twp., Montgomery co.]
461. M[aria] H[eebner] [She was born June 7, 1833; died February 1, 1889; married William A. Schultz on October 18, 1859. Daughter of Anthony S. and Lydia Krauss Heebner she was from Worcester twp., Montgomery co. This is the same Maria Heebner who painted the watercolors seen in the book, Folk Art of Rural Pennsylvania by Frances Lichten, pp.222, 223.]
462. MARTHA R HERR/ 1883
463. 1831/ Elizabeth Hershy [From Millersville area, Lancaster co.]
464. Maria Leaman is my name heven/ is my situation lampeter is my twel/ ing Place christ is my salvation the/ rose is ret the leavs are green the day/ are Past witch I have seen when I am/ dead and in my grave and when my/ bones are all roten and when this yo/ u see remember me unless I be forgoten/ [Spelling as found on towel.] Maria/ Leaman/ Abraham Leaman/ Barbara Leaman/ David Buchwalter Maria

274

Buchwalter [Maria B. Leaman was born November 11, 1834; died January 9, 1870; married Daniel L. Book, b. 1828. Their daughter Amendo Book married Christian H. Herr and inherited the towel afterwhich it was inherited by their daughter Maude. Maria Leaman was a sister to Catharine Leaman. cf. 539, 540; Figure 286]

465. BARBARA BAMBERGER/ OEHBDDE 1833/ A B/ Pb Fb/ 1835/ M B A B/ When I am Dead and Buried and all my Bones are Rotten/ When this you see remember me Leist [sic] I should be For gottn/ [sic] BARBARA BOMBERGER/ F S B S/ E B M B/ JOHN KRALL IS BORN TH G 11 OCTOBER/ 1839/ E B M B/ B A [From the Reistville area, Lebanon co.; Figure 88; Plate 37]

466. The Grass is Green The Rose is Red/ Here is my name when I am dead Elisabeth Frey/ She marked this towl [sic] one [sic] the 4th day of October A D 1843/ When I am dead and in my grave/ and all my bones are Rotten/ When this you see Remember me/ Lest I Should be Forgotten/ Elisabeth Frey A D 1843/ OEHBDDE [Elisabeth Frey was born October 7, 1824 in Lancaster co. Thornton Catalogue, January, 1977, 49; cf.755; Figures 24, 187, 473; Plate 29]

467. DAS HAN/ DUC HAPIC MERI WEINHOLT GENET IM/ IAHR 1839/ [I Meri Weinholt stitched this towel in the year 1839] A B C D E F G H I/ K L M N O P Q R/ S T U V W X Y Z/ L I [Mary Weinholt, nee Sollenberger, was born November 8, 1804; died January 9, 1880; married George Weinhold June 9, 1830. They had six children and are buried at the Muddy Creek Church, Lancaster co. Garvan and Hummel, p. 31, attribute this towel to Mary Weinholt, nee Sollenberger. It is unlikely that a woman with several small children in 1839 would have found time to make a to make a towel. On the assumption that Mary had a sister Rebecca (cf. 255), who made a similar towel, then this may be Mary, daughter of Peter and Elizabeth Grill Weinhold who also had a daughter Rebecca, the only members of that family in that generation to have daughters with both names; Figure 77, 165]

468. A H/ [In cross stitch in English.] Anna Herr/ [Sewn in German script.] 1816 [From the Millersville area in Lancaster co; cf. 285, 392; Figures 149, 324]

469. LYDIA KURTZ/ 1846 [Garvan and Hummel, p. 189; Figure 136; Plate 12]

473. MARIA/ LESCH/ 1828/ OEHBDDE/ D D [This Maria Lesch was probably born ca. 1808 in Lebanon co., daughter of Benjamin and Catharine Lesch; she married a Boeshore. Plate 1]

474. 1856/ Catharina G Sauder [LCHS]

475. SALOME/ BARTHIN [Thought to be from Lebanon co.; LBCHS]

476. ANNA KRIEBEL/ A K/ 1842 [Anna Kriebel was born December 15, 1827; died August 25, 1881; married Ephram Kriebel February 20, 1851 who was Salome Kriebel's (towel 453) brother. They lived in Worcester twp., Montgomery co. Married second to Jacob Fisher, January 25, 1868. She was the daughter of George and Sophia Kriebel. Figure 298]

478. 1842/ A[nna] K[olb]

479. Anna Anganey/ 1833

480. Iohannes/ Willmina Leise/ Hetwig Leise/ 1811 [From the same family as Ann Kolb cf.478.]

481. M A H [Thought to be for Maria Heebner.]

482. SUSANNA HEEBNER

485. M H

486. CATHARINE BITTING

488. MARIA BOLLINGERN/ MERI B

490. IUDITH MARTIN [cf. 912, 1031]

491. CADARINA/ C F

492. OEHBDDE/ CATARINA REB[?] LI[?]/ 18[?]

493. LIDIA HUNSIKERN

494. A A [sic] B C D E F G H I K L M N/ O P Q R S T U V W X [Y] Z S H 1809

496. 1815/ E E/ ELISABET/ EBERLIN/ A B C D E F G H I J K L M N O P Q R/ [In cross stitch.] S T U V W X Y Z [In drawn thread panel.]

497. S B/ 1829 [In drawn thread panel.]

501. U Q R T V W X Y Z/ E R 1831 A B C D E F G H I K L M N O P/ CADARINA SIER/ 18[ ] [A note attached to the towel reads, "Catharine Sier, now spelled Searer made this towel in 1833 in Thompsontown, Pa. Married to Christ Martin died in Wakarusa, Ind. June 19, 1882. Sent to me Neon N. Mouser July 1, 1942 by Elymra Hoofnagle Martin Catherine's daughter-in-law. 1833 date in the black thread look close. Catherine Sier or Searer now. She married Christian Martin December 12, 1839 in Thomsontown Penn. Died June 19, 1882

in Waharusa, Ind. Daughter Seanah Roher died near Wakarusa Ind. December 12, 1884. Son Jacob Searer Martin died February 22, 1922 Elkhart. The family came to Ind. 1849 the towel from 1833, 1884, 1922, 1942 to hers." HMAL]

502. G.H. DANNER/ 1888 M H/ Born 1799 [HMAL]

508. CATHARINA CASSEL 1816 [Catharina Cassel was born in 1801; died in 1885; never married. She lived on what is now called Stump Hall Road in Skippack, Montgomery co. and is buried at Upper Skippack Mennonite cemetery.]

509. [DCHS]

510. S F [Purchased in Lancaster co.; Figure 94]

511. I H/ 1822 [Purchased in Berks co.]

512. CATARINA HUNSIKER [Purchased in Chester co.]

513. 8 M S I S N H A P [Purchased in Elizabethtown, Lancaster co.]

514. H [?] HANNA ST[?] U [?] T/ 18[??] [Purchased in Berks co.]

515. 1820 [Purchased in Mt. Airy, Lancaster co.]

516. A B C D E F G H I J K L M N P P P O/ [sic] R S T U V W X Y Z [Purchased in Emmaus, Lehigh co.; Figures 55, 56, 147]

517. MARIA SEM/ 1827/ EBERLI [Purchased in Chester co.]

519. 1834 E A D/ ELEZABETH/ ALDERFER/ IST GEBORN/ DEN 6 IUNE IM/ IAHR 1815 [Elizabeth Alderfer was born June 6, 1815; died September 29, 1894; married December 18, 1836 Abraham G. Delp; buried in Salford Mennonite cemetery. Father Abraham R. Alderfer, mother Susanna Shoemaker; lived in Lower Salford twp., Montgomery co. Figure 319]

520. OEHBDDE/ ANA THUMA [Purchased in Chester co.]

521. M E [Purchased in Willow Street, Lancaster co.]

522. E L [Purchased in Manheim, Lancaster co.]

523. 18 B K 24 [Purchased in Lancaster co.; cf. 527]

527. B K [cf. 523]

528. L H S/ E L S [Purchased in Upper Hanover twp., Montgomery co.]

529. ESTHER BINKLY [PFMLV FM25.289; cf. 530, 531]

530. E[sther] B[inkly] [A tag attached to the towel reads, "Linen towel made by Esther Binkly 1820."; PFMLV FM25.274; cf. 529, 531]

531. E[sther] B[inkley] 1820 [PFMLV FM25.276; cf. 529, 530]

532. E S/ 1814 [PFMLV FM25.277]

533. [PFMLV FM25.284]

534. [PFMLV FM25.286; FM25.285]

535. 1828/ B L CL AL/ A B C D E F G H I J K L M N O P Q R S T U V W X Y Z [These initials mark names on towels 539, 540; PFMLV FM28.152]

536. M H [PFMLV; FM25.153]

537. 18 22/ ANEA MUSSELMAN [PFMLV FM 74.4.11]

538. [PFMLV FM74.4.14]

539. Catharine Leaman is my name/ heven is my situation Lampeter/ is my tweling Place christ is/ my salvathion the rose is ret/ the leavs are green the day a/ is Past witch I hav sean wh/ en I am dead and In mI gra/ ve and when m I bones are/ all roten and when you Se/ this remember me unless I/ be forgoten/ [Spelling as found on towel.] 1851/ Catharine B. Leaman/ DAVID BUCKWALTER/ MARY BUCKWALTER/ ABRAHAM LEAMAN/ BARBARA LEAMAN [Catharine Leaman, 539, 540, and Maria Leaman 464 were sisters, daughters of Abraham and Barbara Buckwalter Leaman whose names appear on each daughter's towel. David and Mary Buckwalter were their maternal grandparents; PFMLV FM24.820; Gehret and Keyser (1976), pl.44; cf.464, 540]

540. Catharine Leaman/ A L B L/OEHBDDE OEHBDDE [PFMLV FM24.821; Gehret and Keyser (1976), pl.43; cf. 464, 539; Figure 277]

541. [PFMLV NUN] [Figure 52]

542. BETZ HUHN/ [In cross stitch.] B H [In drawn thread panel.] [PFMLV FM74.4.16]

543. ANNA HORST/ OEHBDDE [PFMLV FM74.4.13

544. There is an hour When i must die/ Nor do i know how soon twill come/ How many children young as i/ Are called by death to hear their doom/ Let me improve the hours i have/ Before the day of grace is fled/ There no repentance in the grave/ Nor pardon offe to the bead/ [Spelling as found on towel.] Elizabeth Rohrer 1836 [PFMLV FM25.150]

545. CATARINA/ HEGE/ C H/ OEHBDDE [PFMLV; Figures 322,350]

546. K W [PFMLV FM74.4.9]

547. A B C D E F G H I K L M N O/ P Q R S T U V W X Y Z [PFMLV FM74.4.12; Figure 456]

548. M 18 27 W [PFMLV FM63.19; Gehret and Keyser (1976), pl.48, 48A]

549. [PFMLV FM74.4.17]
550. Mary Kreider/ 18 35 [PFMLV FM25.151]
552. E L [Purchased in Ephrata, Lancaster co.; Figures 216, 247, 386]
553. IAC COB/ GR AF/ 1822 [Figures 273, 344]
554. ELIZABETH HARBOLD [Figure 414]
555. 1841/ Anna Hess
556. IACOB 1835 HESS
557. ANNA/ WEAVER/ 1846
558. 1836/ OEHBDDE/ CATRINA ZARTMAN
559. GEORGE HOKE/ M H [Figures 135,369]
560. ELIZABETH/ DAMY MY HAND/ AND NWEDLE/ C S [sic] A B C D E F G H I J K L M/ N O P Q R S T U V W X Y Z CHRISTOPHER/ DAMY CATHARINE/l DAMY A D 1836/ [cf. 1335; Plate 14]
561. SUSANA ROCK/ S R/ [In cross stitch.] S R [In drawn thread panel.] [Figure 426; Plate 22]
562. SARAH SHIMP [Figures 148, 387]
566. ELISABETH L/ FRANK A B C D E [Figure 152]
568. SUSANA HUNSI[CKER] [Figure 376]
569. M OEHBDDE H [From Hanover, York co.; Figure 442]
570. CATARINA WITMER [From near Hanover, York co.]
571. When I am dead and/ Buried and all my/ Bones are [word missing] when/ This you see remember/ me Leist [sic] [missing word] should be/ forgotten Catharina Frankhauser/ C F/ [In cross stitch.] C F [In drawn thread panel.] [Figure 311]
573. R H/ M[ary] 1825 S[tauffer] [Mary Stauffer, born 1813, married Samuel Behm. She lived in the Hershey-Annville area as a child, but after marriage moved south of Annville and Palmyra into Derry twp., Lebanon co. She is buried at Spring Creek Church of the Brethren, Hershey. Family tradition states that a friend Ruth Hoppel made the towel for Mary. Initials "R H", the top border, and the legs on a deer motif were replaced about a generation ago. Figure 547]
574. 1839/ Fanny Nissley/ is My Name Rapho To/ wnship Lancaster County and/ State of Pennsylvania Fany/ [sic] Nisley is My name the rose is/ red the lives [sic] are green the days/ are Past which I have seen/ I Mark this Hand/ Toul [sic] the 4/ May [Fanny Nissley was born December 3, 1821 in Rapho twp., and married October 21, 1841 Jacob Snyder (1820-1910). She died in 1888. Fanny was one of five daughters of Martin (1788-1872) and Anna Bomberger Nisley (1791-1881). She made two samplers, one dated 1836, and another dated 1839 (Garvan, p.283; PMA 69-288-145) with designs and inscriptions similar to those sewn on her own towel, her sister Mary's sampler and towel (cf. 856) and sister Anny's sampler. If Anna also made a towel, it has not been found. She was born in 1819 and married in 1845 to Emanuel Cassel. Figures 103, 399]
575. Catharine Halanah Minnich Her Towel L/ March the 14th L In the Year of our Lord/ A D 1850/ Within thy courts one single/ Day Tis better to attend than/ Lord In any other Place A/ Thousand Days to Spend/ Catharine Halanah Minnich is My/ Name And Heaven is my Station/ And Lancaster County Is my/ Dewlling [sic] Place And Christ is My/ Salvation And When I am dead And in/ My Grave and all my bones are rotten/ If this You see Remember me or else I/ Must be Foregotten [sic] And Fore ever/ [sic] Amen/ This ring/ Is round it has/ No end when I/ Look on this ring/ Then I can see/ How kind my sist/ er was to me/ Rebecca J M/ innich/ And We soon shall hear/ Him say Ye Blessed/ Children come. He soon/ Will call us henec [sic] away/ And take his wanderers/ Home [Catharine Halanah Minnich was born 24 March, 1845, daughter of John and Barbara Johnson Minnich. She was one of twelve children and a sister to Emanuel J Minnich (towel 18). Their sister Rebecca J Minnich made a decorated towel for both Emanuel and Catharine as well as a sampler in 1843 that has sewn on it, "Rebeca Minnich 1843 daughter of John and Barbara Minnich." Family information is from the Minnich family Bible. cf. 1054; Plate 43]
576. S/ A/ R/ A/ A/ N/ N/ A/ X/ H/ O/ L/ L/ O/ B/ U/ S/ H/ 1840 [Sara Anna Hollowbush waas born in 1826, daughter of Richard Hollowbush and Margaret Wölker, Upper Frederick twp., Montgomery co. She married Jacob Stauffer in 1846 who was from Colebrookdale twp., Berks co. cf. 275, 276; Figure 151a]
577. M R 1827
578. MARIA BENNER 1829/ OEDHBDDE [From the Richland-Quakertown area in Bucks co. Maria Benner was related by marriage to Hannah Walp, towel 274.]
579. ELIZABETH FRANKENFIELD 1820/ OEHBDDE [Born ca. 1803; married Christian Hager of Haycock mountain, Bucks co.]

580. NANCY WEAVER/ 1836/ OEHBDDE [In cross stitch.] N W [In drawn thread panel.] [Figure 393]
581. 1797/ MA[RI] HO[CHSTETTER]/ [In cross stitch.] MARI HOCH[STETTER] [In drawn thread panel.] [From Lancaster co. A note with the towel reads, "Maria Hostetter (Aunt Polly) sister of grandfather Benjamin Hostetter....''; Figure 150]
583. M L [PMA 55-94-61; Garvan, p.271]
584. L M L [Thought to be from a Ziegler family, Skippack, Montgomery co. ca. 1800-1840; PMA 20-35-1; Garvan, p.271]
585. A R/ A H/ 1839 [PMA 70-132-2; Garvan, p.274]
586. KATARI/ 1838/ NA NS [PMA 55-94-62; Garvan, p.274]
587. M L [PMA 55-94-58; Garvan, p.271]
588. MARGRET KRESMAN/ 1827 [PMA 55-94-59; Garvan, p.273]
589. CADARINA MILER/ 1834 [PMA 55-94-65; Garvan, p.274]
590. ANNA LEMIN/ 1818/ OEHBDDE ANNA LEMIENDE [PMA 28-16-1; Garvan, p.273]
591. 184[?]/ Alithebeth ebersole hand and thread/ Here is my name When i [sic] am dead/ When i [sic] am dead and in my Grave/ And all my bones are rotten/ If this you see i think on me/ Or else i [sic] shall be for goten [sic] Alithebeth ebersole is my name the rose is red/ The leaves are green the days are Past Wich [sic] i [sic] have seen/ Remember me [PMA 55-94-64; Garvan, p.275]
592. The Grass is Green The Rose is Red Here is/ my Name When I Am Dead FIANN BUCKWALT/ ER She Marked This Towel Done The 30 Day of April/ When I am dead and in my/ Grave and all my bones/ Are Rotten A D 1856 When/ This you See remember me/ Lest I Should Be Forgotten/ FIANN Buckwalter is my/ Name and heaven is my/ Salvation Pennsylvania/ Is my dwelling place/ And christ [sic] is my sustation/ F B/ OEHBDDE [PMA 28-10-115; Garvan, p.276; cf. 362]
593. Sophia Elizabeth G Witmer 1860 [Thought to be from Montgomery co. PMA 55-94-60; Garvan, p.276]
594. MARY CASSEL/ OEHBDDE/ 1828 [Thought to be from Norriton, East Norriton twp., Montgomery co. PMA 70-132-3; Garvan, p.273]
595. E H/ 1842 [Thought to be from Berks co. PMA 55-94-63; Garvan, p.275]
597. MARGARET/ KOLB 1849
598. H G/ 1853
599. REBECAK GROS/ 1832
600. A K 1826
601. A F/ [In drawn thread panel.] A FABER MAHL EIN IAHR/ EIN TAG VER FLOSS SEN/ NA HEYZU DER EWIGK/ EIT WIEEIN PEILWIRT/ ABGE SCHOSENSOVER/ GEHET MEIZEIT/ [Again another year (day) has flown nearer to eternity as an arrow forth is blown so goes time away from me.] ACHWIEBETRVBTSINDFROMESELEN EW [Oh how troubled are pious souls] [All inscriptions in cross stitch. Thought to be from Montgomery co. The first hymn verse is from a hymn which may be sung at the end of any day or at the end of the year by the insertion of the proper word Jahr (year) or Tag (day). It was a popular hymn among all Pennsylvania Germans. Figure 475]
602. C Z [In cross stitch.] C Z F [In drawn thread panel.] [Figure 532]
604. M[ariah] G[etz]/ E E/ [In cross stitch.] M G M G [In drawn thread panel.] [For Mariah Getz Landis.] [Figure 312]
606. MARIA DILLIER HAT DAS GENETH/ IM IAHR 1827 [Maria Dillier sewed this in the year 1827.] A B C D E F G H I J K L M N/ O P Q R S T U V W X Y Z A B C D E F G H I K L [Incomplete.] [cf. 231, 232, 660, 687]
608. MAGDALENA EDRIS/ L K 18 41 M E [Figures 137, 242]
609. ESTHER NISZLY/ 1821 MEY 2/ OEHBDDE [Esther Niszley was born on May 4, 1799, married Abraham Long, and died October 12, 1865. She is buried in the Frey graveyard near Chambersburg, Franklin Co. cf. 1415. Plate 3]
611. Susan C Killefer/ is my name/ the 30 day/ of September/ in the year of/ our Lord 1829/ I was received/ into the comm/ union of the Ger/ man reformed church on the/ 21 days of Febr/ uary in the year/ of our Lord 1846/ S K/ 1847/ S K/ 1847/ Susan Killefer/ 1847 [Garvan and Hummel, pl.133; Figure 433]
612. FERONICA WITMER/ 1826 [Figure 107]
613. LID SCHMCH/ 1827
614. ELISABETH GRUBER/ 1829
615. HANNA KRESSMAN/ 1827
616. SUSANA 1824 IORGIN
617. LIDIA STIERLE/ 1831

619. MARIA KURTZIN/ EDEL HERTZ [noble heart] [NMFM; Figure 446]

620. My/ parents/ are Geor/ ge and M/ atty Meck/ 1841/ Catharine Meck is my name/ for you to see when i [sic] am dead/ and am laid in my grave and all/ my bones are rotten here is my/ name for you to see or else i [sic] am/ forgotten/ Nun lasst uns gahn und trattan/ met sengan und met batan zum/ harrn dar unsarm laban beshea/ har kraft gafaban/ Wer gahn dahen und wandarn/ fon aenam eahr zum andarn wer/ laban und gadahan fom altan bes/ zum nauan [Now let us go and step on with singing and with praying to the Lord who hitherto has given strength to our lives we go thence and wander from one year to the next. We live and thrive from the old to the new.] [The first two stanzas of a popular German New Year's hymn written by Paul Gerhard; NMFM Figures 207, 296, 413, 427]

624. Susan Hochstittir is my name/ S H/ S H/ 1824/ 1824/ S H [In drawn thread square.] S H [In drawn thread panel.] NMFM [Probably related to 634, 635 Figures 213, 282, 408]

625. 1816/ E H/ [In cross stitch.] E H/ [In drawn thread panel.] ELISABETH HISTAND [In cross stitch.] [NMFM; Figures 138, 155, 290, 291]

626. BARBARA KURTZ/ 1811 1811 [NMFM]

627. Anna Kurtz/ 18 44 [Probably born 1820, a daughter of Christian Kurtz and Catharine King, married after 1855 Jacob Stoltzfoos and died 1889. Fisher 3239.1)

628. 1845/ MARY KURTZ [NMFM; Probably related to 627, 629, 630, 967]

629. ANNA KURTZ/ 1839 [NMFM; cf. 627, 630]

630. A[NNA] 1846 K[URTZ]/ OEHBDDE [NMFM; cf. 627, 629]

631. ANNA EBERLY/ 18 OEHBDDE 38 [NMFM; Stoudt (1964), Fig.221]

633. L H/ LOH N HOSTITTER [NMFM]

634. Susan Hostitter/ 1822/ 8 [NMFM; Probably related to 624, 635]

635. Susan N 10 Hostetter/ 1830 [NMFM; Probably related to 624, 634. Susan Hochstetter also made a sampler, 1823.]

636. Maria Leaman

637. Anna G. Herr [In black ink stamp.] [Anna also stamped her name onto a tablecloth on which she inserted bobbin lace identical to the lace found on towel 814 and another tablecloth initialed, "SA SK 1841." Plate 47]

638. CLINTON EBERSOLE/ 1888 [Made for Clinton Ebersole (1866-1934) of Lebanon co., who married in 1891 to Fannie K. Shanaman (1872-1893). His parents were Elias A. and Catharine Longenecker (1844-1915) Ebersole. Figure 195]

639. ANNA MEYER/ 1846/ OEHBDDE. [Grow Catalogue, 157]

640. I W F/ 1853 MM

641. Barbara Landisen/ 1846/ B L E L/ B 1846 L [cf. 863; Plate 42]

642. M C/ 1836/ MACDALENA CROBB/ OEHBDDE [Plate 44]

643. 1838/ MARIA BESHOR

644. MARY HOFFER/ 1890/ M H [From Mt. Joy area, Lancaster co.]

645. MARIA KRIEBEL/ M K [Maria Kriebel, daughter of Melchior and Rosina Kriebel, was born December 16, 1826; died October 30, 1859; married Rev. Reuben Kriebel November 30, 1848; lived in Worcester twp., Montgomery co.; cf.646]

646. Maria Kriebel/ M K/ 1842 [cf.645]

647. MARY/ 1836 [Wetzel Catalogue, 1751]

649. MAGDALENA BRAUN [Wetzel Catalogue, 1751]

651. MAGDALENA STAUFER 1842 [Wetzel Catalogue, 1751]

652. C P/ M K/ A B C D E [Incomplete.] [Wetzel Catalogue, 1752]

653. CATHERINE BITTING [Wetzel Catalogue, 1753]

655. ELIZABETH BROWER/ 1813/ OEHBDDE/ E B [Wetzel Catalogue, 1753]

657. SUSANN/ BRUB/ ACHER/ 1844 [Wetzel Catalogue, 1809]

658. SARA WEBER [Wetzel Catalogue, 1810]

659. I I M H R 1819 [Wetzel Catalogue, 1810]

660. MARIA DILLIER 1831 [Wetzel Catalogue, 1811; cf. 231, 232, 606, 687, 1410,1411]

661. ELISABETH/ BUCHWALTER/ 1846 [Wetzel Catalogue, 1812]

662. MAGDALENA BARTHOLOMEW DECEMBER 23, 1831/ A B C D E F G H I J K L M N O P Q R S T U V W X Y Z [Wetzel Catalogue, 1838]

663. MAGARETHA ARNOLD 1855 [Wetzel Catalogue, 1839]

664. catarine derr/ A B C H 4 Year 1854 MAY THE 19/ Catharine Derr hand and thread/ Here is my name when I am dead/ When I am dead and in my grave/ And all my bones are rotten/ If this you see O think on me/ Or else I shall be forgotten/ CATHARINE DERR/ Catharine Derr is my name The rose is red/ The leaves are green the days are past wich [sic] I have seen/ Remember me [Wetzel Catalogue, 1840]

665. A B C D E F G H I J K L M/ N O P Q R S T U V W X Y Z [Wetzel Catalogue, 1874]

666. CADARINA BECHTEL 1830 [Wetzel Catalogue, 1875]

667. CATHERINE WELKER 1849 [Wetzel Catalogue, 1875]

668. ELISABETH HOFMAN 1814 [Wetzel Catalogue, 1875]

669. MATTY GUTH 1844 [Wetzel Catalogue, 1875]

670. REBECCA FOLTZ 1842 [Wetzel Catalogue, 1876]

671. ELIZABETH LONGENECKER/ April 7, 1840 [Wetzel Catalogue, 1877; cf. 15, 90]

673. CATHERINE KREITER [Wetzel Catalogue, 1877]

675. SALOME IRLING 1817 [Wetzel Catalogue, 1901]

676. 1831/ KATHARINA BRAND [Wetzel Catalogue, 1901]

677. HENRY RINKER/ SARAH STAHR/ 1848 [Wetzel Catalogue, 1902]

678. ELISABETH WISLER [Wetzel Catalogue, 1902]

679. A B C D E F G H I J K L M N O P Q R S T U V W X Y Z [Wetzel Catalogue, 1902]

680. ELIZABETH MINICH/ SEPTEMBER 30, 1840 [Wetzel Catalogue, 1902]

681. LEISEBLE 1827 [Wetzel Catalogue, 1904]

682. SUSANA/ HILLER/ 1813/ [In cross stitch.] SH [In drawn thread panel.] [Wetzel Catalogue, 1928]

683. CATHARINA 1819 BINDER [Wetzel Catalogue, 1929]

684. I H [Wetzel Catalogue, 1931; May be European.]

685. L E [Wetzel Catalogue, 1945]

687. SUSANNA DILLIER 1832 [Wetzel Catalogue, 1947; cf. 231,232, 606, 660, 1410, 1411]

691. HEDDY OXENFORT/ 1839 [Thought to be from Boyertown area, Berks co.; cf. 708, 933; Figure 214]

692. M K/ MARIA KREID[ER?] [Figures 170, 295]

693. HENRY KIEFER/ 1858 [cf. 694; Figure 162]

694. CATARINA KIEFER/ 1854 [cf. 693, brother and sister; Figure 163]

695. K N S 1832 [Figures 307, 345]

696. M S/ 1845 [In drawn thread panel.]

697. IENNER 1820/ [January 1820] M A L E/ Veronica Rutt [cf.751; Figures 22, 81a, 8b, 541.]

699. M A E R/ 1808 [Figures 38, 59; Plate 23]

701. 1837/ ANNA BRUBACHER/ [In cross stitch.] 1841/ A B/ [In drawn thread panel.] anna brubacher elizabeth tounship lancaster county state Pensylvania [Spelling as found on towel. In cross stitch.]

702. 1839/ OEHBDDE/ NENCY GREYBILL [Figure 58]

703. LIDIA DUNDOR [A Berks co. name.]

704. M F [Figure 554]

705. MARIA STAUFFER/ 1835

706. ELESEBETH/ H ORT E/ DEN 15 MERZ/ [March 15] C 1854 M/ a b c d e f g h i J k l m n o p q r s t/ u u [sic] v x y z [Figures 180a, 412.]

707. 1814/ ANNA ERHARDIN

708. 1838/ ESTHER OXENFORT [cf.691, 933; Figure 372]

709. M R/ 1817 [Figures 76, 266]

711. OEHBDDE/ 1799/ HANNA BRENNEISEN [Hanna Brenneisen was born January 2, 1782, a daughter of Conrad and Maria Elisabeth Brenneisen, baptized March 24, 1782 at Trinity Lutheran Church, Lancaster. She was confirmed in 1798 at Trinity Lutheran Church, New Holland and married March 6, 1803, Johann Sensemann of Cocalico twp. Conrad Brenneisen appears on Earl twp., Lancaster co. tax lists and census records throughout the period of Hanna's childhood and adolesence. Figures 184, 204, 320]

712. OEHBDDE/ 18 09/ CATARINA KINTZ I SI [Figure 335]

714. [MMA 13.111]

715. M F I F/ Fear none of those things which thou shalt/ suffer behold the devil shall cast some of you/ into Prison that ye may be tried and ye shall/ have tribulation ten days be thou Faithful unto/ death and i [sic] will give thee a crown of life/ [Rev. 2:10] and i [sic] heard a loud voice saying in heaven now/ is come salvation and strength and the kingdom/ of our god [sic] and the power of his christ [sic] For the/ accuser of our brethren is cast down which ac/ cused them before our god [sic] day and night [Rev. 12:10] [MMA 13.108.6; Figure 178]

718. HEDDED MEIER HOTS/ GEMACHT IM IAHR 1827/ [Hedded Meier made it in the year 1827] OEHBDDE R/ RAYEL ZIEGLER [Probably worked by both women. Workmanship and designs differ from top to bottom. Figure 127]

719. LID BAC/ 1831/ LYDIA BACHMAN [Figure 27]

720. 18 46/ M H

721. NANSEY 18 32 HAPPEL [Penciled on the back upper right corner "Ida Troup."; Figure 35]
722. LEA STOLSFUSZ [cf.241; Plate 21]
723. M 1855 W/ M W [Figure 365]
724. IOSEP H LANG/ 18 12
726. SARA S/ CHENCK [cf. 429, 430]
727. 1830/ BARBARA MEYER
728. SARA MOKA WEH SO KAN IC ZEITVERTREIWEN 1820/ [Thus I pass time.] SA RA MO KA WE H
729. 1820/ ELISABETH MILLERNI
730. SUSANNA 18 32 HUBER
731. 1853/ B C E C [Figure 245]
732. CATARINA [Figures 39, 267, 499]
733. E B [Name tag sewn on back of towel reads, "C M Cusler."]
734. A [?] HU [?] [Too much missing to read the name.]
735. M R
736. ANNA LONG/ 18 31
740. A D
741. S B
742. A H [In drawn thread panel.]
743. ESTER WEISER
744. C R 1821 [Figure 232]
745. E S/ [Sewn in German *fraktur* type face] 1809 1809
746. E K 1845 S I [Figure 377]
747. M D MARY DELLINGER/ 1841
748. E L
750. A B C D E F G H I J [?] K L M N/ O P Q R S T [U] V W X Y Z/ ANNA E. HABECKER/ 1839 [Thought to be from Lancaster city, Figures 182, 347, 348, 403]
751. 1820/ VERONICA RUTT [From Elizabethtown, Lancaster co.; Figure 156]
752. OEHBDDE/ 1888/ ANNA/ WEAVER/ E[lizabeth] B[uchwalter]/ 1847 [Elizabeth Buchwalter who made this towel was born 1830 in East Earl twp., Lancaster co.; died 1907; married Peter Brubaker 1850; buried in Pike Church cemetery, Ephrata. Her daughter, Anna Weaver, later sewed her name and date on the towel. The present owner remembers the towel hanging inside the bedroom closet door in her grandfather's house. cf. 764]
753. Catherine Ebersole/ 1848 OEHBDDE [Purchased in Dillsburg, York co. There was also a chest with CATHERINE EBERSOLE 1847 on the lid. Figure 220]
755. Anna Frey 1848/ The Grass is green The Rose is Red/ Here is my Name when I am dead Anna Frey/ She Marked This Towl done the 2th day of October/ A D 1848/ When I am dead and in my grave/ and all my bones are Rotten/ when This you See Remember me/ Lest I Should be Forgotten/ Anna Frey is my name/ and Heaven is my station/ Pennsylvania is my dwelling Place/ And Christ is my salvation' [Anna Frey, born December 1, 1825, was a daughter of Johannes Frey (1796-1872) and Anna Tschantz (born 1795). From Lancaster co. Her sister Elisabeth sewed a towel with similar motifs. cf. 466]
756. ANNA 18 25 CARLE [Anna Charles (1804-1872), daughter of Jacob Charles and Barbara C. Herr married after 1848 to Jacob Seitz (1812-1892); lived in Manor twp. Lancaster co. and buried in Habecker Mennonite Cemetery. No issue. Her sampler is dated 1832. cf. 1110; Figures 74, 79, 209a, 317]
757. ELIZABETH TRAUB/ 1835 [Elizabeth Traub was born December 3, 1813; died January 2, 1880; married April 28, 1833 Philip Traub, Esquire; daughter of Wendell Heimbach and Susanna Bittenbender; buried in St. Peter's cemetery, Sieshozville, Berks co.]
758. Clary Hallman/ 1841 [Possibly from East Greenville, Upper Hanover twp., Montgomery co.; Figure 97]
759. LIDI/ LANC/ IOSEP/ SMIDT
762. C B [In drawn thread panel.]
764. E B E B/ 1846/ ELIZABETH BUCHWALTER [cf.752]
765. HANNA ZIEGLER [Name in drawn thread panel in two parallel columns spelled from the bottom to the top. Thought to be from Bucks co. Figure 327]
766. B E
769. Eliza Brackbill/ Ann 1847 [Lichten, p. 58; Figure 265]
770. SUSANNA HERR/ OEHBDDE/ 1843/ S H [Figure 208]
771. SUSANNA GROFF 1840/ SUSANNA GROFF 184[?] [Susanna Groff was born October 17, 1829 in Earl twp., Lancaster co.; married September 25, 1862 Isaac Carter Evans; died October 20, 1906.]
772. MARIA GENEGE [Maria Genege was born 1821 Mifflin co.; married Isaac Hertzler 1847; died 1896.]
774. CATHERINA WEAVER 1834 [From the Weaverland-New Holland area in Lancaster co. Catherina Weaver married Mar-

tin Good. cf. 775]
775. CATHERINA WEAVER 1836 [cf.774]
776. BARBARA BRACKBILL 1834 [Barbara Brackbill, daughter of Benjamin Brackbill and Elizabeth Hershey, was born November 27, 1815; married Benjamin Hoover, November 22, 1836; died September 25, 1892; buried in Hershey Cemetery, New Miltown, Lancaster co. Plate 28]
777. MARIA METZLER/ 1819/ OEHBDDE
778. ELIZABETH HUBER/ DAVID BUCHWALTER/ [?] BUCH-WALTER [cf. 1330; Plate 33]
780. 1843/ MARYAN FOLS [NYHS 1941-942]
781. 1835/ [In cross stitch.] 1829 [In drawn thread panel.] [NYHS 1941-941 Figure 154a]
782. 1848/ ANNA HUWER/ A H OEHBDDE
783. R M
784. L K [In cross stitch.] L K [In drawn thread panel.]
785. M H [In drawn thread panel.]
787. SERER EN NO A B C D E F G X [Sarah Renno, probably from Mifflin co.]
788. ANNA MOSSER
789. E W 1833 [RM]
790. ANNA HUBER 1833 [Woods, p. 48]
791. G B 1813 [RM; Woods, p. 48]
792. LYDIA PEPLEY 1825/ LP 18 25 [RM; Figure 415]
793. H 18 35 M [RM]
794. MARIA BRUBAKER [RM; Woods, p.49]
795. M M/ 1832
796. M[ary] D[eardorff]/ M 1821 D [Mary Deardorff was born June 11, 1815 Franklin co.; married Samuel Koser December 28, 1837; moved to Gettysburg 1868; died January 3, 1894. Figure 409]
797. BARBARA LEHMANIN/ BER LEH/ 1828/ OEDHBDDE/ A H D L/ BERBARA L/ LULZ EDMD/ AGSF VMTI/ ENDE EDNE [Figures 215, 478, 479]
798. I Just dropt in to See You all and ax You how you do/ I'll sing You a song it is not very long itts about my/ Long tail blue/ Just look at my long tail blue o how do you like my/ blue ill sin you a song it is not very long itts about/ my long tail blue/ Some niggars they have but one coat but i you/ [Spelling as found on towel. Folk song.] 1838/ OEHBDDE/ Maria Young workd in The 19teen Year of her March/ David Backer/ JY MY SY MY MY CY AY LY SY/ LY RY SM CM CM FY EY MY [Probably from Lancaster co. Figure 474]
799. 1826/ ANNA HIETHWOLE [Anna Hiethwole was born June 4, 1808 Rockingham co. Va.; died March 12, 1834; married Daniel Suter in 1828. Her father was David Hiethwole from Lancaster co. Pa. who moved to Virginia 1795-1796. Towel was always inherited by daughters. Figure 2]
800. Sarah Hager/ 1843/ [In cross stitch.] S H [In drawn thread panel.]
801. MAGDALENA GROSS/ OEHBDDE/ M G 1829 [Christensen, p.10; Lichten, p.56]
802. FANNEY WHITMER/ IS BORN IN THE YE/ AR 1832 AUGUST T/ HE 28 1852 END [Fanney Whitmer, aged seventeen, was a member of the household of Christian and Mary Wohlgemuth Witmer in Mount Joy twp., Lancaster co. in 1850; cf. 63, 67, 250, 440]
803. Maria B Kreiders work done 1859/ OEHBBDE/ J Y A K M K D K J K A K E K/ My parents there parents/ John and Anna Kreider and Jacob and Maria/ Baslar/ This work of mine my friends may have/ When I am in my silent grae [sic]/ Look on this work then you shall see/ How kind my parents where [sic] to me/ Daniel and Anna Kreider [Maria B Kreider was born September 20, 1835, to Daniel (1801-1861) and Anna S. Bossler (1811-1859). She married Isaac Kauffman and died March 5, 1882.]
804. E H/ S H/ 1839
805. 1858/ ELISAB/ ETH MO/ SSER
806. SOPHIA EBY
807. CATARINA FRANCK/ 1822 [Family tradition states Catarina was fifteen years old when she made this towel. She married Christian Hostetter. Her sampler dates 1820. Figure 99]
809. 1820 IUNIUS/ [June 1820.] ANNA RUTT [NSDAR 62.213]
810. M A M N/ [In cross stitch.] 1797/ [In drawn thread panel.] MARGETHA MINSEN/ [In cross stitch.] M A M N [In drawn thread panel.] [NSDAR 62.212]
811. R[ebecca] B[ushey] [Made ca. 1850 by Rebecca Bushey, born June 8, 1820; died October 1, 1898; daughter of Nicholas Bushey (1799-1887) and Christina Nell (1788-1869). Family tradition states Rebecca made four towels. Her mother Christina sewed a sampler dated 1813.]

813. BARBARA LEHN/ OEHBDDE
814. S V M I [cf. 637; Figure 505]
815. M A I G I [SI T.18231]
816. M F/ M A F/ [In cross stitch.] M D/ 1823 [In drawn thread panel.] [SI T.18230]
819. [Thought to be "part of the wedding outfit of Catharine Mill, Pittman or Red Banks, Shenandoah co. Virginia."] [SI T.12182]
820. C A E N/ 1841/ A B C D E/ F G H I K/ L M N O P/ Q R S T U/ V̆ W X Y Z [SI T.17292]
821. 18 34/ P W̆ [SI T.17291]
822. MARIA A/ STEWER/ 1823/ [In cross stitch.] OEHBDDE [In drawn thread panel.] [SI T.17290]
823. 18 34/ BARBARA ESCHLIMAN [SI T.17294]
824. 1838/ M A [SI T.17293]
825. ALIAN SMITH/ 1851 [SI T.17295; Stoudt (1973), 156]
826. ELISABETH FLUMM/ 1830 [SI T.10870]
827. [Thought to be from Bowmansville, Lancaster co. Figure 546]
828. ELIZABETH/ IUNI WALDSCHMIDT 1824 [June 1824.]
829. CATHARINE ACKER 1842/ C A/ C A 1846 [HCLC]
830. 1838/ OEHBDDFM/ FANNY MEYER [HCLC; Figures 181, 206.]
831. JOHN D SENSENIG/ M S/ 18 46/ M S B S [Thought to be from Quarryville area, Lancaster co.; HCLC; cf. 832, 833, 834, 945]
832. B D/ B D/ B D/ B 1825 D [HCLC; cf. 831, 833, 834, 945]
833. B D/ B 18 C D 25 D [HCLC; cf. 831, 832, 834, 945]
834. MARY SENSENIGS [HCLC; cf. 831, 832, 833, 945]
835. E H
836. 18 G G 75 [PMA 03-116; Garvan, p.272]
837. [PMA 55-94-67; Garvan p.272]
838. 1818/ MARGARETA GUTBROR [PMA 03-120; Garvan, p.272]
839. 18 ELI[ZABETH] KAU[FFMAN] 40 [PMA 03-119; Garvan, p.274]
840. ANNA 1848 MEYER [PMA 55-94-66; Garvan, p.275]
842. B R [Figure 549]
844. S W/ isaac weidman susanna weidman peter weidman christina weidman/ L C Z 1837 [Schiffer, p.151; cf. 379, 1047]
845. MATTY WISMER 1867 [Seen at Allentown Antiques Show, November, 1981.]
846. SOPHIA WIRMAN 1844 [Seen at Montgomery co. flea market, 1979.]
847. LIDIA WICHTERN
848. E V 1819
849. J S/ JACOB STOUFFER THIS TOWL/ I MADE FOR SAKE OF THE WHEN THIS YOU SEE REMEM/ BER ME 1847 [Lichten, p.57]
850. SARA STEWER 1825 [Seen at a Montgomery co. antiques show, 1979.]
851. E R 1833
852. M L R 1827 [Pennypacker Catalogue, (ca. 1938), pl.N]
853. S E R 183[?]
854. MARY/ REIST/ 1850 [Stoudt (1964), Fig. 223; Stoudt, (1966), p.354]
855. C P 1819/ A B C D E F G H I J K L M N O P Q R S T U V W X Y Z [Pennypacker Catalogue, (ca. 1938), pl. 5]
856. MARY NISSLY/ OEHBDDE/ Mary Nissly is my station Heaven/ is my dwelling place and Christ is my Salvation when I am/ dead and in my grave and all my bones are rotten when/ this you see remember me or Else I Shall be Forgotten/ Rapho Township Lancaster County and State of Pennsylvan/ ia/ I markd [sic] this hand toul [sic] January the 2 1841 [Mary Nissly, sister of Fanny Nissley, 574, was born June 17, 1824. She married Benjamin Musser (1825-1892) and died in 1898. She made a sampler, dated 1839, 1840, with designs and inscriptions similar to those sewn on her towel. Schiffer, p.151; Garvan and Hummel, p.190]
857. MARIA MUSSELMAN 1821 [Seen at Allentown Antiques Show, November, 1981.]
858. 1844/ MARY MARTIN/ A B C D E F G H I J K L M N O P Q R S T U V W X Y Z [Stoudt (1966), p.356]
859. S[usanna] L[e] F[ever] [Seen in private photograph collection.]
860. LEDYA LUTZ/ OEHBDDE/ THE YEAR 1829 [Stoudt (1966), p.359]
861. ELIZABETH LIEB 1833 [Pennypacker Catalogue (Flack, 1976), p.102]
862. CATHARINA LAUDENSCHLAGER 1833 [Little, p.198A]
863. Barbara Landisen/ 1838 [Stoudt (1964), Fig. 223; Stoudt (1966), p.354; cf. 641]
864. CADARINA KUNS/ C K 1827 [Lichten, p.58; Stoudt (1966) p.357]

865. CATHERINE KREITER [Wetzel Catalogue, 1877]
866. POLLY KAUFMAN [Seen in private photograph collection.]
867. C H/ 18 Catharina Hoch 44/ [In cross stitch.] C[atharine] W[eidner] [Catharina Hoch's mother. In drawn thread panel.] [Stoudt (1964), Fig.224; Stoudt (1966), p.359]
868. 1816/ A G [Schiffer, p.152]
869. L E [Pennypacker Catalogue (ca.1938), pl.9]
870. FRENI FRICK 1835
871. ANNA ESHLEMAN 1851
872. E B D/ 1820/ ELISABETH BIEMERSDERFFER/ OEHBDDE/ [In cross stitch.] E B [In drawn thread panel.] [Stoudt (1964), Fig. 220; Stoudt (1966), p.365]
873. SARAH DORNBACH [Seen in private photograph collection.]
874. Catharina Deimer May 6, 1833 [Stoudt (1966), p.356]
875. ELIZABETH DANNER [Seen in private photograph collection.]
876. A B 1827
877. A B
878. MARY BUBEACHER [Seen in private photograph collection.]
879. ELIZABETH BUCHWALTER [Lichten, p.58]
880. LEHE BOWMEN 1836 [Seen at Allentown Antiques Show, 1981]
882. MAGDALENA ALBRECHT [Stoudt (1964), Fig.223; Stoudt (1966), p.354]
883. ELISABETH HALTEMAN [Woods, p.49]
884. [Stoudt (1973), p.154]
885. FIANNA LANDIS 1832 [Kauffman, p.113]
886. ANO · 1 · 795 · DEN/ · 27 · SEPTEMBER/ · BALLI WEISER [Examined in Guy F. Reinert Photograph File. Figure 120]
887. N A/ MARIAAN 1834 HEIMBACH [Examined in Guy F. Reinert Photograph File.]
888. L[ydia] 1851 S[chlabach] [Examined in Guy F. Reinert Photograph File; cf. 889]
889. L[ydia] S[chlabach] [Examined in Guy F. Reinert Photograph File; cf. 888 Figure 122]
890. MARIA BECHTEL/ 1841 [In cross stitch.] M B [In drawn thread panel.] [Examined in Guy F. Reinert Photograph File.]
891. R[egina] S[chultz] / 1841 [Regina Schultz was born 1816; died 1902; married 1845 to Abraham Kriebel; lived in Upper Hanover twp., Montgomery co. Examined in Guy F. Reinert Photograph File; cf. 892; Figure 123]
892. R[egina] 1841 S[chultz] [Examined in Guy F. Reinert Photograph File; cf. 891; Figure 123a]
893. M 1819 M [Examined in Guy F. Reinert Photograph File.]
894. A B C D E F G H I/ K L M M [sic] N O P Q/ R S T [U] V W X Z [sic] Y/ BARBARA/ LATSCHAR [Examined in Guy F. Reinert Photograph File.]
896. OEHBDDE/ MARY FRETZ/ 1846 [Examined in Guy F. Reinert Photograph File.]
897. ELIZA FRETZ/ 1848/ OEHBDDE [Examined in Guy F. Reinert Photograph File. cf. 1291]
898. A/ N N/ A RIEG/ ER/ T [Examined in Guy F. Reinert Photograph File.]
899. REGINA SCHULTZ/ 1837 [Examined in the Guy F. Reinert Photograph File.]
900. P G/ 1818 [Thought to be from Womelsdorf, Berks co.; AARFAC 75.608.1]
901. Anna Roland is my name Rapho/ is my station heaven is my dwelling/ Place and christ is my salvation the rose/ is red the leaves are Green the days are/ Past which i have seen when i am dead/ and in my grave an my bonse are/ rotten When this you see remember me/ let all the rest forgotten this/ towl i made in the year 1846 [Spelling as found on towel.]
902. LEA STOLTSFUS 1830
903. CATHARINE BITTING
904. HENRY BUCH 1829
905. MRA WEBER
906. ROSINA OTH 1814
907. E L B A 1832
908. SARAH LAPP 18[?]3
909. 1826 BAR/ BARABA/ UMAN A B C D E F G/ H I K L M N/ O P Q R S T U V W X Y/ Z [Purchased in Sunbury, Northumberland co.]
911. A B/ annie bonholtzer/ 1850
912. JUDITH MARTIN/ OEDHBDDE AMB [cf. 490, 1031]
913. P B [In drawn thread panel]
914. ELISABETH BORG/ HOLDER 1831/ OEHBDDE [Encyclopaedia Britannica, vol. 8, pl. XII]

915. ELIZABETH HERR/ 18 46/ OEHBDDE/ Elizabeth Herr is my name/ [missing] is my station/ Pennsylvania is my dwelling place/ And Christ is my salvation/ When I am dead and in my grave/ and all my bones are rotten/ When this you see remember me/ lest I should be forgotten [Kleinfelter Catalogue, 1979]
916. ANNA MYERS 1846 [Keggereis Catalogue, 191]
917. ANNA SCHENEIN [Keggereis Catalogue, 192]
918. LEAH KELLER 1831 [Keggereis Catalogue, 195]
919. SARAH HOFFMAN [Kleinfelter Catalogue, August, 1981]
920. ELIZABETH HUNSICKER [Kleinfelter Catalogue, August, 1981]
921. ANna Huber 1831 [Thornton Catalogue, January, 1977, 314]
922. MAGDALE/ NA/ MESNER/ 1844 [Thornton Catalogue, January, 1977, 312]
923. CATHARINE ANN FRETS 1844 [Grow Catalogue, 158; cf. 325]
924. ANNA HARTMAN 1837 [Renner Catalogue, 828]
926. A M C [Figure 151]
927. R S [Figure 133]
928. BARBARA MEYERN
930. MARIA FAUST
931. S M/ 18 43
932. MARIA MASTELLER/ 1848 [SL]
933. Esther Oxenfort/ 1844 [Thought to be from Boyertown area, Berks co. This is one of three known towels by the Oxenfort sisters. Esther's initials, "E OF" are sewn on her blue and white linen bolster case. cf. 691, 708; Figures 212, 263]
934. SARA ANN REX/ A B C D E F G H I K L M N O P Q R S T U V W X Y [Z] [Sarah Ann Rex, born April 21, 1847; died August 24, 1919; daughter of Maria Krauss (339, 340, 935); sister of Rosa Ann Rex (341). From Heidelberg twp., Lehigh co.; Figure 161]
935. M[aria] K[rauss]/ 1836 [cf. 339, 340, 341, 934; Figure 160]
936. Mary Landis made this hand taul/ 1836
937. B D [Thought to be from Lancaster co.]
938. CATARINA RIEGEL/ 1798
939. S D 1836 S D
940. BARBARA MARTIN/ 1838/ A B C D E F G H I K L M/ N O P Q R S T U V W X Y Z/ B M
941. 1846/ E K/ L H
942. M S/ Was Grandfathers/ Moses Smoker/ Died October 7 1876/ age 49 years/ Then Fathers/ Eli A Smoker/ Died September 18, 1932/ Age 65 years/ Now Mary B. Smoker 1934 [Moses J. Smucker (1827-1876) married Cathrine Summers (1832-1870); son: Eli Smucker (1867-1932) married Susan Beiler (1865-1944); daughter Mary B. Smoker (1898). Fisher #1820]
943. 1851/ U L/ A B C D E/ F G H I J/ K L M N O/ 'P Q R S T/ U V W X Y/ Z
944. 1842 March 3/ OEHBDDE/ FAYANNA WENGER
945. M K ? D [HCLC; cf. 831, 832, 833, 834]
946. LEA LAPP 1855 [cf. 327, 328]
947. 1851 Anna Eshleman
948. N K C B 1820
949. OEHBDDE/ 1849 [Lichten, p. 56]
950. 1807 [In drawn thread panel.] [Schiffer, p. 151]
951. SUSANNA HERR/ S/ 1827/ S H [Stoudt (1966), p.358; Schiffer p. 151; cf.770]
952. NANCY BACHMAN/ OEHBDDE/ 1832 [Stoudt (1966), p. 358]
953. LIDI LANG [Stoudt (1966), p. 358]
954. FRONICA GEHMAN/ 1827
956. ELIZABETH STAUFFER/ A B C D E F G H I K L M N/ O P Q R S T U V W X Y Z [Seen in private photograph collection.]
957. ELIZABETH/ [?] 1838 [?] / OEHBDDE [Seen in private photograph collection.]
958. ELIZABETH STRICKLER/ 1824 [Seen in private photograph collection.]
960. C S [In drawn thread panel.] [From East Greenville, Upper Hanover twp., Montgomery co.; cf. 961]
961. 1825 [In drawn thread panel.] [From East Greenville, Upper Hanover twp., Montgomery co.; cf. 960]
962. ELISABETH STAUFFER/ 1821/ OEHBDDE/OEHBDDE A/ B/ C/ D/ E/ F/ G/ H/ I/ K/ L/ M/ N/ O/ P/ Q/ R/ S/ T/ U/ V/ W/ X/ Y/ Z/A/ B/ C/ D/ E/ F/ G/ H/ I/ K/ L/ M/ [Arranged vertically on left side of towel.] N/ O/ P/ Q/ R/ S/ T/ U/ V/ W/ X/ Z/ A/ B/ C/ D/ E/ F/ G/ H/ I/ K/ L/ M/ N/ O/ P/ Q/ R/ S/ T/ U/ V/ W/ X/ Y/ Z [Arranged vertically on right side of towel.] [Elisabeth Stauffer was born 1804; died 1842; married John D. Overholt 1822 and had seven children. She was a daughter of

Rev. Abraham Stauffer from North Huntington twp., Westmoreland co.; WM-FHSM TX82-12-1; Figure 177]
963. S[arah] B[urkholder] / 1831 [From Kurtz family, Ephrata, Lancaster co.]
964. Nathanael answered and saith unto him Rabbi thou art the son of God [St. John 1:49a; Seen at a Lancaster co. flea market, 1984.]
965. 1834/ ELISABETH LANDES [From Franconia twp., Montgomery co.]
967. CATHARINA KURTZIN [From Ephrata area, Lancaster co. Probably related to 627, 628, 629, 630]
968. Catharina Lapp/ Sweet Home/ A D OEHBDDE 1857
969. ANNA STOLZFUSZ/ MARY LAPP/ 1896/ CADHARINA STOLZFUSZ/ FANNIE KING/ 1948 [This towel was begun by Cadharina Stoltzfusz. Catharine Unsechar (apparently a widow, died 1866) became the second wife of Bishop John Stoltzfus, Sr., (1776-1857) after the death of his first wife Veronica King (died 1827). The towel was next worked on by Anna Stoltzfusz. She was a step-granddaughter of Catharine Stoltzfusz, and a daughter of Bishop John Stoltzfus (1805-1884) and Mary (Mast) Stoltzfusz. Nancy or Anna Stoltzfusz (October 8, 1831 - May 14, 1900) mararied in 1849 Stephen Blank (January 30, 1826 - January 18, 1851). This indicates the towel dates between 1828 and 1849 after the marriage of Catharine Unsechar, but before the marriage of Anna Stoltzfusz. The towel was next worked on by Mary B. Lapp a granddaughter of Nancy (Stoltzfus) Blank and a daughter of John Lapp (1849-1926) and Fannie (Blank) Lapp (851-1893). Mary Lapp was born May 24, 1879; died July 7, 1942. She married Benjamin L. Lantz (April 7, 1872 - August 26, 1947) on December 14, 1897. The last generation to work on the towel was Fannie King a daughter of Mary B. Lapp and Benjamin Lantz. Fannie L. Lantz was born January 25, 1909 and married Aaron K. King (born September 16, 1903) son of David S. and Mattie (King) King. They were members of the Old Order Amish church. Fisher, #3595; Figure 167]
970. MERI MILLER/ 1831/ OEHBDDE [From the Lititz area, Lancaster co.; cf. 1046]
971. Jacob Blank he yos born the 20/ march Septemer the 8 1857/ Mary Blank She was born The 2 decemr/ The 1st october/ David Blank he was born/ The 20 novemr the 2 october Fanny Blank/ she was born 23 november aPril the 8 1858/ Mary Blank was born aug the 11th 1858/ [Spelling as found on towel; on left side of towel.] John Blank he was born the/ 27 July the 5 m october/ Nancy Blank she was/ Born the 25 december/ Sary Blank She was born/ the 29 december 13 october/ F K[ing] [Spelling as found on towel; on right side of towel.] [All names appearing on this towel are children of Jacob Blank (March 28, 1816 - February 28, 1893) son of John Blank and Fanny (Lantz) Blank. Jacob married Mary Stoltzfus (September 2, 1819 - April 1, 1893) daughter of David and Anna (Fisher) Stoltzfus. This family was Old Order Amish and resided in Lancaster co. Below is a list of their eight children: 1) Fannie Blank (November 23, 1839 - January 29, 1902; married Jacob Stoltzfus); 2) David S. Blank (November 20, 1841 - December 13, 1926; married Mary L. Byler); 3) John S. Blank (July 27, 1844 - December 19, 1918; married Fannie Renno); 4) Nancy Blank (December 25, 1848 - February 22, 1925; married John Miller); 5) Sarah Blank (December 29, 1850 - March 8, 1924; married Simeon Stoltzfus); 6) Mary Blank (August 11, 1858 - November 24, 1925; married Eli Smucker); 7) Mary Blank; 8) Jacob Blank. These two names appear on the towel, but are not in the Fisher genealogy, apparently died young. The initials F K are apparently those of the maker. The date April the 8, 1858 appears to be the date the towel was completed. The birth of Mary Blank on August 11, 1858 was added later by a different worker. cf. 973 Fisher, #2988]
972. LEA BEILER/ SARAH YODER/ 1852 [Sarah Yoder, born June 16, 1834; died June 20, 1897; married February 10, 1857 to Joseph W. Byler (February 13, 1828 - May 25, 1905). She was a daughter of Nicolas and Leah (Yoder) Yoder. This family was Amish and residents of Mifflin co. Their daughter added her name to towel. Leah Y. Beiler (October 4, 1861 - June 24, 1922; married January 14, 1879 to Eli B. Zook). Fisher, #5202]
973. 1815/ M N/ FRENI KINIG/ IMI AHR/ 1839 [In the year 1839] F K Z/ 1893/ 1917/ A Z [This towel was begun in 1815 by M[attie] N[isley] who married Abraham King (Kinig) born June 10, 1786. Abraham is said to have been an immigrant. This family was Old Order Amish and resided in Lancaster co. In 1839 this towel was decorated by their daughter Freni Kinig (Veronica King) born July 30, 1818; died March 7, 1877. On February 20, 1848 she married Andrew Diener

(September 19, 1820 - March 1, 1897) who was Old Order Amish, a linen weaver and immigrant from the Alsace in 1837. They lived near Monterey, Lancaster co. In 1893 their daughter Frany Diener (April 7, 1855 - March 22, 1937) added her initials (married) and some embroidery. Frany was the second wife of Joel Zook (August 13, 1847 - September 25, 1927) who was ordained a minister in the Old Order Amish church in 1878. In 1917 their daughter Anna D. Zook (October 7, 1895 - July 13, 1962) added her initials and additional embroidery. On December 13, 1917 she married Jacob K. Zook (born September 7, 1895) who was ordained a minister in the Old Order Amish church in 1925. This couple resided at Gap, Lancaster co. cf. 971 Fisher, #3058.1 Figure 166]

974. MARGRET 1840 BEYER/ MARGRET BEYER/ OAHBDDE/ Mary 1840 DETWEILER [Thought to be from Skippack area, Montgomery co.]

975. S 1854 E/ H A/ N D/ T O/ W L/ SARAH EBY [From Lancaster co.; Figure 462]

976. ELIZABETH BINKLY/ 1832

978. E G [From Godshall-Keeler family, Harleysville, Lower Salford twp., Montgomery co.]

982. C[arrie] R[osenberger]/ 1787 [Carrie Rosenberger was the mother of Elisabet Rosenberger, 983; Franconia twp., Montgomery co.]

983. ELISABET ROSENBE/ RGER 1822 A B C D E F [Elisabet Rosenberger was the daughter of Carrie Rosenberger, 982; Franconia twp., Montgomery co.]

984. 1818/ P

985. ELISABETH LANDES/ 1844 [Also a sampler and needle-worked picture, both without date, but with similar motifs. From Franconia twp., Montgomery co.]

986. DINA BENNER/ 1842 [From Marlborough twp., Montgomery co.]

987. C B/ CATHARINA EMRICH [From Quakertown, Bucks co.]

988. I H/ C H [From Quakertown, Bucks co.]

989. LIDISTOWER [Figures 43, 70, 71]

992. S W/ SUSANA W 1797

993. A C

995. R[euben] K[riebel] [From Montgomery co.]

998. S G/ C B [Figure 41]

999. E Z

1000. Sarah Kulp/ [Black ink stamp.] ELIZEBETH DITWILER [In cross stitch.] [From Montgomery co.; Figures 80, 328, 507]

1003. E B

1006. M E W

1007. ELISABEB ROSENBERGER [Date missing. Needleholes indicate it might be 1810. In cross stitch.] / E R B [In drawn thread panel.]

1008. M W

1010. 18 R F 16

1011. SALLIE L HALTEMAN/ 1896/ OEHBDDE [Sallie L. Halteman, daughter of Levi S. Alderfer and Sarah M. Landis, was born in Lower Salford twp., Montgomery co., April 2, 1877; died 1920; married Joseph H. Halteman October 10, 1896; buried at Franconia Mennonite cemetery. This towel made after marriage. cf. 1012]

1012. S[allie] L A [lderfer]/ 1896 [This towel made prior to marriage. cf. 1011]

1013. C H/ 1822/ MARY HERTZLER/ in the year of our lord/ 1840 [Workmanship indicates towel was made by two women. Seen at a Lancaster co. antiques show, 1984.]

1014. E L I Z U G I H M I A H R 1842 [Eli Zug in the year 1842] [Eli Zook was born December 12, 1821; died February 2, 1904; married January 10, 1843 Rebecca Lapp who was born December 30, 1820; died February 15, 1901 and a daughter of Michael and Barbara (Stoltzfus) Lapp. The towel was likely made by his fiancee Rebecca Lapp. Eli was ordained as a minister in the Old Order Amish church in 1859, ordained bishop in 1867 and resided in Lancaster co. Fisher, #3625; Plate 20]

1015. S B/ 1831 [Seen at a Lancaster co. antiques show, 1984.]

1016. Anna 1836 Huber/ The grass/ is green/ the rose/ is ret/ Heir is my/ name wen/ i am thet/ Ann Huber/ [Spelling as found on towel.] Wie sicher lebt der mensch der staub sein leben ist ein/ fallent laub und dennock schmeikelt er sich gern/ der tag des totes sey noch fern [How securely man made of dust lives. His life is a fallen leaf and he fools himself about it gladly the day of death is still quite far off. [A German hymn. Lefevre catalogue, June, 1984]

1017. MATLENA SPENGLERIN/ A B C D E F G H I/ [J] K L M N O P Q R S/ T [U] V W X Y Z 1826/ M S [Lefevre catalogue, June, 1984; cf. 1318]

1019. ANNA MARIA NIES/ 1816 [Lefevre catalogue, June, 1984]

1020. C L/ M 1831 Y [Lefevre catalogue, June, 1984]

1021. A B C D E F G H I J K L/ M N O P Q R S T U V W X Y Z/ M H 18 [?] M H [Lefevre catalogue, June, 1984]

1022. HANNAH WISMER/ 1853 [Lefevre catalogue, June, 1984]

1023. BARBARA PEFFLY/ 1826 [Lefevre catalogue, June, 1984]

1024. CATHARINA LATSCHAR/ 1826 [Lefevre catalogue, June, 1984]

1027. S G [In drawn thread panel.] [Probably for Susanna Weigner Gery of Hereford twp., Berks co.; born July 24, 1770; married a John Gery. cf. 1028]

1028. C K [Probably for Catharine Glausen, born January 1, 1799; died February 7, 1884. She was the daughter-in-law of Susanna Gery, 1027.]

1029. C[atharina] S[techman or Steinman] [From Hereford twp., Berks co.]

1030. ANNA A KREIDER/ IS MY NAME AND HEAVEN IS MY STATION/ PEQUA TOWN IS MY DWELLING PLASN AND/ CHRIST IS MY SALVATION THE ROSE IS RED THE LEAVES ARE GREEN THE DAYS ARE PAST/ WICH I HAVE SEEN WHEN I EM DED AND IN/ MY GRAVE AND ALL MY BONES ARE ROTTEN/ IF THIS YOU SEE REMEMBER ME AND AT LAST I/ WILL BE FORGOTTEN LOOK ON THIS WORK MY/ FRIENDS AND SEE HOW KIND MY PARENTS/ WAS TO ME MY PARENTS ARE GEORGE AND MARIA/ KRIEDER/ A D 1858 [Spelling as appears on towel.]

1031. JUDITH MARTIN [cf. 490, 912; Figures 13, 188]

1032. MARY KREIDER 1828 [BF]

1033. IHM/ 1849/ M S/ IAHR/ G K [In the year 1849] [BF]

1034. ELISABETH BORGHOLDER/ 1839 [BF]

1035. ELISABETH SCHMELTZER [BF]

1038. 1852 [BF; Figure 435]

1039. E F 1824 [BF]

1040. ELISABETH HORST/ [In cross stitch.] 1820 [In drawn thread panel.] [BF]

1041. CADARINA BEZN 1831 [BF]

1042. 1844/ A B C D E F G H I [J] K L L [sic]/ M N O P Q R S T [U] V W X Y Z/ CHRISTINA/ BORKHOLDER/ ICH WEIS/ IEN BLUMLEIN/ HUBSCHUND FEIN [I know a little flower beautiful and fine.] [First line of a German hymn/ BF]

1043. 1846/ CATHARINE KURTZ BARBRA KURTZ [BF]

1044. E B P B/ E T [BF]

1045. R S [BF]

1046. SARA MILLER/ 1823 [In cross stitch.] SARA MILLER [In drawn thread panel.] [Probably related to Meri Miller, 970; BF]

1047. CATHARINA WEIDMAN C W/ OEHBDDE/ OEHBDDE/ catharina b. weidman peter weidman christina weidman george weidman/ susanna weidman daniel weidman joseph weidman/ catharina weidman/ margaret weidman/ peter weidman/ emanuel weidman/ israel weidman/ elisabeth weidman/ my andy catharina sees my andy elisabeth yundt/ my hand lydia sally maria weidman mardaw/ 1838 [BF; cf 379, 844; Figure 90]

1048. MARGRAT APPEL/ [In cross stitch.] 1841 M M [In drawn thread panel.] [BF]

1049. M E I M ELISABETH/ ROTH/ 1818 [BF]

1050. 18 22 [BF]

1051. ELISABETH 1845 STONER [BF]

1052. E F 1825 [BF]

1053. E U/ 1819

1054. Farewell dear friend/ s i must be gone i/ have no home or sta/ y with you ill take/ my staff and travel/ on till i a better wo/ rld do view/ Chorus. - Farewell/ Farewell farewell/ my loving friend/ farewell/ Farewell young/ Cnverts of the cros/ Oh labor hard for/ Christ and heavn/ Youve counted all/ things here but dross/ Fight on the crown/ will soon be givn/ Farewell & c/ Farewell poor/ Careless sinners too/ It grieves my heart/ to leave you here/ Eternal vengeance/ waites for you turn/ and find salvation/ near o turn o turn o/ turn and find/ salvation near/ Maria Minnich her/ towl August 25 1842/ [On left side of towel.] st sophia at/ Constantinople/ [On center top of towel.] Hosanna to the Prin/ ce of light That cloth/ ed himself in clay/ Entered the iron gates/ of death and tore their/ bars away/ Death is no more the/ King of dread since chri/ st our lord arose he/ took the tyrants sti/ ng away and spoiled/ our hellish foes/ See how the conqu/ ror mounts aloft/ And to his Father/ flies with scars of honnor in his flesh/ And triumph in his/ eyes/ There our exaulted/ Saviour reigns And/ scatter blessing/ down our Jesus/ fills

281

the right hand/ seat of the celesti/ al throne/ Maria Minnich her/ towl and in the year/ of our lord/ august 25 1842/ [On right side of towel.]

Maria Minnich this work of mine I leave here for my parents and my friends/ to look upon when I am dead and gone Maria Minnich her toll August 24/ [Across width of towel.] Maria Minnich her toll the rose is red the grass is green the time is past Where I/ have seen the grass is green the rose is red here is my name when i am dead [Across the width of towel.] [All spelling as found on towel. Maria Minnich was born February 26, 1822, to John and Barbara Johnson Minnich. She was the oldest of twelve children and sister to Emanuel (towel 18) and Catharine (towel 575). She died February 4, 1844 aged twenty one years, eleven months and nine days. Information from the family Bible. Figures 476, 477]

1056. R S
1057. ABRAHAM PETERSHEIM/ 18 55
1058. S W/ A B [Appears to be made by two different women.]
1059. This towl was mad bY Your aut Susana bruba/ cherin manor tounsShiP lanCaSter CountY State of/ PennSYlvania in march the 2 .. a.d. 1839 For Anna Brubacher [Spelling as found on towel.]
1060. 1839/ Feronica Schyffer/ F OEHBDDE S/ F S [Feronica Schyffer, daughter of Isaac and Feronica Martin was born in 1821; lived in West Earl twp., near Farmersville, Lancaster co.; never married; buried at Groffdale, Lancaster co. Design layout similar to towel 1061. cf.7, 1061, 1063, 1064, 1106; Figure 466]
1061. 1836/ B OEHBDDE S/ Elisabeth Schyffer/ A B C D E F G H I K L M N O P Q R S T U/ V W X Y/ [In cross stitch.] B S [In drawn thread panel.] [Elisabeth Schyffer was born February 26, 1825; never married; lived in West Earl twp., near Farmersville, Lancaster co.; buried at Groffdale in 1865. cf. 7, 1060, 1063, 1064, 1106; Figure 467]
1062. E/ ELISABETH/ Eichholtz 1837
1063. 1838/ FENNY SCHYFFER [Probably related to towel 1060. Figure 465]
1064. 18 43/ DANIEL BUCH [Thought to be made by his wife Magdalena Schyffer who also made towels 7 and 1106. Magdalena (who went by Martha) Schyffer was born in 1819; lived in Earl twp., Lancaster co.; buried at Groffdale Mennonite Cemetery, Lancaster co.; cf. 1060, 1061]
1065. 1814/ ELISABET DORNBACH/ OEHBDDE/ [In cross stitch.] ELISABED [In drawn thread panel.]
1069. 1804/ E H [Figure 145]
1070. B 1824 H [In cross stitch.] B H [In drawn thread panel.] B H [In cross stitch.] [Figure 134; Plate 30]
1071. 1858/ M P
1072. B G/ 1863/ BARBARA B GISHS
1073. CADARINA MOHR
1074. E L
1075. M E
1076. E M
1077. LIDIA GEHMAN
1080. 18 38/ MARY HERSH
1082. ANNA STAUFFER 1824/ A K S T A S T
1087. 1833/ G B [uch]
1088. H H/ 18 HENRY 34/ HOTTENSTEIN/ C H
1089. SUSANNA MILLERIN
1090. [?] R [?] E/ H R [?] T[?]/ FRE[?]NE/ DENLINGER
1091. REBECCA R L LAPPIN/ 1835
1094. ESTHER KÖNIG 1848
1095. LYDIA SOLLE
1096. SUSANNA MILERIN
1097. 1799/ H E B V/ A H B V
1098. A B C D E F G H I K L M N O P Q R S T/ U V W X Y Z ANNA BENDER 1837
1099. 1838 Fanny Meyer [Kleinfelter Catalogue, November 19, 1960]
1100. MARGARET WEIDMAN 1835 [Kleinfelter Catalogue, November 19, 1960]
1101. L E [Kleinfelter Catalogue, December 15, 1941]
1102. ELISABET NISLISIN/ 1832/ E N [Gilbert and Kleinfelter Catalogue, April 20, 1936. Listed as "Fine Dated Linen Door Panel."]
1103. 1838 S R [Kleinfelter Catalogue, November 19, 1960]
1104. 1824 ELIZABETH EBY [Kleinfelter Catalogue, November 19, 1960]
1105. MARIA/ SAHM/ A B C D E F G H I K L M N O P Q R S T Y[sic] V W X Z [sic]
1106. 1835/ MAGDALENA SCHYFFER/ M S [Figure 464]
1108. C E D I W U [?] S Z
1109. A N S H N I

1110. Frances 18 32 Charles [cf. 756; Figures 203, 2096, 211, 248, 254, 321.]
1111. M E P E
1112. 1834/ ESTHER BAUMAN
1113. [A B] C D E F G H J [sic] I K L M N P [sic] O Q R S T U V W X Y Z CATHARINA GLEIM 1820
1114. J M H I/ G M 1818
1115. ELISABETH H. SPICKLER/ 1826
1116. Elizabeth W Hunschberger/ 1849 [Figure 482]
1117. I G/ 1823/ [In cross stitch.] I G [In drawn thread panel.] [Figure 32]
1118. H S
1119. ESTHER FUCHSIN/ OEHBDDE/ [In cross stitch.] OEHBDDE [In drawn thread panel.] [Figure 438]
1120. ANNA/ HERR/ 1858
1121. CHRISTINA SCHULTZ/ 1836
1122. MARIA WEBER/ M W 1824 B S
1123. EVA [?] EICI
1124. M F 1843 [cf. 1288]
1126. E E W
1127. 1840 [In drawn thread panel.]
1130. 1810/ OEHBDDE [In drawn thread panel.]
1131. 1812 [In drawn thread panel.]
1132. MAGDALENA/ GANTZIE/ 1819/ P R Q/ M W H [Figure 159]
1133. HORNUNG 1828/ [February 1828] MARIA RUTT/ [In cross stitch.] OEHBDDE OEHBDDE [Figure 157]
1134. 1855/ ANNA SHENK
1135. BAL OER/ 1820 [Figure 49]
1136. MARIA GUTH/ 1831
1137. L H C H/ S H 1831
1138. E V H E
1139. A N Z O R/ 1833/ A B C D E F G H I K L M/ N O P Q R S T U V W X Y Z
1140. Sarah Landis/ 1823 [In cross stitch.] S L/ S L [In drawn thread panel.]
1141. S A H M/ OEHBDDE
1142. 1826/ ELISABETH NOLT
1143. ELISABETH SCHWAR [?]/ 1819/ BENJAMIN STEMAN/ 1837/ BENJAMIN STEMAN/ 1838/ Lizzie 18 99 Stehman
1144. ANNA EBERSOL/ IENNER 1847 [January 1847] OEH [Figure 221, 447]
1145. S 1831 M
1146. 1836/ M L/ Barbara Beiler/ 1863/ SAVILLA FISHER/ 1928 [Mary Lapp (1822-1899) married Christian Beiler, 1843; daughter Barbara Beiler (1844-1912); niece Savilla Fisher (1899). Fisher #3626.]
1147. E B/ ELIZEBETH BARNDT 1831 [cf. 101, 188]
1148. BANJAMIN AND 1834 EVE REICHERT
1149. Anna Burkholder/ 1840
1150. SUSZEN/ 1834
1151. Mrs. Lydia Claytons' Needle Work./ Lydia Clayton March 4th 1859 [cf. 258; Figures 171, 251]
1152. ANNA BAUMAN/ 1837
1153. H S
1155. C U [In drawn thread panel.]
1156. I E N N E R 1820/ [January 1820] PETER RUTT
1157. MARCRYDHICK
1160. 1831/ ELISABE/ THGEHMAN
1170. B M [In drawn thread panel.]
1171. E M/ C G [Figure 224]
1172. 1833/ LIDIA SENSENIG
1173. 1827
1174. E L [?] T A [?] E[?]H HERR/ 1834
1175. SUSANNA MOSSER 1848
1176. Frany Fretz/ 1833
1177. SARA KALBACH
1178. E L/ [In cross stitch.] EVA LANI [In drawn thread panel.]
1179. MERY EN GROF/ 1839/ [In cross stitch.] 1831/ M E G R [In drawn thread panel.]
1180. MARGARETWE/ IDMAN ABCDEF
1181. B E [Figure 48]
1184. 18 ANNA KINSY 44
1185. BEZI HLEIB [In drawn thread panel.]
1187. L W/ OEHBDDE
1188. 18 31/ MARY BRUBAKCH/ ER
1189. ELizabEth L BearD is My name Heaven/ is my Station America is my Dwelling Place and christ [sic] is My salvation ELISABETH BEARD/ OEHBDDE/ 1835
1190. S B
1191. 18 43 [Figure 458]
1192. 18 4[?]/ ANNA GEHMAN

1193. NANCY BACHMAN/ 18 34/ OEHBDDE
1194. SUSA NNA/ FISC HER/ IHM IAR/ 18 41 [In the year 1841.]
1195. S K
1196. F H/ F 1808 H [Figures 30, 174]
1197. S B S/ 1838
1198. Susanna Martin/ 1854
1199. MARIA 18 22 KNECE
1200. 1815/ ANNA RUTTIN
1201. MARIA KLEIN
1202. I M I A R/ 1838/ [In the year 1838.] S U S T/ [In cross stitch.] S [In drawn thread panel.]
1203. ELISABETH DANNER
1205. 1807
1206. Sarah Fretz/ 1846 [Figure 50]
1207. 18 43/ S K [In cross stitch.] S K [In drawn thread panel.] [Figure 551]
1208. CATHARINE OVEr/ 1827 [Figures 401, 428]
1210. S D [Figure 429]
1211. Fianna Grube/ F G/ 1850 [Figures 169, 340]
1212. I M I A H R 1833/ [In the year 1833] MARIA/ WIT-MEYER
1213. CHRISTINA CROBBIN/ 1848
1214. D 1832 W/ M G
1215. LIDIA GABI/ 1833
1216. MARIA GEISSINGER/ [In cross stitch.] 1837 [In drawn thread panel.]
1218. Hannah Meyer [Figure 354]
1219. S B/ 18 12
1220. CATRINAHE/ RSCHBERGERN
1221. LYDIA KRONA 1823/ [In cross stitch.] LYDIA KRON [In drawn thread panel.]
1222. C M
1223. ANLIS KILMER/ 1795 [In drawn thread panel.]
1224. S K/ a b c d e f g h i j k l m n o p q r s [a long "s"] s t u v w x y z/ Sara Krumbein 1843
1225. MARIA SCHEIRICH 1827/ MEINE ZU IRIEDENHEIT STEHT IN FERGNIGLICH KEIT VAS ICH NIGHT ENDERN KAN NIHM ICH GEDULTIG AN/ [My contentment rests in fulfillment. What I cannot change I accept patiently.] HOFF-NUNG LASZ FIR UND FIR BLEIBEN DEIN SCHIFE PAN-IER SIEHT ES HEUT STIRMISCH DREIN MORGEN WIRDS STILLE SEIN [Allow hope to be your ship's banner forever and ever. If it looks stormy today tomorrow it will be still.] [The first and fourth verses of the hymn, Meine Zufrie-denheit steht in vergnuglich keit. Figure 455]
1226. 18 D S 27
1227. MARGRETA/ MASE
1228. LIDI LANG/ 18 29
1229. 1836/ MARIA/ BECKER
1230. C L
1231. E B B E R
1232. CADARINE IREY 1806/ A B C D E F G H I K L M N O P
1233. CHRISTINA SCHULTZ/ 1830
1234. ARNAEM
1235. A N 1849 B K
1237. A S/ E S/ 1838
1238. I H OEHBDDE CH/ H H F H/ C H A H [Figure 231]
1240. 18 47/ MARIA/ WEBER
1241. REBECA STOLSFUS/ 18 L B 33
1242. E Z
1243. 1828/ A B A B
1244. 1844/ MARY MARTIN/ A B C D E F G H I J K L M N O P [Q] R S T U V W X Y Z
1245. 1814/ SARA DORN/ BACH
1246. D L/ L K 1848 M S
1247. C K/ OEHBDDE/ CATHARINE KRATZ/ 1838 [Plate 24]
1248. 18 33/ A B C D E F G H I K L M/ N O P Q R S T [U] V W X Y Z/ ELISABETH/ EBERSOHL/ S U H M E H B G
1249. MA RY/ HARMAN/ C T/ 1837
1250. MICHAEL/ MEZER 1842 [In drawn thread panel.]
1251. SUSANNA LEFEVER/ 1855
1252. CATARINA/ K L I C [In drawn thread panel.]
1253. Catherine Strome 1835
1254. 1823/ SARA WALMER
1257. A B G [sic] D E F G H I J K L M N O P Q R S T [U] V W [X] Y/ [Z] Barbara 1846 Hernley/ P H/ E H. [Renner Catalogue, 829; Figures 189, 283]
1258. I M Y a h r/ [In the year] Catharina Ebersol/ [In cross stitch.] B E [In drawn thread panel.] [cf. 1424]
1259. MAGDALENA/ 1821/ GANTZI/ RZ [at the top] E S [on right side] E D O [at the bottom reading left to right] H I [on left side] [These initials surround a motif similiar to the OEHBDDE design. Figures 158, 443]
1260. CATHARINA SCHNEIDER/ 1828/ OEHBDDE
1261. ANNO/ 1799/ CHRISTINA RIBLI [Figures 72, 146, 432]
1262. 17 87/ LIS BEDB
1263. BarBara Leaman 1846/ BarBara HuBer [Figure 193]
1264. MAGDALENA WEAVER/ 1848 [Figure 382]
1265. Franey Kulp/ J K B K/ A K J K F K/ E K 1861 [In cross stitch.] F 18 61 I [In drawn thread panel.] [Figure 86]
1266. SUSANNAH TI/ ABARNHARDK/ A B C D E F G H I J K/ L M N O P Q R S T U V W X Y Z [In cross stitch.] CATAH-RINEK [In drawn thread panel; Figures 153, 218]
1267. FIANNA HOOBER/ 1854
1268. ANNA 1837 ROYER
1269. LYDIA BACHMAN 1831
1270. MAGDA 1812 LEHNA/ BEC KER [cf. 1271]
1271. ANNE. B. BAKER/ 1853/ OEHBDDE [Probably related to 1270. Figure 404]
1272. 1859/ ELISABETH CLEMMER/ A B C D E F G H/ I K L M N O P Q/ R S T [U] V W X Y Z
1275. CATARINA GUTH/ 1852 [Figures 180, 379]
1277. G R/ 1810
1278. E H/ 1845/ ELISABETH odehbdde HERSHEY/ A B C D E F G H I K L M N N [sic] O P Q R S T U V W X Y Z [Figures 380, 381, 445]
1279. 18 55/ ELIZABETH B. KEENER [Figures 168, 284]
1280. Catharina Balmer May 6 1833 [Figures 172, 173]
1282. F B/ 1811
1284. CHRISTINA REBER [Figure 528]
1285. 1827/ A B C D E F G H I K L M N O P Q R S T U V W X Y Z/ OEDHBDDE/ ELISABET STAUFER/ A B C D E F G H I K L M N/ O P Q R S T U V W X Y Z [Figures 31, 430, 431, 449]
1288. M F 1842 [cf. 1124]
1290. OEDHBDDE/ Mary Meyer./ 1821 [Mary Meyer was born December 3, 1812; died February 15, 1895; married Abraham K. Hunsberger, April 1833 a Mennonite farmer from the Hill-town area, Bucks co. Their daughter Maria Hunsberger, born February 6, 1840, married William H. Fretz. cf. 1291]
1291. ELIZA FRETZ/ 1846/ OEHBDDE [Eliza Fretz was a sister or niece of William H. Fretz who married Maria Hunsberger. cf. 1290 May also be related to towel 897; Figure 186]
1295. A O B C D E F G H I K L M M N O/ P Q R S T U V W X Y Z A A B C/ D G A M P W 1 2 3 4 5 6 7 8 9 0 &/ OEHBDDE [Huntley, p. 3]
1298. CHRISTINA FEIC[K ?]/ 1831/ [In drawn thread panel.] [BF]
1300. The grass is green The rose is red/ here is my name when I am dead C Kreiter/ OEHBDDE [BF]
1301. Ma[r]y Mast/ This work of mine my fri[e]nds may have when i am in my silent gr [a] ve/ Look on this work and then you see How [ki] nd my pa [re] nnts w [he] are to me [BF]
1302. Anna Sch/ lebach/ [18] 17 [BF]
1304. ELIZABETH HERMAN/ 1835/ EH DS/ 1838
1306. BARBARA BENDER/ 1847 [Sold at public auction, Lancaster co., July, 1984]
1307. CATARINA KURZ/ 1836/ SEREYEN KAUFMAN/ 1840 [From the Bernville area, Berks co.]
1308. CRISTINA FRAN/ 1816
1309. M B/ HAND TUCH/ [Hand towel] OEHBDDE/ mery burck-hart/ MARIA BURCKHART [From the Denver area, Lancaster co.]
1310. M 1826 R/ M R
1311. E D
1312. FANNY HESS/ FANNY HESS/ 1843 [Figures 194, 268, 361
1313. BARBARA MARK [Figure 179; Plate 43]
1314. D H [In drawn thread panel.] DINA HAVTZ [In cross stitch.] [Figures 143, 411]
1315. MARIA HEEBNER [Figure 556]
1316. A S/ ANNA SHELLY 1833 [Figure 331]
1317. 1827/ 1 2 3 4 5 6 7 8 9 [Plate 45]
1318. SARA/ SARA SPENGLER/ A B C D E F G H I K L M N/ O P Q R S T [U] V W X Y Z [A note attached to the towel states, "Sara Roth Spengler Amanda Roth Lan's Aunt (father's sister circa-1835"; cf. 1017; Figure 550]
1320. LEAH KELLER 1831/ [In cross stitch.] L K [In drawn thread panel.]
1321. 1820/ V R G S/ VERO NICA
1322. CATHARINE BARR/ 18 31
1323. B 1859 M/ S D/ [In cross stitch.] B M [In drawn thread panel.]

1324. FIAHNA LANDIS IS MY NAME MANHEIM TO/ UNSHIP
IS MY TWELING PLACE HEAVEN IS MY/ STATION
CHRIST IS MY SALVASION THE ROSE/ IS RET THE
LEAVES ARE GREEN THE DAYS ARE/ PAST WICH I HAVE
SEEN AND WHEN I AM DEAD/ AND IN MY GRAVE AND
ALL MY BONES ARE ROT/ TEN REMEMBER ME WHEN
THIS YOU SEE/ LET ALL THE REST FORGOTTEN/
1835 [Spelling as found on towel.] [Figures 191, 233]

1326. C H
1327. ANNA MOSSERIN 1802
1328. FRO/ NICA/ HABE/ CKER/ 1805
1329. 1814/ A[nna] [Musselman] L. [Landis] [Anna Landis (1781-
1861) was wife of Henrich Landis, Warwick twp., Lancaster co.
Towel descended to Mary Landis Royer, to Lavina Royer
Bender, to Benjamin R. Bender, to Lillie Bender Hess, to present owner.]

1330. Mary Buckwalter 1864 Anna B. Huber/ OEHBDDE/ A[nna]
H[ostetter] K[ilheffer] [Anna Buckwalter Huber was the ninth
child of ten to John Eshleman Huber and Fanny Buckwalter
Huber. Anna Hostetter Kilheffer was granddaughter of Anna
B. Huber. cf. 778]

1331. K H
1332. 18 25/ E H [Thought to be from a Hostetter family south of
Lancaster.]

1333. WEST HEMPFIELD TOWNSHIP/ 1841/ Mary Hershey is
my name/ North america is my station m h/ West Hempfield
is my DWiling [sic] Place/ And christ is my salvation/ Now
be the Gospel banner

1334. 18 S[usan] M[artin] 39 [From Manor twp., Lancaster co. Susan Martin was the great-great aunt of present owner.]

1335. MARIA/ MAGDALINA DAMY/ MY HAND AND NWEDLE/
HF/ A B C D E F G H I J K L M N O/ P Q R S T U V W
X Y Z 1836/ CHRISTOPHER/ DAMY CATHARINE/
DAMY A D 1836 [Maria Magdalena Damy, daughter of Christopher and Catharine Damy, married Henry Fenstermacher August 31, 1837. He died in 1842. Her sister Elizabeth, cf. 560,
was born December 14, 1812, married Christian Simon on November 21, 1837, and died on or about April 25, 1843. This
family were members of Salem Lutheran Church at Rohrerstown; some of them are buried at the Rohrerstown cemetery.
Figures 236, 237, 239, 240; Plate 13]

1338. IHM IAYR 1828/ Beniamin Kinig/ 1862/ Lidia Kinig [cf.
117, 186]

1339. MA HE/ [In cross stitch.] M H [In drawn thread.]
1340. ELISABETH 1835/ SCHWARTZ
1341. MARY FUNK/ 1819/ This is The Text of my Fathers funeral
Psalms the 23d C 4 Verse [Figure 472]

1342. C 18 35 Z/ FRENI FISCHER
1343. 1 2 3 4 5 6 7 8 9 0/ ANNA HOSTETER/ 1842 [Figure 119]
1344. SUSANA RUDY [Figure 453]
1345. 18 40/ BARBARA
1346. MACDALENA BAMBERER

1347. CATHARINA 18G55 SAUDER/ EEDL HERTZ/ IACOB
SAUDER IST GE/ STORBEN DEN 1 AUGUST/ IM IHAR
1842 UND SEIN/ ALTER WAR 64 IHAR 8/ MONAT UND
12 TAG/ [Jacob Sauder died 1 August in the year 1842 and
his age was 64 years 8 months 12 days] MARIA SAUDER IST
GE/ STORBEN DEN 8 APRIL/ IM IAHR 1843 UND IHR/
ALTER WAR 24 IAHR/ 7 MONAT UND 7 TAG [Maria Sauder
died 8 April in the year 1843 and her age was 24 years 7 months
7 days] [cf. 1348; Figure 470]

1348. HANNAH 1846 SAUDER/ EEDL HERTZ/ IACOB SAUDER
IS GE/ STORBEN DEN 1 AUGUST/ IM IHAR 1842 UND
SEIN/ ALTER WAR 64 IHAR 8/ MONAT UND 12 TAG/ [Ja-
cob Sauder died 1 August in the year 1842 and his age was
64 years 8 months 12 days] MARIA SAUDER IST GE/
STORBEN DEN 8 APRIL/ IM IAHR 1843 UND IHR/ AL-
TER WAR 24 IAHR/ 7 MONAT UND 7 TAG [Maria Sauder
died 8 April in the year 1843 and her age was 24 years 7 months
7 days] [cf. 1347; Figure 469]

1349. H G
1350. SUSANA DER/ ANNA DER/ H D E D S D
1351. M E [In drawn thread panel.]
1353. C H
1355. ELIZABETH RODEBERGERN
1356. E S/ ESTHER SAUDER/ OEHBDDE
1357. BARBARA LEFEWE/ R/ 1834
1358. CADARINA KUNS/ MARIA KUNS/ M K/ M
1359. ESTHER KREIDER/ 1831/ [In cross stitch.] E K [In
drawn thread panel.]
1361. M D

1362. Rebecca Lentz/ 1853/ R L/ Sarah Lapp/ Rebecca Smoker/
1903/ Sarah Beiler/ 1928 [Rebecca Lantz (1839-1917) married Michael K. Lapp, 1858; daughter Sarah L. Lapp (1865-
1902) married Levi K. Smoker, 1887; daughter Rebecca L.
Smoker (1888-1927) married David K. Beiler, 1916; daughter
Sarah S. Beiler (1918) married 1967. Fisher, 580.1]

1363. M S/ 5/ M S
1364. K B [Plate 32]
1365. V M/ 1818
1366. CATHARINA GERBER/ IACOB GERBER 1814 MARIA
GERBER
1367. I K E K/ B L C L/ Esther Kreiber/ 1835/ OEHBDDE/
G K E K M K B K F K G K E K E K A K A K G
K C K
1368. SUSANA SUSA
1370. SALLY GEHMAN
1371. R M/ Rachel 1834 Miller R M [A handwritten note attached
to towel states, "This door panel was made by Rachel Miller
mother of Mrs. Evans whose daughter Rachel was married to
Jacob Bowers New Holland Lancaster Co., Penna. and bought
from her son Horace Bowers Lancaster Penna. September 1937
Mrs. Charles S Brenneman."]

1372. 1829/ EWA BABBARF
1373. I RABACA OBERLI/ 1834
1374. 1837/ MARIA K E ENPORTZ
1376. 1842/ LEISL BECKER
1377. MARIA HIRSHIN 1832/ M H
1379. BARBARAH BAMBERGER/ OEHBDDE/ 1825 [Name
handwritten in ink on back of flap Annie B. Risser.]

1380. M M [In drawn thread panel.]
1381. A B C D E F G H I J K L M N O P Q R S T/ U V W X Y
Z S M 1838/ SUSANA MARTI 1839
1383. SUSANA BEILER
1384. A H
1386. A B C D E F G H I J K L M N O P Q R S T U V W X Y Z
E S/ BARBARY MYERS
1387. 1820/ L S
1388. REBECAK HIRSCHIN 1826/ R H
1389. A W
1390. ANN 18 32 EBY/ OEHBDDE [In cross stitch.] OEHBDDE
[In drawn thread panel.]

1391. S U H O
1392. FANNY STAUFFER/ 1841
1393. 18 64/ MA RY/ KAUF FMAN
1394. ELIZABETH REIFF [Bean]
1395. 1831 [Bean]
1396. SUSANNA HALDEMAN/ 1801 [Bean]
1397. JOHN GERHARD/ 1818 [Bean]
1398. 1842 [Bean]
1399. 1810 [Bean]
1400. ESTHER ORTT/ 1831 [Bean]
1401. SOPHIA WALT/ 1831/ 1803 [Bean]
1402. BETSY MARKLEY/ 1819 [Bean]
1403. 1799/ IN DEM LE/ BEN WAR IC/ H DEIN IN/ DEM
TOD/ VER GES/ NET MEIN/ [In life I was yours in death
forget me not] E[lizabeth] B[enner] [Burnham and Burn-
ham, p.123; D. 65.63.1; Figure 471]

1404. ELIZABETH R DECKERT 1847 FEBRUARY 8 M K L H
B J M [Purchased in Neffsville area, Lancaster co.]

1405. 1845/ B S [From an Amish Stoltzfus family, Whitehorse,
Lancaster co.]

1406. 1862/ PETER LEHMAN [Probably from Berks co.]
1407. ANNA H
1408. CATARINA GANTZ/ 18/ 41
1409. A B C D E/ F G H I K/ L M N O P/Q R S T Y/ U W X Z/ [Sic]
MARIAN/ NA BOHR [?] [Seen in a private photograph collection.]

1410. SUSANNA DILLIER 1837. [Seen in a private photograph
collection. cf.231, 232, 606, 660, 1411; Figure 176a]

1411. SUSANNA DILLIER HA/T DAS GENETH IM IAHR/1846/
THE HUNTING HORSE. [Seen in a private photograph collection. cf. 231, 232, 606, 660, 1410; Figure 176a]

1412. Mary R/ Gamder/ 1841 [Seen in a private photograph collec-
tion]

1414. MARY [?] 1846 [?] LARDET [?] [Seen in a private photograph collection.]

1415. Esther Nisly [cf. 609]
1416. REBE WEIN [HOLD]/ A B C D E F G H I K L M N O/ P Q
R S T [U] V W X Y Z [cf. 467; Figure 164]

1418. ANNA BECHTEL/ 1833/ A B [In cross stitch.] 1832 [In
drawn thread panel.]

1419. ANI BRUBACHER

1421. 1842 [From East Hempfield twp., Lancaster co.]

1422. ANASCHENK 1837 A E G D/ IESUSBL(?)EIBIN MEIN-HAUS/ [Jesus, stay in my house] S F. S. B. [Towel made by Anna Schenk (1820-1842) of Heidelberg twp., Lebanon Co.; married to Joseph Bucher (1820-1894); passed to only child Fanny S. Bucher (1841-1910) married to Simon B. Snyder (1836-1907) of Clay twp., Lancaster co.; towel passed to her daughter Barbara B. Snyder (1862-1922) married to John M. Stoner (1862-1946); towel passed to her daughter Ida S. Stoner (1891-1977) married to Reuben S. Horst; towel passed to grandson.

1423. IHM IAR/ 1848/ CED/ EKI/ NIG/ B K/ Rebeca Beiler [In the year 1848. Cedi [Katy] Kinig] [Probably from Lancaster co.]

1424. A D 1873/Mary Ebersol [Mary Ebersol was a daughter of Christian and Elizabeth (Stoltzfus) Ebersol. She was born October 19, 1848, married Christian Lapp March 12, 1874, and died December 22, 1936. Her sister Barbara (1846-1922) is remembered by family members to have made towels. Barbara also made bookplates for members of the Old Order Amish church of which these women were members.]

BIBLIOGRAPHY

1. Manuscripts

Metz, Benjamin A. and Lizzie R. Family Record. Mennonite Library and Archives, Kulpsville, Pa.

Rex, Samuel. Day Books: Nos. 1-20. Schaefferstown, Lebanon county, Pennsylvania (1798-1820). Private Collection.

Stetler Store Account Book. Frederick, Montgomery co., Pa. (1839, 1840). Private Collection.

Weber, Anna. Accounts and Diary of Anna Weber. West Earl township, Lancaster county, Pa. (1838-1843). Private Collection.

2. Articles and books

A Dictionary of Textile Terms, Danville, Virginia: Dan River Mills, 1967.

A Pennsylvania German Sampler. Sandwich, Massachusetts: Heritage Plantation of Sandwich, 1984.

Ames, Kenneth L. *Beyond Necessity—Art in the Folk Tradition.* Winterthur: The Henry Francis duPont Winterthur Museum, 1977.

Bean, Theodore W. *History of Montgomery County, Pennsylvania.* Philadelphia, 1884.

Beck, Thomasina, *Embroidered Gardens.* New York: The Viking Press, 1979.

Becker, Karl August, *Die Volkstrachten der Pfalz.* Kaiserslautern, 1952.

Bishop, Robert; Secord, William; and Weissman, Judith Reiter. *The Knopf Collector's Guides to American Antiques, Quilts, Coverlets, Rugs and Samplers.* New York: Alfred A. Knopf, 1982.

Bolton, Ethel Stanwood, and Coe, Eva Johnston. *American Samplers.* New York: Dover Publications, 1973.

Brecht, Samuel Kriebel, ed., *The Genealogical Record of the Schwenkfelder Families.* Pennsburg, Pa,: Rand & McNally & Co., 1923.

Burnam, Harold B. and Dorothy K. *"Keep Me Warm One Night."* Canada: University of Toronto Press, 1972.

Caulfield, Sophia Frances Anne, and Saward, Blanche C. *The Dictionary of Needlework.* New York: Arno Press, 1972.

Christensen, Erwin O. *The Index of American Design.* New York: Macmillan Co., 1959.

Clabburn, Pamela. *The Needleworker's Dictionary.* New York: William Morrow Co., 1976.

Coats Sewing Group. *Fifty Counted Thread Embroidery Stitches.* New York: Charles Scribner's Sons, 1977.

Davis, Mildred J. *Early American Embroidery Designs.* New York: Crown Publishers, 1969.

Decorative Needlework of the Pennsylvania Germans. Hershey: Hershey Museum of American Life, 1979.

deDillmont, Th. *Encyclopedia of Needlework.* D. M. C. Library

Deneke, Bernward, *Volkskunst; Führer durch die Volkskundlichen Sammlungen.* München: Germanisches Nationalmuseum Nürnberg, 1979.

Diener, Menno A. *History of the Diener Family.* Aylmer, Ontario: Pathway, 1964.

Egeland, Janice A., ed., *Descendants of Christian Fisher and other Amish-Mennonite Pioneer Families.* Baltimore: Moore Clinic, Johns Hopkins Hospital, 1972.

Egelmann, J. C. F., *Verbesserter Calender auf das Jahr 1844.* Reading, Pa.

Egelmann, Carl Friederich. *Deutsche & Englische Vorschriften für die Jugend.* Reading, Pa. 1831.

Emery, Irene. *The Primary Structure of Fabrics—An Illustrated Classification.* Washington, D.C.: The Textile Museum, 1966.

Encyclopedia Britannica. 1963 ed. s.v. "Embroidery-United States," by Mildred L. Davison.

Erich, Oswald A., Beitl, Richard and Beitl, Klaus, *Wörterbuch der deutschen Volkskunde.* 3rd ed. Stuttgart, 1974.

Fabian, Monroe. *The Pennsylvania German Decorated Chest.* New York: Universe Books, 1978.

Fangel, Esther; Winckler, Ida; and Madsen, Agnete Wuldem. *Danish Pulled Thread Embroidery.* New York: Dover Publications, 1977.

Fletcher, Stevenson Whitcomb. *Pennsylvania Agriculture and Country Life 1640-1840.* Harrisburg, Pa.: Pennsylvania Historical & Museum Commission, 1950.

Foris, Andreas and Maria. *Charted Folk Designs for Cross Stitch Embroidery.* New York: Dover Publications, 1975.

Garvan, Beatrice B. *The Pennsylvania German Collection.* Philadelphia: Philadelphia Museum of Art, 1982.

Garvan, Beatrice B., and Hummel, Charles F. *The Pennsylvania Germans A Celebration of Their Arts 1683-1850.* Philadelphia: Philadelphia Museum of Art, 1982.

Gehret, Ellen J. "O Noble Heart . . ." *Der Reggeboge,* 14 (July, 1980): 1-14.

Gehret, Ellen J. *Rural Pennsylvania Clothing.* York, Pa.: George Shumway, 1976.

Gehret, Ellen J., and Keyser, Alan G. *The Homespun Textile Tradition of the Pennsylvania Germans.* Harrisburg, Pa.: Pennsylvania Historical and Museum Commission, 1976.

Gibbons, Phebe Earle. *The Pennsylvania Dutch and Other Essays.* Philadelphia, Pa.: J. B. Lippincott and Co., 1882.

Gockerell, Nina. *Stickmustertücher.* Kataloge des Bayerischen Nationalmuseums, Bd. 16. München: Deutscher Kunstverlag, 1980.

Gröber, Karl. *Schwaben. Deutsche Volkskunst.* Frankfurt: Weidlich Reprints, 1982.

Harbeson, Georgiana Brown. *American Needlework.* New York: Bonanza Books, 1938.

Heads of Families At The First Census of The United States Taken In The Year 1790 Pennsylvania. Washington: Government Printing Office, 1908.

Heisey, John W. *A Checklist of American Coverlet Weavers.* Williamsburg, Va.: The Colonial Williamsburg Foundation, 1978.

Herr, Theodore W. *Genealogical Record of Reverend Hans Herr and his direct lineal descendants.* Lancaster, Pa., 1908; reprint ed., Lancaster, Pa.: Lancaster Mennonite Historical Society, 1980.

Hitz-Caflisch, F. *Alte Bündner Kreuzstichmuster.* Klosters: M. Buff-Müller, 1976.

Hoffmann-Krayer, E., and Bächtold-Stäubli, Hanns. *Handwörterbuch des deutschen Aberglaubens.* Berlin and Leipzig, 1930-1931.

Holroyd, Ruth N., and Beck, Ulricke. *Jacob Angstadt Designs Drawn From His Weavers Patron Book:* Hartford, Conn.: Ruth N. Holroyd, 1976.

Houck, Carter. *Whitework,* New York: Dover Publications, 1978.

Huish, Marcus. *Samplers and Tapestry Embroideries.* New York: Dover Publications, 1970.

Huntley, Richmond, "Door Panels Adhere to Oldest Sampler Form," *American Collector,* November 29, 1934: 3.

Kauffman, Henry J. *Pennsylvania Dutch American Folk Art.* New York: Dover Publications, 1964.

Kaufmann, Gerhard. *Stickmustertücher aus dem Besitz des Altonaer Museums.* Hamburg, 1975.

Keyser, Alan G. "Gardens and Gardening Among the Pennsylvania Germans," *Pennsylvania Folklife* 20 (Spring 1971): 2-15.

King, Donald. *Samplers.* London: Her Majesty's Stationery Office, 1960.

Klees, Fredric. *The Pennsylvania Dutch.* New York: The Macmillan Co., 1951.

Krueger, G. Lee. *A Gallery of American Samplers The Theodore H. Kapnek Collection.* New York: E. P. Dutton, 1978.

Lichten, Frances. *Folk Art of Rural Pennsylvania.* New York: Charles Scribner's Sons, 1946.

Little, Frances. *Early American Textiles.* New York: The Century Co., 1931.

Melen, Lisa. *Drawn Threadwork.* New York: Van Nostrand Reinhold Co., 1972.

Meyer-Heisig, Erich. *Weberei Nadelwerk Zeugdruck.* München: Prestel-Verlag, 1956.

Meulenbelt-Nieuwburg, Albarta. *Embroidery Motifs From Old Dutch Samplers.* New York: Charles Scribner's Sons, 1974.

Nichols, Marion. *Encyclopedia of Embroidery Stitches Including Crewel.* New York: Dover Publications, 1974.

Nordfors, Jill. *Needle Lace and Needle Weaving A New Look At Traditional Stitches.* New York: Van Nostrand Reinhold Co., 1974.

One Hundred Embroidery Stitches. Stamford, Conn.: Coats & Clark, 1975.

Parolini-Ruffini, Elvira. *Charted Swiss Folk Designs.* New York: Dover Publications, 1978.

Patterson, Nancy-Lou. "The Iconography of the Show Towel," *Waterloo Historical Society,* 64 (1976), 49-69.

Pennsylvania Dutch Folk Arts . . . From the Geesey Collection and Others. Philadelphia, Pa.: Philadelphia Museum of Art.

Pennsylvania Folk Art, Allentown: Allentown Art Museum, 1974.

Reinert, Guy F. *Coverlets of the Pennsylvania Germans.* Yearbook of the Pennsylvania German Folklore Society, vol. 13. Allentown, Pa., 1949.

Ring, Betty. *Needlework An Historical Survey.* New York: Universe Books, 1975.

Roan, Nancy, and Gehret, Ellen J. *Just A Quilt or Juscht en Deppich.* Green Lane, Pa., Goschenhoppen Historians, 1984.

Robacker, Earl F. *Old Stuff in Up-Country Pennsylvania.* Cranberry, N.J.: A. S. Barnes Co., 1973.

Rosatto, Vittoria. *Leavers Lace: A Handbook of the American Leavers Lace Industry.* Providence, Rhode Island: American Lace Manufacturers Association, 1950.

Safford, Carleton and Bishop, Robert. *America's Quilts and Coverlets.* New York: Barre Publishing Co., 1974.

Schiffer, Margaret B. *Needlework of Pennsylvania.* New York: Charles Scribner's Sons, 1968.

Snook, Barbara. *Needlework Stitches.* New York: Crown Publishers, 1974.

Stoudt, John Joseph. *Pennsylvania Folk-Art An Interpretation.* Allentown, Pa.: Schlechter's, 1948.

Stoudt, John J. *Early Pennsylvania Arts and Crafts.* New York: A.S. Barnes & Co., 1964.

Stoudt, John Joseph. *Sunbonnets and Shoofly Pies A Pennsylvania Dutch Cultural History.* New York: A.S. Barnes & Co., 1973.

Swan, Susan Burrows. *A Winterthur Guide To American Needlework.* New York: Crown Publishers 1976.

Swan, Susan Burrows. *Plain and Fancy, American Women and Their Needlework, 1700-1850.* New York: Holt, Rinehart and Winston, 1977.

Swank, Scott T., et. al. *Arts of the Pennsylvania Germans.* New York: W.W. Norton and Company, 1983.

Weiser, Frederick S., and Heaney, Howell J. *The Pennsylvania German Fraktur of the Free Library of Philadelphia.* Breinigsville, Pa.: The Pennsylvania German Society and The Free Library of Philadelphia, 1976. 2 vols.

Wingate, Isabel B. *Fairchild's Dictionary of Textiles.* New York: Fairchild Publications, 1970.

Woods, Jean. *The Germanic Heritage.* Washington county, Md.: Washington County Museum of Fine Arts, 1983.

Zink, Theodor. *Die Pfalz. Deutsche Volkskunst.* 12 Frankfurt: Weidlich Reprints, 1982.

1976 Antiques Show A Benefit For The Hospital of The University of Pennsylvania. Philadelphia, 1976.

Catalogues of auctions in the Gilbert, Kleinfeiter and Pennypacker auction galleries, Lebanon and Reading, Pa., 1936-

INDEX

289

291

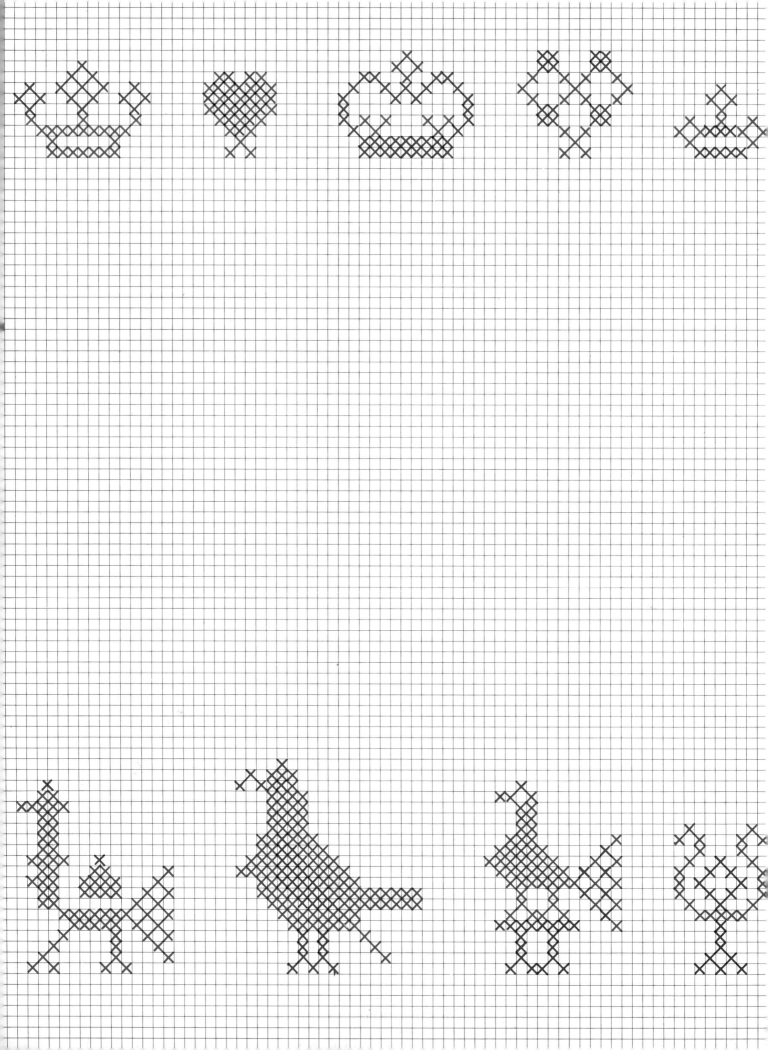